HISTORY PLAY

HISTORY PLAY

The Lives and Afterlife of
Christopher Marlowe

RODNEY BOLT

BLOOMSBURY

Published by Bloomsbury Publishing, New York and London
Distributed to the trade by Holtzbrinck Publishers

All papers used by Bloomsbury Publishing are natural, recyclable
products made from wood grown in well-managed forests. The
manufacturing processes conform to the environmental regulations
of the country of origin.

Library of Congress Cataloging-in-Publication Data
has been applied for.

ISBN 1-59691-020-8
ISBN-13 978-1-59691-020-1

First U.S. Edition 2005

1 3 5 7 9 10 8 6 4 2

Typeset by Rowland Phototypesetting Ltd,
Bury St Edmunds, Suffolk
Printed in the United States of America
by Quebecor World Fairfield

For my parents

About anyone so great as Shakespeare, it is probable that we can never be right; and if we can never be right, it is better that we should from time to time change our way of being wrong.

T. S. ELIOT

Contents

PART III

Acknowledgements

My heartfelt thanks go to David Miller, Ravi Mirchandani, and Arabella Pike, who were all instrumental, in their different ways, in bringing this book to life. And a special thank you, too, to Amanda Katz for transferring that life successfully across the Atlantic.

I am deeply indebted to earlier Marlowe biographers, most notably William Urry, Leslie Hotson, John Bakeless and in particular Charles Nicholl. Their painstaking and serious scholarship has been of great value to me, and I can only hope that they do not thump their desks too hard, or (in some cases) turn in their graves at what I have done with it.

While every effort has been made to trace owners of copyright, I would be happy to rectify any errors or omissions in future editions. I am grateful to the Master and Fellows of Corpus Christi College, Cambridge, for their assistance with accommodation, and to the staff of the Parker Library at the college for their help and attention to my requests. Dr Mara Kalnins, a Fellow of the college, and Dr Linne Mooney, very kindly gave their permission to reproduce the letter included in Appendix III. Staff at the University of Padua Library, too, were very helpful and tolerant of odd requests.

Roon van Santen generously offered his design services in

pursuit of a maverick idea, which Allan Grotjohann superbly put into effect. Frank Wynne came up with ingenious last-minute suggestions. Ton Amir, Sandra Ponzanesi, Massimo Scalabrini, Isabel Cebeiro and Pierre Bouvier all helped in recondite corners of translation. Fausto Schiavetto put me up in Padua, and Vitorina Côrte offered refuge when I needed it. Warm thanks to all of them.

But my deepest debt of all is to Hans Nicolaï, Gerard van Vuuren and Andrew May, who have borne my obsession with this book for the past three years with fortitude, even giving practical help with research. Anna Arthur, Chris Chambers, Iris Maher and Dheera Sujan have also been stalwart in their support. Without them, the task would have been tough indeed.

Foreword

How curious and interesting is the parallel – as far as poverty of biographical details is concerned – between Satan and Shakespeare. It is wonderful, it is unique, it stands quite alone, there is nothing resembling it in history, nothing resembling it in romance, nothing approaching it even in tradition. They are the best-known unknown persons that have ever drawn breath upon the planet. By way of a preamble to this book, I should like to set down a list of *every positively known* fact of Shakespeare's life, lean and meagre as the invoice is. Beyond these details we know *not a thing* about him. All the rest of his vast history, as furnished by the biographers, is built up, course upon course, of guesses, inferences, theories, conjectures – a tower of artificialities rising sky-high from a very flat and very thin foundation of inconsequential facts.

FACTS

He was born on the 23rd of April, 1564.

Of good farmer-class parents who could not read, could not write, could not sign their names.

At Stratford, a small back-settlement which in that day was

shabby and unclean, and densely illiterate. Of the nineteen important men charged with the government of the town, thirteen had to 'make their mark' in attesting important documents, because they could not write their names.

Of the first eighteen years of his life *nothing* is known. They are a blank.

On the 27th of November (1582) William Shakespeare took out a licence to marry Anne Whateley.

Next day William Shakespeare took out a licence to marry Anne Hathaway. She was eight years his senior.

William Shakespeare married Anne Hathaway. In a hurry. By grace of a reluctantly-granted dispensation there was but one publication of the banns.

Within six months the first child was born.

About two (blank) years followed, during which period *nothing at all happened to Shakespeare,* so far as anybody knows.

Then came twins – 1585. February.

Two blank years follow.

Then – 1587 – he makes a ten-year visit to London, leaving the family behind.

Five blank years follow. During this period *nothing happened to him,* as far as anybody actually knows.

Then – 1592 – there is mention of him as an actor.

Next year – 1593 – his name appears in the official list of players.

Next year – 1594 – he played before the Queen. A detail of no consequence: other obscurities did it every year of the forty-five of her reign. And remained obscure.

Three pretty full years follow. Full of play-acting. Then

In 1597 he bought New Place, Stratford.

Thirteen or fourteen busy years follow; years in which he accumulated money, and also reputation as actor and manager.

Meantime his name, liberally and variously spelt, had become associated with a number of great plays and poems, as (ostensibly) author of the same.

Some of these, in these years and later, were pirated, but he made no protest.

Then – 1610–11 – he returned to Stratford and settled down for good and all, and busied himself in lending money, trading in tithes, trading in land and houses; shirking a debt of forty-one shillings, borrowed by his wife during his long desertion of his family; suing debtors for shillings and coppers; being sued himself for shillings and coppers; and acting as confederate to a neighbour who tried to rob the town of its rights in a certain common, and did not succeed.

He lived five or six years – till 1616 – in the joy of these elevated pursuits. Then he made a will and signed each of its three pages with his name.

A thorough businessman's will. It named in minute detail every item of property he owned in the world – houses, lands, sword, silver-gilt bowl, and so on – all the way down to his 'second-best bed' and its furniture.

It carefully and calculatingly distributed his riches among the members of his family, overlooking no individual of it. Not even his wife: the wife he had been enabled to marry in a hurry by urgent grace of a special dispensation before he was nineteen; the wife whom he left husbandless so many years; the wife who had had to borrow forty-one shillings in her need, and which the lender was never able to collect of the prosperous husband, but died at last with the money still lacking. No, even this wife was remembered in Shakespeare's will.

He left her that 'second-best bed'.

And *not another thing*; not even a penny to bless her lucky widowhood with.

It was eminently and conspicuously a businessman's will, not a poet's.

It mentioned *not a single book.*

Books were much more precious than swords and silver-gilt bowls and second-best beds in those days, and when a departing person owned one he gave it a high place in his will.

The will mentioned *not a play, not a poem, not an unfinished literary work, not a scrap of manuscript of any kind.*

Many poets have died poor, but this is the only one in history that has died *this* poor; the others all left literary remains behind. Also a book. Maybe two.

If Shakespeare had owned a dog – but we need not go into that – we know he would have mentioned it in his will. If a good dog, Susanna would have got it; if an inferior one his wife would have got a dower interest in it. I wish he had had a dog, just so we could see how painstakingly he would have divided that dog among the family, in his careful business way.

He signed the will in three places.

In earlier years he signed two other official documents.

These five signatures still exist.

There are *no other specimens of his penmanship in existence.* Not a line.

Was he prejudiced against the art? His granddaughter, whom he loved, was eight years old when he died, yet she had had no teaching, he left no provision for her education although he was rich, and in her mature womanhood she couldn't write and couldn't tell her husband's manuscript from anybody else's – she thought it was Shakespeare's.

When Shakespeare died in Stratford *it was not an event.* It made no more stir in England than the death of any forgotten theatre-actor would have made. Nobody came down from London; there were no lamenting poems, no eulogies, no national tears – there was merely silence, and nothing more. A striking contrast with what happened when Ben Jonson, and Francis Bacon, and Spenser, and Ralegh and the other distinguished literary folk of Shakespeare's time passed from life! No praiseful voice was lifted for the lost Bard of Avon; even Ben Jonson waited seven years before he lifted his.

So far as anybody actually knows and can prove, Shakespeare of Stratford-on-Avon never wrote a play in his life.

So far as anybody actually knows and can prove, he never wrote a letter to anybody in his life.

So far as anyone knows, he received only one letter during his life.

So far as anyone *knows and can prove,* Shakespeare of Stratford wrote only one poem during his life. This one is authentic. He did write that one – a fact which stands undisputed; he wrote the whole of it; he wrote the whole of it out of his own head. He commanded that this work of art be engraved upon his tomb, and he was obeyed. There it abides to this day. This is it:

> Good friend for Iesus sake forbeare
> To digg the dust encloased heare:
> Blest be ye man yt spares thes stones
> And curst be he yt moves my bones

Sam L. Clemens, D.Litt,
Missouri, USA

A Dead Man in Deptford

Friends in high places can give you a pain in the neck, and Eleanor Bull's connections were positively stratospheric. She was cousin to Blanche Parry, who was a close confidante of the Queen, and also related to Lord Burghley, Elizabeth's chief minister and the most powerful man in the land. She had an ear in court when she needed one, but was a servant of the court when her connections required it. They had made inconvenient demands of her before. But this time it was different. This time she had a dead poet on her hands.

Widow Bull had a maxim: 'A friend i' th' court is better than a penny in purse.' She had said it to the poet that morning. In a later age she might well have embroidered the wisdom and had it framed, hanging above the fireplace. Her husband Richard, sub-bailiff at the local manor house, had died three years earlier, leaving her with some standing but little money. It was her friends in court who helped put the pennies in her purse; in return they called on her discretion and enlisted her hospitality. Mrs Bull ran what we would today call a 'safe house' and letter-drop, in Deptford Strand.

History has dealt Eleanor Bull a double blow. It has turned her respectable, if somewhat clandestine establishment into a rowdy tavern, and it linked her name for ever with the death of the brilliant young poet and playwright Christopher Marlowe, who (as tradition would have it) was 'killed in a drunken brawl over a bill in Deptford'. We now know that was not the case. Recent research suggests that Marlowe was murdered as a consequence of his involvement in the shady world of Elizabethan espionage and behind-the-scenes politicking. The subsequent obfuscation of the story was deliberate.

Deptford, in 1593, was an ideal location for a safe house. It was within easy reach of London, and a convenient dock for ships that trafficked the Thames, to and from the open seas. Queen Elizabeth's favourite residence, and a frequent meeting place of her cabinet, the Privy Council, was less than a mile down river at Greenwich. Two shipyards, one for the navy and one for merchant ships, filled the air with the smells of pitch and fresh-sawn timber as they churned out vessels to plunder Spanish treasure, explore the globe, and protect the realm. The Admiral of the Fleet, Lord Howard of Effingham, had a house on Deptford Green. Foreign musicians from the Queen's consorts and the Chapel Royal choir lived in Deptford, as did the joiners, chandlers and ropemakers of the ship industry, cadets from the naval college at Trinity House, and a transient population of seamen . . . and spies. Sailors, travellers, foreigners and minor courtiers could mingle unheeded on the streets. English and French, German and Dutch might be heard around tables in taverns. Some 4,000 incomers arrived to live in Deptford in the 1590s, and most of them descended on the lodging houses in the riverfront area known as Deptford Strand. Mrs Bull's 'victualling-house' would not have stood out at all.

She was used to taking in tired travellers from across the Channel – the 'projectors' and 'intelligencers' of the secret service network controlled by the Secretary of State, Sir Francis Walsingham, and after his death by Lord Burghley's hunchback son, Sir Robert Cecil. She soothed spies ravaged by seasickness with her famous posset (milk and egg yolks 'seethed on a fire', poured from on high into a bowl of warm ale or sack, and with a little 'ginger and synomon cast on'*), passed on letters and packages from one unnamed man to another, or waited quietly out of earshot while visitors spoke to men from court.

Of the four men who arrived at Eleanor Bull's on the morning of Wednesday, 30 May 1593, two were known to her. The poet had been coming in every morning at 'the tenth hour before noon' for the past ten days. No reason was given. He simply stayed for an ale, then left. She knew not to ask any questions. It was something to do with Sir Robert Cecil. She was to send Cecil a message 'incontinent' (immediately) if the poet did not appear. She didn't like Sir Robert. An ambitious little bunch-backed toad, she thought, and had said as much to the poet. She was generally wise enough to keep such opinions to herself, but she had liked the poet, and he seemed to hold no high opinion of Sir Robert himself.

She may well have heard of Christopher Marlowe before he started appearing daily on her doorstep. Just a few years earlier his play *Tamburlaine* had been the talk of London, even in respectable circles, and he had followed it with further successes. But then, in Elizabethan times, it was the theatre company not the playwright that took the credit, and a play's title not its author that achieved renown. If the name Kit Marlowe was familiar to her, it was more likely that she had heard it murmured during quiet conversations under her own roof.

The second man she knew better, though not always by the same name. Robert Poley was a frequent visitor – a university man with a flattering tongue; a king of smiles and a beguiler of women. 'Sweet Robyn' they called him. Lately, he was close with Sir Robert, and seemed to have some position of control. He frequently arrived to collect packages from other visitors, or (it

---

* Gertrud Zelle, in *The Bare Truth: Stripping Spies' Cover*, gives Eleanor Bull's recipe for posset in an appendix.

seemed) to pass on instructions or make introductions. Often he had about him large amounts of good gold. In the past few months he had been travelling a lot to the Low Countries. Word slipped out about who was boarding which ship, even when coins closed lips and eyes. The other two men, she was to learn later, were Ingram Frizer and Nicholas Skeres. Of them she could say nothing, except that Skeres was most certainly not a gentleman.

They had come at about ten o'clock. The poet and Frizer arrived together. Sweet Robyn and Skeres were there to meet them. She had given them a room apart, as asked. They talked 'in quiet sort together' most of the day, but this was not unusual. Eleanor Bull was accustomed to the hushed back-and-forth tones as agents imparted their information. She gave them a passable lunch: pottage, neat's-tongue pie, a little cold lamb ('goode from Easter to Whitsun' – she had just made it, Whitsun in 1593 fell on the following Sunday), a 'sallat' of boiled onions served with vinegar, oil and pepper, capon with prunes, currants and dates, and as a treat 'baken stagge' (another May favourite, probably gained through one of her connections – there were royal hunting grounds at Lewisham and Blackheath).* That would customarily have been at eleven o'clock. Later they walked in her garden, staying there until six, when they came back to the same room for the supper she had laid out. Sweet Robyn took her aside to talk about the bill. She didn't see the others come in.

The poet Marlowe was resting when the supper was cleared. There was one bed in the room, against the wall. In front of it, Robert Poley and Ingram Frizer were seated playing 'tables' (backgammon). Skeres was drinking ale. Later, voices were raised and there were sounds of a scuffle; she was called in to the room. Frizer had two gashes on his head and the poet was dead. He had been stabbed above the eye, and his face was covered in blood. (The blade severed the internal carotid artery,

---

* Zelle, *Bare Truth*, p. 234.

and probably also caused an air embolism.) Sweet Robyn hastened to calm her. It was too late for a surgeon, and he didn't call the watch. Instead, they waited for the coroner.

It was thirty-six hours before a coroner came. Not the district man, but William Danby, 'Coroner of the household of our . . . lady the Queen'. Normally, such a grand official wouldn't be bothered for a minor stabbing, but Danby had jurisdiction 'within the Verge', defined as the area within a twelve-mile radius of the body of the sovereign. Eleanor Bull's house was under a mile from the palace at Greenwich, and the Queen was in residence. At the trial, sixteen mostly local men made up the jury: gentlemen and yeomen, a couple of bakers, a grocer and the miller of Deptford. They were told how 'malicious words' were uttered between 'Christopher Morley' (Marlowe) and Ingram Frizer about the 'payment of a sum of pence, that is, *le recknynge*', and that Marlowe, who was lying down, 'moved in anger' against Frizer, who was sitting at the table with his back to the bed, with Poley and Skeres sitting on either side. Drawing Frizer's dagger 'which was at his back', Marlowe attacked him from behind, wounding him twice on the head ('two wounds . . . of the length of two inches & of the depth of a quarter of an inch'). In the struggle to retrieve his dagger (valued at 12*d*) Frizer stabbed Marlowe, causing a wound 'over his right eye of the depth of two inches & of the width of one inch', killing him instantly. Frizer 'neither fled nor withdrew himself', and the inquest found that he had acted 'in the defence and saving of his own life, against the peace of our said lady the Queen, her now crown & dignity'. Frizer was briefly imprisoned but quickly received a royal pardon. The body was carried that day along the Common to St Nicholas's church, and buried in an unmarked grave.

If Eleanor Bull wondered why Ingram Frizer's dagger was so easy to get at, why the argument with Marlowe reached such a pitch without Frizer turning to face him, why the other men appeared not to intervene, or how in the struggle Frizer had managed to dispatch the poet with such apparent neatness and efficiency, she wisely said nothing. William Danby was an experienced and high-ranking official, a friend of her kinsman Lord Burghley from their days together at the Inns of Court. Perhaps she scented the hand of Sir Robert Cecil in this. But Eleanor Bull never made a fuss and, as ever, Robert Poley paid her handsomely. With a little extra for the inconvenience. We can only imagine her displeasure with the world of spies as she cleaned away the blood and set her room to rights. Assignations are one thing, assassinations quite another.

There we could leave Widow Bull (she died peacefully three years later), were it not for something that not even she suspected.

The body on the bed that May evening was not that of Christopher Marlowe.

PART I

CHAPTER ONE

Prefaces to Shakespeare

In the year that Calvin died and Galileo was born, when the world was racked by religion and beginning to dream of science, two babies were baptised whose lives fortune's fingers would entwine in a knot that we still cannot completely untie. In the parish of St George, near the great cathedral in Canterbury, Christopher Marlowe, the newborn son of a local shoemaker, was carried howling to the font on Saturday, 26 February 1564. Exactly two months later, on 26 April, in the country town of Stratford, William Shakespere, mewling son of a glovemaker, was entered in the parish register. By the late 1580s they would both be living in London and working for the same company of players, their affairs becoming increasingly entangled. Then in 1593, Marlowe would disappear from view and Shakespere would publish *Venus and Adonis,* calling it 'the first heir of my invention'. The two events were not unconnected. We have learned that the incident in Widow Bull's house in Deptford was not all we perhaps thought it was – or rather, that it was a little more than we thought it was. To reconstruct what happened up to that point, we begin with the story of baby Marlowe.

The infant that Goodwife Roose, the local midwife, pronounced 'lusty and like to live' was John and Katherine Marlowe's second child in a string of nine, and by far the brightest. Perhaps he owed that to his father, who – fairly uncommonly for a shoemaker at the time – could read. Perhaps it was from his father too that little Christopher inherited a venturesome curiosity, which at times could be insatiable. No-one knows from whom he got his beautiful singing voice. For his infant howls soon transmuted into a tinkling treble, far superior to the singing of any of his siblings, and he was taken up by Thomas Bull, the cathedral organist and master of the choir, who lived almost next door to the Marlowes near St George's church.*

John Marlowe (or Marloe, or Marley, or Marlyn, as he was also known in that lackadaisical way Elizabethans had with spelling in general and surnames in particular) was an immigrant to Canterbury. In the mid-1550s, when he was about twenty, he had walked there from Ospringe, near Faversham in Kent. Soon after arriving he took up an apprenticeship with one Gerard Richardson, a shoemaker, and by the end of April 1564 was already a freeman of the city. This would suggest that he was at least part-qualified when he arrived in Canterbury, and that his apprenticeship was something of a ruse as a short cut to citizenship (apprenticeships usually lasted seven years and began at the age of fifteen). Being a freeman was a coveted position that raised a man a notch above his fellow artisans, enabling him to have his own shop ('hold craft and opyn windowes withoute leve'), take on apprentices and participate in city council meetings. Marlowe married Katherine Arthur, whose family came from Dover, and they settled in the parish of St George.

Leafing through the Canterbury borough plea books, we find John Marlowe to be belligerent and litigious, setting himself terrier-like against everyone from fellow shoemakers to the local gentry. In return, there were various suits launched against him, once for assaulting his apprentice and drawing blood, but mostly for debt. He did not pay his rent, he did not pay his rates, and

---

* See Julia Wells, *Tho's a Dear: Bull's Boys*, pp. 16–17.

his business finances were generally in a state of chaos. This lack of business sense was something else his son was to inherit. That and a sharp temper. Life in the little house behind the cobbler's shop was not calm. At least one other of the Marlowe brood, Christopher's younger sister Anne, showed the characteristic family quarrelsomeness. Later in life she was publicly criticised for being 'a scowlde, comon swearer, a blasphemer of the name of god', and as a fifty-five-year-old widow laid into one William Prowde with 'staff and dagger', and the following year with 'sword and knife'. Nor was the family home in a particularly reposeful part of town. St George's parish, though close to the cathedral, lay between the cattle market and the butchers' shambles. This may have been convenient for the leather that was the material of John Marlowe's trade, but it wasn't terribly salubrious. Just yards away, animals would bellow and scream as they were herded to slaughter. Barrows of blood and stinking entrails were trundled past the Marlowe front door (cf. 'Have I lived to be carried in a basket, like a barrow of butcher's offal?' *Merry Wives* III v). The acrid smell of crowded cattle and the earthy pungency of manure hung in the air and clung to clothes. We may imagine that the young Marlowe whiffed. He certainly knew his blood and butchery. The knowledge he shows in his plays of how blood spurts 'like a fountain', how it darkens as it coagulates, forms black clots, and follows a withdrawn knife, is impressive; and his haunting recollection of a slaughterhouse quite moving:

> And as the butcher takes away the calf
> And binds the wretch, and beats it when it strays,
> Bearing it to the bloody slaughter-house . . .
>
> And as the dam runs lowing up and down,
> Looking the way her harmless young one went,
> And can do naught but wail her darling's loss . . .
> (2 *Henry VI* III i 210–16)

5

He also, incidentally, shows a fine knowledge of leather, no doubt gleaned from his father's workshop. He knows, for example, that cow's leather was used for shoes, sheep's leather for bridles, and how far cheverel will stretch.

As if the screams of cattle and cantankerous sisters were not enough, the sturdy steeple of St George's housed the great waking bell, which was rung at 4 o'clock every morning and was loud enough to get the whole town out of bed. Just across the way from the church tower was Newingate, the medieval gate that was the highest point in the city wall. Scholars have argued that these two looming structures inspired the 'Two lofty Turrets that command the Towne' mentioned in *The Jew of Malta.*

The town that these turrets commanded was not a large one. A point of pilgrimage ever since the assassination of Thomas à Becket in 1170, Canterbury was also renowned for its cloth market and the quality of its fish, and in the late sixteenth century had a population of somewhere between 3,000 and 4,000. It was, as the Marlowe biographer William Urry points out, a city close to the countryside: 'Cows grazed within a hundred yards of John Marlowe's shop and local women went milking every morning. Gleaning went on at harvest-time in Barton Fields, stretching into St George's parish. Fifteen minutes' walk would have taken the young Marlowe far out into the meads, the orchards and primrose lanes. His contact with the open countryside was as close as that of the small boy Shakespeare.' We know that he enjoyed country jaunts. It took just ninety minutes to walk to the stretch of coastline between Sandwich and Deal, a trip he made often with his father, and perhaps also with a playmate Nat Best, the son of a tanner from Wingham (a village just six miles east of Canterbury) with whom John Marlowe had business dealings. Later in life Marlowe was to leave us an extraordinarily evocative recollection of how, as a young boy visiting his maternal grandparents in Dover, he would lie at the very edge of the cliffs, gazing below him or staring out to sea.

> ... How fearful
> And dizzy 'tis to cast one's eyes so low!
> The crows and choughs that wing the mid-way air
> Show scarce so gross as beetles. Half-way down
> Hangs one that gathers samphire – dreadful trade!
> Methinks he seems no bigger than his head.
> The fishermen that walk upon the beach
> Appear like mice; and yond tall anchoring bark
> Diminish'd to her cock; her cock, a buoy
> Almost too small for sight. The murmuring surge
> That on th' unumb'red pebble chafes
> Cannot be heard so high. I'll look no more;
> Lest my brain turn, and the deficient sight
> Topple down headlong.
> (*King Lear* IV vi 11–23)

Young Christopher got on well with his irascible father – though rather less so with his mother, who like her daughter Anne was sarcastic, frosty and domineering. As Tony Bordel points out, most of the families in Kit's plays are single-parent ones, or involve step-parents. Sons and mothers – such as Hamlet and Gertrude, or Coriolanus and Volumnia – have especially volatile relationships.*

Fiery he might have been, but John Marlowe had a sharp wit and amongst his friends a reputation as a raconteur. A court case of 1565 gives us a glimpse of the company he kept. He was called to testify in the defamation hearing of *Hunte* [or Hurte] *alias Chapman v. Applegate*. His close friend, the Canterbury tailor Laurence Applegate, who had a shop on the High Street near

---

* Tony Bordel, *Word Plays*, p. 222.

the Vernicle alehouse on the corner of Iron Bar Lane, had been sowing scandals about Godliffe, the daughter of Goodwife Chapman. On the road to Dover, one summer's day in 1564, Applegate had boasted to John Marlowe that he had 'hadd [his] pleasure of godlyve Chappmans Daugher'. Though he made Marlowe promise to keep it secret, the news was soon all round the town, and an outraged Goodwife Chapman in retaliation refused to repay Applegate two shillings she owed him. Applegate was heard to say in mixed company in the Vernicle tavern, and later in the shop to two of John Marlowe's apprentices (and, it would seem, anywhere else where Marlowe could egg him on to tell the tale, at 'divers tymes syns and in sondrie places'), that it was quite a bargain 'for that I occupyed Godliffe hir Daughter fower times which was for everie tyme vj d [i.e. sixpence – the sums do work out, as the old shilling was worth 12d, so that two shillings equalled four sixpences]'. As Godliffe was about to get married, an outraged Goodwife Chapman took Applegate to court. The case was inconclusive, but Applegate had to perform public penance.

Such stories linger, and this one was no doubt still being narrated with embellishment and delight by the time Christopher was old enough to listen in. Wisps from the world of adults float in to young minds; sometimes they snag and remain, perfectly preserved if not fully understood. Later we may re-examine them: odd, untarnished strands in our fabric, suddenly seen with a fuller perception. In Christopher's case, he worked them into his plays.

Two other stories gleefully gossiped around St George's reached the ears of the little boy who, watchful and inquisitive, was known to eavesdrop from the corner of his father's shop, or from behind the thin walls of the family house. The first, the tale of Dorothy Hocking, happened in the year Christopher was born, but so delighted the good folk of Canterbury that it was firmly lodged in local legend for years to come.

Dorothy was comely but a little dim, and was kept in drudgery and virtual imprisonment by her mother and stepfather. They lived in the parish of Holy Cross, near Canterbury's Westgate and next door to the tailor Robert Holmes. Between the 'backsydes' (back yards) of the houses there was a wall. It was built of stones and earth, bonded with hair and coated with lime or roughcast. It probably had a capping of thatch to keep off the rain, and it certainly had a hole. We know this because Dorothy Hocking's dog had nipped through the gap and stolen a conger eel from the Holmes's yard. Under the pretext of discussing this incident, Robert Holmes's wife drew Dorothy 'from her mothers busyness in hir mothers backsyde' for a secret discussion through the hole in the wall. Dorothy had fallen in love with one Richard Edmundes, and Goodwife Holmes had a mind to help her out. It was 'about five or six of the clock in the afternoon'. Dorothy agreed that Goodwife Holmes should send for Richard, so she could speak to him through the hole in the wall. Robert Holmes found him nearby, playing bowls in 'the backsyde of goodman podiches house', and brought him to the hole. By then Dorothy's parents had gone out. Goodwife Holmes took Dorothy's hand through the wall, and gave it to Richard to hold by the finger, asking 'knowe youe who this is that hath youe by the finger'. Dear but dull-witted Dorothy answered 'no not yet'. Robert Holmes told her 'it is Richard Edmundes', and open-mouthed she asked 'what . . . he wold have with her?'. Richard replied: 'well my wench I beare youe good will and if thow canst find it in thie harte to love me and wilbe ruled by me I will delyver thee out of thye miserie'. She answered she could 'find it in her hart to love him above all men', and Edmundes asked her how old she was, saying, perhaps with a fillip of flattery, 'I thinck you bee neere hand 16 or 17 yeares of age'. This seems to have somewhat thrown Dorothy who replied 'yea that I am, for I am neerer 20 yrs ould but my age is kept from me'. Edmundes then asked her if she was betrothed to anyone else,

9

and when she answered 'no' said, 'can you finde in your harte to forsake father and mother and all men lyving for my sake?', and she replied with a heartfelt 'yea'.

We are told that Robert Holmes then called his journeyman, Harry Jenkinson, from indoors to act as a witness. 'Where and whan, Edmundes toke Dorothie by the hand throughe the hole in the wall and then said Dorothee unto Edmundes these words, viz. I Dorothee take youe Richard to my husband forsaking all other for your sake and thereupon I give you my faith and trouthe. Then said Edmundes, in faith wench, I were too blame if I would not speak the like woords unto thee.' He did so, and 'called for a drinck and dronck to Dorothy', giving her 'an ould angell [gold coin]' to seal the ceremony. Now that she was betrothed, Dorothy – perhaps not so dim after all – was freed of her parents' tyranny. As soon as her circumstances had changed she broke off the engagement, bringing down a breach of contract case against herself, thus leaving us a record of her story. This droll titbit of Canterbury gossip was, of course, to re-emerge as the story of Pyramus and Thisbe in *A Midsummer Night's Dream*.

The second Canterbury tale overheard by the young Marlowe, perhaps from customers in his father's shop, perhaps as he slipped in and out of neighbours' kitchens, centred on William Darrell, who was a canon at the cathedral, and Clemence Ward, a notorious harlot. The story was told by Goodwife Pratt as she sat working at her door at harvest-time 1575, with Goodwife Thomasina Newen, overheard by the newly widowed Goodwife Culverhouse as she suckled her child, and repeated by a Mrs Hunt to Goodwife Joan Moyse, who told it in her kitchen to Clemence Ward's landlord John Foster. Clemence lived near the Marlowes, in the neighbouring parish of St Alphege, and was of sufficient 'suspect behaviour' to be required to do penance clad in a white sheet on the porch of St Alphege before the Sunday morning service, and to be excommunicated when she refused to comply. Goodwives Newen and Pratt opined 'Yt is a pity she is not carted out of the town.' However the core of the tale they told sitting at Goodwife Pratt's front door at harvest-time concerned something Goodwife Lea had witnessed in the cathedral precincts. She had seen two people staggering with a peculiarly heavy laundry basket, through the Christchurch Gate, along the great length of the cemetery, through the Norman gateway to the inner cemetery until they came to Canon William Darrell's house, where they put the basket down among a clump of oak trees. But soon, seeming to act on a tip-off, one of the cathedral's lay clerks – Mr Whyting, perhaps, or Mr Wade – appeared, drew his dagger and plunged it into the basket. Out leapt a furious Clemence Ward, wounded in the arm. We do not know if it was this that destroyed Canon Darrell's reputation (he had already been accused of misbehaviour at court while chaplain to Queen Elizabeth, and had run up considerable debts), but he was eventually suspended from his canonry. The canon's downfall inspired Falstaff's nemesis in *The Merry Wives of Windsor*, in which the sack-swilling knight is tricked into hiding a laundry basket during his attempt at seducing Mistress Ford.

Noisy, nosy and malodorous though the parish of St George was, it was home, in addition to the goodwives and gossips, to a number of artists and musicians. Residents included Thomas Bull, the cathedral choirmaster; William a Lee, a tabor player; and John Johnson, who in addition to painting, made rude labels to pin to witches. It is a city quarter that was also evidently a nursery for playwrights. In Sun Street, in the parish of St Alphege near the cathedral gate, lived John Lyly. Some ten years older than Marlowe he was to become famed for his *Euphues*, a prose romance written in a peculiar, heightened style, giving us the word 'euphuism'. Like Marlowe, he was to move to London, and in the 1580s and 1590s wrote plays – not the rough-and-tumble theatre preferred by the young Kit, but finely

crafted dramas for court and boy actors. However the neighbour who perhaps most influenced the course of Marlowe's
youth was Stephen Gosson, a grocer's son who was the same age
as John Lyly, and who was also to become a dramatist. New
evidence, in what appears to be rough copy for a pamphlet on
Marlowe, probably written in the early 1590s while Gosson was
rector of Great Wigborough, and recently discovered among
material that once belonged to the great Elizabethan actor
(and Gosson's lifelong friend) Edward Alleyn, points to a relationship between Gosson and his younger neighbour that
amounts to a form of hero-worship on Marlowe's part.* Both
boys appear to show an early desire to escape the stifling air of
St George's, and Canterbury, and it is Stephen Gosson who
shows the way.

In 1568, when Christopher was four, his sister Mary died –
leaving him as the eldest child and, for a while at least, the
Marlowes' only son. It was a hard year for the family. Katherine
gave birth to another son at the end of October, but he survived
only a few days. John's business, however, was doing well enough
for him to take on a third apprentice, Richard Umbarffeld. But
it was neither to Richard nor his fellow apprentices Lore Atkyn-
son and Harman Verson that little Christopher looked as a role
model. Christopher's earthly paragon had walked into the shop
when the lad was three, to get a pair of new shoes. Stephen
Gosson was about to enrol at The King's School, quite a step
up for a grocer's son, and one that evidently warranted being
better shod.

---

* Found in the extensive, but uncatalogued collection of theatre
   memorabilia belonging to the late Jack Gielgaffe. The pamphlet is
   entitled 'The Alchemist of Eloquence' (a phrase lifted from Thomas
   Nashe), and is hereinafter referred to as *Alchemist*.

According to tradition, the school, which occupied part of the cathedral precinct, had been founded by Archbishop Theodore in the year 600. What is known for certain is that it was re-established and given its royal title by Henry VIII in the 1540s, and that by Marlowe's time it enjoyed a brilliant reputation. Stephen, who was thirteen at the time he enrolled, later described the little boy he encountered in the cobbler's shop as a 'prating, parlous boy' with a 'sharp-provided wit, ingenious, forward, capable' – a babbling, shrewd boy with a quick wit, clever, precocious and gifted.* The lad could already read well. John Marlowe, himself educated beyond his station, had taught Kit using his own old horn-book – a suitably indestructible reading aid comprising a tablet of oak inscribed with the alphabet and Paternoster and covered with a protective sheet of transparent horn. It was an English invention, and John would himself have used it at a 'petty' or 'ABC' school, which (not being quite as 'forward' or 'capable' as his son) he would have attended from the age of four. Possibly he had also kept his *ABC and Catechism*, a volume combining the Lord's Prayer, the Apostles' Creed, the Ten Commandments and short catechistical exercises, which was the follow-on from the horn-book (cf. 'to sigh like a school-boy that had lost his ABC', *Two Gentlemen of Verona* II i, and 'That is question now;/And then comes answer like an Absey book', *King John* I i, and the pedantic Holfornes who 'teaches boys the horn-book' in *Love's Labour's Lost*).

Writing was an altogether different matter. It was not a skill taught at the ABC school, though we do know that John Marlowe could write a few words – he was sometimes called in during business negotiations as a witness, or to draw up inventories, and in 1589 was elected to the responsible position of warden and treasurer of his guild, the Shoemaker's Company (an office

---

* *Alchemist*, folio 3.

he held with characteristically disastrous consequences, being completely unable to balance the books at the end of the year). The usual recourse was for townspeople to call on a peripatetic scrivener, or the local clergy ('a pedant that keeps a school i' the church'). Unfortunately for St George's, its rector, the Reverend William Sweeting, was, as William Urry reveals, none too literate, leading to his parish registers becoming muddled. Nor, it seems, was he much good at preaching, bringing in another clergyman to do it for him or encouraging his flock to go to the cathedral and listen to the sermons there.

These regular cathedral appearances may be the reason that, a year after starting ABC school in 1568, Christopher left and came under the private tutelage of Thomas Bull, the cathedral organist and choirmaster, who was a neighbour of the Marlowes. Certainly, Christopher hated the ABC school. The monotony of the lessons blunted his quick mettle, and he was indeed the 'whining school-boy, with his satchel/And shining morning face, creeping like a snail/Unwillingly to school' (*As You Like It* II vii 145). He also developed a lasting scorn for his windy Welsh schoolmaster, and was to lampoon him as the pedagogue cleric Sir Hugh Evans in *The Merry Wives of Windsor*. (William Urry points to what he calls the 'strong Welsh contingent' of Davys, Joneses, Vaughans, Williamses and Evanses that along with Germans, Italians, the Spanish, French, Dutch and Walloons made up the extraordinarily ethnically diverse population of Canterbury.)

Where the money to leave the ABC school and study under Thomas Bull came from is not clear. Though John Marlowe was frequently in court over debts and financial squabbles with his neighbours, he seems also to have been a bit of a '*Johannes factotum*', a Jack of all trades, dipping into all manner of affairs. City records offer hints of prosperity alongside proof of poverty. Perhaps the newly made freeman, upwardly mobile and himself benefiting from his learning, made his son's education a financial priority. As Richard Mulcaster (the schoolmaster who championed the teaching of vernacular English, favoured proper schooling for girls, and encouraged music and drama in education) wrote in 1581: 'The middle sort of parentes which neither welter in to much wealth, nor wrastle with to much want, seemeth fittest of all ... to bring forth that student, which must serve his countery best.' Or perhaps Thomas Bull knew talent when he saw it and Christopher, like an exact contemporary of his, one R. Willis in Gloucester, moved in as one of the pupils who boarded with his new Master:

> The Master Downhale having very convenient lodgings over the school, took such a liking to me, as he made me his bedfellow (my father's house being next of all to the school). This bedfellowship begat in him familiarity and gentleness towards me; and in me towards him reverence and love; which made me also love my book, love being the most prevalent affection in nature to further our studies and endeavours in any profession.

Julia Wells suggests it was Christopher's singing as much as his learning that attracted Bull's attention, and indeed, even when his voice 'got the mannish crack', it was to develop into a fine tenor that would stand him in good stead his whole life. But we have it from Stephen Gosson that Christopher's sights were set higher than reading with his choirmaster through the *Primer*, a dismal devotional book containing prayers and metrical versions of the psalms, the successor to the *ABC*. Besides, Bull was too busy with his other activities in the cathedral to give the boy the attention he demanded. And the boy did demand. Although Stephen would not have had much free time as a scholar at The King's School (school kept six days a week, from six in the morning until seven at night, with only short vacations and the odd church holiday) Christopher clung to Stephen every moment that he could, 'like fruit unripe sticks upon a tree'.*

Kit would accept nothing less than the King's School. Behind him loomed the goodwives of St George's, and worse – Mother Bassocke who begged from door to door, holding out her apron for scraps; or poor 'Agnes that makes strawen hattes'. Up ahead were the sons of local landowners, professional men, royal servants and clergy, who took their lessons at the school that had been founded by the Queen's father. He was determined that whatever his background, that was where his future lay:

> What glory is there in a common good,
> That hangs for every peasant to achieve?
> That like I best that flies beyond my reach.
> Set me to scale the high Pyramides . . .
> (*The Massacre at Paris* I ii 40–3)

Christopher's knight errant appeared in the form of Sir Roger Manwood, an awesome – and it would seem incorrigibly corrupt – Justice of the Peace, who lived in the manor house of Hawe, two miles outside Canterbury in the village of Hackington. Known as the 'scourge of the night prowler', he was a taker of bribes and a bender of justice. (Maybe it was he who inspired the lines 'Hark, in thine ear: change places and, handy-dandy, which is the justice, which is the thief? . . . Robes and furr'd gowns hide all', *King Lear* IV vi 153 ff.) Years later Marlowe was to encounter him from the wrong side of the bench, and the Latin epitaph on Manwood's magnificent marble monument in Hackington church bears Marlowe's name as author.

But in the 1570s it was Sir Roger's interest in the clever young boy that would give him the step up he desired. He promised his patronage to ease Marlowe's passage to The King's

---

* *Alchemist*, folio 4. In the light of the future course of their relationship we must allow for a little churlishness on Gosson's part.

School.* First the boy had to improve on his basic education, and was sent, at the age of seven with Sir Roger's support, not to one of the two grammar schools in St George's parish, but to a superior establishment in St Peter's Street, founded by Matthew Parker, the Archbishop of Canterbury, in 1569. So once more he joined the other boys as they tramped to school with heavy looks. He began to study Latin grammar, later venturing into composition, and reading works such as Cato's *Puerilis* and Aesop's *Fables*. After a year or two his masters switched to Latin, rather than English, as the medium of instruction, and he may even have begun a little Greek – all the better to equip himself for his next school. But as time wore on and Kit became easily eligible for King's, Sir Roger appears to have become curiously unwilling to pay for his protégé. Whether or not he still enjoyed Sir Roger's patronage when he got to King's is unclear. Cathedral accounts for the school show that 'Chr'opher Marley' received a scholarship payment of £1 a quarter under a statute that allowed 'fifty poor boys, both destitute of the help of friends, and endowed with minds apt for learning' and who were over nine and younger than fifteen, to enrol. And it was not until Christmas 1578, when he was just a few months short of the maximum admission age, that he finally made it to the exalted institution in the cathedral precincts.

Stephen Gosson was not there to greet him. In 1572 he had gone up to Oxford, giving Christopher a new goal, but leaving him bereft of a soul mate. The boy who filled Stephen's place in Christopher's quiver of friends was Oliver Laurens (or Lourens).†

---

* Seb Melmoth's facetious comments in his address 'Rogering Sir Roger: Only a Manwood', reprinted in the *Annals of the Fitzrovian Society*, need not concern us here.

† I am deeply indebted for my information on Oliver Laurens, both at this stage and in his later life, to Dr Bernard Rosine of the Bernhardt Institute in Paris, who gave me unlimited access to original documents and to his unpublished biography of Laurens, *Oliver Laurens: The Man who Brought us Shakespeare*.

Oliver was the same age as Christopher, and he had just escaped from France with his life. Tension between the Catholic monarchy (dominated by the house of Guise) and the Protestant Huguenots had bristled yet again into violence. In the summer of 1572 the Duc de Guise, at the instigation of the Queen Mother Catherine de' Medici, fired up a rabid Catholic mob in Paris to an act of shuddering ferocity. Hundreds of Huguenots had gathered in the city for the wedding of the Protestant Henri of Navarre to Catherine's daughter, Marguerite de Valois. Juan de Olaegui, secretary to the Spanish ambassador, reported the atrocity:

> On Sunday, Saint Bartholomew's Day [24 August] at three o'clock in the morning, the alarm was rung; all the Parisians began killing the Huguenots of the town, breaking down the doors of the houses in which they lived and pillaging what they found within.
> [The Duc de] Guise, Anevale and Angoulême went to the Admiral's [the Huguenot leader Coligny's] house ... they went up to his room and in the bed where he was lying, the Duc de Guise shot him in the head with a pistol; then they took him and threw him naked out of the window into the courtyard ...

Some 4,000 Huguenots were slaughtered, and the unrest spread to the provinces where it lasted for weeks. Another witness to the massacre was Francis Walsingham, the man who was one day to control a network of spies across the continent, but was then the English ambassador in Paris. It was to sour his attitude to Catholics for life.

By 27 August, crowds of terrified Huguenot fugitives began to arrive at Rye from Dieppe. So many made their way to Canterbury that the cavernous cathedral crypt, which had been allocated to them for worship, could scarcely contain 'such a swarm'. According to Urry they were not unwelcomed by the people of Canterbury as the refugees looked after their own poor, gave jobs to locals and took over dilapidated property, even though they sometimes packed in four or five families to a house. Many settled in the neighbourhood of St George's, though it is most likely that Christopher met Oliver Laurens through Stephen Gosson, before Stephen left for Oxford at the end of the year. We know that Stephen's father was a foreigner: Cornelius Gosson is described as an 'alien' in local tax lists, and Stephen referred to himself as a 'mule' (i.e. half foreign by birth). French Protestant refugees had been arriving in Canterbury since the 1540s and there was a family of Gossons with the new wave of refugees – quite possibly relations of Stephen's own family.

Curious young Christopher's instinctive reaction to being surrounded by the cosmopolitan Gossons and Laurenses was to learn their language. Oliver's father made a little money by teaching French, and a 'C. Marle' appears as a student in his account books as early as Christmas 1572. By adulthood Marlowe's grasp of French would be very good, as was later evident in the courtship scene in *Henry V*; and in *The Merry Wives of Windsor* he would gently mock his friend's dapper, rather exuberant father – a 'musical-headed Frenchman' with an explosive temperament – in the character of Doctor Caius.

> *Caius:* Vat is you sing? I do not like des toys. Pray you, go vetch
> me in my closet un boitier vert – a box, a green-a box. Do
> intend vat I speak? A green-a box . . .
> You jack'nape; give-a this letter to Sir Hugh; by gar, it is a
> shallenge; I will cut his troat in de park . . .
>   (*The Merry Wives of Windsor*, I iv 39ff)

Here Christopher cheekily sets his French teacher off against his former ABC school teacher, as Caius 'shallenges' Sir Hugh Evans to a duel.

No doubt in his French lessons Christopher used the book of dialogues brought out by the London-based French teacher Claudius Hollyband a few years earlier, which in an admirably taut definition of the process of language teaching, claimed to accustom the learner to 'the true phrase of the language' and teach him 'the perfect annexinge of syllables, wordes and sentences' and also 'in what order they ought to be uttered'. The book would also have given Christopher a glimpse of one of the problems of cultural adaptation his new friend was having to face, as in one dialogue a shocked French boy named Francis demands of his nurse: 'Wilt thou that I wash my mouthe and my face, where I have washed my handes, as they doo in many houses in England?' (an echo of the horror shown by mainland Europeans that the British enjoy soaking in their own dirty bath water). It is probably at this stage of his life, too, that Christopher, fired by his new discovery of foreign tongues and sustained by his evident ability with them, sought out one of the Flemish refugees who lived in Canterbury and began learning Dutch. Both languages were to prove invaluable to him. English, in the sixteenth century, was unimportant and decidedly insular. That he was keen to learn French and Dutch, an important language of trade, appears to indicate that he had already set his sights and his ambitions on the Continent.

Oliver's family came from Paris. Together with a small group of fellow Huguenots, they had fled their homes when the killings started, but were set upon once again when they were found huddled and praying in nearby woods. The Laurenses were one of the few families to survive the slaughter. Later, as they grew to have more language in common, Oliver would tell Christopher of his horrors, tales that were to resurface years afterwards:

               . . . 'Kill, kill!' they cried.
Frightened with this confused noise, I rose,
And looking from a turret, might behold
Young infants swimming in their parents' blood,
Headless carcasses pil'd up in heaps,
[Women] half-dead, dragg'd by their golden hair . . .
Old men with swords thrust through their aged sides,
Kneeling for mercy to a [lad],
Who with steel pole-axes dash'd out their brains.
(*Dido, Queen of Carthage* ii 1)

The boys re-enacted the scenes Oliver had witnessed, shouting *Tue, tue tue!* (Kill, kill, kill!), a phrase which haunted Marlowe and was chillingly echoed in his version of *The Massacre at Paris* (*c.* 1590), and later also in the assassination of Coriolanus. Marlowe's subsequent Puritanism also possibly springs from this time. Certainly, Oliver was to become a lifelong – at times it would seem his only – friend.

One event in 1573 was to brighten the boys' lives considerably. In September, Elizabeth I arrived in Canterbury to celebrate her fortieth birthday. Christopher had never seen anything like it in his life. Perhaps this was the awakening of the taste for pomp and splendour and a fascination for England's history that he would display in his early plays. Certainly, the royal visit gave him a tantalising glimpse of the world beyond St George's. Royal progresses were awesomely extravagant combinations of ritual and spectacle, and this one was magnified not only by birthday celebrations, but by the arrival in Plymouth the month before of the adventurer Sir Francis Drake with tens of thousands of pounds' worth of shiny plundered treasure. What pageantry, what feats, what shows, what minstrelsy and pretty din the people made in Canterbury to meet the Queen. The city had been preparing for months. The revelry would indeed be unprecedented, if the frantic activity of their neighbours in

Sandwich (through which the Queen passed on the way) was anything to go by: here buildings had been repaired, 'beautified and adorned with black and white', the town had been gravelled and strewn with rushes and herbs, great bows put on doors and festoons of vines and flowers hung across the streets; the brewers had been enjoined to brew good ale for her coming, the butchers had to cart their offal out of town, and someone was employed especially to keep the hogs out. The Virgin Queen stayed in Canterbury for fourteen days, and would have passed close by the Marlowes' house for the celebrations on the exact occasion of her birthday, 7 September. That day she was met by Archbishop Parker at the west door of the Cathedral, and before she had even dismounted from her horse heard a nervous Grammarian (a scholar from The King's School) make his oration. As a member of the cathedral choir, Christopher would have had a fine view, as they 'stood on either side of the church and brought her Majesty up with a square [solemn] song, she going under a canopy, borne by four of her temporal knights'. City officials were adorned in every bit of silk, velvet and ermine that their livery afforded, even the ordinary burghers were fitted with finery that amounted almost to fancy dress. There were lavish entertainments, masques and musicians, elaborate feasts, and a showering of Gloriana with sumptuous gifts. And there were players.

Christopher had seen players before. William Urry observes that there is a record of travelling troupes coming to Canterbury in almost every year of Marlowe's boyhood. The Lord Warden's Players, for example, came in 1569/70, and the city accounts for December 1574 record: 'Item payd to the Lord of Leycester his players for playing.' Perhaps, like his Gloucester contemporary R. Willis (the boy who had been the bedfellow of his teacher Master Downhale), Christopher had been taken by his father to see a morality play in the market place, standing 'between his leggs, as he sate apon one of the benches'. For Willis, '[t]his sight tooke such impression in me, that when I came towards man's estate, it was as fresh in my memory, as if I had seen it newly acted'. The pageantry and supposed idolatry of medi-aeval mystery plays was disapproved of by stricter adherents of the Reformation, but an old Catholic pilgrimage town like Canterbury, one that a contemporary traveller noted was a 'harborowc[r] of the Devill and the Pope', still abandoned itself to such wickednesses as Maygames, bonfires in the streets and bell ringing on saints' days, and may well have indulged itself in the odd performance of a miracle play.

But something was happening in the 1560s and 1570s that made the shows Christopher saw very different, more alluring than the old Mystery cycles, and perhaps even a little more wicked. Already in the first decades of Elizabeth's reign, the tradition of religious and civic performances had begun to give way to troupes of strolling players who offered spicier fare. There was a move from morality to mirth, from the didactic to the entertaining. Theatre was becoming more fun. In London in 1567, the Red Lion, the first commercial playhouse with a paying audience, had opened. The amphitheatre-like design of the Red Lion playhouse, based itself on the buildings used for bear-baiting and other earthy entertainment, became the model for the Theatre, which opened in Shoreditch on one of the main roads leading out of London, three years after Queen Elizabeth's visit to Canterbury (and, incidentally, lodged the word in English with its modern meaning). These new public playhouses offered 'gallimaufreys' – hotchpotches of romance and drama, narra-tives with 'many a terrible monster made of broune paper', amorous knights, acrobatics and knockabout clowns. These med-leys, Philip Sidney's 'mungrell Tragycomedie', catered to a new body of urban playgoers who were looking for something in between community religious drama and the stiffer plays per-formed in private homes and after banquets. Powerful men such as the Lord Chamberlain and the Earl of Leicester, Robert

Dudley, began to sponsor the playhouses, as presenting the new drama at court became a sign of their status and standing with the Queen, with rival companies doing battle over who was chosen to perform the Christmas entertainments. At first, this was a London-based phenomenon and the provinces lagged behind, but go-ahead companies such as 'the Lord of Leycester his players' would have brought the drama that so captivated Christopher Marlowe to Canterbury.

What is more, Stephen Gosson was once again showing the way. He had begun to write plays. None has survived, but the author Francis Meres ranked him 'the best for pastoral', and Gosson himself mentions a tragedy, *Cataline's Conspiracy*, a comedy, *Captain Mario*, and a moral play, *Praise at Parting*. According to Gosson, it was *Cataline's Conspiracy* that Marlowe was first to see, when he was ten, in 1574 – the year that 'diverse strange impressions of fire and smoke' appeared in the night skies over Canterbury, and the heavens seemed to burn 'marvellously ragingly', with flames that rose from the horizon and met overhead, 'and did double and roll in one another, as if it had been in a clear furnace'. It was a magnificent display of the aurora borealis, but to the impressionable Christopher it seemed a portent. If Stephen could do it, so could he.

The King's School, when Christopher finally made it there in 1578, greatly improved his formal education and unlike his earlier schools it also gave him the freedom and opportunity to strut his hour or two upon a stage. Like the grander English public schools, The King's School had a lively tradition of performance. The acting of plays there was not only well established, but during Marlowe's lifetime even threatened to get a little out of hand as 'playing had become such an accomplished diversion among the schoolboys that it posed a problem of discipline'.

The boys were renowned for Christmas entertainments in the cathedral, 'settynge furthe of Tragedies, Comedyes, and inter-ludes' in costumes that involved considerable expenditure – the headmaster one year receiving an astonishing £14 6s 8d for Christmas plays. Their efforts at least once so impressed some passing professionals that they 'dyd anymate the boyes' to run away and join their troupe, promising them a princely £4 a year in earnings, and later again inveigled the boy players 'to go abrode in the country to play playes contrary to lawe and good order' – far more tempting than the school plays, which were performed in Latin and Greek, but Christopher resisted.

Like Stephen Gosson, Christopher aimed at university, and on writing plays rather than acting in them. But in 1578, univer-sity was barely within his reach. At his new school he embarked upon more complex Latin grammar, later voyaging into Greek and the deeper waters of prose and poetry, before casting up on the rocks of rhetoric. Mere learning was not enough, 'rhetoric' helped translate language into persuasive action. He had to recognise rhetorical forms and devices used by the ancients, to master the skills of clear expression and to discriminate between good and bad style. He had also to learn how to make links between history and present behaviour. As Richard Grenewey, who translated Tacitus in the 1590s, put it: 'History [is] the treasure of times past, as well as a guide an image of man's present estate: a true and lively pattern of things to come, [and], as some term it, the workmistress of experience . . .'. So Chris-topher read the poets and the historians – the chaste bits at least – of Terence, Virgil, Ovid, Plautus and Horace; Sallust, Cicero, Caesar, Martial, Juvenal and Livy, and also such moderns as Erasmus and Baptista Mantua. In his final year he would have had to deliver several formal declamations.

Like Stephen before him he was a day boy, starting school at six in the morning with prayers and psalm-singing in the cathedral, before passing back under 'the Dark Entry', the low passage between the cloisters and the school, to his lessons (cf. 'There's a dark entry where they take it in . . .', *The Jew of Malta* iii 4). Money was deducted from his scholarship allowance to pay for lunch at school: breast of mutton, according to one kitchen account, with peas and prunes; fish every Friday, and salt fish and herring during Lent. The cobbler's boy from St George's parish began to make friends above his station – like Samuel Kennet. Sam and Kit were new boys together and left school in the same year. Sam's father had served in the royal households of both Henry VIII and the present queen, and his great-great-grandfather had been standard-bearer to Henry V at Agincourt. He had Kit enthralled with family stories of knights and the glory of England, and was even more awe-inspiring for his glittering treasure of first-hand tales of court life.

Now that he was rubbing doublets with the gentry, Kit had to brush up on his manners. The instructions to young Francis – the French boy he encountered in the language book he had used with Oliver's father – would have helped: use a napkin, not your hand to wipe your mouth; don't touch food that you are not going to eat yourself; don't lean on the table ('Did you learne to eat in a hogstie?'); clean your own knife and put it back in its sheath (forks were not yet widely used in England); don't pick your teeth with your penknife (use a 'tooth-picke of quill or wood'); and be sure not to get your sleeves in the fat.

And as Christopher had done with Stephen Gosson, so Oliver tagged along with Christopher at every free moment. Records are scanty, but documents in the Bernhardt Institute collection help build up a picture of the two boys at the time. An 'apprisement of suche goodes as were Mr Oliver Laurens's' (dated 1609), made after his death, includes a list of books, some of which must date back to his boyhood.* 'Nowels Catechismes

---

* Bernhardt Institute, Laurens box, folder 6.

one in Latin, one in Englishe' and '*Luciana dialogi Latini et hist*', which has an annotation in a different, unidentified hand, revealing that Oliver was taught Latin as a child by 'the atheist Marloe'. If the Lucian indeed included *The True History*, then the boys at least had some fantasising fun during their after-hours lessons, as the book claims to describe a journey to the moon. Dr Rosine cites an account of Oliver taking Christopher to worship at a Huguenot chapel, and we find Christopher getting into trouble when he 'solde his poyntes' to a scrivener in exchange for teaching Oliver to write – 'poyntes' were tagged laces for tying doublet to hose. These were apparently special silver-tipped ones given to Christopher by Sir Roger Manwood. This account was in a copy of a deposition by the ever-litigious John Marlowe, though the case is surprisingly absent from Canterbury records.*

Christopher spent just two years at The King's School. In 1580 – not quite in the footsteps of Stephen Gosson, who had gone to Oxford – he was promised a scholarship to Corpus Christi College, Cambridge. His voice as well as his learning had got him there. The scholarship, one in a long line established by Archbishop Parker, himself Master of Corpus Christi from 1544 to 1553, had been set out in the archbishop's will and provided for a scholar of The King's School who was Canterbury born and bred. It required that:

> . . . schollers shal and must at the time of their election be so entered into the skill of song as that they shall at first sight solf [sing to the sol-fa syllables] and sing plaine song. And they shalbe of the best and aptest schollers well instructed in their grammer and if it may be such as can make a verse.

---

* Laurens box, folder 8.

Young Christopher could do all that, and well. Even at the age of sixteen he could 'make a verse' better than the rest. With the scholarship, he had almost reached the peak of the first 'high Pyramide' he had set himself to scale, in a climb that had begun the day that Stephen Gosson had walked into John Marlowe's shop to buy new shoes for school.

Stephen's life, however, had suddenly and radically changed course. He had failed to take his degree, had hived off to London to write plays, and now, suddenly, in the year before Marlowe went up to Cambridge, had done a complete about-face and published the *Schoole of Abuse*, one of the most vituperative anti-theatre diatribes of the time, railing on (once he had finished with the evils of plays and players) against the decay of the English spirit. According to Gosson's *Alchemist* pamphlet, Marlowe was deeply affected by the book, and had, by the time he went up to university, become a Puritan. His friendship with Sam Kennet, who was about to embark upon his career as 'the most terrible Puritan' in the Tower, would seem to bear this out. But even if this is so, it was not a state of grace that was to last very long. The prods and tugs of Kit's new fortune would propel him in alarming new directions. The boy who had thought: 'That like I best that flies beyond my reach' was about to stretch himself further than he had ever done before. In 1580 – the year in which earthquakes shook England, setting church bells pealing unaided, and a blazing star appeared in Pisces – Kit Marlin (as he had started to style himself) sloughed off Canterbury and set out for Cambridge.

CHAPTER TWO

Une Histoire Inventée

Sir Francis Walsingham, the English ambassador who had been so appalled by the St Bartholomew's Day Massacre, was back in England by the time Kit left Canterbury, and an increasingly potent force in foreign affairs. Elizabeth had made him Secretary of State the year after the massacre and knighted him four years later. He had been involved with Lord Burghley's spies for years. Now he himself was beginning to throw out the first strands of a net of espionage that he was to knot, weave and twitch for the rest of his life. A silent, labouring spider, he spun his web to snare his enemies and serve his Queen. It obsessed him. So much so that he sunk his personal fortune into it and died in poverty.

Sir Francis was a thin man. He held himself straight, and his beard was perfectly clipped and combed. He had the sort of mouth that settles naturally into a slight downward curve, and eyes that seemed to show permanent, personal moral disapproval. His Queen called him her 'Moor', perhaps because of his reputation for scheming (attributed variously in Elizabethan times to Moors or Jews), coupled with his swarthy complexion and a fondness for wearing black. The historian William Camden labelled him 'a sharp maintainer of the purer religion', a fervent Protestant, if not a Puritan, who dedicated himself to the exposure of Catholic plots against the realm and believed 'that devilish woman' Mary, Queen of Scots, was a danger as long as she lived. Under the Catholic Mary Stuart he had fled England to study at the tolerant University of Padua, and was fluent in both Italian and French. In foreign affairs he was an ardent interventionist, advocating aggressively anti-Catholic policies. In this he was opposed to the conservative Lord Treasurer Lord Burghley, and by the Queen herself, who was unwilling to be drawn into a Protestant crusade that might unite Spain and France with Scotland, against her. But Elizabeth was certain of one thing about her 'Moor': only death would end his consuming loyalty. 'Mr Secretary' would adoringly, doggedly, dutifully perform her will, even if he disagreed. Disagreement was allowed. Sir Francis fearlessly argued his position, driving his monarch to outbursts of screaming fury, but, once a course was settled, he was a servant of the Queen, not an adviser.

The issue that most exercised Elizabeth, Lord Burghley, Sir Francis and his fellow hawk, the Queen's current favourite, the Earl of Leicester, was the situation in the Low Countries, then the main battleground between Protestantism and Catholicism in Europe. In 1572, the same year as the St Bartholomew's Day Massacre, the Protestant Dutch had seized part of their territories back from the occupying Spanish. After the Dutch Revolt, the northern provinces (roughly approximating to the Netherlands of today) had united in a Protestant bloc, while the southern part (much of which is now Belgium) was still controlled by Catholic Spain, which also ruled over much of Italy and had ambitions in France and England. Whilst the United Provinces in the north declared their independence, forces led by the Duke of Parma were conducting an increasingly successful reconquest of the Low Countries from the south. Walsingham and Leicester pressed for military intervention: in the Low Countries to help William of Orange against the Spanish, and in France to assist the Huguenots in their struggle against the pro-

Spanish Guisards. If England did not help, reasoned the interventionists, this brought the prospect of direct Spanish invasion of the island even closer. The Queen demurred, and was supported in her reluctance by moderates, such as Lord Burghley, that ever-adroit, politically pliable kinsman of Eleanor Bull, a man who had served under both Catholic and Protestant queens, who carried a copy of Cicero and the Protestant *Prayer Book* in his pocket, but at home kept a certificate signed by the vicar of Wimbledon, proving he had attended Catholic mass under Mary, just in case.

In 1578 Elizabeth had further complicated matters by entering into negotiations for marriage to François, Duke of Anjou, hoping, it seems, to ensure French help against the Spanish, and put a brake on those of her ministers pressurising for English involvement in the Low Countries. Though the duke was a Catholic, anti-Spanish feeling was feasibly strong enough for the French to be persuaded to aid the Dutch rebels, allowing England to side-step the conflict. In 1581, after some years of uncertainty, Elizabeth announced her intention to go ahead with the marriage. This horrified Walsingham, and caused alarm among the Protestant populace, who feared the consequences of a marriage to a Catholic prince (they had been down that road before with Mary I), and that England might become a satellite to a foreign Catholic power. So back home Elizabeth was having to prove her Protestant credentials. And the proof came in the persecution. Execution of Catholic priests began in 1577 and increased sharply from 1581. The Recusancy Act of 1581 upped penalties for absence from church services to £20 a month (about 500 times a workman's daily wage).

What was guaranteed to unite Burghley, Leicester and Walsingham was the belief that English Catholics were involved in an international popish plot to overthrow the Queen. There were indeed plots to kill Elizabeth, to assist foreign invasion, and to put Mary Queen of Scots on the throne. Catholicism became defiant, dangerous, extreme – and, perhaps just for those reasons, alluring to hot-headed young men. In the very year that Kit began at Cambridge, Jesuits from abroad had set up a network there to recruit students to the faith.

Such were the political winds that were blowing as Kit Marlin trudged, through biting winter air from Saffron Walden, on the last leg of his journey to Cambridge. But Rome's 'wicked ways' offered no allure to the conservative, puritanical, sixteen-year-old who arrived at Bene't College – as Corpus Christi was then known – just after Christmas in 1580. It had been a long and arduous journey, and he immediately spent 1*d* on a meal, just enough for a little ale and a warming pottage (winter vegetables boiled with eggs, milk, saffron and a scraping of ginger) and perhaps, given the season, a mince pie made with mutton, beef suet, 'various kinds of Spicery' (nutmeg, mace cinnamon, depending on what could be afforded), orange and lemon peel, and perhaps a dash of 'sack' (sherry). His expenditure is recorded in the college buttery book, a patchily extant record of what students spent on food and drink, which together with the college account books give us an idea of Kit's movements during his years at Cambridge.

Just getting started at Bene't was an expensive business. The account books record 'Marlin' as paying a heavy 3*s* 4*d* as an admission fee to the college, and he also had to find 4*d* for the college gatekeeper (followed by another 4*d* when he was officially admitted as a scholar). To make matters worse, Christopher Pashley, his predecessor as Canterbury scholar, was tardy in packing his bags, and it was not until May that Kit Marlin officially took up the scholarship and matriculated. Just how he survived during these expensive first months is unclear; no doubt he was admitted on the strength of the scholarship that was to come, but somebody seems to have been supporting him. Perhaps Sir Roger Manwood once again came to the rescue, ascertaining a well-made Latin epitaph from the clever young man who could already 'make a verse' better than his contemporaries.

Kit joined the other two Canterbury scholars, Robert Thexton and Thomas Leugar, in a small chamber that had been converted from a 'stoare house' in the north-west corner of what is now Corpus Christi's Old Court. He was a lanky youth, with the sort of shining, marble-white skin that seems visibly to tingle; and sparkling, sun-bright eyes, part flint, part green (a besotted elderly Fellow has left us a record).* We know from Stephen Gosson that even as a child Kit had a 'sharp-provided wit', and at Bene't he impressed immediately with his 'nimble mind' and 'retorts dextrous'. He also made a mark with his consumption of ale. Will Dukenfield, the malmsey-nosed tavern keeper of the Eagle & Childe (now the Eagle), two steps and a stumble from the Bene't College gate, in his very old age remembered young Marlin as being addicted to 'wine, women and watching [staying up all night]' and 'sitting at good ale, swilling and carousing' all day long. Dukenfield's recollection is itself no doubt ale-washed and subject to a certain lack of focus, so we cannot really be certain of its veracity, much less pinpoint it in time, and it should be noted that all this was reported by Dukenfield's grandson many years after Marlowe and the flame-faced old tavern-keeper himself had died.†

However, quite soon after arriving in Cambridge Kit's puritanical carapace was starting to crack. Initially, part of his attraction to the university, and to Bene't College especially, had been its Puritan reputation. Bene't was pre-eminently a Puritan

---

* This is revealed in Beryl Tondo's paper 'Five Hundred Years of Corpus Recollections', and is the first indication that his eyes were hazel, and not brown, as in the retouched portrait at Corpus Christi College. Later paintings bear this out.

† W. C. Dukenfield, *What a Man!*, p. 53.

college. Dr Aldrich, the Master until just five years before Kit arrived, was a leading partisan supporting the Puritan Thomas Cartwright, who had famously clashed with Bishop Whitgift, and been deprived of the chair of Divinity. Robert Browne, the founder of the 'Brownists', the forerunners of Congregationalism, completed his degree there in 1576, and had preached without licence in St Benet's church in 1580. The church, which doubled as a college chapel, was well within earshot of Kit's room. He had swapped the noise of the St George's great waking bell, for the regular toll of St Benet's (cf. 'The triplex, sir, is a good tripping measure; or the bells of Saint Bennet, sir, may put you in mind – one, two, three', *Twelfth Night* V i 34–5).

Kit held his scholarship for the full course of six years, to Masters degree level, rather than for the four-year bachelor of arts degree. (An MA ordinarily took seven years, which probably explains why he had to find some other sort of funding for the first few months.) Under the terms of Archbishop Parker's scholarship, which aimed at staffing the established church, this meant that he had said that he would be taking holy orders. Either young Kit was sincerely intent on life as a clergyman – be it Protestant or Puritan – or he was showing a cool Machiavellian approach to getting the best education he could. However it was not unknown for other young men in similar situations to change their minds about religion. Stephen Gosson had abandoned playwriting in favour of railing against the sins of the theatre, and later entered the church; his friend Sam Kennet, who was already terrorising Catholic prisoners as yeoman warder in the Tower of London, would before Kit had finished his degree be converted to Rome. And Kit soon discovered that at Cambridge, in addition to 'minds of the pure religion', there was a knot of rebellious, rather clever young men who deplored what the poet John Donne (whose time there overlapped in part with Kit's) called the 'plain, simple, sullen, young, contemptuous' features of Puritanism. One of this clutch of rebels was Thomas Nashe, a bright, skinny, boyish student who came up to St John's College within a couple years of Kit entering Bene't; he would soon become his close friend and collaborator. But even before he met Thomas Nashe, Kit's perspectives were shifting.

Ours is not the only era in which young men between the ages of sixteen and twenty are ambitious, kick against fortune and convention, question their lot, and reinvent themselves a thousandfold. It is clear that Kit Marlin, at the tumultuous age of seventeen, was developing his own style, and a bit of a swagger – according to Gosson, the cobbler's eldest son was becoming a 'malapert [impudent] full-mouth, breathing defiance'.* And there are hints that, during his first months at Bene't, Kit was rudderless and malcontent. Part of the reason for this had to do with his status. Even more than at that 'seminary for gentlemen', The King's School, he now found himself exposed to the nobility and upper classes. Archbishop Cranmer had argued when re-founding The King's School that it was 'through the benefit of learning and other civil knowledge, for that most part, [that] all gentle[men] ascend to their estate'. Tudor humanists, the historian John Adamson points out, had for some time been arguing that learning, manners and deportment were no less conferrers of gentlemanly virtues than noble lineage. Kit felt this keenly, but at Cambridge social rank was structured and glaring. The sons of the nobility and gentry were counselled to 'Consort yourself with gentlemen of your own rank and quality.' Though some students ostentatiously glittered, others were dismally poor. On the one hand were rich young blades such as Robert Devereux, the Earl of Essex, who spent a

---

* *Alchemist,* folio 12.

mighty £7 on refurbishing his room at Trinity College, putting extra glass in the windows and buying wall hangings for his study; on the other were those like the wretched youth who owned little more than 'a thinne Chest', a hat, a hooded gown, a chair, one pair of hose, an old shirt, a meatknife, eight books, a lute, three sheets, and 'a very old Blankett'. Kit fell somewhere in between. College records place the new scholar 'Marlin' in the *convictus secundus,* the 'second list' of students who were neither poor 'sizars', who had to perform menial tasks for other students (such as cleaning and waiting at table) to pay their way – the fate of a cobbler's son, had it not been for the Parker Scholarship – nor 'fellow-commoners', rich boys like Essex, whose parents filled pockets and college coffers with gold, who dined at the Fellows' table, and who were generally allowed to proceed to their degrees without the bothersome intervention of examinations.

For Kit, certain of his intellectual superiority, this social inferiority smarted. John Bakeless reads this resentment into lines from *Hero and Leander*: 'And to this day is every scholar poor,/Gross gold from them runs headlong to the boor', and you can hear Kit's frustration in the lament: 'Alas, I am a scholar!/How should I have gold?/All that I have is but my stipend . . . /Which is no sooner receiv'd but it is spent' (*The Massacre at Paris* I vii 18–20). At first, it would seem, he tried rather foolishly to buy himself into favour. Urry notes that 'Marlin's' expenditure in his second week at college was a lavish 3s 1½d, an amount he never again equalled, not even in his heady final years, and a huge extravagance for someone who was supposed to be getting by on a shilling a week. But Kit soon realised that conspicuous consumption or headlong hospitality (whatever it was that demanded such spending) was pointless, and instead fell back on a more sustainable resource: his 'ingenuity'. He reacted to this world of gentlemen who demanded deference and respect, with pride, rebellion and a deployment of ready wit – a response he would recall years later when he wrote *Edward II*:

> . . . you must cast the scholar off,
> And learn to court it like a gentleman.
> 'Tis not a black coat and a little band,
> A velvet-cap'd cloak, fac'd before with serge,
> And smelling to a nosegay all the day,
> Or holding of a napkin in your hand,
> Or saying long grace at table's end,
> Or making low legs to a nobleman,
> Or looking downward with your eyelids close,
> And saying 'Truly, an't may please your honour,'
> Can you get any favour with great men.
> You must be proud, bold, pleasant, resolute,
> And now and then stab, as occasion serves.
> (*Edward II* II i 30–42)

It was not deference that would get you high friends and favour, it was spark. Not for Kit the making of low legs to noble-men, the downcast eyes and 'May it please your honour'. He was proud and resolutely cocky, but a charmer. The lanky lad with a sharp wit and a ready retort made friends easily, even, it soon became clear, across social barriers that were not usually breached. The stabbing part ('now and then stab') was to come later.

At the same time Kit shed his Puritanism. What replaced it? A curious and previously unnoted interlude in his first year at Bene't gives us a clue. Urry hints at it when he reveals that: 'In 1581 one William Peeters, during Marlowe's absence, was granted Marlowe's food, which was charged against him in his absence . . .'. Other biographers have simply let this pass, but what young Kit got up to in those weeks has a curious link with the murder in Deptford twelve years later, and casts some light on the course his life was taking. People he met during this short absence from Cambridge were one day completely to redirect his life. The evidence lies in two unexpected places: an archive in Belgium, and the Vatican.*

William (or Willem) Peeters was from Flanders. An erstwhile student of the University of Leiden, he arrived in Cambridge as an 'instrumentalist' with a group of travelling players. This is not unprecedented. Strolling troupes did pass through the town, and foreign musicians were not uncommon. Two broad types of theatre were performed at the university in Kit's time. The colleges staged performances as instructive academic exercises, mostly in Latin, sometimes in Greek, and occasionally venturing lighter fare in English; wilder, wickeder and more exciting drama came in the form of comedies and satires performed by commercial players. The authorities frequently tried to discourage such wanton revels. Lord Leicester's Men, whom Kit had already seen perform in Canterbury, had been prevented from performing in Cambridge in 1579. The following year, Lord Burghley, who was chancellor of the university, recommended that his son-in-law the Earl of Oxford's men come to Cambridge. Though the company had just performed for the Queen, the vice-chancellor politely scotched Burghley's request, pleading the dangers of plague at public assemblies, and sniffily stating that commencement (the time of conferring degrees) was upon them and this 'requireth rather diligence in stodie than dissoluteness in playes'. Even the Queen's Men, three years later, were sent off with a payment of 50 shillings for *not* performing, 'forbidding theim to playe in the towne & so ridd theim cleane away'.

But other troupes did perform, and English plays were becom-

---

* The Geenstad city archive has a box of documents and letters relating to Peeters, hereinafter referred to as *Peeters* with the appropriate document number; the Vatican source is the rarely consulted 'Miscellaneous Papers' of Pope Vicarious I (Vat. Vic. Misc).

ing wildly popular with student actors too. We know that *Gammer Gurton's Needle* was performed at Christ's College and the lively satire *Tarrarantantara* wowed audiences more than once at Clare. At Trinity, Kit and Thomas Nashe enjoyed *Pedantius*, which scoffed at the Puritan Gabriel Harvey, who was a Fellow of Trinity Hall and a mutual enemy of theirs. The players mimicked Harvey's mannerisms perfectly and, said Nashe, 'delineated [him] from the soale of the foote to the crowne of head'. Another play, *Duns Furens* so lambasted 'the little Minnow his Brother' Richard Harvey that, according to Nashe, '*Dick* came and broke the Colledge glasse windows', and was put in the stocks till the show was over, and for most of the next night too. Furious fenestraclasm seems to have been a favourite mode of dramatic critique. In 1583 Trinity paid 'for lv foot of newe glasse in the hall after the playes', and subsequent to that took the precaution of 'taking downe and setting vp the glasse wyndowes' for the duration, while St John's paid for 'nettes to hange before the windowes of ye Halle', before giving up on such flimsy protection and following Trinity's lead. 'Stage-keepers', sometimes armed and often equipped with visors and steel caps, were employed to try to keep order. But audience participation remained energetic. Sir John Harington, who was a 'truantly scholar' at King's around 1580, noted that the antics of the stage-keepers often made matters worse, as they went up and down 'with vizors and lights, puffing and thrusting, and keeping out all men so precisely, till all the town is drawn by this revel to the place; and at last, tag and rag, fresh men and sub-sizers, and all be packed in together so thick, as now is scant left room for the prologue to come upon the stage'.

In the Bene't college accounts for 1581, we find a payment of 10*d* 'made to one Lamb and Porter' 'for making houses at the Comaedie' and another 'In Largeis to the Actors for a Beaver [visor]'. Was this perhaps the company William Peeters was with, unused to rumbustious Cambridge audiences, and having to provide themselves with a 'stagekeeper'? Certainly Peeters joined a company of English players in Leiden early in 1581, and was back at the university in late 1582.* Printed bills announcing English players are mentioned in a Dutch document from 1565, and organised groups of professional players from England became increasingly common on the Continent from the 1580s onwards. The troupes managed to travel through war zones, and indeed accompanied military leaders, sometimes appearing to perform for soldiers and citizens on both sides of the conflict. Such troupes would play an important part in Kit's life over the next few years.

Just how Kit made contact with William Peeters is uncertain, though it is conceivable that his prowess with the Dutch language, picked up in Canterbury, provided the introduction, or possibly it was his interest in drama. It would certainly seem that despite the implicit reprimand he had received reading his friend Stephen Gosson's *Schoole of Abuse*, Kit's enthusiasm for the theatre was very much alive. He was quickly giving up on Stephen's Puritanism. 'Will not a filthy play,' ranted a Puritan preacher, 'with the blast of a trumpet, sooner call thither a thousand, than an hour's tolling of a bell bring to the sermon a hundred?' That, for the future playwright, was precisely the attraction.

Obscurity surrounds the arrangement Kit made with Peeters, but whatever it was, it would appear to have had the blessing of the college authorities. Students were supposed to stay up at university full time, though with permission they could absent themselves for four weeks a year. The malapert Marlin appears to have persuaded the college to allow a similar arrangement to that practised by students at the Inns of Court, who would pay someone else to be at the meals that were a compulsory part of attendance requirements.† Perhaps he convinced them

---

* *Peeters* Aa5.
† *Peeters* Aa7.

that he could benefit from a period of study at Leiden, temporarily taking Peeters's vacated place, and thus effecting one of
the world's first ever student exchanges. Certainly the famous
university at Padua welcomed a great many foreign students,
often from middling or lower ranks, who did not register officially for the 'studium', but followed courses of study on an infor-
mal basis for a short period of time. Perhaps Marlin convinced
the authorities that he was going to do the same at Leiden. In
any event, the college tolerated his absence, and charged him
for Peeters's meals. But Leiden was not his destination. In the
late summer of 1581, he was in Francc.

We get glimpses only of Kit on his first journey abroad. It would
seem that he travelled with the players as a musician – most
likely a 'singing-man' – and under Peeters's name. This was
daring, but would have obviated the need for a passport. The
English, unless they were merchants, had to obtain a licence to
travel to foreign countries. This was issued by a court official or
nobleman, and often had conditions attached, such as strictures
on visiting Rome or other places where there were Catholic
seminaries. A similar arrangement existed for troupes of players
moving around the Continent, where local notables or city
fathers would provide them with written permission to proceed,
and sometimes a promise of protection along the way. The passport issued to Will Ireland and his troupe still included Peeters's
name at the time when he was eating Marlin's meals in Bene't
(see Appendix I). In an age with no photographs, it was simple
enough for Kit, an accomplished linguist, to assume the persona
of the Fleming, and head off on an expenses-paid adventure.
Such flits happened. The players that 'dyd anymate the boyes'
of the King's School 'to go abrode in the country to play playes
contrary to lawe and good order', lured them with promises

of good earnings. A letter from one J. Beaulieu to William Trumbull, the English envoy at the court at Brussels, requested: 'I send you a note of my Lord Deny for the finding of a certain youth of his, who hath been debauched from him by certain players, and is now with them at Brussels'. Kit, obviously, did not want to relinquish his scholarship, nor to travel with the players forever – hence his contrivance with Peeters and dissembling of college authorities – but it is clear that the twin lures of theatre and travel were irresistible to him, even at this stage.

The players were heading for Paris, in all likelihood following in the train of a diplomatic mission sent to discuss the marriage between Queen Elizabeth and François, Duke of Alençon (later Duke of Anjou), the Queen having just announced her intention of marrying the French prince. Whether or not she meant this is unclear, but she sent a reluctant representative, Sir Francis Walsingham, to Paris to negotiate the match. He was also charged with carefully putting together an Anglo-French treaty intended to muzzle Spanish aggression (this was the whole point of the proposed nuptials), and to divine the attitude of Anjou's brother King Henri, without whose support the scheme would be worthless. Sir Francis was accompanied by his young second cousin Thomas, who was just a year older than Kit and was acting as a courier. Thomas Walsingham had in his company an Englishman called 'Skeggs', who Charles Nicholl convincingly surmises is none other than Nicholas Skeres, one of the fateful four who were in Eleanor Bull's house in Deptford that day in May 1593. Also in the party was Thomas Watson, a young Catholic poet who had once been resident in Douai and who was also carrying messages for Sir Francis. Tom Watson and Kit were to become close friends and one day to end up in jail together. Kit and Tom Walsingham would become even closer. Many years later, when he was writing *Meliboeus* as an elegy to Sir Francis, Tom Watson would dedicate the poem to Thomas Walsingham, and recall with affection these days in Paris, when they were living 'by the banks of the Seine'.

Espionage historian Gertrud Zelle has uncovered an account that gives us one brief flash of Kit and the two Thomases on their evening revels around town, consuming large quantities of wine, tucking in to wild boar (cheaper and more readily available than in England), capons with oranges (to them a novel combination) and mounds of bread (far more than was the customary back home), all the time Kit's dazzling wit and facility with French easing the way.* The only other evidence indicating that Kit may have been in Paris is circumstantial: a story about an affair in the upper echelons of Parisian society was doing the rounds in the city's taverns at the time, and it emerged many years later as the plot for *Measure for Measure*. The French scholar Georges Lambin uncovered the Parisian tale, and found that it is used in the play with barely disguised names: Angelo for Angenoust, Claudio for Claude Tonard, Varrius for de Vaux, and so on all the way down to one Ragosin, who appears as Ragozine the pirate.

After Kit had been in Paris just a few days, somebody – most likely Thomas Walsingham, but maybe Sir Francis himself – gave him the task of going to Rheims, to collect a 'Note'. Rheims was the location of an English Catholic seminary, a honeypot for converts and between 1580 and 1587 believed to be the source of almost every plot against Elizabeth. The English College had been founded in Douai, in Flanders, in 1569, but had been forced to move to Rheims when Protestants took over the town in 1578. It soon became a focal point for English Catholics of all classes, a source of anti-Elizabethan pamphlets and banned devotional books (such as the Rheims Bible), and a training ground for missionaries – like the Jesuits who had arrived to

---

* Zelle, *Bare Truth*, pp. 238–40, cites an unsigned letter mentioning the antics about town of one 'Christophe Merlin'.

garner converts in Cambridge, just as Kit was beginning his studies. There was, as Gray puts it, a 'perpetual leakage' of students from Cambridge to Rheims, which increased markedly after 1580. Robert Parsons, who like his associate Edmund Campion toured England luring youth to Rome, reported back to Claudius Acquavivia, the Superior General of the Jesuits, that: 'At Cambridge I have at length insinuated a certain priest into the very university under the guise of a scholar or a gentleman commoner and have procured him help from a place not far from town; within a few months he has sent over to Rheims seven very fit youths.' So Kit would have heard of Rheims. Maybe he rather wanted to go there himself, flirting with the views of Catholic rebels, as he slid back from 'plain, sullen' Puritanism. It may even have been the very reason he accompanied the players to Paris.

If Kit made friends in Paris, he made a lifelong enemy at Rheims. Richard Baines had been a gentleman pensioner at Christ's College in Cambridge, and had later moved to Caius, a seedbed for young Catholics, before enrolling at the seminary in Rheims in 1578. By the time Kit arrived to collect the 'Note' from him, Baines was already a deacon and set for full ordination in a matter of weeks. But things were not as they seemed. Baines was spying for the English government. He was hobnobbing with his superiors, trying to find out secrets about the English College president Dr William Allen 'and set[ting] them down in writing, with intent to give the note of the same to the [Privy] Council'. He was insinuating himself among younger students too, who (in a monastically austere, religiously fanatical environment) he thought 'might easily be carried into discontentment' and encouraged 'to mislike of rule and discipline, and of subjection to their masters'. Not content with sniffing out secrets and stirring rebellion, he had a plan to kill off the entire college population by poisoning the well water. That sort of melodramatic gesture befitted him well. A fluttering, flattering 'water-fly',* he was also the 'fawning spaniel'† who would obsequiously contradict himself as he stumbled along behind the prevailing opinion of a conversation. He was verbose, full of 'pretty scoffs' and 'wicked words' (though more so in speech than in the tittle-tattling 'Notes' he wrote), admitting that he 'had a delight rather to fill [his] mouth and the auditors' ears with dainty, delicate, nice and ridiculous terms and phrases, than with wholesome, sound and sacred doctrine'. Soft, rather than purposefully fat, he greedily desired 'of more ease, wealth and . . . of more delicacy of diet and carnal delights than this place of banishment [Rheims] was like to yield . . .', and he had an eye for a 'well-looked boy'.

There was a vindictive streak, too, and in situations where he did not feel he was the weaker participant, he could be a bully. Charles Nicholl argues that it could very well be Richard Baines who is the 'Mr Wanes' in Paris in the spring of 1580, who 'came unto one Henry Baily, a young youth, & demanded of him who was come of Rhemes and what their names were, having the boy in a corner of a chamber'. With his juniors he was also affected and boastful. This, where Kit was concerned, proved his downfall. Baines, who of necessity had to be reticent about his prowess for plotting, was bursting to tell the well-appointed young courier what he had been up to. Kit in turn told the college president, Dr William Allen. Just why he did this is not clear. Perhaps he had taken an instant dislike to Baines. Perhaps he did already have Catholic sympathies. It is also possible that this was the secret brief for Kit's journey in

---

* This according to Dr William Allen (Vat. Vic. Misc. Allen 3/6). The term is best explained by Samuel Johnson in his dictionary: 'A water-fly skips up and down upon the surface of the water, without any apparent purpose or reason, and is thence the proper emblem for a busy trifler'.

† Allen again (Vat. Vic. Misc. Allen 3/6), who appears to enjoy zoological metaphor.

the first place: Rheims conveniently focused anti-English government activity, and to have the college wiped out at a single sip by an egotistical maverick agent would not have been helpful to Sir Francis Walsingham. It is conceivable, too, that one of the Thomases was behind the exposure. We know that Thomas Watson had interests in both camps, as a Catholic in government service; and Thomas Walsingham had been involved in negotiations with Mary Stuart's official ambassador in Paris.

As it turns out, Dr Allen already knew. In a letter to the Jesuit and college warden, Alfonso Agazzari, in May 1582, William Allen says Baines had been an *explorator* (spy) for four years – ever since his first admission. Allen bided his time, 'unmasked' the interloper some months after Kit's visit, and locked him up for nearly a year. We know of Kit's part as an informer through a second letter, from Dr Allen to an unnamed priest.* What Allen knew, Baines could only suspect. He was certain Kit had a role in his exposure, but then he had also been indiscreet with a fellow seminarist to whom he offered untold wealth (quite unjustifiably, on behalf of Sir Francis Walsingham) to join him in his treachery. So he could not be sure who had caused his downfall. Nevertheless, in his lonely cell he had plenty of time to fuel his loathing. Years later, Kit would secretly mock him in *The Jew of Malta*, in which Barabas the Jew is said 'to go about to poison wells', succeeding (unlike Baines) in doing away with an entire nunnery: 'Here's a drench to poison a whole stable of Flanders mares: I'll carry't to the nuns with a powder.' (*The Jew of Malta* III iv 113–14). There are also shades of Baines in *Hamlet*'s camp, contemptible Osric, the verbose courtier who presides as a referee over the rapier fight in which Hamlet dies – taking the name 'Osric' from an earlier play, *A Knack to Know a Knave*, which is something Baines most certainly did not display

---

* Vat. Vic. Misc. Allen 4/6.

at the time. In his dank dungeon, with no proof of Kit's hand in his predicament, Baines could only silently seethe.

He was to have his revenge.

CHAPTER THREE

Catch My Soul

Kit was back in Cambridge by Michaelmas 1581. It had been a whirlwind tour of the Continent – just four or five weeks, much of the time would have been spent in transit, and at least part of this on horseback. The players had a wagon, but once Kit left them for Rheims, travelling by horse rather than walking was an expensive choice, which seems to indicate that (unless his time with the players had been especially lucrative) he was being funded by someone else.

College life was surely dull by comparison, just a little less hard and humdrum than a day at St John's College described by the preacher Thomas Lever in the 1550s:

> There be divers there which rise daily betwixte foure and five of the clocke in the morning, and from five until six of the clocke, use common prayer with an exhortacion of gods worde in a common chappell, and from six unto ten of the clocke use ever either private study or commune lectures. At ten of the clocke they go to dinner, whereas they be content with a penye piece of biefe amongest .iiii. having a fewe porage made of the brothe of the same biefe, with salt and otemell, and nothinge els.
>
> After this slender dinner they be either teachinge or

learninge untill v. of the clocke in the evening, when as
they have a supper not much better than their diner.
Immediatelie after the whiche, they go either to reasoning
in problemes or unto some other studye, until it be nine
or tenne of the clocke, and there being without fire are
faine to walk or runne up and downe halfe an houre, to
gette a heate on their feete whan they go to bed.

Lever was probably painting a heroically severe picture to
impress his congregation. Kit didn't have to run up and down
to warm his feet before going to sleep, but he was cooped up
with his fellow scholars – the senior Robert Thexton hogging
the big bed, while he and Thomas Leugar slept on hard 'truckle-
beds' that slid out from underneath, in a room that smelled of
burning animal fat from the rushlights they worked by after
dark. Though not quite as dissolute as the dramatist Robert
Greene, who admitted to 'consum[ing] the flower of my youth'
at Cambridge 'amongst wags as lewd as myself', Kit liked a jovial
cup in the company of the bacchanalian blades who came up
to college almost on a part-time basis, with no intention of taking
a degree but simply of filling in time before studying law in
London, or travelling on the Continent – 'a wild and wanton
herd . . . of youthful and unhandled colts' who spent their time
fencing and dancing, whose behaviour resulted in an increasing
number of vice-chancellor's injunctions against playing football,
going to bear-baiting and plays in the town, and whose first
element of knowledge was 'to be shown the colleges, and
initiated in a tavern by the way'.* They were a Babylonical bunch
with insatiable appetites, but unlike them Kit had a thirst for
learning as well as revelry, and the ability to indulge all his
cravings at once.

---

* The behaviour of Kit and his friends is mentioned in a letter cited by
  Tondo in 'Five Hundred Years of Corpus Recollections', p. 286.

In his first year, the rigid Cambridge curriculum officially confined his studies to Rhetoric. After that he could look forward to a year of Logic, then one of Philosophy, and later Greek, drawing and astronomy before moving on to a Masters degree. His quick mind raced beyond such limits, and he responded to academic circumscription with tangents of intellectual adventure. Cambridge allowed this. Attitudes to study underwent a radical change in the years before Kit arrived. Instead of merely lamenting the fact that lectures were so poorly attended, the authorities addressed themselves to the reason for the decline, and realised (about 100 years after the event) that the accessibility of printed books meant that students were no longer reliant on lectures for basic information. This revelation led to a new approach in which college tutors (rather than lectures) played an increasingly important role in a student's education, and good tutors turned their charges' minds and eyes to studies outside the curriculum, to books that brought them up to date with contemporary thought, and skills that would equip them for modern life. So Kit studied modern languages: French (in which he was already fluent) and Italian (which he became desperate to master), and read the controversial logician Ramus (who gets a brief critique, and is then gorily killed in *The Massacre at Paris*), Machiavelli (who delighted him) and, hot off the press, essays by Montaigne. Gabriel Harvey sourly noted the subversive course Cambridge studies were taking, complaining 'You cannot step into a scholar's study but (ten to one) you shall lightly find open either Bodin's *De Republica* or Le Roy's exposition upon Aristotle's *Politics* or some other like French or Italian politic discourse'.

Much to Kit's chagrin his curriculum did not include music, as it might have done at Oxford, and he could not afford the usual recourse of a private tutor. Ever since Thomas Bull had picked him out to sing in the Canterbury cathedral choir, and all through his time at The King's School, Kit had a passion for music. As he later put it: 'The man that hath no music in him-self,/Nor is not mov'd with concord of sweet sounds,/Is fit for treasons, stratagems, and spoils;/The motions of his spirit are as dull as night,/And his affections dark as Erebus./Let no such man be trusted' (*The Merchant of Venice* V i 83–8). The young malcontent Kit Marlin, in some turmoil over religion, full of rage and questioning, fired by new learning and excited by new friends, found counterpoise in 'the sweet power of music' – on at least one occasion in the home of the great composer and organist, William Byrd.

It is tempting to accept that the musician once dubbed as *homo memorabilis* is the 'William Byrd' who is paid 10 shillings in Bene't College accounts, and who was a university wait. 'Waits' were municipal musicians – originally watchmen who played their instruments to assure citizens that all was well, but by the sixteenth century they performed at civic occasions and hired themselves out privately. Byrd's biographer Edmund Fellowes refutes the possibility of this being the same William Byrd, pointing out that the name was a common one, and the position at this stage of his career too menial. Intriguingly, another Wil-liam Byrd (alias Borne) was a close friend of the actor-manager Edward Alleyn, became a shareholder in the Admiral's Men (the company that staged Christopher Marlowe's plays), and was paid for his additions to *Doctor Faustus*. (It is thought that he used the alias Borne to disguise his identity on religious grounds.)

But it seems Kit's contact with the composer Byrd came through theatre and his new friend from Paris, Tom Watson. Byrd composed music for *Ricardus Tertius*, a play by the Master of Caius, Thomas Legge ('an horrible papist'), which was staged a number of times in the early 1580s. Tradition has it that it was at a performance of *Ricardus Tertius* that Kit first met the young Earl of Essex, who was at Trinity, and that both men disliked the play. Whatever the truth of this, it is evident that Kit thought he could do better than Legge, and would use the same subject matter to much better effect in one of his very first history plays.

Kit was already familiar with Byrd's work – as a choirboy in Canterbury he had enjoyed singing from the composer's *Sacred Songs*, which Byrd had published with his tutor Thomas Tallis in 1575, so delighting the Queen that she granted them a countrywide monopoly in printing church music. But it was at Cambridge that he first encountered Byrd's secular music. And he liked it. He must have mentioned this to Tom Watson, because in 1582 he received an invitation, through Watson, to meet the composer (who was now approaching forty, and living in Middlesex). This may have been Tom Watson flaunting his connections, or it could quite arguably have been the Catholic net slowly closing in on Kit.

The Bene't accounts and buttery books for 1582 and 1583 show that Kit was away from college for between five and seven weeks during the summer of 1582. At the time, Tom Watson was temporarily back from Paris and was living in the parish where he had been born, St Helen's, Bishopsgate, in London. Seven years Kit's senior (Kit was still just eighteen), he seems to have stepped in to the position of older friend and mentor, from which Stephen Gosson had been tumbled by his Puritanism. Tom had come down from Oxford without taking his degree, had been a law student in London without becoming a lawyer, and now lived off his wits as a poet and playwright – with, as we have seen, the odd foray into the shadier corners of diplomacy for the 'master spyder', Sir Francis Walsingham. And he was a Catholic, a recusant whose name occurs in the St Helen's parish list of 'strangers who go not to church'. Kit joined him for a summer of writing poems, reading the classics, going to plays, and not going to church.* Tom was finishing his

---

* See Charles Parker, *Byrd*, p. 55, who cites a diary reference to 'one marlyn of Benets lying [i.e. lodging] with Watson'.

The ʾΕϰατομπα Θια or *Passionate Centurie of Love*, a series of eighteen-line poems, which he called 'sonnets', often based on classical, French or Italian sources. Kit was beginning a translation of Ovid's sensual *Amores*, relishing the chance to improve his Italian (Tom had introduced him to the poems of Tasso), and honing his poetic skills, fascinated by the form of Watson's sonnets, but not quite convinced he had got it right.

In the afternoons they went to plays – not polite indoor dramas like those written by his former Canterbury neighbour John Lyly for boy companies and courtly audiences, but rollicking gallimaufreys that coupled clowns with kings, and leashed in the odd musician and a number of nifty jiggers, too; plays the authorities disapproved of, which took place beyond City jurisdiction in the open amphitheatres of the Curtain or the Theatre, where there was 'no want of young ruffins, nor lacke of harlots, utterlie past all shame', and where law students from the Inns of Court created much the same sort of rumpus as hooligans at modern-day football matches. Here, from the gallery, they could heckle Richard Tarlton, the dumpy man who in all likelihood gave common currency to the word 'clown', and whose cross-eyes and cheeky expression had the audience wetting themselves as soon as he put his head through the hangings at the back of the stage:

> Tarlton when his head was onely seene,
> The Tirehouse dore and tapestrie betweene,
> Set all the multitude in such a laughter,
> They could not hold for scarse an houre after.

Tom and Kit were among the few who could match his banter. As the theatre historian Andrew Gurr points out, Tarlton was by the 1580s in one sense at least already a bit old-fashioned. His direct address to the audience, the gap he created between himself as clown/player and his role (a technique we would now view as distinctly post-Brechtian), was about to give way to a more illusionistic drama, where actors disappeared behind the characters they portrayed, more in the manner of cinema today. Kit, perhaps already grappling with his own first play, watched carefully, enjoyed the repartee, but did not approve. His plays were among the first to be different. Tamburlaine would edge Tarlton into the wings, as poetic tragedy supplanted knockabout. This was where he wanted to make his theatre, appealing to an amphitheatre audience, but he would draw its focus in a new direction. In the prologue to the first *Tamburlaine the Great* he promised to lead the audience away 'From jigging veins of rhyming mother-wits,/And such conceits as clownage keeps in pay.' The urbane fool Touchstone in *As You Like It* stands in direct contrast to knockabout Arden rustics, and of course there is the writer's *cri de coeur* in Hamlet's 'And let those that play your clowns speak no more than is set down for them . . .' (*Hamlet* III ii 36).

A rough new theatre was emerging from a turbulent world. It needed a figure of genius to give it fresh language and direction. Kit knew that he could do that. It is he, in the blank verse of *Tamburlaine*, his first solo effort, who would give Elizabethan drama its rhythm.

Tom had also introduced Kit to his London circle – a brood of poets and pamphleteers that burgeoned through the 1580s and 1590s, and who centuries later would be dubbed the 'University Wits' (by the wine connoisseur and doyen of Victorian literary taste, George Saintsbury). If any remnant of Puritanism still clung to Kit, it was dispelled by parley over the tavern table with Thomas Lodge, whose *Defence of Poetry Music and Stage Plays* had just unsheathed daggers against Stephen Gosson's ranting *Schoole of Abuse*. Like the others, Kit frequented St Paul's Churchyard, the centre of the printing (which then also meant publishing) and bookselling, where there were already over twenty 'stationers' at trade (the modern word has its origin in these licensed booksellers who traded from 'stations', rather than being itinerant). Kit's childhood friend, Oliver Laurens, was unhappily apprenticed here to the epitome of Sloth, so vividly described by Thomas Nashe as:

> . . . a Stationer that I knowe, with his thumb under his girdle, who if a man come to his stall and aske him for a book, never stirs his head, or looks upon him, but stands stone still, and speakes not a word: onely with his little finger points backwards to his boy, who must be his interpreter, and so all the day gaping like a dumbe image he sits without motion, except at such times as he goes to dinner or supper: for then he is as quick as other three, eating six times every day.

Oliver was later to enter into a more fruitful arrangement with the publisher Thomas Thorpe, with whom he was to work for years to come. It was with Oliver that Kit went to see the premier tourist attraction of the time, Sir Francis Drake's ship, the *Golden Hind*, moored down river at Deptford. The adventurer had returned from his circumnavigation of the globe, his ship stuffed with treasure, on a Sunday in September 1580, causing such a stir that nobody went to church that day. In the summer of 1581 the Queen visited him on board, handed a sword to the ambassador of her suitor, the Duke of Anjou, to knight him, and declared the ship a national monument. For the past year, hordes of visitors had swarmed over the ship, chipping off bits as souvenirs. Over eleven years later, when Kit was sipping ale at Eleanor Bull's house on Deptford Strand, nothing was left of the *Golden Hind* but a few skeletal timbers, sticking up from the dry dock like a rotting ribcage.

Though Kit could range around London with Oliver, he was not able to see his other old friend, Sam Kennet. The one-time 'terrible Puritan', scourge of Roman Catholic prisoners in the Tower, had himself become a convert, and by the summer of 1582 was a seminarist at Rheims. Was Kit also already a Catholic? It is hard to tell. Charles Nicholl makes the point that there was at that time something seductive about Catholicism, something forbidden that made becoming a Catholic a gesture of defiance, especially attractive to those who deplored the spread of Puritanism, and among the young literary set. Thomas Lodge would one day convert, as would the philosophically fickle Stephen Gosson, who after writing plays, then puritanically ranting against them, went off to Rheims – though he later relented and returned to England to become an Anglican vicar. Tom Watson was of course a Catholic, and when he took Kit to stay at Harlington, William Byrd's house in Middlesex, he was transporting the young man to an anteroom of Rome. Byrd's home was a resort for Catholics; it is included in a list now housed at the Public Record Office of 'places where certaine Recusantes remaine in and about the city of London: or are to be com by uppon warninge'. Though himself loyal, a Gentleman of the Chapel Royal and (it seems) enjoying special protection from the Privy Council, Byrd was a close friend of the staunch Catholic Charles Paget, and had possibly also known the plotter Anthony Babington and the recent Jesuit martyr Edmund Campion. Hovering on the edge of this circle was Robert Poley – 'Sweet Robyn' – who was to be so charming to Eleanor Bull, and who earlier that year had married Tom Watson's sister. Even more curiously, both Poley and Tom Watson were by then in the employ of Sir Francis Walsingham.

The purpose of Tom and Kit's visit to Harlington was 'to make good pastime', and was apparently innocent. Although such gatherings were not uncommon, it is not entirely true that music filtered through every aspect of Elizabethan life, as a sort of merrie muzak with citizens singing at their work, madrigals after dinner and everyone as adept as their Queen at a range of instruments; at one end of the scale (as it were) there was church music, and at the other 'that lascivious, amorous, effeminate, voluptuous music' in theatres. While perhaps many houses did have viols hanging up for guests to use, and a 'lute, cittern, and virginals, for the amusement of waiting customers, were the necessary furniture of the barber's shop', the much-quoted passage from Thomas Morley's *Plain and Easy Introduction to Music* is something of an exaggeration. Morley wrote:

> But supper being ended and music books (according to custom) being brought to the table, the mistress of the house presented me with a part earnestly requesting me to sing; but when, after many excuses, I protested unfeignedly that I could not, every one began to wonder; yea, some whispered to others demanding how I was brought up . . .

Morley, however, had a vested interest in presenting lack of musical knowledge as a social faux pas. Not only was he author of a teach-yourself music textbook, but also a composer of popular songs. After-dinner music was more likely to be presented by professionals, or talented members of the household. Yet Byrd himself had also made a famous appeal to everyone to sing, maintaining that not only did it 'strengthen all the parts of the brest' and 'open the pipes', but that the 'exercise of singing is delightful to Nature & good to preserve the health of Man', ending his uplifting evocation with the jingle 'Since singing is so good a thing/I wish all men would learne to sing'. As the syllables of the couplet make a perfect sol-fa ditty, one can imagine hapless students of Byrd forever singing these words as they practised vocal scales. Fortunately for posterity, Byrd seldom wrote his own words in his secular work, rather using poetry by the likes of Sir Philip Sidney, the Earl of Oxford, and later Kit himself, for his songs.

The gatherings at Harlington were different from the after-dinner norm; these were masters coming together to make music. That summer they sang madrigals. It was a form that was becoming increasingly fashionable in England – Tom Watson had already translated a few. *The first sett, of Italian madrigalls Englished* would be published in 1590, and dedicated to the Earl of Essex, who was also briefly of the party that summer. According to a note, which appears to have been written by an informer sent to report goings-on at Harlington, they sang the madrigal 'Why do I use my paper, ink and pen?', which had been written the year before by Henry Walpole, after a spot of Edmund Campion's blood splattered onto his coat during the execution, and which Byrd set to music. Thanks to this singing spy, we know that Byrd also set two of Kit's songs during the visit: *O mistress mine* and *It was a lover and his lass.** Eventually, Kit would use somewhat altered versions of these songs in plays, but the score Byrd later published is the original one written that summer. Kit left Harlington with two successful songs to his credit, and if not a convert to Catholicism, he did at least become a devotee of the madrigal.

There is a theory that Kit did not go directly back to Cambridge after Harlington, but was the 'Christoffer Marron' who accompanied William Stanley (then twenty-one, later to be the sixth Earl of Derby) to the Court of Navarre, and perhaps further on to Spain. The letter in which the name is mentioned survives not in its original form, but in a contemporary manuscript copy, in which other mistakes with names are made, including at least

---

*   D. J. Cornwell, *The Arts of Espionage*, p. 62.

one transposition of an 'l' to an 'r', so reading 'Marlon' for 'Marron' is not so far-fetched.* Unfortunately, no further proof exists, though it is true that Kit was later involved with the Stanley family, and the French scholar Abel Lefranc makes a convincing argument that *Love's Labour's Lost* includes scenes, characters and events that only someone with intimate knowledge of Henri of Navarre's court could have written. The Protestant Henri Bourbon was separated from his wife Marguerite de Valois, sister of the King of France, but in 1578 in an attempt at reconciliation Marguerite had returned to Navarre, where Henri held court with a learned and highly cultured male coterie. Lefranc points out the distinct parallels between real life and the plot of *Love's Labour's Lost*, where a king (in the play called Ferdinand, the name of William Stanley's older brother, later Kit's friend and patron) and three courtiers devote themselves to study and self-denial (mainly of women), but are frustrated by the arrival of the Princess of France. Lefranc quotes Montégut, the French translator of the play, as saying that the conversations, witty skirmishes and even the bad taste is so totally French that it must have been written by an insider, and points out that the three courtiers are given almost their actual names: Berowne for le baron de Biron, Longaville for le duc de Longueville, and Dumain for le duc du Maine. Furthermore, the pedantic schoolmaster Holofernes is modelled both on Kit's much-hated Welsh schoolmaster in Canterbury, and on Richard Lloyd, William Stanley's tutor and companion on the tour. Holofernes presents a pageant of the Nine Worthies in the play; Lloyd wrote a long poem on the same topic. No other source for *Love's Labour's Lost* is known. Lefranc also points out a parallel between a love story current in court, and the story of Hamlet and Ophelia. There is also the possibility of a later visit, as a 'Mr Marlin' is a messenger for Sir Henry Unton, the English

---

* Reproduced in Zelle, *Bare Truth*, pp. 263–4.

ambassador who accompanied Henry of Navarre in the wars of
1591–2. But in the absence of further evidence, we must leave
Kit's visit to Navarre dangling as an enticing possibility.

Back in Cambridge, Kit was beginning to cut quite a dash,
showing a fashionable taste for 'gorgeous attire', dressing like a
London dandy in a doublet with 'a collar that rose up so high
and sharp as if it would have cut his throat by daylight', volumin-
ous breeches 'as full and deep as the middle of winter' and soft
leather boots 'in such artificial wrinkles, sets and plaits, as if they
had been starched lately and came new from the laundress's'.
But skull caps and sombre ankle-length gowns were what the
university wanted. Such insobriety fell foul of national Sumptuary Laws, which set out a strict dress code designed to curb
extravagance and remind people of their station in life. Flouting
these laws showed just the sort of defiance that *arrivistes* like Kit
and other rebellious young 'malcontents' were notorious for,
and seems to have been quite common. Fighting a losing battle
against the flouncing ruff and dangling aiglet, the university
authorities passed a series of injunctions during the 1570s and
1580s against flashy dressing. Wearers of 'great galligaskins'
(wide breeches) and other outrageous attire would be 'ordered,
reformed and punished . . . both for stuffe, fasshion and colour'.
The 'stuffe' that courted disapproval was anything 'in upon or
about [the] doublett, coates, Jerkyn, jackett, cassock or hose,
of velvet or silke'. Unseemly 'fasshions' included too-baggy
breeches, fancy doublets, and the ruffled silks of the malcontent.
Even minimalist, rather desperate gestures like allowing your
gown collar to 'fall' rather than 'stand' were forbidden, and as
for finer details, the authorities knew them all: nothing should
be 'embrodred, powdred, pynked, or welted . . . gathered,
playted, garded, hacked, raced, laced or cutt'. Furthermore,
'long lockes of Hayre uppon the heade' gave them the horrors.
Hair had to be 'polled, notted or rounded', and nothing else.
Graduates had to forswear brightness and wear gowns made only

of 'wollen cloth of blacke, puke [a 'dirty brown' or the 'camel's colour', eclipsed in candour only by 'goose-turd' – yellowish-green], London Browne, or other sad colour'. Kit, of course, favoured 'lustie-gallant' (light red) and primary colours that showed up well in candlelight, or the newly fashionable pale tints such as 'cane' and 'milk-and-water'. Again, we hear the echo in Spencer's speech in *Edward II*, 'you must cast the scholar off,/And learn to court it like a Gentleman', and of Dr Faustus who wants to 'fill the public schools with silk'.

Despite chasing fashion, getting drunk and avoiding fines, Kit was working hard. He continued with his translation of Ovid's *Amores* – often quite racy love elegies. Bene't buttery and account books show that he was in full residence for a long and studious stretch up to gaining his BA in April 1584, though both Urry and Moore-Smith point to an absence of six or seven weeks in the summer of 1583. The recent rediscovery of a curious piece of late sixteenth-century pornography, *First suckes at the brestes of Venus*,* throws some light on what he may have been up to.

Erotic verse, upmarket literary pornography, was a legitimate source of sexual titillation for pent-up, post-pubescent Elizabethans sweating away at their studies. Thomas Nashe was later to pen the bawdy burlesque *Lenten Stuff*, and even more pithily *The Choice of Valentines* (also known as *Nashe's Dildo*), a tremendously lascivious piece about one prematurely ejaculating Tomalin and his bawd Frances, who after taking his 'silly worm' in hand, 'rolled it on her thigh ... And dandled it and danc'd it up and down', but in the end must needs resort to the services of her 'little dildo' that 'bendeth not, nor foldest any deal,/But stands as stiff as he were made of steel,/And plays at peacock

---

* Usually known as *First suckes*, with, of course, the common Elizabethan *s/f* visual pun. The work has only recently come to light, in the private possession of the American collector Julius Marx.

twixt my legs right blithe'. The fruitier bits of Kit's translation of Ovid, and later poems such as *Hero and Leander* can be seen in this light, though he seems to have disapproved of masturbation, once rebuking the 'tender churl' who 'mak'st waste in niggarding' (Sonnet 1).

First suckes seems to have been inspired by an earlier work, *I modi*, sixteen prints of 'postures' of love-making, each accompanied by an explanatory sonnet. The book was banned in Italy and though hard to come by, highly popular in England among students and lawyers at the Inns of Court. The prints in *I modi* are by 'that rare Italian master' Giulio Romano, the poems by Pietro Aretino, whom Thomas Nashe in *The Unfortunate Traveller* called 'one of the wittiest knaves that ever God made'. When it was first published, *I modi* enjoyed extensive circulation among the upper clergy and was furiously suppressed by Pope Clement VII – to the extent that almost every trace of it was eliminated. By the mid-1850s, Count Jean-Frédéric-Maximilien de Waldeck, an adventurer and amateur archaeologist, who had fought for Napoleon at Toulon and in Egypt, then escaping the English had travelled down the east coast of Africa, and later to Chile and Guatemala, came up with ink-and-wash reconstructions of *I modi*, based on prints he claimed to have seen in a monastery in Mexico. These tallied with fragments in the British Museum. The accompanying sonnets surfaced in a copy of *I modi* that was found for sale in Italy in 1928 by Walter Toscanini, son of the famous conductor. Assiduously kept from public gaze by Toscanini, it is now in the hands of another private collector. From the same source in Italy, an American collector bought *First suckes* (which seems to indicate that the two volumes were once owned as companion pieces). He keeps his find just as jealously guarded.

Like *I modi, First suckes* comprises sixteen prints and sonnets; each one deals with the loss of virginity. In eight of the poems a maid is deflowered, and in the other eight a young man has his first sexual experience – though it must be said that in each case the focus seems primarily on male enjoyment. Also, whereas the women are sexual caricatures, the poems about men appear to be based on the true experiences of real people, probably friends of the poet. There is a further link with *I modi* in that a quote from one of the Aretino poems appears on a separate leaf (apparently included as a prologue), beneath a portrait of a pleasured maid:

> *Che per mia fé' questo é, miglior boccone*
> *Che mangiar il pan unto apresso il foco.*
> (I believe this is a tastier feast
> Than eating larded bread before a fire.)

It is not known who made the prints for *First suckes*, but the poems have been attributed to Thomas Nashe. *Sonnet 6* is evidently about Kit Marlin, and hints at his Catholic (or even atheist) proclivities. The young man in a gondola in the accompanying print bears a striking resemblance to the Kit of the Corpus portrait, and he is punningly referred to as 'Merlin' (cf. Robert Greene in *Epistle to Perimedes*, '. . . mad and scoffing poets, that have propheticall spirits as bred of Merlin's race'). The sonnet tells how young Merlin is most capably projected into the realm of the sexually experienced by one Bianca, 'a cunning whore of Venice', and how she feeds him fat black olives, takes the pips from his lips, sucks them quite clean and threads them into a rosary, for protection against the pox. The young man is 'not yet two score', which, if he is Kit, would make the year 1583. 'Bianca' is quite possibly the same 'La signora Bianca' who is twice mentioned on a list of 'public whores condemned for transgression of the laws', and fined ten and then thirty ducats. Venice was famous for its courtesans – they had their own ghetto, the Carampane, where they paraded on the Ponte delle Tette (literally 'Bridge of Tits') naked from the waist up (the authorities thought the sight of bare breasts would help prevent sodomy). This was in singular contrast to conservative English attitudes. Contemporary English manuals such as Thomas Cogan's *The Haven of Health* advised frisky young men to control their ardour by sitting on cold stone, plunging themselves into icy water, or dousing their genitals in vinegar. Yet in Venice there were catalogues and guides to pleasures and prices, and many a young Englishman's first carnal thrash occurred between the canals. Sir Philip Sidney cavorted in Venice when he was twenty, though a young Sir Henry Wotton (one day to be British ambassador there), 'not being made of stone' fled the wicked ladies to the safety of academic Padua.

If Kit was busy losing his virginity in Venice in 1583, he would have had to have been quick about it. He was away from Cambridge for a maximum of seven weeks. Andrew Badoer, an envoy in a hurry in the early sixteenth century, made it from Venice to London in twenty-six days, riding 'incessantly, day and night' – though he was in his sixties, and grizzled 'nor do I know what more could have been expected of a man at my age'. Queen Elizabeth's tutor, Roger Ascham, called the Queen of Hungary 'a virago' because she rode from Augsburg to Flanders (part of a possible route between England and Venice) in thirteen days, 'a distance a man could scarce do in 17'. In 1589 Henry Cavendish, admittedly travelling a long and leisurely route via Hamburg and down through 'Jarmany', took nearly a month to get to Venice. It could be that Nashe sets the event in Venice because of the racy, romantic image the city enjoyed, and that it in fact took place in the stews of London. On the other hand, Richard Lassels, a tutor who had been five times to Italy, lamented that the courtesans of Venice were such an attraction that some young men would 'travel one month for a night's lodging with an impudent woman'. Kit did have a rosary made of olive pits. He kept it for years, though it eventually ended up among the possessions of the enigmatic Elizabethan astrologer Dr John Dee, and was discovered in 1662 in a secret drawer of a cedar chest, by a confectioner called Robert Jones.

Fast travel and expensive living could only mean one thing: Kit had another source of income. The evidence is elusive and needs careful sifting, but it would seem that by 1583 he was already in the service of Sir Francis Walsingham, at first (in modern-day spy parlance) as an 'irregular' – used only occasionally, while his worth was being tested – but after 1584 as an active member of the network. His links with Sir Francis Walsingham could even have begun as early as 1581, when he was befriended by Thomas Watson and Thomas Walsingham in Paris. Also in Paris at the time was one Nicholas Faunt, who like the two Thomases was working for Sir Francis, and was a Bene't man. Though his time at college pre-dated Kit's, it is very possibly Faunt who made the first introduction to the Walsinghams. Recruitment in 1581 might explain Kit's presence in Rheims that year, and would make more sense of that curious visit to Navarre. The English would have been interested in intelligence from Henri's court. After the Duke of Anjou, Henri was next in line to the French throne, and though the champion of the Huguenots, he had briefly converted to Catholicism after the St Bartholomew's Day Massacre and was now being courted again by Catholics. We know that the agent Anthony Bacon was gathering information about developments concerning Henri, and passing it on to Walsingham in 1584. Kit's nascent Catholicism would not have been a barrier to his recruitment. Indeed, Walsingham made something of a speciality of 'turning' Catholics, and had a number of supposedly Catholic agents spying for him. With all the trappings of a new convert, Kit was ideally placed to inform on the activities of the Jesuit missionaries who had newly arrived at Cambridge in 1581. Perhaps, also, it was Kit who was reporting back on Byrd's circle at Harlington in the summer of 1582.

Kit had entered an uneasy world of duplicity and betrayal, a realm of cold falsehood and calculated hypocrisy, where trust had been sucked hollow by cynicism. Information was its currency, and worth was judged by tangible results. Just what moved him to such an existence? To some extent it was the sheer pressure of necessity: he needed the money. When his time at Cambridge came to an end, the cobbler's son from Canterbury would have had few options (given that he already seemed intent on reneging on his scholarship obligation to enter the Anglican church). He could become a tutor perhaps, a secretary to some notable, or even a poet in an aristocrat's retinue, traipsing along forever in the train of high society. But this was not Kit's style. For a young man of 'vaulting ambition', who like Tamburlaine felt that he had 'an aspiring mind' and a soul 'whose faculties can comprehend the wondrous architecture of the world . . . climbing after knowledge infinite', who was restless, rebellious, willing to live on his wits and certain of his ability, working for Walsingham offered a way forward. It may be distasteful, it would almost certainly be dangerous, but Kit knew that to take the position he wanted in the world, he had to be 'proud, bold, pleasant, resolute,/And now and then stab, as occasion serves'. Those stabbings might be literal, or metaphorical: in the back. Friends became enemies at a shrug. 'To some perhaps my name is odious,' says Machevill (Machiavelli) in the Prologue to *The Jew of Malta* but, 'Admir'd am I of those that hate me most . . . Let me be envied and not pitied'.

From the privileged viewpoint of posterity it is easy to raise a moral eyebrow and lament Kit's decision to join this secret world. But, as Charles Nicholl puts it: 'Our regret has no real claim on him. Posterity prefers poets to spies, but this young man could not be so choosy. He lived on his wits or else went hungry, and he was probably rather better rewarded for spying than he was for the poetry we remember him by.' It is clear from his later plays, written long after he had stopped spying, that he had his own regrets, and that the evils of duplicity, ambition and betrayal ever occupied his mind: the spying servant, the spying friend, the spying husband, the spying courtier, the spying duke never quite leave the stage.

Deception simultaneously fuelled and consumed the secret service. 'Treason begets spies and spies treason,' noted Queen Elizabeth's godson, Sir John Harington, wearily. Or as John le Carré put it centuries later: 'You teach them to cheat, to cover their tracks, and they cheat on you as well.' The dour Sir Francis watched over his web with care. Gathered close around him was a small core of men operating more or less permanently as controllers; beyond that was a haphazard, freelance band whose motivation was as likely to be money as politics – patriots and ne'er-do-wells, former pages and would-be ambassadors, the desperate, the greedy, men he had blackmailed, gamblers who had bankrupted themselves, vain adventurers, bored gentlemen, turncoats and zealots. Walsingham's favourite maxim was: 'There is less danger in fearing too much than too little, and there is nothing more dangerous than security.' He checked and he double-checked. He sent out spies to confirm other spies' information, spies to check on the other spies themselves, then another to inform on them all; he placed moles in Catholic organisations and set *agents provocateurs* among conspirators, ran double-agents, and was himself the victim of treachery. He had men pretend to be spies to discredit the opposite side, and found his agents snooped on by rival factions from his own side. He infiltrated conspiracies, undermined intrigue, and sometimes even made up plots from scratch to snare unsuspecting traitors.

Spanish invasion and Catholic conspiracy were the twin bugbears. Subtle, dedicated Sir Francis gathered intelligence from abroad and effected counter-espionage at home all to serve his queen, but this was by no means a national organisation. The Elizabethan secret service was a privately run affair. Lord Burghley had a web of informants too, as later did his son, Sir

Robert Cecil (he whom Eleanor Bull so disliked), and the Earl of Essex – ambitious men all, who were often acting in their own self-interest and sometimes with a competition that verged on hostility. Intrigue went on at lower levels too, all the way down to one-man bands – quite literally in the case of one Richard Foley, an ironmaster from Stourbridge who disguised himself as a minstrel and wandered through Belgium, Germany, Italy and Spain collecting information on new iron-founding techniques. Walsingham did eventually persuade Elizabeth to finance his activities, but it was never enough. Perhaps he would have derived some comfort in his poverty-stricken last years to know that technically this royal funding made his network the first ever professional English secret service.

Intelligence also came in on a casual basis from letter-writers (it was around this time that 'intelligence' began to take on the additional meaning of information gathered by spies). Sir Francis had well over a hundred such correspondents abroad every year after 1577. In a sense, this was innocent intelligence, simply keeping him in touch in an age without media, performing much the same function as a newspaper, but its value should not be underestimated. For Elizabeth and her government there was simply no other way, apart from emissaries' reports, of getting basic news about what was going on in the world. There was a darker side too – secret, more devious, requiring agents with particular skills – and here poets and students were an able bag to scoop from. Writers made good spies: 'They knew the international language, Latin, and the literary tastes of the day gave them a good smattering of French and Italian. They were mobile people: geographically mobile – young men disposed to travel and to see the world – but also socially mobile. In a class-ridden society, the literary *demi-monde* floated free, touching at once the back-streets of London and the heights of the nobility.' So, as a budding poet, Kit was a good catch.

As regards his activity at this time, again Bene't account and

buttery books are revealing. After the stretch of hard study leading up to his BA he is away again, in the autumn of 1584. There
is a discrepancy in the records in that the account books indicate
he was away for nine out of the twelve weeks of term, yet the
buttery records indicates that he was in college in the second,
third, fourth, seventh, eleventh and twelfth weeks. Moore-Smith
maintains he was also away for two weeks in the summer. This
accords with the idea of a period of probation. After one or two
initial forays in the early 1580s, Kit is being more earnestly
recruited, tested on short but increasingly important local missions, snooping about in grand houses and taverns before being
trusted with work on the Continent at the slightly more repu-
table edge of the profession. Overseas couriers and agents
abroad were paid, on presentation of a warrant signed by
Walsingham, by the Treasurer of the Queen's Chamber, for
'carrying letters for Her Majesty's special and secret affairs' or
being 'employed in affairs of special importance'.

With his wit, 'sparkling, sun-bright eyes', nimble mind and
easy manner Kit wore his motley well, mobile and fluid with his
friendships, flitting in and out of all sorts of social circles. From
snippets – an entry in household accounts, a diary anecdote, a
letter deriding 'the man Marlin'* – gradually a picture forms of
the people he is beginning to mix with. We learn of his contact
with Henry Percy, his exact contemporary and soon to be 9th
Earl of Northumberland – the 'Wizard Earl' who built up one
of the greatest libraries in the country, who while on a visit to
Paris in 1582 had had to write reassuring his father that the
exile Charles Paget (an associate of the composer William Byrd)
was not trying to convert him to Catholicism. Paget himself had
written to Sir Francis denying the charge, and Sir Francis no
doubt wanted to keep an eye on the young Lord Percy, especially

---

* Zelle, *Bare Truth*, pp. 267–70, yet again uncovers more than one
  could have hoped for.

as his inclination to learning drew him towards the 'wizardry' of alchemy, new science and adventurous thinking. Kit was even more intimate with Percy's close friend and later chief scholar Thomas Hariot, who, it was said, was the first Englishman to smoke a pipe, and from whom Kit picked up the expensive tobacco habit. This was itself tinged with the hue of rebellion. In casting round for a verb to describe the intake of tobacco, the first English users alighted on 'drink'. It was not until well into the seventeenth century that people began to 'smoke' tobacco. This gives us a hint of the attitude those first tobacco-nists (as they were called) had to the leaf. Using the word 'drink' to describe the process indicates a mind-expanding experience. You drank tobacco like you drank in a view, or a new idea. Or the way you drank sack – and the effects were similar. Upright public opinion railed against this 'filthy novelty', King James himself damned it as 'harmful to the brain'. So Kit and his fellow early experimenters with the weed can in some sense be seen as miscreant drug users.

Through Percy and Hariot, Kit met Sir Walter Ralegh, a gambling friend and intellectual confidant of the earl, who frequented the Northumberland seat, Petworth in Sussex, and whose agent Robert Browne created a rumpus over wine prices in Cambridge in 1585, leading to riots between town and gown and Sir Walter's personal intervention. Kit also flirted with Ralegh's arch rival, the handsome young Earl of Essex, Robert Devereux, who had just been propelled into Elizabeth's inner circle by his stepfather, the Earl of Leicester. At Cambridge he befriended the twelve-year-old Henry Wriothesley, Earl of Southampton, the era's most renowned pretty-boy, whose pink-petal eyelids and long, curled locks would inspire some of Kit's finest verse. And, in a rare moment of calm, he relaxed at the stationer's in St Paul's Churchyard with his old friend Oliver Laurens. Gertrud Zelle argues that Kit also met up with Thomas Watson in London during one of Tom's brief descents from the

Continent, and that Kit was becoming increasingly 'close with' Thomas Walsingham, who had returned from France to a large house in Seething Lane, owned by Sir Francis, which served as the London headquarters of the network. Thomas had been promoted and was now in a position of control, a channel through which minor agents could gain access to Sir Francis. One of these informers attendant upon Thomas, wishing 'secret recourse to Mr Secretary', was none other than 'Sweet Robyn', Robert Poley. In the tangled brier of names that grows to fill Kit's early life, this is one to be remembered, a bud to be plucked and placed alongside those of Wriothesley, Thomas Walsingham and Tom Watson, as we carefully watch them blossom.

As this social brier spread, so Kit's intellectual tendrils curled and thrust themselves in unexpected directions. Friends such as Ralegh and Northumberland encouraged the questioning that had begun during his first days at Cambridge, a journey from the Christian viewpoint where doubt was a sin, to one where it was a virtue. Europe had been rocked by the claims of Copernicus, and the discovery of cultures that seemed to predate the Creation. It was a philosophically alarming world, where two great Christian factions were clashing, but where for people like Kit, God could no longer be trusted. If you wanted knowledge you had to flirt with the Devil. Or worse. It is around this time that rumours grew of Kit's 'atheism' and his interest in the occult. He is supposed to have won over one Thomas Fineaux, who began studies at Bene't in Kit's last term there. In a way rather reminiscent of Doctor Faustus conjuring 'in some bushy grove', Fineux 'would go out at midnight into a wood, & fall down upon his knees, & pray heartily that the devil would come, that he might see him (for he did not believe there was a devil)'.

Kit was not alone in his dilemma. Scientific curiosity had doubt as a handmaiden. The question arose that if you could no longer trust God, then whom could you trust? This was a time of psychological turbulence, uncertainty, reinvention – the figures that emerged from it as rock-like have become fixed as cultural icons. It is not for nothing that we now prefer to call this English Renaissance the 'Early Modern Period' – it is the period of upheaval during which England's cultural world was made.

CHAPTER FOUR

Gentlemen of a Company

As the recall of Thomas Walsingham to become a controller of London headquarters at Seething Lane in 1584 shows, Sir Francis was, by the mid-1580s, beginning to formalise his organisation and expand. In April 1583 he had three men reporting from Paris, nine from Antwerp, and two from Middelburg and Strasbourg; by 1585 his intelligencers abroad had grown to fifty. The reason for such expansion lay primarily in events in the Low Countries. The Duke of Parma's campaign against the Protestant north was reaching a high point. Antwerp had been drawn into the battle zone and by June 1584 was under siege; in the same month Parma's key opponent, William of Orange, was assassinated. Just a few weeks before, François, the Duke of Anjou, had died and with him the hope of French resistance to Parma, as the country sank into internal conflict over succession to the throne. England was now being drawn into the fray.

In May 1585 the Dutch were to offer sovereignty of the United Provinces to Elizabeth. The hawks on the Privy Council, Walsingham and Robert Dudley, the Earl of Leicester, said 'aye', but Lord Burghley and the doves gave a firm 'nay', as they thought that such a move risked outright war with Spain. In the end, Elizabeth turned down the Dutch offer because she too foresaw 'long, bloody wars' with one of the most powerful countries in Europe. She had already dispatched embassies to Denmark and to German princes to see if they would join in a Protestant League against the Spanish, but to no avail. English involvement was inevitable. Eventually, in August, she signed the Treaty of Nonsuch at the sumptuous pleasure palace built by Henry VIII at Cheam – so named because there was '*none such* like it in the realm' (the royal equivalent of calling your house Dunroamin').

Elizabeth agreed to send a force to support the Dutch, reluctantly naming Robert Dudley commander, with the warning not to 'hazard a battaile without great advantage'. When Leicester precociously named himself 'governor-general' of the United Provinces, a move that implied sovereignty and which riled the Spanish, she was furious. Meanwhile, the Dutch had found a military genius in William of Orange's successor, Maurice, who was hotly intent on war with Spain, and good at it.

Throughout all of this Elizabeth needed intelligence from France, the Low Countries and from Spain. She also needed to know what was going on in Leicester's camp, to monitor the movements of the increasingly powerful Maurice of Orange, and to judge the mood in the courts of Denmark and of the German princes. This was the field in which Kit became engaged. Curiously, it was his interest in theatre that got him the job. Dramatists, as one would imagine, were more suited to spying than other writers, given the cloak-and-dagger antics of Elizabethan espionage. Complicated ciphers and invisible inks were commonplace; messages were smuggled inside beer barrels; seals were forged, couriers drugged; men disguised themselves as beggars and passed themselves off as members of other nationalities. Tradition has it that Kit deeply impressed Sir Francis with a scheme of getting a cipher-key to the conjuror Dr Dee (who was by this time living in Bohemia). He proposed shaving the head of a servant, who had eye trouble, inking the code on his pate, then allowing the hair to grow back and hide it. The man was sent to Dr Dee on the pretext that the writing on his head was a part of a spell that would help the great doctor effect a cure. The advantage of the plan was that not only was the message invisible in transit, but that the unsuspecting servant, who had been told that revealing the presence of the spell would destroy it, could not double-cross them. (Servants were usually the weakest link in a chain of espionage as their loyalty was easily bought.) Maybe Sir Francis would not have been so admiring had he known that the young poet had stolen the idea directly from Herodotus. Kit also came up with the idea (taken this time from Aeneas Tacticus) of writing a message on a tree leaf which was used to cover an apparently putrid ulcer on the leg of someone disguised as a beggar. Plagiarism, as well as deception, was evidently becoming something of a strong point.

Such disguises and complicated plots of betrayal and counter-betrayal were very much the stuff of the theatre of the time. What is more, if one is looking for the perfect cover, a travelling theatre company proves ideal – it would have access not only to burghers and market place, but to the heart of the local court. A player could pick up on gossip below the stairs, and would be within earshot when the lords were drunk, and a poet with such a company would penetrate upper social strata with an ease that few other means would allow. An English theatre company on the Continent might move with the immunity of jesters where English diplomats feared to tread.

Such companies existed. Kit had already briefly travelled with one, on his jaunt replacing William Peeters. Not only were companies touring on the Continent, but there were English players wherever an eager spymaster might have wished them to be. There are records of Maurice of Orange licensing English players, a troupe accompanied Leicester to the Low Countries; there were English players in the Danish court on at least two occasions, and in towns all over Germany throughout the period.

Known generically as the *Englische Komödianten* or 'English comedians', these troupes of players were resoundingly popular. They performed in the energetic, rag-bag gallimaufrey style that had so enthralled the young Kit in Canterbury, which corrupted students at Cambridge, and which was filling the London amphitheatres to the brim: a mixture of music, playing and acrobatics that quite astounded those who saw it. The English comedians' spontaneity and vividness so enthused audiences that it revolutionised northern European theatre, turning what had previously been stiff, formal recitation into drama. For the first time this was theatre in its own right, not presented for religious instruction or as part of a festival. And people turned out in their thousands to watch. In Frankfurt, according to the sixteenth-century traveller Fynes Moryson, both men and women 'flocked wonderfully to see their gesture and Action, rather than heare them, speaking English which they understand not', and at Elsinore in 1585, the citizens flocked so 'wonderfully' to a performance in the town hall courtyard, that they broke down a wall. This popularity is especially surprising because, as Fynes Moryson remarks, so few of the audience understood the language. English was an island tongue with little continental currency. In court, a simultaneous translator might be employed as a sort of living surtitle, but this did not often happen in the market place. (Perhaps a parallel can be drawn with the popularity among British audiences in the 1980s and 1990s of, to them, largely incomprehensible Polish and Czech theatre companies, and later of Japanese *noh* and *kabuki* performances.)

The heyday of good English drama abroad was short-lived. One of the effects of performing for non-English audiences is that the companies preferred to stage high-action plays with spectacular visual effects. Kit wrote *Tamburlaine* and *Titus Andronicus* for such an audience. As troupes relied on memory and improvisation rather than carrying around cumbersome prompt-books, texts soon became corrupted and grossly simplified, leaving a flotsam of tenuously linked violent and sensational scenes as subtlety receded. Language restrictions meant that performance style rapidly degenerated into clowning, extempore bawdy and highly exaggerated acting, as the companies became the refuge of second-rate actors. Hamlet knew what he was up against when he tackled the travelling players at Elsinore. The Danish prince remarks that he has seen players – and ones that are highly praised at that – who 'have so strutted and bellowed that I have thought some of Nature's journeymen had made men, and not made them well, they imitated humanity so abominably'; he says it offends him to the soul 'to hear a robustious periwig-pated fellow tear a passion to tatters', and demands that the players' clowns 'speak no more than is set down for them' (*Hamlet* III ii). By the early 1600s most troupes had given up on English and were performing in German, and indeed comprised mainly German and Dutch actors who only called themselves 'English comedians' because it meant good business.

In the halcyon days of the 1580s and 1590s, however, when Kit was first touring with English comedians, the companies were in the vanguard of theatrical change. Players like the clown Will Kemp went on to fame in London; their performances had huge impact, yet still showed a finer touch – they were known 'partly by their pretty inventions, partly by the gracefulness of their gestures, often also by the elegance of their speaking'. There were the germs here of what became known in England as 'personation' rather than playing – the fuller and more subtle representation of character, which Kit mastered so triumphantly in his later work.

And it paid well. Players could earn far more on the Continent than they could at home. In a pamphlet entitled 'The Run-away's Answer' a group of poor, debt-withered actors defended themselves against Thomas Dekker's reproaches for skipping the Channel with: 'We can be bankrupts on this side and gentlemen of a company beyond the sea: we burst at London, and are pieced up at Rotterdam.' To Kit, with his costly taste for tobacco-drinking and his failing for the garlands of fashion, this was no unwelcome news. He would be rewarded not only for his intelligencing, but also well paid for his cover. The benefit was not all on his side. He was a profitable addition to a travelling troupe. A poet alone would be dead wood, but although Kit 'lacked voice' as a player, he could cope with smaller parts and could sing well – and his ability with French and Dutch was a decided benefit in the Low Countries. The Bene't accounts and buttery books show that Kit's absences from college increase dramatically from 1585. He was away for eight weeks between April and June in 1585 and for nine weeks to the end of September, then again for nine weeks from April to June of 1586. These absences coincide perfectly with the spring and late-summer touring seasons of the English players.

We owe what knowledge we have of Kit's first foray as a player/spy, in April and May of 1585, to material uncovered by the theatre historian Joseph Keaton.* Using the alias Timothie Larkin, Kit travelled to the Low Countries with John Bradstriet's players. 'Tim Larkin', as Keaton points out, is an anagram of Kit Marlin. Spies seeking aliases sometimes succumbed to the Elizabethan delight in wordplay, in which anagrams were a particular obsession. Bad auguries, for example, were seen in that the name of the king of France, Henry (or Henri) de Valois could be rearranged as Vilain Herodas, or O crudelis hyena. The name John Bradstriet (sometimes written as Bradstreet or Breadstreet) also smacks of alias: Bread Street was the location of the Mermaid Tavern, the great literary watering hole of the time. Breadstreet appears on lists of players all over the Continent, but there is no record of his existence as one in England.

The troupe seems to have had some connection with Charles Howard, who had a personal company of players, and who

---

* See Joseph Keaton, *Luvvies' Labours Lost, a History of Forgotten Acting*, p. 23ff.

became Lord Admiral in 1585. John Bradstriet's name occurs a few years later on a passport for a number of players, led by one Robert Browne, which is signed by Lord Howard. Robert Browne, the actor who again and again comes up in the records as the leader of a troupe of English players, was a member of the Admiral's Men (as Lord Howard's Men became known after 1585), the company that was first to stage Kit's plays in London.

Kit's introduction to Bradstriet was made through Thomas Walsingham, which indicates that Bradstriet himself might have been an intelligencer, and that Kit perhaps was still on pro-bation. The mission was a simple one. In the months running up to the Treaty of Nonsuch, as it became increasingly evident that England was going to be militarily involved in the Low Countries, the government needed as much information as poss-ible about troop movements and numbers on the ground. A group of strolling players had some mobility even through Spanish-held territory. Travellers of the time seemed anyway somewhat nonchalant about moving through war zones, appar-ently seeing battles as nothing more than a bit of localised bother: Richard Lassels, the gentleman traveller, on the road to Italy some decades later, 'chose to steer towards Genoa by the low way' in order to avoid two armies 'which lay in the way'. William Lithgow in his *Rare Adventures and Painefull Peregrinations* similarly mentions 'leaving both armies barking at each other like wolves' and happily treading off in another direction. Brad-striet and his troupe were probably in more danger from deserters and brigands than from soldiers, who frequently escorted convoys of merchants' wagons to ensure safe passage. Like one Wychegerde, a grain and sundries merchant sent by Sir Francis Walsingham a few years later to spy on Spanish-held towns and enemy garrisons, Kit probably had to climb through ditches and plod across soggy polders secretly to count Spaniards in their camps.

But he did also have some fun. The English players were

not only innovative, spontaneous and acrobatic, they were sexy. Keaton mentions an account of 'untold young virgines, enamoured of the players that followed them from citty to citty till the magistrates forbad them to play' (the traveller Fynes Moryson noted a similar phenomenon in his *Itinerary* in 1592). A poem published in 1597 in Frankfurt, where the September book fair was a favourite players' destination, lets us in on some of the excitement:

> The tumbler also did us please,
> He sprang high in the air with ease . . .
> His hose they fitted him so tight,
> His codpiece was a lovely sight.
> Nubile maids and lecherous dames
> He kindled into lustful flames . . .
> For, know that those who paid their fee
> To witness a bright comedy,
> Or hear the tunes of fine musicians
> Were more entranced by the additions
> Of bawdy jests and comic strokes,
> Of antics and salacious jokes,
> And what, with his tight-fitting hose
> The well-bred tumbler did disclose.

At the more serious end of the players' activity, Kit was writing. His play *Pyramus and Thisbe* was first performed by Bradstriet's men, and was still in English comedians' repertoires in 1604. *Tamburlaine* was formed, not in the isolation of a Cambridge college (the solitary author in a garret is a creation of Romanticism), but in the rough and tumble of working with a real theatre company. Kit also translated and adapted Plautus's *Menaechmi*, which sparked his fascination with twins and mistaken identity, and was later to form the basis of *The Comedy of Errors*. It was around this time too that he marked his transition into a new phase of life with another name change. As Moore-Smith points out, after 1585 the Marlin, Marlen, Malyn or Marlyn in college records becomes Marly, Marlye, Marley or Morley. Even given the vagaries of Elizabethan spelling, these two clusters of variance are different enough to be significant. Kit Marlin was a new man, and now styled himself Kit, or more often Christopher, Marley.

'Marley' returned to Cambridge in the early summer of 1585 buoyed by his new position and with his pockets (or to be exact, his sleeves and codpiece, which served as pockets in Elizabethan dress) filled with gold. Never was there cobbler's son so full of pride. Immediately he did something that no-one in his family had ever dreamed of doing, something that at once showed soaring insolence, announced his arrival in society, and cryptically boasted about what he was up to. He had his portrait painted.

The old Master's Lodge at Bene't College housed a wood-panelled gallery dedicated to the display of paintings depicting important national figures, notable college academics and other worthy alumni. With astonishing hubris for someone of such youth and humble origins, when he left the college in 1587 Christopher gifted his picture to the Master – and indeed in the years that immediately followed, his success in London made him arguably one of Bene't's living luminaries, perhaps warranting a portrait prominently on show. After the incident at Deptford in 1593 and his public disgrace, Christopher Marley's painting suddenly disappeared. It resurfaced at Cambridge only in 1953 (a numerical anagram that some scholars find intriguing in itself). A passing student noticed two panels of wood sticking up out of a pile of builders' rubble when the Master's Lodge was being renovated. Though faded, scratched and splattered by rain, they bore the shadow of a Tudor portrait. This fact was later confirmed by the National Portrait Gallery, and restoration work began. The Canadian scholar Calvin Hoffman was the first to suggest, in 1955, that the portrait was of Marlowe, and subsequent research using a computer programme that ages faces, convincingly connects the subject of this portrait with that of the painting (known as the Chandos portrait) made of him in his forties (see Appendix II).

Poets and players of the period did sometimes hire painters to record their likenesses for posterity – or rather to contrive an image of themselves and project it into the world, showing them in the way they wanted to be seen. Like successful merchants, they commissioned portraits to show that they had arrived in their particular profession. Even people involved in seamier activities had paintings made as mementoes of significant moments in their labours. In 1586 the plotter Anthony Babington and his fellow conspirators posed for portraits on the eve of what they thought would be the toppling of Elizabeth and the raising of Mary Queen of Scots to her rightful position. Kit, at the age of twenty-one, was brazenly celebrating his arrival in society, and hinting perhaps that he was in the secret service. He posed with his arms folded, not a common posture in Elizabethan portraits. Sir Roy Strong interprets this as indicating a fashionable melancholy, the humour of the disappointed lover and those of artistic temperament. But it can also indicate that the sitter has something to hide. A. D. Wraight suggests that the pose imparts the message 'I am one who is entrusted to keep secrets.' And Charles Nicholl goes so far as to wonder whether he has a dagger up his sleeve, no doubt to 'stab, as occasion serves'. An ideal posture, then, for the dreamy young poet who has entered the world of espionage.

Two inscriptions appear in the top left-hand corner of the Corpus portrait. The one, '*ætatis suae* 21 1585' gives Kit's age when the picture was painted. The other is a motto that reads

'*Quod me nutrit me destruit*' – 'That which nourishes me destroys me'. Some take this as a statement of the consuming passion of unrequited love. Others see it as a confession of Kit's predicament at Cambridge – he is under obligation to the Parker Scholarship, which is paying his way, to take holy orders, while the thought of life as an Anglican priest appals him. But the motto is also eerily prescient. It reflects the paradox of Christopher's new world, a life (as we have seen) simultaneously fuelled and consumed by deception. He is beginning a brilliant new career, but one that by definition is infected with the germ of his downfall. As he moves deeper into the world of espionage, he comes closer to the moment where someone wants him dead, a step nearer to Eleanor Bull's house in Deptford. He seems to have a disturbing premonition of what he is letting himself in for. The motto recurs decades later, in a sonnet Kit wrote not long before he died, in which he seems to regret the youthful fury that, if it did not cause his death, very nearly destroyed his life:

> In me thou see'st the glowing of such fire
> That on the ashes of his youth doth lie,
> As the death-bed, whereon it must expire,
> *Consum'd with that which it is nourish'd by* [my italics].
> (Sonnet 73)

Kit stares out of the painting with eyes rather darker than in later portraits and an insolent, supercilious expression, matched by a half-curled smile. It is just a twitch short of a sneer. He is pale, almost pallid, but with a touch of youthful colour (or is it the flush of temper?) in his cheeks. A downy moustache tops a wispy 'mouse-eaten' beard that 'groweth but here a tuft and there a tuft', softly following his jaw line. His folded arms give him a slightly defensive look, but a full lower lip adds an air of sullen defiance, an edge of spoilt child, of someone who knows he can offend and has the protection of people more powerful than the viewer.

And he certainly was transgressing. He is blatantly defying both university dress regulations and the Sumptuary Laws. His bouffant hair is nowhere near the 'polled, notted or rounded' style that university authorities required. The open-throated shirt he wears, with its flopping collar of gossamer-fine linen, 'a falling band of cobweb lawn', is at the absolute peak of fashion in 1585. So is his magnificent doublet – close-fitting with prominent 'wings' on the shoulders and big padded sleeves, narrowing 'bishop-style' to a tight wrist. It is made of black fabric slashed to reveal a reddish velvet lining, and adorned with a dazzling set of huge, decorative gold buttons, up each sleeve as well as down the front – in substance, style and splendour contravening every rule of sober dressing. Here is a young man who is not only breaking the law, but has the defiance to have himself painted while doing so. A young man who goes even further and publicly hands over this evidence to the very authority who should discipline him. A young man who is certain of the protection of very powerful friends.

He is also a young man on a spree.* His spending in the buttery in 1585 spiralled from a few paltry pennies a week to a heady 18*d* and 21*d* extravagances. The portrait is a flash of

---

* Even so, very much in the style of a true young blade about town, Kit seemed reluctant to pay for the portrait. A document, found behind a skirting board during restoration work in the Corpus Old Court and appearing to be a letter to the Master from one William Larkin (one wonders if this name is the source of Kit's alias when travelling with the players), complains that 'maistcr marley, a scoler wythin yowre colege' has contracted a painting for which Larkin 'can in no wayes receyve of him payment. for that he Sayth yt ys noo goode lykenes, but al men Sayth yt ys'. Perhaps here we also have a clue as to why Kit parted so readily with the work when he left the college. The letter, circulated among Fellows by Drs Mara Kalnins and Linne Mooney on 1 April 1996, now lies sealed in a conservation box in the Parker Library (see Appendix III).

prestige, its very existence a boast; it is painted on high-quality oak, sawn radially on the tree – better than most other paintings of the period in the college. His doublet, Charles Nicholl estimates, even second-hand would have cost thirty shillings or more (about £750 by today's reckoning). Perhaps the only reason for the folded arms is to show off as many as possible of its forty oversized gold buttons.

Once again all is not what it seems. Kit had borrowed the doublet from a fellow novice spy, Roger Walton, who had been a page to the old Earl of Northumberland, and like Kit moved in the circle of Henry Percy, the young 'Wizard Earl'. By 1586 Walton was working in France for Sir Francis Walsingham, and a short while later the doublet (no longer quite so fashionable, but still worthy of remark) would again be captured for posterity when the English ambassador in Paris complained to Sir Francis of a young man who sounds remarkably like Kit himself, but whom the ambassador thinks is Roger Walton. This young disrupter 'to some . . . showeth himself a great Papist, to others a Protestant, but as they take him that haunt him most, he hath neither God nor religion, a very evil condition, a swearer without measure and tearer of God, a notable whoremaster . . . a little above twenty, lean-faced and slender, somewhat tall, complexion a little sallowish, most goeth appareled in a doublet of black carke, cut upon a dark reddish velvet'.

We know Kit himself was in France during his second long absence from college in 1585, in the late summer. He appears momentarily at the baths at Plombières, which suggests he had again been at Rheims or possibly in Strasbourg, where Walsingham also ran agents and which was a popular destination for troupes of English comedians.* This is the first hint we have of what was to become a lifelong predilection for public bathing.

---

* Kit's visit to Plombières and other spas was first noted in Toby de Lorn's *The Craving of the Stew*, p. 17 ff.

At times the reason for this may have been plain lust – the vapour baths or 'stews' of London were notorious brothels for both sexes – but house rules at Plombières stated quite clearly that: 'All prostitutes and immodest girls are forbidden to enter the said baths, or to approach the same within five hundred paces, under penalty of being whipped at the four corners of the said baths . . .'. It seems more likely that one of the 'untold virgins' that followed Bradstriet's players had not been so virginal after all, and that despite the protection of the olive-pip rosary so carefully made for him some years before by Bianca, the Venetian courtesan, Christopher had a dose of the clap – or in Elizabethan parlance, he had been 'burned'. Hot baths were considered an effective cure for the searing pains of gonorrhoea. In Sonnet 153 Kit plays with the idea of Love's 'burning'. He has been 'burned' but a 'maid of Dian's' steals Cupid's brand and (in an apparent early form of inoculation) plunges it into a fountain, creating 'a seething bath, which yet men prove/Against strange maladies a sovereign cure . . . I, sick withal, the help of bath desired,/And thither hied, a sad distempered guest,/But found no cure.' In Sonnet 154 he once again goes for a cure to a bath that is 'a healthful remedy/For men diseased', but finds that neither treatment nor disease diminishes his ardour: 'Love's fire heats water, water cools not love'. Was he suffering from the more dangerous, often fatal, syphilis? In later life he shows a good knowledge of the disease and supposed cures, such as 'villainous saffron' in *All's Well That Ends Well*; or mercury fumigation, as Doll Tearsheet undergoes in *Henry V.* Timon displays a detailed awareness of such symptoms as baldness and disintegration of the nose when he berates Phrynia and Timandra in *Timon of Athens*; and Lucio in *Measure for Measure* makes one of the earliest references in English literature to the disease being transmitted by a drinking vessel.

The glimpse we are given of Kit's visit to Plombières is through a document written by an unnamed secretary of the essayist

Montaigne, noting a conversation held in the seething waters between 'an Englishman T. Larkkin' and his master. The same secretary had, during an earlier visit, helped Montaigne write up his journal when the essayist was too ill to do so himself. That document survives, but the fragment mentioning Larkin appears to be part of a second journal, now lost.* Montaigne had just finished his second term of office as Mayor of Bordeaux and was taking his family wandering, as he put it, to avoid the plague. Five years earlier, while on a grand tour of the spas of Germany and Italy in an attempt to cure his gallstones, he had especially enjoyed Plombières, and was back for more – astonishing regulars who came only to bathe by also drinking four pints of the waters every morning. He particularly liked the sweet, cool waters of the Queen's Bath, which he said tasted of liquorice with a faint tang of iron. Montaigne and his man stayed at the Angel, where the cooks were good but the wine and bread bad, and where the chambers had private galleries that gave access to the baths. Kit's lodgings were less grand.

The pair took to the waters in their regulation skimpy briefs (Montaigne notes that although the baths were mixed, it was considered 'indecent for the men to bathe otherwise than quite naked, saving a little pair of drawers, and for the women, saving a shift'), sitting on the steps of the large oval principal bath, separated from each other by stable-like bars and sheltered from the sun by slatted planks. Hot water bubbled up from underground springs, as cooler waters from across the valley flowed in 'to temper the bath according to the wish of those taking it', and Kit, who had dipped into the new edition of Montaigne's *Essais*, eagerly pestered the older man into conversation.

At first he singularly failed to engage the philosopher, but after a confession of his own 'painefull pissing', managed to

---

* Parts of this second journal are quoted in de Lorn, *The Craving of the Stew.*

87

elicit a long monologue on the nature of Montaigne's stools, 'voiding gravel, black threads and bubbles that are a long time in bursting', 'wind about the groin' and the benefits of various purges and waters, all faithfully recorded by the secretary. (Further details of Montaigne's ailments are expounded at length in the journal of his travels in Italy.) But buoyed by his feats with Bradstriet's men, Kit appears to have tried a different approach, posing as a successful poet of the new drama. This had a little more success, provoking a discussion of the 'great conflict and power of imagination', and of the quest of the writer:

> *Mont:* It is ... *le passage!* To examine the verie movement of the mind, and ye the Poet should pierce and usurp the senses of other men.
> *Lark:* Are not Actors but the ciphers of the tale?
> *Mont:* The sacred inspiration that stirs thee as Poet unto a choler, unto griefe, unto fury and beyond thyself, shoulde by thee strike and enter into the Actor and thus the multitude ...

The following day, Kit was, according to the secretary, given the customary viewing of Montaigne's famous medal, struck on one side with the inscription, *Que sçais-je?* – 'What do I know?' – and on the other, in Greek, 'Restraint' – a virtue which did not at that time hold much appeal for him. They spoke of doubt and knowledge, the master exhorting his disciple to question and re-question, urging that it was 'but his thinking that made the taste of good or bad', and that he should look to within himself to find truth – advice that the fledgling spy was not perhaps ready for. The secretary records that his employer was 'animated by the spirit of young Mr Larkkin', who spoke in both Latin and French, but the dialogue seems to have run aground on the subjects of sensuality and affection – on friendship, physical beauty and the love permitted by the Greeks. On the third day Montaigne was reluctant to speak. On the fourth he appears to have relented, but began on safer ground with tales of the Indians of Brasil who had lived thousands of years before Adam, disappointed that Kit had not read his essay 'On Cannibals'. Once again Kit seems to have offended the Frenchman, and after that there is silence.

By April of 1586 (during yet another lengthy absence from Cambridge), Kit was back with the English comedians.* This time not with Bradstriet's company, but with a troupe that followed the Earl of Leicester, into the bowels of battle in the Low Countries. No doubt Leicester thought the players appropriate to his prestige as self-styled governor-general, though it was not unknown for musicians and actors to accompany military leaders to war. The composer Claudio Monteverdi travelled as *maestro di cappella* with the Duke of Mantua into battle with the Turks in 1595, a harrowing experience he recalled vividly for decades, and which emerged in his *madrigali guerrieri, et amorosi* or 'Madrigals of Love and War', in his setting of battle scenes from Tasso's *Gerusalemme liberata*, and in a fascination with scenarios of affray.

Kit did not travel out with Leicester's original party, but was sent later by Sir Francis Walsingham. The Queen had been infuriated when Leicester unilaterally assumed the title 'governor-general', as it implied that he was accepting sovereignty over the United Provinces on her behalf, and this was a direct challenge to Spain. Perhaps Elizabeth herself was behind Walsingham's decision to send someone to spy on Leicester (who was, after all, a fellow 'hawk'). However it seems more likely that the old spymaster had something else in mind, for very soon after Kit's arrival, Leicester instructed the players to leave for the Danish court at Elsinore.

---

* Keaton, *Luvvies' Labours*, p. 86.

The dramatist Thomas Heywood, in his 'Apology for actors', tells us that the King of Denmark 'entertained into his service a company of English comedians, commended unto him by the honourable the Earl of Leicester', and the household accounts of the Danish court also record the presence of English players in the summer of 1586. Was Elizabeth perhaps still entertaining the idea of Denmark joining a Protestant alliance against the Catholic League, and therefore eager for an ear in the Danish court? This is possibly so, but it seems the Queen had an even more pressing reason for wanting to know who might be coming and going in Elsinore, and what the courtiers might be whispering to each other in castle corridors. There was talk of marrying Princess Anna of Denmark to James I of Scotland, something Elizabeth was anxious to stall, as she favoured a match with Catharine of Navarre. She needed to know how the nuptial negotiations were going, for some of the buzz of court gossip to be transmitted to London. (She was, in the end, unsuccessful in obstructing the marriage, and in 1589 James sent an embassy to Denmark to fetch his young bride.)

So Kit's sojourn with Leicester's soldiers was brief. The only evidence we have of it is his remarkable ability to write battle scenes (as with Monteverdi, his experiences remained extraordinarily vivid), and a curious passage from the second *Tamburlaine*. This snippet of tactical know-how appears to be a result of a conversation with Paul Ive, another Walsingham spy who operated mainly in the Low Countries. The play, written around 1587, includes a technical speech about fortifying a garrison which closely mirrors a military manual written by Ive, but published only in 1589. In 2 *Tamburlaine* we have:

> It must have privy ditches, countermines
> And secret issuings to defend the ditch.
> It must have high argines and covered ways
> To keep the bulwark fronts from the battery.

And in Ive's book:

> It must also have countermines, privy ditches, secret issuings
> out to defend the ditch, casemates in the ditch, covered
> ways round about it, and an argine or bank to impeach the
> approach.

A little more is known about Kit's activity with Leicester's players
through research conducted by Joseph Keaton. It seems that
this time, perhaps to facilitate social mobility in the Danish court,
he joined the troupe not as an actor or musician, but as a poet.
Keaton argues that he is the 'Daniel Jonns' who like the other
players received payments of six thalers a month from the Danish
court, though he leaves Elsinore before the others. Also in the
company (pre-dating Kit's arrival) was Will Kemp, the clown
who, in his own words, 'spent his life in mad Jigges and merry
jestes', and for whom Kit was one day to create such roles as
Launce in *The Two Gentlemen of Verona*, Peter in *Romeo and Juliet*,
and Dogberry in *Much Ado about Nothing*. Like Kit he eventually
went back to London, to join Lord Strange's Men. His rough,
physical style of clowning and penchant for ad-libbing grated
with Kit, but the time they spent together in the Low Countries
helped cement a functional, if not over-friendly, working
relationship. A letter to Walsingham from his son-in-law Sir
Philip Sidney, written in Utrecht in March 1586, is carried 'by
Will, the Lord of Lester's jesting plaier', but there is no reason
to suspect Kemp was also spy – if he was, he was either incompetent or working for someone else, as he had delivered an
earlier letter from Sidney, about Leicester and intended for
Walsingham, to Leicester's wife. He did, however, rejoin the
company in Elsinore, after Kit had left. A 'Wilhelm Kempe
instrumentalist' appears in the royal household accounts along
with the other players in July and August.

Soon after presenting *The Forces of Hercules* in Utrecht at the end of April, the troupe 'began frolickly to foote it' to Elsinore, travelling through the popular playing spots of Bremen and Hamburg. Their presence was ostensibly part of ongoing festivities at Kronborg Castle, the new royal residence at Elsinore, begun in 1574 and completed the year before they arrived. The halls and high ramparts of Kronborg, the sagas and stories Kit heard there, the friendships he formed during his stay and even the little Danish he picked up, formed the first small fragments in the mosaic of *Hamlet*. It is he who departs from other tellers of the story, such as the Danish chronicler Saxo and the Frenchman Belleforest, to set the play in Elsinore rather than Jutland, and he even anachronistically locates it in Kronborg, with some poetic colouring in the addition of cliffs and mountains. Later scholars offer a detailed identification of this setting, from the 'platform before the castle' and ghost-walked ramparts, to Polonius's house and Ophelia's stream. The existence of a chapel on the passage used by the Queen from the Riddersal (where the players would have performed) to her apartments, for example, making topographical sense of Hamlet encountering Claudius at prayer while on his way to his mother's chamber after the performance of *The Mousetrap*.

Kit and the players arrived in Elsinore in a clamour of drums and trumpets, an attention-grabbing ploy that was used by English players, though not by others in Europe at the time (cf. Parolles in *All's Well that Ends Well*, who says that Captain Dumain 'has led the drum before the English tragedians'). Complaints of magistrates in contemporary records of towns around the Continent bear witness to the English players' deafening arrival – the genteel folk of Cologne on three separate occasions forbade them to make noise with their drums. But then the English were generally known as a clamorous lot. Paul Hentzner, a German travelling through England in the 1590s, noted somewhat wearily that they were 'vastly fond of great noises that fill the ear, such as the firing of canon, drums and the ringing of bells, so that it is common for a number of them, that have got a glass in their heads, to go up into some belfry, and ring the bells for hours together, for the sake of exercise'. In Denmark the rowdies met their match, both in noise-making and in drinking. The Danes had the reputation of being the heaviest drinkers in Europe and, as William Segar, a member of an English embassy in 1603 reported: 'It would make a man sick to heare of their drunken healths . . . Every health reported sixe, eight or ten shot of great Ordinance, so that during the king's abode the ship discharged 160 shot.' Hamlet also notes these noisy toasts, remarking that 'no jocund health' is drunk by the king but that 'the great cannon to the clouds shall tell' (*Hamlet* I ii 125–6), and the guns are joined by drums and trumpets:

> And let the kettle to the trumpet speak,
> The trumpet to the cannoneer without,
> The cannons to the heavens, the heaven to earth,
> 'Now the King drinks to Hamlet'.
> (*Hamlet* V ii 267–70)

It is, Hamlet drily notes, 'a custom more honour'd in the breach than the observance'.

If Danish troupes had a lesson in publicity to learn from the English players, Kit and his company took a valuable playing tip from their hosts. A dumb show preceding the drama was a Danish convention (then unknown in England), as the Danes still performed in Latin and used mime to get the message across to illiterate audiences. It is, of course, an ideal technique when performing in a language the audience does not understand, and such dumb-show prologues became a feature of performances by the English comedians on the Continent (and also in the provinces back home) – indeed, the strolling players in *Hamlet* offer one (III ii).

The image we have of Kit in Elsinore is of someone moving fairly freely through a relaxed court, developing an intimacy with Danish customs, eating 'dainties' of bacon and salt meats with dark bread ('very black, heavy and windy' according to Fynes Moryson) and learning a little of the language (his Dutch probably helping here). *Hamlet* shows a knowledge of Danish words and names that is not gleaned second-hand. When Polonius asks 'Inquire me first what Danskers are in Paris' (II i 7) this is not only grammatically sound, but is the only such correct use of the word '*Danskers*' in English literature of the time. Kit introduced the Danish word *rus* (meaning a full draught, or bout of drinking) into English – as 'rouse' ('And the King's rouse the heaven shall bruit again', *Hamlet* I ii 127), and he carefully changes non-Danish names into Danish ones when he draws on Belleforest's French version of the story. His Latin and nascent Italian eased his access to upper echelons of the court (the Earl of Rutland spoke Italian with the King on his diplomatic mission in 1603), and he even made friends with a couple of fellow students – admitting to them that he was 'no mere plaier', though probably not revealing his true identity. With his new friends he talked about the university at Wittenberg (the favourite of the Danish nobility of the time), and 'fair Padua, nursery of the arts' (which all three wanted to visit). The trio achieved a bemused notoriety for their 'Bachinall entertainments' and for 'reeling the streets' of the fishing village beside the castle – young, blithe and 'gilded with grand liquor'.* Perhaps it was beside tavern fires that Kit first heard old Danish chronicles, or perhaps he was inspired by the magnificent chamber in the castle which so impressed William Segar that it was the only one he fully describes:

---

* According to a report by a Danish court aide, possibly assigned to spy on them, quoted in Keaton, *Luvvies' Labours*, p. 261.

> ... it is hanged with Tapistary of fresh-coloured silke, with-
> out gold, wherin all the Danish kings are exprest in antique
> habits, according to their severall times, with their armes
> and inscriptions, containing all their conquests and vic-
> tories: the roofe is of inlett woods and hung full of great
> branches of brasse for lights.

Segar further notes that the 'queen's closet' was also splendidly
hung with these tapestries. Is this perhaps what Kit had in mind
when in the chamber scene Hamlet entreaties Gertrude, after
he has stabbed Polonius, to 'Look here upon this picture, and
on this,/The counterfeit presentment of two brothers' (III iv
53–4). Since the Restoration, performances of *Hamlet* have had
Hamlet produce miniatures of Claudius and the old king at this
point. This raises the question of why on earth Hamlet would
be carrying a portrait of Claudius next to his bosom. It makes
some sense that he is referring either to wall paintings or to two
tapestries – raising the symbolically deft possibility that one of
them is the arras behind which Polonius hides. His stabbing of
Polonius through an arras bearing the portrait of Claudius would
add acid irony to the lines 'Is it the King? . . . I took thee for
thy better . . .' (III iv 25–32). A movement made by someone
hiding behind the arras of the old king gives an intriguing dramatic colour to Hamlet's seeing the ghost of his father in the
dark room, while Gertrude does not.

Working with his Danish student friends, and using their copy
of Saxo's *History of Denmark*, Kit wrote *Hamlet* for the court at
Elsinore as part of his obligation for the monthly 6 thalers. This
is not the *Hamlet* we know today, but a much simpler play that
was to remain in the repertoire of various English comedians'
companies for decades, and influence a German version of the
story called *Der Bestrafte Brudermord*. Scholars refer to this elusive
early play as the *Ur-Hamlet*. We know little about it, but like
Kit on his missions of espionage, it makes mysterious single

appearances, even in England, until the *Hamlet* we are now familiar with definitely arrives in 1600 or 1601. In 1589, soon after Kit had finished the early version, his Cambridge friend Tom Nashe wrote in his 'Epistle' to Greene's novella *Menaphon*: 'Hee will afoord you whole Hamlets, I should say, handfuls, of Tragical speaches'. In 1594 his one-time employer the theatre manager Philip Henslowe noted in his account book, 'Received at hamlet viijs [eight shillings]'; and in 1596 Thomas Lodge (who, like Kit, worked with the Admiral's Men, and whose novel *Rosalynde* was the source for *As You Like It*), wrote in *Wits Miserie*, '. . . ye Visard of ye ghost which cried so miserably at ye Theator, like an oister wife, "Hamlet, revenge"'.

Kit left Elsinore suddenly, without the other players, some time in June 1585. Perhaps he simply had to get back to Cambridge, possibly his mission was accomplished – or maybe his cover was blown. It does seem that he later came to suspect his two Danish friends of treachery, though he was to meet them again, in Italy. According to the University of Padua archives, Rosencrance was a student there from 1587 to 1589, and Guildenstiene registered a few years later.

Kit returned to England, with at least one new play in his bag, during a barren summer with a thin harvest in prospect. After two decades of plenty, 1585 and 1586 were years of hardship and shortage. War in the Low Countries further sucked the country dry – and the plants that most prospered on this stony ground were paranoia and persecution. Catholics at home were yoked with enemies abroad. From 1585 Catholic priests and all who helped them were by law to hang. Parishes were searched, householders questioned, and the shadow of Richard Topcliffe, Lord Burghley's notoriously sadistic torturer, elongated across the land. Conspiracy was detected everywhere, and as the pressure to squeeze out traitors intensified, so the number of plots – both real and imaginary – grew. We can count them off on our fingers over the next few years – the Stafford plot of 1587, the Lopez plot of 1594, the Squire plot of 1598 – but the one that wrenched the frame of the nation, that led ultimately to the execution of Mary Queen of Scots, was the Babington plot in 1586. The machinations of the plot, and the cynical way in which Sir Francis used it to further his long-held aim of eliminating Mary, give us a flavour of the world in which Kit now moved. At least one of his spy friends was involved.

In late May, some weeks before Christopher arrived back, Anthony Babington – twenty-four, handsome, rich, a Catholic and a law student at Lincoln's Inn – met with one John Savage and an altogether shadier character, Father John Ballard, a Jesuit priest who, disguised as the dashing Captain Fortesque, his cape trimmed with gold, silver buttons on his hat and sporting a satin doublet, had travelled abroad and returned to report that 60,000 troops (French, Italian and Spanish) were poised to invade England in the summer. Ballard asked Babington to sound out Catholic gentry in Scotland and to help raise English support as a fifth column to the invasion. He also planned to assassinate Queen Elizabeth. This was something John Savage, the third man at the meeting, had vowed to do, but it had been a government agent, Gilbert Gifford, who had incited that oath. Sir Francis had agents provocateurs – 'projectors' – attached to all three men. Ballard's ever-present sidekick and fixer, Barnard Maude, was a Walsingham agent, and soon to charm his way into Babington's affection was Sweet Robyn, Robert Poley. At the beginning of July, Babington rather naïvely wrote to Mary to tell all, believing her royal assent would give the final stamp of legitimacy to their efforts. As Nicholl points out, the plot bears Babington's name not so much because he was its instigator, but because he was its weakest link. His letter was long and recklessly specific, listing the conspirators' main aims: to lay the way for a

Catholic invasion; free Mary from captivity, and finally to despatch 'the usurping competitor', Elizabeth. Mary replied point for point. The problem for the plotters was that Mary, in an Elizabethan sense, had been bugged.

The system had been set up by Gilbert Gifford. Incarcerated in Chartley Hall in Staffordshire, Mary nevertheless believed she had secret contact with the outside world through messages smuggled in and out in beer barrels – arriving in waterproof pouches, and leaving in the empty kegs. Sir Francis was intercepting the letters and deciphering them, before resealing them and sending them on. Mary's reply to Babington was what Sir Francis had long been waiting for, a plot that irrevocably implicated the Queen of Scots. In August Sir Francis pounced. Ballard was arrested while meeting with Babington at Robert Poley's house. Poley went off, ostensibly to plead Babington's case to Sir Francis and stay his arrest, but when he hadn't returned by evening, Babington himself fled, leaving Poley a letter aching with hurt, desperately trying to hold together a crumbling trust: 'I am the same I always pretended. I pray God you be, and ever so remain towards me ... Farewell, sweet Robyn, if as I take thee, true to me. If not, adieu ...'. He was arrested a few days later, along with a number of other conspirators, after hiding out in St John's Wood and disguising themselves as labourers by cutting their hair and staining their skins with walnut juice. They were all gruesomely executed.

At the last moment before the arrests, Sir Francis, tugging and twitching from the centre of his web, lifted his hands and receded. It is his deputy Thomas Walsingham who is seen coming to Poley's garden house on the morning that Ballard is apprehended; it is the Lord Admiral not Sir Francis who signs the warrant, and the affair is, in the words of another Walsingham agent, 'handled so circumspectly that neither you nor any of yours need be known in the matter'. But we do find a deepening of the working relationship between Thomas Walsingham and Sweet Robyn, and lurking on the edges of the scene as another government plant in Poley's house during the arrest set-up, is someone who was also hovering around Thomas Walsingham on the banks of the Seine back in 1581, the man Eleanor Bull thought not a gentleman – Nicholas Skeres, one more in that little party at Deptford in 1593, here again involved in intricate duplicity.

Kit's attendance at Bene't was exemplary up until Michaelmas, as he sunk himself into work for his Masters degree. Unlike many fellow dramatists, who slipped from university into London life without taking a degree, the qualification mattered to Kit as a firm seal to his status as a gentleman. Both Urry and Nicholl point to absences before his scholarship expired in March 1587, but most of his forays were to London, or back into the circle of Thomas Walsingham and the 'Wizard Earl' of Northumberland. Their mutual friend Tom Watson had just written a paraphrase of Coluthus's *Raptus Helenae*, a long poem about Helen of Troy, which he dedicated to Northumberland, and which Kit translated into English. Kit's version is now lost, though perhaps we have a teasing echo of it in the 'face that launched a thousand ships' in *Doctor Faustus* (V i 97), and the 'pearl/Whose price hath launched above a thousand ships' in *Troilus and Cressida* (II ii 82–3). The echo in *Faustus* adds force to the intriguing possibility that later in the year Kit once again joined the player troupe of Bradstriet or Browne for their regular tour to the Frankfurt book fair. In 1587, one of the new books introduced at the fair was the *Faustbuch*, a fantastical 'biography' of a real-life peripatetic scholar and magician, Georg or Johannes Faustus. Kit used this story for his *Doctor Faustus* – though his Faust is not a simple magician, but a man with a Tamburlaine-like ambition and lust for power, one who wants to be 'great Emperor of the world'. Early versions of the play were performed by Bradstriet's men on the Continent (two very dissimilar texts have come down to us), but the first performance recorded in London is only after events at Deptford, when the impresario

Philip Henslowe notes receipts from a 'doctor ffostose' on 30 September 1594. Intriguingly, the *Faustbuch* may not have been Kit's first knowledge of the magician – in 2002 Dr Christopher de Hamel, Donnelley Fellow Librarian at Corpus Christi College, discovered in a 1469 edition of Aquinas, one of the first printed books, an annotation by Archbishop Parker himself ascribing the semi-magical art of printing to 'John Faustus'.

During these last months at Cambridge, Kit formed ever stronger bonds with Thomas Walsingham and Tom Watson. 'Witty Tom Watson', as a contemporary dubbed him, was famed for his Latin and English poetry, his stage plays, and the 'froth of [his] jests'. Francis Meres noted that he was one of the best for tragedy, and Tom Nashe (along with most other literary figures of the time) 'dearly loved and honoured' him, writing that 'for all things he hath left few his equals in England'. He had been Kit's introduction to London intellectual circles, and though only a few years older had become something of a mentor and father-figure. Kit, for his narrative poetry, was seen as 'Watson's heir'. With Thomas Walsingham – part Kit's employer as a spy, part his patron as a poet – Kit was entering into what one writer has called the 'flower-strewn world' of Elizabethan intense male friendship. And it would be Thomas Walsingham who would tip Kit off about a threat to his standing at Cambridge.

Richard Baines, the sybaritic spy who had insinuated himself into the seminary at Rheims, who had plotted to poison the well water there, and whom Kit had sent tumbling into jail, was out for revenge. He had nothing more solid than a seething suspicion of the young Christopher Marley, and even this was something that in a world of leaking secrets, shifts of power and sudden counter-thrusts, he had to be cautious of exposing. But he knew how to strike Kit where it hurt, yet remain invisible himself. He started a rumour at the university that in his absences from Bene't College, Marley had gone over to Rheims. In an atmosphere of anti-Catholic paranoia, this would cost the

bumptious arriviste, the cobbler's boy made good, his degree.
A Cambridge man himself – he had been a prosperous 'gentleman pensioner' at Christ's College, and then moved to hotly
Catholic Caius College – Baines knew where to drop his chance
remarks, and carried enough of a whiff of popery about him
for them to be believed. The idea was easily creditable, given
young Marley's reputation as a malcontent and rebel. However
Baines did not reckon with Kit's powerful friends.

On 29 June 1587, the Privy Council met at St James Palace
in Westminster. Part of its business that morning was to draw
up a letter to the Cambridge University authorities. The letter
is missing from the university archives, but we get the gist of it
from Privy Council minutes:

> Whereas it was reported that Christopher Morley was deter-
> mined to have gone beyond the seas to Reames [Rheims]
> and there to remain, their Lordships thought good to certify
> that he had no such intent, but that in all his actions he
> had behaved himself orderly and discretely, whereby he had
> done her majesty good service, and deserved to be rewarded
> for his faithful dealing: Their Lordships' request was that
> the rumour thereof should be allayed by all possible means,
> and that he should be furthered in the degree he was to take
> this next Commencement: Because it was not her majesty's
> pleasure that anyone employed as he had been, in matters
> touching the benefit of his Country should be defamed by
> those that are ignorant in th'affairs he went about.

'Christopher Morley' was rolling out very big guns indeed. He
had not only done Her Majesty 'good service' while he was away,
'in matters touching the benefit of his Country', but he deserved
reward, and the 'ignorant' people who defamed him had better
hold their tongues. He got his degree. Richard Baines could
only further fume and secretly bide his time.

Interlude

Long before a horseman was carrying the Privy Council's letter to Cambridge, the malapert, ambitious, subversive, talented young Christopher Marley had followed up the connections he had made through players on the Continent and set himself up with the Lord Admiral's Men in London.

And what of that other babe baptised back in 1564, Will, mewling son of a glovemaker and child of small-town Stratford? It is now, in London, that he re-enters our tale.

The lives of the two young men reflect each other, like those of twins in Kit's plays, one favoured by fortune, the other not. Perhaps, like Kit, Will went to an ABC school to pick up the elements of reading. Maybe a passing scrivener taught him how to write. As Dr Clemens points out in his Foreword, we can be sure his illiterate father did not help him out (in the same way that Will would fail to educate his own children), and he was never registered at the local school, nor did he go to university. But, like Kit, he developed an early fascination for the new theatre, and strolling troupes visited Stratford at least as often as they came to Canterbury or Cambridge. Warwick's Men were paid a handsome 17 shillings to perform there in August 1575, though Leicester's Men had to make do with a measly

1 shilling in 1573; Strange's, Oxford's and Worcester's Men all came to town. And in 1587 a visit by the Queen's Men was to change the direction of young Will's life. The Stratford Corporation was happy to splash out a hefty 20 shillings for the star troupe, and the town's good citizens appeared to have had a riotous time: another 16*d* had to be found to repair a broken bench.

Vigorous actors they may have been, but the Queen's Men also had something of a reputation for violent affray. In Cambridge a few years earlier they had been paid 50 shillings *not* to perform. In 1583 in Norwich two of the players had chased an audience member who had sneaked in without paying, and so beat him about the head that he died. And just a few weeks before coming to Stratford, two of the leading men, John Towne and William Knell, had pursued each other with swords around the town of Thame, and up 'a close called the White Hound', where Towne had fatally pierced Knell through the throat. So the Queen's Men were two players short when they reached Stratford, with one dead and one in jail. Leaving behind his wife, daughter and toddler twins, twenty-three-year-old Will stepped into the breach. After touring briefly with the Queen's Men in the provinces he came back to Stratford, but only to make arrangements to re-join them in London. Just what attracted Will to the players? Possibly he had the same motives as Kit. Indeed, they shared similar backgrounds, both being the sons of upwardly mobile craftsmen. Will's father had left rural life to become a glovemaker, and had risen through a sweep of public offices, from ale-taster to petty constable and eventually Chief Alderman and Justice of the Peace. Maybe Will felt the need to make his own mark, to better himself, even though the law famously deemed actors 'rogues and vagabonds'. Money may also have been an incentive – at the time his father's fortunes were in a slump. But most of all (especially for someone who had married young and almost immediately found himself responsible for three children), joining the players was an act of rebellion. The troupes offered young men a yeasty admixture of public popularity and social defiance. Not only the Puritans railed against theatre. London authorities disapproved and so, in general, did the Establishment (apart from a few frivolous aristocrats who bankrolled the companies, as indeed did the monarch herself). The emergent middle class was wary of innovation, staunchly moral and utilitarian, demanding piety or at least worthiness in drama, not the flash, fire and frolics of the strolling players. Companies like the Queen's Men offered a new and hazardous career, a fast raft to leap onto at a time of cultural turbulence, especially for a burgher's boy of limited prospects. It was a hard life, but one that glinted with possible gold and the lure of fame. Kit, destined by his Cambridge scholarship for the clergy, had forsaken the hundred people summoned to a sermon by 'an hour's tolling of a bell', for the thousand called forth to a 'filthy play' by a trumpet. Like his move into the secret service, it was a step of dissent, tinged by social ambition and spurred by financial need. So, too, with Will.

And so 1587 found young Will Shakspere and Christopher Marley both on the road to London. Of course, Will went as a 'mere player', not a poet, for although he was not without literary ambition, he lacked talent.

PART II

CHAPTER FIVE

West Side Story

The London that lured these two young travellers – Will Shakspere walking from the west, through Oxford and Wycombe, past the gallows at Tyburn and the palaces of Westminster; Kit Marley, riding down through Saffron Walden and Epping Forest, traversing 'villainous boggy and wild country' to approach the city across Hackney Marshes – was, from a distance, a prickle of spires. Five score parish churches poked up their steeples in a small patch around the great, looming Gothic mass of St Paul's, the predecessor to Wren's domed church, and just as awe-inspiring (despite its own tall tower having been somewhat truncated by a bolt of lightning early in Elizabeth's reign). The only non-ecclesiastical competitors for the skyline were the Tower and the tiered turret of the Royal Exchange – or perhaps as you drew closer, the forest of masts of ships on the Thames. Closer still, and the bristling plume of churches matted into a tangled, infested profusion of tenements and taverns, palaces and grim alleys, gardens, slaughterhouses, plague-pits, theatres and stews. Over 100,000 people were crammed into a tiny area within or just outside the City Walls – and the population was swelling, and not just with Englishmen. There were Germans and Dutchmen, Switzers and Danes, Protestant refugees from Flanders and France –

but, according to a 1580 census, only 116 Italians and (until Cromwell changed discriminatory laws) barely a handful of Jews.

Kit, of course, had seen it all before. But the parvenu from Stratford was taking his first plunge into the city's swift current, swept along by the thrust and turmoil, avoiding restless ripples of violence, gasping at the novelty and merry motley. Yet London seemed already familiar to Will, a picture the players had painted for him often before. Over ale in Stratford, he had in his mind sucked good oysters in Bread Street and drunk cups of sack at the Boar's Head in East Cheap; he had seen street jugglers and duels with rats, learned the curses and insults of the watermen who plied the Thames, and had taunted 'Sir Tom', who wore a tattered doublet, a codpiece as a hat, and howled maudlin drunk through the night near St Helen's. He expected the roar you could hear half a mile from the city, that fragmented into cries like 'Buy my great eeeels!', 'Any work for John Buckle?' and 'Sir Francis Drake His Triumph in Cadiz!'. He felt he had already reeked the tallow by Paternoster Row, and knew the stink of Pissing Alley. He had choked on the fug of sea-coal fumes, gagged at the seeping stench of the burial grounds, but also breathed in the scents of oranges and of markets in herb-time.

Not everything was filth and flying ordure. The commonplace that London was dirty and Elizabethans ignorant of personal hygiene is misleading. Kit does write of the 'stinking breaths' of the common people in *Coriolanus*, and 'the Rabblement' in *Julius Caesar* throw up their sweaty night-caps and utter 'such a deal of stinking Breath' that the great man chokes and swoons. But then Kit might very well have been writing about Rome. The German traveller Paul Hentzner, who visited London in 1598, was impressed at how 'handsome and clean' the streets were. Soap had been brought back centuries before by the Crusaders. The young lad Francis in Claudius Hollyband's sixteenth-century language-teaching book undergoes extensive morning ablutions, and in a similar book, *The French Garden*, the mistress of the house is scoured with paste of almonds, refuses to wear a dirty ruff support, and later sends drinking glasses back to the kitchen because they are grimy. Nor should we forget that the frequently cited instances of people being prosecuted for mis-placed 'dungheaps' are records of transgressions. To deduce from these that everyone piled their faeces outside their front doors would be the equivalent of some future social historian deducing from a few twenty-first-century speeding tickets that all motorists tore about the country at 100 miles per hour. Citizens were required to burn their rubbish three times a week. It is clear that among the richer classes and in some parts of town, cleanliness could prevail, the difference from today being one of starkness of contrast. The stench of London was of the poor. The problem for people like Kit and Will Shakspere, who attempted to straddle both worlds, was of not carrying the odours of one into the other.

In London lay riches and wonders and wit. Like so many aspiring young men of his generation – a rising class that realised they could make their own future – Will wanted to grasp it all. As he walked down the Oxford road, and through the Wall at Newgate, the picture he had formed of London had to shift only slightly to adjust to the city he found. Perhaps he had underestimated the persistent grip of anxiety – the constant edge of fear of robbery, of murder, of the noises of night, of the plague which came suddenly and scythed swathes through the populace. The world beyond England, with all its dangers, seemed closer here, too. Foreign tongues could be heard in the streets, and the rumours that filtered from court were cold with the terror of Spanish invasion. Heads of traitors stared down from stakes on London Bridge; the spurting neck of Mary Queen of Scots was still fresh in the minds of people he passed.

And so much was new. Tall, steep-roofed houses – a cellar, a shop, two more floors and a garret – thrown up quickly to accommodate the thousands of incomers. The chronicler John

Stow, well into his seventies by the time he compiled the *Survey of London* in 1598, lamented a city 'pestered' with new construction, the gardens of his youth suddenly sprouting tenements; hills and fields 'incroched upon by building of filthy Cottages'. Throughout the 1580s laws were passed to control new building and prevent the sardine-packing of families into old ones. But it was futile. London became a teeming press of inhabited cellars and backstreet hovels, hard up against the grand houses of the rich.

The rich were very much in evidence. Elizabeth's court was a flame that drew politics and society to London. Of course, sessions of Parliament and the law courts played their role, but it was the Queen who exercised a pull that could be felt throughout the land. She had palaces in town at Westminster, Whitehall, St James's and the Tower, and more just a barge ride away, at Greenwich, Hampton Court and Richmond. Paul Hentzner gives us a picture of her at the time, her face 'oblong, fair but wrinkled; her Eyes small, yet black and pleasant; her Nose a little hooked, her Lips narrow, and her Teeth black' (the latter, he notes, being 'a defect the English seem subject to from their great use of sugar'). He registers her 'false hair, and that red' and her 'uncovered bosom, as all English ladies have it till they marry', and especially admires her small hands, long fingers, stately air and mild and obliging manner of speaking. She is dressed in white silk, bordered with pearls 'the size of beans', with a black mantle of the same fabric shot with silver threads. Fluttering around this figure were the 1,500 or so members of the royal household, but it was not just they who spurred excitement and generated wealth. The circles that surrounded Elizabeth – the household (the lord chamberlain dealing with upstairs, the lord steward with downstairs and the master of the horse with outdoors), the Privy Council, the courts, and the exchequer – fed their influence out across London, whether or not the Queen was in residence. The royal wardrobe was in the

City, the mint was in the Tower. Half the aristocracy owned London houses: a Westminster or Strand address became an exclusive one as a royal village grew around the palaces and the road that connected them to the City. Lord Burghley and Sir Walter Ralegh had houses on the Strand, Sir Francis Walsingham had one within the Walls, and the earls of Southampton and Essex lived lavishly in town. This was a celebrity culture, where fame and fortune were speedily gleaned by reflection or association. Anyone enjoying high office or royal favour had their own stable of hopefuls, alert for preferment while themselves passing down privilege for a fee. Thousands of tradesmen catered to their whims. Tailors and goldsmiths drifted westwards towards Westminster; and purveyors of silks and plate, of fine foods and entertainment filled their coffers, supplying the people that swarmed around the body of the monarch.

Fashion filtered down the line. Fynes Moryson noted that: 'All manners of attire came first into the City and Countrey from the Court, which being once received by the common people, and by very Stage-players themselves, the Courtiers justly cast off, and take new fashions'. Any courtier so misfortunate as to appear in last season's cut of doublet would find that 'men looke upon him as upon a picture in Arras hangings [tapestries]'. The practice of wearing aristocrats' hand-me-downs meant that the players presented a splendid appearance, a phenomenon marvelled at by the young Swiss student Thomas Platter after a performance of *Julius Caesar* in 1599. The play-actors, he remarks, were 'dressed most exquisitely and elegantly' and what's more, 'at the end of the play they danced together admirably and exceedingly gracefully, according to their custom, two in each group dressed in men's, and two in women's, apparel'. Dances, too, descended from fashionable halls to the stage, whereupon they 'come to be vulgar' and 'Courtiers and Gentlemen think them uncomely to be used'.

Kit, of course, was astutely aware of these niceties, and had the contacts and extra income to keep up with the Court. Will, in his player's finery, was happy in his delusion. But both knew the power of preferment and of the patronage these great houses afforded.

Will, with an arriviste's characteristic over-reaching, first took wholly unsuitable lodgings in Westminster, nearer to court than the theatres and in too ambitious a social milieu. A copy of a legal textbook (published in 1568) in the Folger Library is inscribed with the name 'Wm Shakespeare', with a note added in an unknown later hand: 'Mr Wm Shakespeare lived at No 1 Little Crown St Westminster NB near Dorset Steps, St James's Park' – though of course we have no way of knowing whether this later note-maker was telling the truth, nor even talking of the same Shakespeare. Our Will was registered at baptism as 'Shakspere', and this is the name used for the baptism of his three children, the burial of his son and marriage of his younger daughter. He was licensed to marry one Anne Whatley under the name 'Shaxpere', and the following day was engaged to Anne Hathwey using 'Shagspere'. All the signatures we have appear to use different spellings, but it would seem that once in London, he began to soften the hard West Country 'shack' of the first syllable for a more cultivated 'shake', as references to him as an actor in London show. All in all there are fifty-seven documented varieties of the family name.

Kit was more canny in choosing somewhere to live, lodging as he had done before with his friend Thomas Watson in St Helen's, before the two moved a step north to Norton Folgate, the area beyond Bishopsgate and the Bedlam hospital, just outside the 'liberty' of the City of London. The City Corporation disapproved of actors and their ilk, and by living a step beyond the liberty, Kit and his friends could shrug off their control.

Norton Folgate was close to the delights of town, yet also home to the Theatre and the Curtain – the leading playhouses of the day, also conveniently beyond City jurisdiction (the Swan and Globe had not yet been built across the river, in the liberty of the Clink, where the Rose was just beginning its life). Together with Shoreditch, its neighbouring liberty, Norton Folgate was a lively den of poets and players, wits and wicked malcontents – the names of the two liberties are sometimes used interchangeably, and often associated with court records of rumpus and mayhem. Robert Poley, Sweet Robyn, was a resident. Realising his mistake, Will very soon moved there too.

If his residence in Westminster was short-lived, his work with the Queen's Men hardly lasted longer. Queen Elizabeth's Men (as they were properly known) were, quite literally, the pick of the bunch, having been formed in 1583 from twelve top players poached from other companies. Once back in London, the star troupe had little need for the inexperienced player employed out of desperation in Stratford. By early 1588 one John Heminges had married the murdered actor William Knell's widow Rebecca, occupying not only Knell's bed but his buskins, as he took over the dead man's roles as well. As his subsequent career shows (he later joined the Chamberlain's Men and became their leading actor after the great Richard Burbage's death), he was a player of superior talent. Even though he edged Will out of his job, the two became lifelong friends – Will leaving him a legacy of 26s 8d to buy a mourning ring.

A 'Lamentable Tragedy' entitled *Locrine*, printed in 1595 gives a clue to the direction Will's career was taking in the late 1580s. On the title page we read that the play has been 'Newly set foorth, overseene and corrected, By W. S'. Biographer Katherine Duncan-Jones suggests that Will began to work as book-keeper and stage-keeper for the Queen's Men. As stage-keeper he had to make sure performers were ready on cue, that all ran according to plan, and perhaps to prompt when necessary. As book-keeper he would have to copy out the 'parts', with single-line cues from the previous actor's speech, to be learned by individual players. It then naturally fell to him to prepare, from prompt-books, 'parts', the author's 'foul papers', and whatever other material happened to be at hand, plays intended for publication. At the same time he was still playing whatever small roles he could garner. It is no wonder, as Duncan-Jones points out, that he was soon to be mocked as 'an absolute *Johannes factotum*', a 'Mr Do-it-all' by Kit's friend Thomas Nashe. But it does indicate that the boy from Stratford must indeed once have benefited from the services of a passing scrivener, and was skilled enough to read and to copy, probably in a neat Secretary Hand – though admittedly, the quality of Will's hand is guesswork. It is well-known that apart from the five (perhaps six) scrawled signatures, no proven examples of his handwriting exist.

It would also seem that early on he had ambitions to write plays as well as act in them. In the same passage in *Greenes Groats-worth of Witte* that marked him out as a Jack of all trades, he would be derided by the playwright-poet as an 'upstart Crow, beautified with our feathers, that with his *Tyger's hart wrapt in a player's hyde* supposes he is well able to bombast out a blanke verse as the best of you' – a pushy young actor, who not content with deriving his glory from words written for him by others, has the gall to think that he can do it himself.

Will Shakspere was indeed leapingly ambitious and determined. He was startlingly confident of his own abilities (as Nashe tells us) and had a greedy eye for gold. It is no chance that the book bearing his Westminster address is a legal textbook – Will was to prove litigious and acquisitive throughout his life. The Queen's Men were often on tour, and it seems he did not join them but instead hawked himself out to other troupes. The two companies that dominated the London scene were Lord Strange's Men, and the Admiral's Men, and it was probably while working for the latter that Will first met the sensational young

Christopher Marley (or Marloe, as he now increasingly styled himself, in yet another of the name shifts that seem to accompany each move into a new phase of his life). Though just the same age, Kit already embodied what Will Shakspere wanted to be. His play *Tamburlaine the Great* had been a huge success. The rhythmic blank verse he wrote it in was revolutionising the way other playwrights worked, and by the time Will came to London *Tamburlaine* already boasted a sequel and was beginning to spawn imitators. The man Marloe had both lustre and a little mystery. He had not only travelled with players abroad, but was rumoured to have visited Italy – quite an achievement for a Protestant Englishman, as much of Italy was in Spanish hands and so virtually at war with England, and what's more, the country was the core of Catholicism. It was forbidden territory. Going there for pleasure would find a modern parallel in a 1950s American going on holiday to the USSR.

This Marloe dressed richly, had aristocrats as friends and all the trappings of a gentleman. It was said he had tumbled with Lord Hunsdon's mistress; there was talk that he dabbled in the occult, that he had once assisted the 'Queen's conjuror', the great Dr Dee, and that in Sir Walter Ralegh's house on the Strand together with the 'Wizard Earl' Northumberland, he courted moral danger and blasphemy. Later, Kit would be suspected of using real spells and necromantic formulae in *Doctor Faustus* and *Macbeth*, and the accusations of atheism would stick.

When in London Kit worked furiously and lived hard (by his own admission he 'conversed more with the buttock of the night than the forehead of the morning'). But he was frequently out of town, and therefore much in demand during the periods he was back. Here was a fat pie for Mr Do-it-all's ambitious finger. By the end of the 1580s, Will 'Shakespere' (as he was now careful to call himself) was helping the busy Christopher Marloe as scribe, transforming his 'foul papers' into fair copy, writing out parts, and transcribing Marloe's work into playhouse prompt-books.* But all the while his eye was firmly focused on collaboration, on an easy vault straight to the top. Fortune was to raise him higher than he could have dreamed.

The theatre managers were hungry gobblers of new plays. London companies operated a repertory system, performing (when not prevented by plague or the authorities) every afternoon except Sunday and during Lent, and offering a new play daily. Of course, works were repeated – the Admiral's Men typically performed fifteen different titles over twenty-seven playing days – but this meant players worked at a tumultuous tilt. As a bit player Will had to keep some thirty different roles in his head, learning them from handwritten 'parts', seldom reading a play in entirety. Mornings were spent in rehearsal, afternoons in performance, hustled on and off stage by the stage-keepers (or himself making sure players were on cue); nights disappeared writing out parts or making some sense of Marloe's scrawl. In between he got on with his theatrical odd-jobbing – 'setting forth overseeing and correcting' other men's words. Though he desperately wanted to bombast out a blank verse of his own, there was precious little time in which to do it.

This does not mean that Kit sat aloof in a garret quilling masterpieces. The notion of a solitary author, dreamily drawing on his own inspiration is another creation of the Romantic era. Kit, as playwright, was very much part of the hurly-burly of Elizabethan theatre, and his plays changed shape with every turn. Even today, the words an audience hears on the first night of a new play are not exactly those the playwright delivered to the theatre on the first day of rehearsal. The text will have been tweaked at by the director, subtly altered by actors, cut, added to, rewritten. An energetic theatre company will continue this process throughout the run. They are the theatrical equivalent of a good editor. Similarly, in the hectic environment of the

---

* Keaton, *Luvvies' Labours*, p. 412.

Theatre, the Curtain and the Rose, the making of a play was an ongoing, collaborative effort. Of course, behind each work there was what Wallace Stevens calls a 'presiding personality', but plays were hybrids of other personalities, too: parts created for a star actor, scenes ad-libbed by clowns, songs added for musicians or slipped in to cover scene-changes, passages inserted to make a contemporary political point. Inspiration came from many sources. The subsidiary ghosts of Richard Burbage, Will Kemp and a host of leapers, jiggers and lute-players, jostle with the dominant spirit of the author of *Othello*, *King Lear* and *Hamlet*.

When it came to publication, even more hands shaped, shaded and changed the text. The focus of public interest at the time was on *performance*. Playwrights did not own their works; these belonged to the company that had paid for them. Plays were published in retrospect, often anonymously and many years after they had been on stage. The first collection of the so-called *Workes of William Shakespeare*, for example, was printed only in 1623, decades after some of the plays had first been performed. A haze engulfs the chronology of Kit's early work – we have to rely on diary entries and second-hand reports to date most first performances, or on when they were first shown to the licenser of plays.

Nor do we have any original manuscripts, though this is not unusual. Although in Elizabethan times autographed manuscripts were sometimes the printers' source material, these were often cut or doctored by the company book-keeper, and plays were frequently published using prompt-books, the author's 'foul papers', scraps of hand-written 'parts' or, notoriously, compiled by dictation from actors' fusty-brained recollections of roles they once played. There are two very different versions of Kit's *Doctor Faustus*; and one of the most famous soliloquies in English comes down to us thus:

> To be, or not to be, that is the question,
> Whether 'tis nobler in the minde to suffer
> The slings and arrowes of outragious fortune,
> Or to take Armes against a sea of troubles,
> And by opposing, end them, to die to sleepe
> No more, and by a sleepe, to say we end
> The hart-ake, and the thousand naturall shocks
> That flesh is heir to; tis a consumation
> Devoutly to be wisht to die to sleepe,
> To sleepe, perchance to dreame, I there's the rub . . .
> (*Hamlet*, Second Quarto)

and thus:

> To be, or not to be, I [aye] there's the point,
> To Die, to sleepe, is that all? I all:
> No, to sleepe, to dreame, I mary there it goes . . .
> (*Hamlet*, First Quarto)

There it goes, indeed. We can almost hear the scatterbrained actor's ramblings, as a scribe witlessly writes them down verbatim. What obfuscates matters more is that we cannot always be entirely certain who wrote what – especially as the absence of copyright laws meant that poets plagiarised each other relentlessly. A neat phrase or a nifty plot spread faster than the pox. Also, one writer might be called in to re-jig another's work, or to add a few scenes – leaving a spoor of personal stylistic imprints through the play to confuse literary bloodhounds for centuries to come. We cannot even be sure that all of Kit's work is his own. Certainly, it seems that bold Will Shakspere ('a slipper and subtle knave, a finder of occasions') persuaded Kit to allow him to collaborate on parts of *Henry VI*, sometime before 1592. And it is possible that the rather nondescript *King John*, probably written a little later in the 1590s, is almost entirely Will's work.

The first loops of the knot that would inextricably bind the names 'Marloe' and 'Shakespere' were beginning to form. According to Norlet Boyd, the two men appear to have got on fairly well, though at first Kit kept his distance.* The sparsely educated glovemaker's son from Stratford, flaming with aspiration yet socially unconnected, was, after all, a little too close to what Kit might himself have been. The two even looked alike – similar wispy beards, domed foreheads and luminous, engaging eyes – though Will Shakespere had more of the burgher in him, and a tendency to run to fat. This is most evident in the only two representations of Shakespere approved by people who knew him, the Droeshout engraving on the title page of the First Folio, and the rather vacant, open-mouthed bust commissioned by his son-in-law for the monument in Holy Trinity Church in Stratford, described by Anthony Burgess as resembling a 'self-satisfied pork-butcher'. The 'Chandos portrait', which was mistakenly said to be of Shakespere in the eighteenth century is, as shall be seen, of Kit, and when compared with the Droeshout rendering highlights differences rather than similarities – Kit's wilder hair, darker eyes and slighter chin.

There is little evidence, though, that the two men socialised together. Kit, like Tom Watson and Tom Nashe, was an habitué of the Nag's Head in Cheapside, and one of the group of poets and intellectuals that later became known as the 'University Wits', who frequented the Mermaid tavern in Bread Street – a sedate and respectable tavern, run by 'the precisest man in England', one William Williamson, who did not even allow musicians to play there. Despite his aspirations to play-writing, Will was more at ease with tumblers and players and was most often found in their company in earthier taverns such as the Garter or the Boar's Head. It was only much later in life that Will ascended to the smarter Mermaid.

---

* Norlet Boyd, *Two's Company*, p. 18.

Though Kit in his plays paints us a delightful picture of the more rumbustious taverns, it was not until this century that we were given an intimate view of the Mermaid. A document recently discovered by Dr Bernard Rosine, of the Bernhardt Institute in Paris, affords us the rare privilege of being able to eavesdrop across four centuries on conversations at the Mermaid.* Coming upon some empty pages bound in with miscellaneous documents pertaining to the Cerne Abbas Commission (a 1594 investigation into Sir Walter Ralegh's supposed atheism), Rosine was put in mind of the conspiracy of the 'Spanish Blanks'. In this affair a Scottish Catholic en route to Spain was found to be carrying mysterious blank sheets of paper each signed by a Scottish nobleman and addressed to the King of Spain, but with space left presumably for the monarch to have written in at his pleasure whatever professions of loyalty or promises of support he required. Rosine had always wondered whether these blanks had in fact not been blank at all, but had contained messages in invisible ink – urine, onion juice and milk all being commonly used as such at the time. He began to consider whether his blank sheets might not also bear a hidden message – one never read, or since faded. After some considerable battle with the archivist he was allowed to treat chemically a small corner of one page. Writing appeared. The pages (once fully treated) were revealed as reports on the Mermaid milieu, written, Rosine suspects, by a spy placed in the tavern by Sir Robert Cecil early in 1591 (a mark '33 E' on one of the sheets could refer to the regnal year). Cecil was probably hoping for damaging information on his rival the Earl of Essex, who had friends among the wits.

The papers are incomplete, and apparently written over a number of weeks. Like an eavesdropper, we do not hear everything said in the busy tavern, but pick up on tantalising snippets

---

* Laurens box, folder 15.

through the hubbub. The Mermaid might have been music-free and respectable, but it certainly was not stuffy. We can hear the toasts: 'Be merry!', 'Here's to you!', 'Here's to thy better fortune and goode stars!'. Tom Nashe in one corner argues vehemently with Kit, 'bounsing with his fist on the board so hard' that the tapster with an 'Anon, anon, sir, bye and bye' brings them more ale by mistake. When someone complains of the 'foul stinke' of Kit's pipe he quips (perhaps not for the first time) that 'all they that love not Tobacco & Boies are fooles'. The overeager eavesdropper speculates (incorrectly) that 'Marley' commits this 'beastlie sinne of sodometrie' not just with boys, but with Tom Watson, and perhaps also another playwright, Thomas Kyd, with whom 'he will soone share a chamber in Sourdich [Shoreditch]'. He picks up on a rumour (correct this time) that Robert Cecil has been knighted, and meticulously records some disparaging comments on this, and praise for Essex. There is some further scoffing about a 'King John' – perhaps not coded conversation, but a dismissal of the play published anonymously that year. Tom Watson derides 'the man Shacksper' as 'a slipper and subtle knave' and later 'a finder of occasions' (an opportunist). There are 'jests' and 'news', and the eavesdropper notes 'combats of wit', but either his shorthand or his brain cannot keep up with them. Once or twice drink dilutes caution, and conversations veer into perilous ground: a snort from somewhere that 'all protestants are Hypocriticall asses'; 'one Chumley', who comes across as a loudmouth and a braggart, falls to 'swearing and cursing, interlacing his speeches with curious terms of blasphemy'; 'Marley' again, jesting that the New Testament is 'filthily written' and that 'if he were put to it to write a new Religion, he would undertake both a more Exellent and Admirable methode'. We are given the sense of a 'deep' crowd that needs to be watched, of 'jesting that is not our jesting', dangerous cleverness, malcontent, whiffs of treachery.

The tavern tattler mentions another name, one as yet

unknown to Will Shakespere but closely associated with Kit – a young man who for a while has been on the edge of our tale, and who is about to move centre stage. The eavesdropper notes him as 'a careful friend' of Kit's, and to pick up his trail we must go back a few years, to the late 1580s. He is Oliver Laurens.

CHAPTER SIX

Gypsy Soul

Oliver, we may remember, was in the employ of a fat and slothful stationer in St Paul's Churchyard, who when asked for a book 'never stirs his head ... but stands stone still, and speakes not a word: onely with his little finger points backwards to his boy'. By 1587, the 'boy' had grown into a handsome young man, adept at stepping nimbly out of range of the little finger of the 'Puddinge of St Paul's'. The one surviving portrait shows him clear-skinned and clean-shaven; his large eyes captured at the moment they dart to look at something over the viewer's shoulder. It shows someone quick, energetic, alert. Dark, rather wayward hair curls down just over his ears. He is dressed simply, in the manner of a scholar – no ruff, just a white linen shirt with a falling collar, a simple black jerkin – and he bends over a writing desk, surrounded by the paraphernalia of a scribe. The painting is anonymous, but Flemish in style, and could very well have been painted in Antwerp, for according to Bernard Rosine, Oliver was already, by the mid-1580s, part of Sir Francis Walsingham's spy web, working mainly in the Low Countries. His natural cover as a St Paul's stationer helped give him access to Roman Catholic book-smuggling rings, perhaps posing as a courier willing to transport 'thornie and insolent bookes' and anti-government propaganda printed in

Middelburg and Antwerp, packaged in with legitimate book orders.*

Oliver appears to have spent some months in Antwerp at the Trognesius publishing house (the Puddinge being easily placable by a substitute boy to respond to his flabby-fingered commands). Antwerp had recently fallen to the Duke of Parma and so was enemy territory to the English, but Oliver's native French meant he could pass himself off as a Walloon. Rosine speculates that he was working on the *Colloquia et Dictionariolum Septem Linguarum*, a handy phrase book for merchants that gives the equivalent of such utterances as 'You did promise me to give me money two months ago' in English, Flemish, German, Latin, French, Spanish and Italian, and was published by Trognesius in 1587.

There was a growing demand for such works. Gentlemen and scholars could travel on their Latin, but what of their serving-men who had to go shopping in foreign markets, arrange for horses to be stabled, and negotiate with inn-keepers? How did merchants from different lands communicate? This is especially pertinent when people of different nationalities were trying to work together in dangerous situations, where efficient communication was crucial. Crews of ships on the high seas were often a mixed bunch – the great Spanish Armada comprised 'captains and crews drawn from many lands and speaking many tongues'. William Blandy described Parma's army as consisting of the 'froth and scomme of many nations', and the Earl of Leicester warned his troops in 1586 that 'whereas sundrie nations are to serve with us in these warres, so as through diversitie of languages occasion of many controversies may arise'. Yet in 1607 Thomas Dekker described a band of English war veterans as a 'mingle mangle of countries, a confusion of languages, yet all understanding each other' – armies seem to have developed what

---

* Rosine, *Oliver Laurens*, pp. 42–50.

Nick de Somogyi calls an Esperanto of War. Merchants, too, developed pidgins, like '*franco piccolo*', a mainly Italian hybrid which used only infinitive verbs, and was the language of commerce through much of the Mediterranean. Many were beginning to resort to early phrase books such as the *Colloquia et Dictionariolum Septem Linguarum*, providing ready employment in publishing houses for polyglots like Oliver (and later also Kit). In early 1588 Oliver was at work on Cornelis Kiliaan's *Dictionorium Teutonico-Latinum*, which was being expanded from its original two languages to include French, English, Saxon, Spanish, Italian and Greek. It was published by the Plantin Press in Antwerp, and here we see the reason for Oliver's (or rather Walsingham's) interest.

Plantin was the leading publisher of his generation. From his presses had come the great maps of Abraham Ortelius, as well as thousands of humanist, religious and academic works which were distributed across Europe and as far as the New World. He was a Catholic, yet managed enough professional flexibility to be (at times simultaneously in different combinations) official printer to the King of Spain, the City of Antwerp, the States General of the Protestant northern provinces, and the Duke of Anjou – an interesting place, then, for Walsingham to have a pair of eyes, especially after the Spanish had recaptured Antwerp. Oliver obliged with a steady stream of intelligence, at one point filching (though probably not from Plantin presses) a copy of a broadside 'Declaration', printed in English and denouncing Elizabeth as a tyrant, being made for distribution when the Armada landed. He also built up an extensive network of contacts in Antwerp, which were to prove invaluable to Kit in 1593.

It is not known whether Kit had anything to do with Oliver's recruitment, but it would appear that sometime in 1588, possibly extending into 1589, the two were together on government work in Italy. They travelled using forged documents bought off a

Jasper Himselroy, who traded in passports at the sign of the Gilded Head in Antwerp. It is unclear why Kit and Oliver travelled together. They may have been on separate but coincidental missions, or perhaps acting as couriers for something so important that back-up was needed to ensure it got through; it may have been for safety, or simply as part of their cover – people travelling together were less suspicious to the 'searchers' who watched foreign comings and goings. The two journeyed, for some of the time at least, as a pair of Catholic priests on pilgrimage to the tomb of St Anthony in Padua. Though perhaps arriving in Padua as couriers, they stayed on as intelligencers. A young student called John Wroth (or Wrothe) was beginning to supply Walsingham with information, and diligent, double-checking Sir Francis wanted a second view on the lad, especially as his agent Stephen Powle, who had probably recruited Wroth, was about to leave the Veneto. Sir Francis always double-checked. For him no action was without a motive, and no motive was above suspicion.

There were broader reasons why agents were needed in Italy. Tension with Spain and fear of invasion were intensifying – by July 1588 the Armada would be off the English coast. Walsingham was increasing the number of spies on the Continent to glean information on naval movements and invasion plans. (It is little wonder that Sir Francis Drake continued with his famous game of bowls. Walsingham's spies were so numerous and industrious that the arrival of the Armada could have come with little surprise.) Italy – the communication line between Madrid, the Vatican and the Holy Roman Emperor in Bohemia, and in large part occupied by the Spanish – was the 'best listening post in Europe', and Walsingham ran a number of agents there, especially in Venice and Padua. The astrologer Dr Dee, then living in Bohemia, had predicted to the Emperor Rudolph that 1588 would be a year of astrological upheaval, together with violent and abnormal storms, which would cause the fall of a mighty Empire. Rudolph was in correspondence with sorcerers throughout Europe, and soon astrologers across the Continent (perhaps because of Dee's high reputation) were warning of terrible tempests and convulsions of earth and ocean. The espionage historian Richard Deacon puts this down to clever exploitation by Walsingham and perhaps by Dee himself, maintaining that it amounted to a subtle psychological warfare, aimed at spreading gloom and despondency. And indeed, the prophecies affected recruitment in Spain, and there were desertions from the fleet.

Dr Dee was not averse to using occult means to practical ends. Some historians believe that his mysterious sidekick Edward Kelley's visions as a 'skryer' (medium) were complex manipulations, or coded espionage messages. Kelley had been in Walsingham's employ since the early 1580s to spy on a Polish prince, Lord Albert Laski, with whom he and Dee were closely associated, and possibly to keep an eye on the great conjuror himself. Dee's espionage connections with both Walsingham and his predecessor as spymaster, Lord Burghley, went back even further. In the early 1560s he had found an extremely rare copy of the *Steganographia* by the medieval abbot and early cryptographer Johannes Trithemius. This was at the very least a complex book of ciphers and codes, but Dee seems excitedly to have believed that it held the clue to transmitting messages over long distances by occult means. This was not dismissed lightly in an age when intelligence could be communicated only as fast as a man or a horse could stumble along appalling (and often impassable) roads. The occult was taken seriously both in espionage and conspiracy – in 1578 the Privy Council had been extremely concerned by the discovery in a stable of three wax images pierced with hog's-hair bristles, one labelled 'Elizabeth'; and the spy and writer Giordano Bruno once plotted to overthrow the papacy by magic.

There is a possible link between the magical duo in Bohemia, and the two fake pilgrims in Padua. The Jesuit scholar Christopher Parkins was in Padua when Kit and Oliver arrived. He had been falsely accused by Kelley of plotting against Elizabeth, but soon after Kit and Oliver were in Padua was himself filing reports on Kelley from Prague, not to Walsingham, but to Sir Robert Cecil. Oliver later became directly involved in the line of communication between Cecil and Prague, so was perhaps also working for Cecil in Italy. If this is so, then Kit's mission to Padua brought him a step closer to being caught up in Cecil's intrigue, and the darkness that would soon engulf him was already beginning to gather.

Kit and Oliver's initial disguise as Catholic priests eased their way, but was not entirely necessary. Although travel in most of Italy was not easy for Protestant Englishmen, it was tolerated in the Venetian republic (which included the cities of Verona and Padua) and in other independent territories in the north. There were English students at the University of Padua and English merchants traded with Venice. Rich, daring young gentlemen like Harrie Cavendish passed through Italy on their way to Constantinople, partly for business, partly for pleasure. The clown Will Kemp (with whom Kit had worked with Leicester's Men) had not only toured in Italy, but was famous there. Kit's friend Tom Nashe – who was in the area at the same time as Kit and Oliver, and could very well have travelled with them – relates that when in Bergamo he had occasion 'to light in fellowship with that famous Francattip harlequin', with whom he talked about English theatre and who asked him if he knew the clown 'Signior Chiarlatano Kempino' (Will Kemp). On saying that he did, Nashe found himself embraced and fêted.

Kit may very well have been with Tom Nashe at Bergamo watching *commedia dell'arte*, the vigorous, improvised Italian theatre which, together with that in England, was remarkable in that it was acted by professionals (the name means 'comedy of the profession'). Certainly he would have seen it in Venice and Padua. The stylish masks and costumes and energetic performances of the Italian actors fascinated him, and strands of *commedia* would run through his work for years to come. Some of the stock characters – the ancient Pantalone, the pedantic lawyer or doctor, the braggart soldier, *dei zanni* (the clumsy, comic servants) – would infiltrate his work. The pedantic Holofernes and the braggart Don Adriano de Armado in *Love's Labour's Lost* come immediately to mind, as do the 'Pedant' in *The Taming of the Shrew*, and perhaps even fussy Polonius in *Hamlet* and the foolish doctor in *Comedy of Errors*. Lucentio in *The Taming of the Shrew* refers to Gremio as an 'old pantaloon' (one of the first recorded uses of the word in English), and the sixth age of man is 'the lean and slipper'd pantaloon,/With spectacles on is nose . . .' (*As You Like It* II vii 158–9). The first use of the word 'zany' in English is recorded as 'Some carry-tale, some please-man, some slight zany' (*Love's Labour's Lost* V ii 463), and this is soon followed by 'these set kind of fools no better than the fools' zanies' (*Twelfth Night* I v 84).

The snappy banter of echoed quips between Beatrice and Benedick in *Much Ado About Nothing*, between Berowne and Katharine in *Love's Labour's Lost*, and between a host of masters and comic servants in other plays is a strong commedia convention, as are rhyming couplets to signify the end of a scene or speech. Allardyce Nicoll sees at least four *commedia dell'arte* masks described in Jacques' 'Seven Ages of Man' speech in *As You Like It*. A renowned scholar of the genre, Kathleen Lea considers the behaviour of Helena, Hermia, Demetrius and Lysander in *A Midsummer Night's Dream* as typical of the vicious circle of enchanted lovers in *commedia*, and gives special mention to Italian sources for *The Merry Wives of Windsor* and *The Comedy of Errors* which were not available in English at the time. The plays of mistaken doubles in *Comedy of Errors*, Lea points out, is a common *commedia* feature, and it is *commedia* that provided Kit's amplifications to the classical source of the play, Plautus' *Menaechmi*. Kit had already translated and adapted the *Menaechmi* for Bradstriet's men in the Low Countries. As he wrote *Comedy of Errors* sometime in 1592, he was perhaps subtly admonishing his would-be collaborator, the 'upstart Crow' Will Shakespere by basing the play on Latin and Italian sources, neither of which Will could read.

The early twentieth-century critic Edward Gordon Craig wrote: 'The naturalness [by which he means popular appeal] of the Dramas was, I believe, wafted to England from Italy. Italy had awakened . . . to a new sense of Drama. It was red hot, spontaneous, natural . . . It was good talk, wonderful patter.' Kit's experiences in Italy were to breathe fire into English theatre. Interestingly, Craig also maintains – nearly a hundred years before scholars would express similar opinions – that 'the Dramas were created . . . in close collaboration with the Manager of the Theatre and with the actors . . . I believe that a glimpse of the manuscript of the plays would reveal a mass of corrections, additions, and cuts made in several handwritings. I believe that the improvisators – and the comedians of that day were great improvisators – contributed a great deal to the Comedies, and not a little to several of the Tragedies.' Of course, sadly, from *Tamburlaine* to *The Tempest*, not a single manuscript remains to bear this out.

It is clear that Tom Nashe did not share Kit's enthusiasm for *commedia dell'arte* – or the passion that was already beginning to grip Kit about Italy. The land that Fynes Moryson called the Queen of Nations, Tom Nashe dismissed as 'the Academie of man-slaughter, the sporting place of murther, The Apothecary shop of poyson for all Nations'. In his novella *The Unfortunate Traveller*, an English earl who has been banished there tells the hero Jack that young men bring from Italy only 'the art of atheisme, the art of epicurising, the art of whoring, the art of poysoning, the art of Sodomitire' (at least four of which arts rather appealed to Kit). The theatre Nashe maligns as comprising 'a sort of squirting baudie [bawdy] Comedians, that have whores and common Curtizens [courtesans] to playe womens partes'. In England, of course, women's parts were played by boys. Many English travellers were shocked to see real women on stage in Italy, and some, like Thomas Coryate, agreeably surprised that they performed women's parts 'with as good a grace, action, gesture ... as ever I saw any masculine Actor'.

But Nashe was having none of it. He went on to complain of actors who would do anything for a laugh; that this was a theatre where Pantaloons and Zanies replaced the more 'stately' English scenes of emperors, kings and princes. Tom Nashe was becoming a little stuffy, and Kit was beginning to drift apart from his once rebellious university friend.

They are pictured at the Saggitari, an airy inn in Bergamo: scrawny Tom Nashe with his buck teeth and 'mutinous unfixed hair' (Kit once quipped that when Nashe was naked he looked for all the world like a forked radish, with a head fantastically carved upon it with a knife), complaining of the dangers and horrors of Italy, while Kit goads him on about women players.* They sit at a table 'spread with white cloathe, strewed with flowers and figge leaves', eating the common Italian fare of huge chunks of white bread, with 'a great Charger full of hearbes, and a little oyle mixed therein', trying for the first time 'the hinder parts of frogs' and snails, or settling for a scrap of roast meat with a delicate Savore sauce, which the traveller Fynes Moryson describes as 'slices of bread steeped in broath, with as many Walnuts, and some few leaves of Marjoram, beaten in a morter, and mingled therewith, together with the juyce of Gooseberries'. A fine feast, it seems, despite the fact that the meagreness of

---

* Laurens box, folder 12 (journal).

portions in Italy (apart from bread and salad) generally troubled guzzling northern travellers – though one William Lithgow notes that when he could not finish a meal, he was given leftovers as 'fragments ... wrapt up in cleane paper'. Like Kit and Tom Nashe, Lithgow enjoyed large quantities of a local wine called Lachrime Christi, complaining: 'I drew so hard at that same weeping Wine, till I found my purse began to weepe also'. Norlet Boyd wonders whether in these bottles lay the inspiration for Tom Nashe's work *Christ's Tears over Jerusalem.** Kit certainly already knew and enjoyed the wine, listing it among the 'dainties of the world' in the second *Tamburlaine*, calling it 'liquid gold' (2 *Tamburlaine* I vi 93–6).

It is around this time that Oliver Laurens began to write the travel journal that helps us keep track of Kit over the next few decades.† He mentions heavy rains and the flood of the Po, which helps date the beginning of his account as 1588. The journal now comprises some 220 leaves of paper, of various sorts, in a folio volume bound in crimson morocco with light gold tooling. The binding dates from at least a century after the journal was written, and the pages would appear to have been gathered from various sources – they are in sequence, but vary greatly in quality of preservation, and there are obviously sections missing. It is written throughout in a small neat English Secretary Hand, with none of the innovation of the Italic script that was taking over Tudor handwriting, but with its own quiet flourishes: a long tendril dropping from the f, a 'p' like a small comet, an elegant double-curved capital T. It's an energetic hand, but one that speaks reliability, constancy and self-control. Parts of the journal are in cipher. There are occasional simple ink illustrations.

Nothing is known of the history of the volume until the late

---

* Boyd, *Two's Company*, p. 34.
† Laurens box, folder 12.

eighteenth century when it appears in France as part of the effects of an elderly Comte, who did not survive the Revolution. For nearly a century it remained the heirloom of a petit bourgeois Parisian family (apparently unread), until as the 'Diary of the Clerk to Mr Shakespere', it was shown to the English ambassador sometime in the 1880s. It then disappeared again (Dr Rosine thinks the ambassador either bought it, or tried to suppress it), and resurfaced after the Second World War when it was catalogued as part of the Huguenot archive at the Bernhardt Institute (the later pages contain some reminiscences of Oliver's childhood, and his account of the St Bartholomew's Day Massacre).

Oliver relates that soon after arriving in Padua, the two abandoned their clerical cover and 'took a lodging fit to entertain such friends as time in the fair city shall beget'. The 'studious universitie' there – older than any Oxford or Cambridge college – was famous for its religious tolerance and liberal ethos, and drew academics from all over Europe. Sir Francis Walsingham had studied law, drunk wine and played the clavichord there in the 1550s, Kit's friend Rosencrance of Elsinore had recently arrived and there were Dutchmen and Germans, students from Illyria, from Bohemia and from Cyprus across the seas. 'More students of forraine and remote nations doe live in Padua,' wrote the 'Odcombian Leg-Stretcher' Thomas Coryate, 'than in any one University in Christendom'. They were organised into nearly thirty different *nationes*, each permitted to recreate the customs and traditions of the homeland, each feeding a little of its essence into the distillation of European life that was Padua. Some of the greatest minds in the world were there, along with freelance tutors and hosts of young men who came not for the official *Studium* but simply to attend a few lectures, follow a short course, learn Italian, or plunge into the cosmopolitan pool. Those who were rich enough or had the right connections were taken up into elite literary circles of Venetian aristocrats and local Florentines. Horse-riding, fencing and dancing were just as enthusiastically pursued as learning, and the pace never faltered, with banquets and tournaments, masquerades and theatre. Kit was in his element.

Oliver – on his first visit to Italy – was awestruck by the light and colour. He writes wonderingly of the brightly painted and patterned walls, of arched stone arcades that keep off 'the greatest raine' and provide shadowy corners for assignations, of the five market places – one where 'Gentlemen and Students of alle nationes meet and walk' – and of the Church of St Anthony, its clustered domes and spindly turrets 'swift transporting me in mind to Constantynople, as on Pacolets horse' (Pacolet was a dwarf magician in the old romance of *Valentine and Orson*. His magical horse could convey you instantly anywhere you desired to go. St Anthony's in Padua is indeed oriental in appearance – though how Oliver could apparently be reminded of Santa Sofia and the Seraglio is unclear, as he had never been to Constantinople). He delighted in the practicalities of their daily life, of the boy Biondello who carried their purchases back in a basket from the market-place for a soll, of the ancient 'Hostesse' from whom they rented their chamber and who found them fine clean 'tableclothes, napkins, sheetes and towels and dresseth our meat in the bargain'. He effuses about the 'sweete Ayre and sunny hills' of the nearby countryside and tells us of Kit's going off to sweat in the waters of Abano, 'which he had heard of Seignyeur de Montaygne' – the thermal springs at Abano, which flow out of the ground at 87°C, had been famed since Roman times. Montaigne had visited them in 1580, and had been impressed by the fact that the very rocks steamed, and had holes pierced in them so that 'a man may lie down in the exhalations and get into a heat and perspiration, which he does very quickly'. He had no doubt recommended them to Kit when they met in Plombières.

Oliver is perhaps just a little too lyrical. Both Montaigne and

Fynes Moryson complained that the arcades of Padua made the streets too narrow, and the Frenchman thought the city downright ugly. The oft-mournful William Lithgow moaned that it was 'the most melancholy City in Europe', that the students committed murders 'with gun-shot or else stilletoes', and that (as in all of Italy, he thought) sodomy was rife: 'A monstrous filthinesse, and yet to them a pleasant pastime, making songs and singing sonets of the beauty and pleasure of their Bardassi, or bugger'd boyes'. Fynes Moryson also notes the high incidence of murder between students, and puts it down to the excessive liberality of the authorities, as 'man-slaiers are only punished with banishment'. There is truth in all this. Murder it was that drove them from Padua, and Kit was taking to buggery with relish.

The *Consiliarius* of the English 'nation' at the time was Richard Willoughby, who had been a fellow at Kit's Cambridge college but had converted to Catholicism and left the country. Gregarious and clever, he entertained most leading Englishmen in Padua, occasionally supplied intelligence himself, and later became a good friend of Galileo. He also offered ingress to smart circles. Kit's spark and easy wit went to work. Oliver writes of a visit to a Venetian *palazzo* which is draped with purple silks and tapestries, where they recline on 'Turkey cushions boss'd with pearl'; and of another to the villa on the mainland built by Palladio for the brothers Barbaro (Daniele, a humanist scholar, and Marcantonio, Venetian ambassador and amateur sculptor) surrounded by forests and fine gardens. Here he marvels at how Veronese's trompe-l'œil mural landscapes blend perfectly with the real vistas, how the music played in the hall escapes into the evening air to mingle with birdsong, how the breeze is so soft that it does not even move the leaves. At night the moon shines bright on the courtyard, and when it is shaded by a cloud, candlelight gently seeps out from the hall to take its place. All is poise and quiet harmony.

Palladio had created such perfectly proportioned villas for a Venetian aristocracy that was beginning to turn away from the merchant life, which had made it so rich, to the pleasures of reading and culture and the delights of a country setting. Summer villas appeared all around the Veneto, and especially along the Brenta river which connects Venice and Padua. Some scholars see these mansions as the image for Portia's Belmont in *The Merchant of Venice*, citing the scene where Portia despatches her servant Balthazar to Padua by the Venice ferry. Contrary to the opinions of those who snigger at Kit's accuracy in these things, ferries did indeed ply the Brenta daily between the two cities. Various travellers of the time note the lock system (which is still in use) and mention boats with arched hatches at the back, sometimes covered in tapestry, and with cushions strewn about for comfort. Other candidates for Belmont include a villa in the town of Montebello, twenty miles from Venice (Portia and Nerissa travel to Venice by carriage with a 'haste away/For we must twenty miles to-day'), and the Villa Barbaro, which Oliver evokes so beautifully, and which is near the town of Montebelluna (the Roman *Mons Bellonae*).

Oliver also mentions a visit to the trimmed, formal gardens of the Conte Guisti in Verona, where, hollowed into a mountain below the Belvedere, is a chapel, nowadays ignored and derelict, that as Friar Laurence's cell and scene for a secret tryst and marriage seems far more authentic than other so-called 'sites' of *Romeo and Juliet* offered up to tourists. At this point Oliver's narrative is lost to us. A few fragments remain on sheets that show substantial water damage (the account resumes on different paper a few years later). One passage refers to a journey to Rome, and another to Milan, though these may have been written during a subsequent visit. Although Milan enjoyed a measure of independence, the Duke was sympathetic to the Spanish, and Rome would have been even more dangerous for Protestants to visit. Yet there is some evidence in Kit's works of a journey to both cities. A. J. Hoenselaars notes that Kit's depiction of Rome in *Doctor Faustus* has few equals in later drama; and A. D. Wraight argues that the 'high pyramides,/Which Julius Caesar brought from Africa' (*Faustus* II 853–7), again mentioned in Sonnet 123 as 'Thy pyramids built up with newer might/To me are nothing novel, nothing strange' dates his visit to Rome as 1589, when the fourth of these obelisks was newly erected and causing some stir among travellers. A visit to Milan may be detected in the scene in *The Taming of the Shrew* where a cultured lord shows the drunken tinker Sly his art gallery and tells him:

> We'll show thee Io as she was a maid,
> And how she was beguiled and surprised,
> As lively painted as the deed was done.
> (*The Taming of the Shrew*, Induction ii 52–4)

Some argue the lines are inspired by first-hand knowledge of Correggio's *Io and Jupiter*, which was on view at the palazzo of the sculptors Leoni and Son in Milan from 1585 to 1600. It is also tempting to see the same lord's references to his 'wanton pictures', and the mention of 'This senior-junior, giant dwarf Dan Cupid' (*Love's Labour's Lost* III i 170) as an indication that Kit had seen Giulio Romano's extraordinarily erotic frescos adorning the Sala di Amore e Psiche, and his terrifying gigantomachy (complete with huge *putti*) splayed across the walls and vault of the Sala dei Giganti, both in the Palazzo Te in Mantua (the first folio has 'This signior Junio's gyant dwarfe', which could be glossed as 'This signior Julio's giant dwarf'). Romano's frequent portayal of stricken youths, such as in *Hylas carried off by the Nymphs* and *The Death of Adonis* very probably inspired the rich poetry of Kit's *Hero and Leander*, and his vivid pictures of the Trojan War are described at length and in detail in *The Rape of Lucrece*, all of which seems to indicate a visit to Mantua. But Oliver is disappointingly mute on this point, or his account is lost.

He does, however, recount the experience that led to their sudden flight from Padua. In a tussle one hot night near the Piazza del Erbe, Kit killed a young German student called Walter Hoochspier. This was not a duel conducted according to formal Italian rules. It was sudden and disordered. The formal steps of picking a quarrel and conventions of combat had been codified earlier in the century, and were taught at the popular fencing schools in Padua. They were laid out in manuals such as Muzio Giustinopolitano's *Il Duello*, which was later plagiarised in an almost direct translation into English by the London fencing master, Vincentio Saviolo, and became much used by English dramatists. Kit mocks these rules through Touchstone's progression from the 'retort courteous' and the 'reply churlish' to 'countercheck quarrelsome' and the 'lie direct', in *As You Like It*; and they inform behaviour in the duels and encounters in *Romeo and Juliet*. Tybalt fights by a 'book of arithmetic', he 'fights as you sing prick-song: keeps time, distance and proportion; he rests his minim rests, one, two, and a third in your bosom' (*Romeo and Juliet* II iv 20–3).

But the ritual and pretty geometry of the fencing schools did not necessarily transfer to the street. Fencing masters and writers of manuals had it in their own interests to stress formality and convention, but in the anarchy of alley assaults, in fury, in battery and battle to the death, rules gave way to dirty tricks and all-in fighting. Heads were smashed, bodies pinned to the ground, testicles crushed, limbs slashed and severed. And Kit's hot temper served him ill. The circumstances of his fight are unclear, as we have only part of Oliver's account (it is in the water-damaged section of the bound journal), but it would appear to have something to do with Rosencrance, who had known Hoochspier in Wittenberg. Perhaps it is at this point that Kit found out about Rosencrance's treachery in blowing his cover at Elsinore. Kit was the betrayer betrayed, the dissembler duped, and angry about it. But it is more likely the cause was immediate

– rivalry for a woman, or a taunt about his 'Bardasso' that flashed Kit into a fury. Whatever his motive, he pursued the Dane down one of the dark, arcaded alleys leading off the piazza towards the Jewish quarter, and attacked him without warning. There are shouts, confusion. Daggers flash, it happens too suddenly for swords. Hoochspier intervenes, closing with Kit and warding off a dagger-thrust with his left hand. Kit stabs twice, wounding Hoochspier down his right side, then severing an artery in the throat. No-one knows quite what is happening until movement and bodies subside. And only then comes the adrenaline rush. In the panic Kit forgets that 'man-slaiers are only punished with banishment', or perhaps he is simply not as well-informed as Fynes Moryson.

Kit and Oliver fled Padua immediately, by horse under bright moonlight to Venice, where at dawn the next day they boarded the first ship that would take them, the *Tiger* bound for Aleppo.

This was probably not the 200-ton *Tiger* under Captain John Bostocke, a noble ship of the Queen's fleet that had helped withstand the Armada the previous summer. Given subsequent events, it is more likely 'the rotten carcass of a bark' of the same name commanded by the Dutchman Captain Barnestrawe (probably an anglicising of Boonstra), who 'was not regarded by the Englishe men but greatlye reviled and called copernose and ... was fitter to drincke ale than to be a Captaine'. Captain Boonstra was probably akin to the commander of the ship the long-suffering William Lithgow boarded in Venice, whose 'Master had no compasse to direct his course, neither was he expert in Navigation', hoisting up the sails at night, and travelling only by day, in sight of land.

The *Tiger* seems to have been caught in a tempest sweeping the Ionian Sea, and blown towards Malta. There is no extant record of their shipwreck, but we can hear the storm throughout Kit's work in the 'hurly-burly in the heavens', the 'deaf'ning dreadful thunders' and 'nimble sulphurous flashes', as ships toss and pitch 'till the brine and cloudy billow kiss the moon', as panicked mariners see the 'ambitious ocean swell and rage and foam,/To be exalted with the threatening clouds' and cannot say 'it is a sea, for it is now the sky: betwixt the firmament and it you cannot thrust a bodkin's point . . . how it chafes, how it rages, how it takes up the shore!' (*Dido* IV i 10; *Pericles* III i 1–6, III i 45; *Julius Caesar* I iii 6; *The Winter's Tale* III iii 83). The storm that engulfed Lithgow 'split our Mast, carrying sayles and all over-board', as sailors fought about who should first leap out, every man with the 'stamp of death in his pale visage'. As tempests rage in Kit's plays, mariners show an expert sense of how to respond to the difficulties they are in, go through the right series of manoeuvres, and use correct professional language. As the weather worsens, they scream to each other: 'Down with the topmast! Yare, lower, lower!' and 'All lost, to prayers, to prayers, to prayers! all lost!', until 'We spilt, we split, we split!' (*The Tempest* I i). We can sense the terror as the ship breaks up, or drifts helplessly to a rocky coast: 'O, the most piteous cry of the poor souls! Sometimes to see 'em, and not to see 'em; now the ship boring the moon with her main-mast, and anon swallowed with yeast and froth, as you'd thrust a cork into a hogshead' (*The Winter's Tale* III iii 88ff). We can almost feel the waves that wind about Leander as he swims through a storm to his Hero, and pull him under.

It is not known how Kit and Oliver survived the wreck. Perhaps, like Sebastian in *Twelfth Night* and Ægeon in *The Comedy of Errors*, they bound themselves to a mast and were washed ashore; maybe, like William Lithgow, they ended up in a cave for three days, without food and water, or were cast up on rocks like Pericles, and helped by fishermen. Kit would develop an aversion to travelling by sea, would feature sea-storms and shipwrecks in twelve of his plays, and has a ship named the *Tiger* in two of them. In *Macbeth* the ship and its captain come in for special malice from the First Witch.

Nor is it known how they made their way back to England. The next that is heard of Kit is in September 1589, when he is arrested for his part in an affray in Hog Lane, near his lodgings in Norton Folgate – back in a London where the older generation of the establishment appeared creakily to be taking a final bow. The Queen's long-time favourite, Robert Dudley, was dead, and his stepson the glamorous Earl of Essex, a wooer of the people, was stepping into his place. Sir Francis Walsingham was ailing, though Kit's friend and tradecraft mentor Thomas Walsingham (who had just inherited family estates at Scadbury), seemed more inclined to life as a gentleman than to assuming his elderly relative's role as spymaster. It was Robert Cecil, the calculating, ambitious son of Lord Burghley, the Lord Treasurer, who had his eye on Walsingham's job; and wily old Burghley, who was also ill and already bereft of his beloved wife, had a mind to help him.

CHAPTER SEVEN

Men of Respect

Lord Burghley said he was as lonely as an owl. His wife was dead; gout chewed at every joint in his body, and he had laboured in government service for over forty years. Punctually, at four every morning, he started work, and led a strictly ordered day. He had no close friends, 'no inward companion as great men commonly have', according to a contemporary, 'nor did any other know his secrets'. Music left him cold, he had no taste for poetry, nor did any private troupe of players ever cavort in his name. And he did look a little like an owl, with his dumpy figure, placid expression, high forehead, feathery white beard and large, watery, old-man's eyes. He was seventy, and Her Majesty had just screamed at him, calling him a 'froward old fool'. But then, she more often called him 'my Spirit', and asked tenderly after his comfort, even allowing him to sit in her presence when his weak hams trembled and his old knees hinged unbidden. He had indeed been bad-tempered and contrary of late; his lifelong forbearance, his bending calm, had become brittle and all too often snapped.

As a younger man he had, with a pliability that is almost suspect, manoeuvred through the turbulence of Tudor succession, changing his allegiance three times in six years. Surviving other men's disgrace, nodding sadly at their executions, he had held on to public office under both Edward VI and Mary I to become the sage and solid stanchion for a flamboyant, inexperienced new Queen. William Cecil, descendant of a poor Welsh squire, had proceeded with certain step to a baronage and the highest office in the land. Along the way he had made a fortune and founded a dynasty. Burghley created networks of obligation and patronage that enriched him (he had an income of £25,000 a year at a time when the revenue of the State itself was only around £300,000) and magnified his power, establishing what Curtis Breight brands a *Regnum Cecilianum*, a Cecilian regime based on paranoia and terror, with surveillance as one of its lynchpins. It was Burghley who, when the Queen elevated him from Principal Secretary of State to Lord Treasurer, had hand-picked Sir Francis Walsingham to take his place, and taught him the value of informers at home and abroad. Yet if there was one thing that rivalled politics in importance to Lord Burghley, it was raising his family's status and perpetuating power through his line. His tomb effigy is in the style of a medieval knight in full armour – an affection of ancient nobility, an illusion of old money.

His eldest son Thomas was a wanton youth and a disappointment to him; his favourite daughter Anne made a seemingly dazzling match when she was just sixteen, to an aristocrat with a gift for poetry, the handsome Earl of Oxford – who went off alone to Italy, and was later reported romping with kitchen boys, swilling in drunkenness and saying scandalous things about the Holy Trinity. Burghley's views on poets, Italy, sodomites, libertines and atheists were not favourable. 'Suffer not [your] sons to pass the Alps, for they shall learn nothing there but pride, blasphemy and atheism,' he warned in a list of ten 'rules and advertisements for the squaring of thy life' intended for his younger son, Robert, on the brink of adulthood. For if anyone was to perpetuate the power of the Cecils, it would have to be this diminutive, crooked second son, whom Eleanor Bull would one day deride to the poet Marloe as a 'bunch-backed toad'.

From a fledgling age Robert had been aimed at high office. His education was full and rigorous, starting early in the morning and consuming most of the day with classics and modern languages, writing, science and theology. After books were closed came the pain and humiliation of fencing and dancing, as he wielded an outsized sword and manoeuvred ill on awkward, splayed feet. And here, to sharpen the shame, another Robert shone, a cuckoo in the Burghley nest, and one that grew resplendent plumage. He was the dashing, handsome and perfectly built Robert Devereux, the young Earl of Essex. The boys were almost the same age, and Devereux's father had died just a few years earlier. Lord Burghley, as Master of Wards, had taken him under his wing. Burghley had established in his household what amounted to an elite school for a handful of young aristocrats, many of whom were his legal wards. Young noblemen and old money were a fillip to family status, and he aimed to create a stable of powerful political supporters. Yet three of his charges, the Lords Rutland, Southampton and Oxford would one day form the heart of the anti-Cecilian faction in the country, and at its head would be the well-favoured Earl of Essex. To Robert Cecil it was as if his father had two sons of the same name, a legitimate one and a usurper; mismatched twins, one bent and graceless, the other manly, popular and athletic. And Robert Devereux did not take to this secretive son of a powerful commoner, whose thin eyebrows seemed constantly arched in disdain, who was clever, subtle and appeared never to sin. The two became rivals for life.

They went to separate colleges at Cambridge, Devereux to Trinity and Cecil to St John's, where he scorned the company of Tom Nashe and his disruptive friends including the malcontent Kit Marlin. The vice-chancellor praised him for his 'godly vigilance' at sermons and debates. At Gray's Inn, among law students notorious as riotous rumpus-makers, terrors of the

London Watch, he singled himself out to the said Watch by passing them by with 'courtly salutation'. Courteousness, sweetness and charm became salient features of his public persona – when he was introduced to the Queen, she called him 'my Pygmy', but on knowing him softened this to 'Elf'. Yet behind this façade he was cool and calculating, and an artful manipulator. As Anthony Bacon later wrote of him to Essex: 'He is a man likely to trust much to his art and finesse (as he that is an excellent wherryman, who, you know, looketh toward the bridge [i.e. London Bridge] when he pulleth toward Westminster [the opposite direction]) that he will hope to serve his turn and yet preserve your Lordship's good opinion.' All the while he was carefully analysing why Sir Walter Ralegh had become unpopular with the people, divining how his monarch reasoned, and assimilating information – which he knew was his most powerful tool. Yet behind his heavy bulwark of privacy he was rash, extravagant, wildly promiscuous, and a reckless gambler, who tumbled into pits of blackest depression. Still, his father steered him firmly towards the top, advising:

> Towards thy superiors be humble, yet generous, with thine equals familiar, yet respective; towards thine inferiors show much humanity, and some familiarity; as to bow the body, stretch forth the hand, and to uncover the head, with such like popular compliments. The first prepares thy way to advancement, the second makes thee known for a man well-bred; the third gains good report, which once got is easily kept; for high humilities take such deep root in the minds of the multitude, as they are easilier gained by unprofitable courtesies, then by churlish benefits . . .

Yet in this blueprint for manipulation of 'the multitude', Burghley sounded a warning: 'I advise thee not to affect or neglect popularity too much. Seek not to be an Essex, shun to be a Ralegh.' The triad of antagonism that would establish itself between his son and the Queen's rival favourites in the late 1580s was already clear in the perceptive old man's mind. The 'Pygmy' could never participate in the coquetry that would win him Elizabeth's personal favour, but both father and son were determined he could grasp high office.

By the time Robert was eighteen, Lord Burghley had already arranged that he be made a Member of Parliament. In 1588, the year Kit and Oliver were sent on the mission to Italy and Sir Francis Walsingham was intensifying espionage activity on the Continent, Robert Cecil is recorded as a confidential messenger, paid for 'bringinge lettres in post, for her majestes affaires, from her highnes Commissioners at Ostend'. Young as he was, he had his eye on the ailing Sir Francis's job, and wove himself carefully into the heart of the secret service. The other Robert was much of the same mind, and was also building up a band of informers. He had been introduced to Court by his stepfather the Earl of Leicester, the Queen's old favourite and Lord Burghley's long-time rival, and by 1587 was Master of the Horse and ascending into Her Majesty's very highest favour. When Robert Dudley died the following year, the battle between Ralegh and Essex for the position of 'favourite' led to open conflict and screaming rows with the Queen, and later almost to a duel, which the Privy Council defused to prevent further indignity. As England moved into a new decade Essex's fortunes were on the rise, and still the Queen seemed reluctant to grant Robert Cecil public office. And then in April 1590, corroded by cancer, Sir Francis Walsingham died.

Robert Cecil immediately conducted a clandestine raid on Walsingham's house, filching material from the archives. Some of the secrets he uncovered he did not even tell his father. A subtle battle ensued to control Walsingham's network, with some agents going over to Essex and others remaining with the Cecils, as Lord Burghley officially re-assumed Sir Francis's role as Secretary of State. He had always run agents of his own, and now that Sir Francis was dead, resumed control of a much-expanded secret service, while Robert increased his activities behind the scenes. But all Burghley's powers of persuasion could not move the Queen to accept his son's appointment to the Privy Council. Even when she relented, and knighted Robert, approving his appointment in August the following year, the position of Principal Secretary seemed way beyond his reach. And the Earl of Essex was coming up close behind.

Essex had begged the Queen on his knees (quite literally – on one occasion for a solid two hours) to be sent at the head of an army to France, and for once Lord Burghley seemed in support of a military campaign, no doubt to remove Essex from the political scene. Robert Cecil's appointment to the Privy Council came a week after the earl set sail. When Essex returned in 1592, after a dismal campaign, he turned his attention from soldiering to politics and his efforts against the Cecils became increasingly apparent. He was already getting the upper hand in his power struggle with Sir Walter Ralegh, who had dramatically fallen from grace in 1592 when he secretly married a pregnant Bess Throckmorton, one of Elizabeth's ladies-in-waiting. A year later Essex became a member of the Privy Council.

For Robert Cecil the situation was becoming fraught. Lord Burghley was increasingly incapacitated by illness, and though Cecil was doing much of the work, the Queen gave no sign of appointing him Secretary. As the astute Thomas Wilkes, a clerk of the Privy Council, had put it to Sir Henry Sidney when Cecil joined the Council: 'Sir Robert Cecil, as you may have heard, is sworn to the Council, though not [as] secretary, whose election will be a bar to the choice of any secretary during the life-time of his father.' While Burghley was alive, the position was safe, but as soon as he died it would be open to all comers. As Burghley declined further, desperate measures were called for. Gradually Robert Cecil came up with a scheme so audacious that he dared not tell even his father – a plan that, if it were successful, would not only earn him Burghley's admiration but the full reward of the Queen's gratitude. It was a low and creeping plot, one that extended as far as Prague, and had a stray tendril that was already winding itself around the ankle of the poet Christopher Marloe.

CHAPTER EIGHT

Shakespeare in Love

Though he was hot-tempered, Kit was not a natural killer. He had been deeply disturbed by the slaying of Walter Hoochspier: 'I know, sir, what it is to kill a man,' he wrote, in a speech he added to the second *Tamburlaine*, sounding a note of sympathy for the 'coward' Calyphas. 'It works remorse of conscience in me./I take no pleasure to be murderous,/Nor care for blood when wine will quench my thirst' (2 *Tamburlaine* IV i 27–30). Oliver Laurens records a remorse that was almost excessive, and wrote that Kit was doubly troubled by Walter Hoochspier's name being a near anagram of his own (in these games a W can be inverted to make an M, so we end up with Christophe Marloe). It is around this time that Kit began the obsessive hand-washing that was to last much of his life.

The Kit that returned to London in early 1589 was a thoughtful, less wild, more sober young man than the one that had left. Perhaps sated by the '*perdona-mi's*' of Italy 'who stand so much on the new form', he was no longer of the sort that might lie ten nights awake, carving the fashion of a new doublet. Life had become weightier. But it would be a mistake to hang all this on a single event. The picture now known as the Grafton portrait, painted in Antwerp for his twenty-fourth birthday in February 1588, as a companion to Oliver's portrait, shows a wan young man, already quieter, more pensive than the cocky sneerer of 1585.

The Hog Lane affray – the first that is heard of Kit after his return from Italy – is much used by biographers to paint his character as murderous and violent. Yet this is unfair. His future room-mate, Thomas Kyd, did say that Kit was given to 'rashnes in attempting soden [sudden] pryvie injuries to men', but Kyd had his own reasons for blackening Kit's reputation – and it is the rashness and spontaneity that must be emphasised, the sudden flare of temper rather than the brutish, belligerent or cruel. Other contemporaries refer to Kit as 'deare unto us', 'kynde Kit Marlowe', or 'that pure elemental wit Chr. Marlow'. Kit was not the antagonist in Hog Lane, but (with Walter Hoochspier still on his conscience) he drew back from the fray, urging calm – like Romeo in the fight between Tybalt and Mercutio. When Romeo finally kills Tybalt it is in 'fire-eyed fury' (*Romeo and Juliet* III i 124). He casts off 'respective lenity' and is transported, as Kit was in Padua, beyond his customary gentleness.

Hog Lane had its source among the tall houses of Norton Folgate, ran south of the Curtain theatre, then beyond the last tenement, and out west through grazing land – Mallow Field on the City side, and to the north High Field, or Finsbury Field, where three windmills creaked and turned, and archers filled the air with the twang and whack of target practice. Men also met there to fight duels. It is up this end of Hog Lane, in the early afternoon of the 18th of September, that Kit encountered William Bradley, son of an innkeeper, resident of Gray's Inn Lane, and bearer of a grudge against Kit's close friend Tom Watson. He was a year older than Kit, a known thug and scoundrel, and he owed £14 to John Alleyn, the brother of the actor Edward Alleyn. Alleyn had made to sue Bradley for his money, and Bradley countered by threatening Alleyn's lawyer Hugh Swift with a severe drubbing if he went ahead with the case. Hugh Swift was Tom Watson's brother-in-law, and Tom was swift to intervene on his behalf. Tension between Bradley and his opponents spiked out into hostility, especially after he somewhat disingenuously petitioned the courts to protect him against violence from Alleyn, Swift and Tom Watson.

What occurred in Hog Lane was not a brawl, but a more formal clash, a fight governed by the 'book of arithmetic'. Bradley was waiting for Watson near the duelling-fields of Finsbury when Kit came along, possibly a little earlier than arranged, to try and make peace. But Bradley attacked him, and they were fighting when Tom Watson arrived, drawing his sword to intervene and stop the fight (or at least that's what Watson told the coroner). Bradley, noticing the man he had originally come to meet, shouted: 'Art thou now come? Then I will have a bout with thee' (the coroner's clerk breaks off his Latin and gives this in English). According to the report, 'Morley seip*sum* retraxit & a pugnad*o* desistit', he lowered his point and withdrew. Tom was wounded and driven up against the ditch at the northern edge of the lane, from where he lashed out, plunging his blade below Bradley's right nipple, and killing him on the spot. Kit did not flee, as he had in Padua, but waited with Tom Watson for the arresting officer (one Stephen Wylde, a local tailor) to arrive. Under English law they had acted in self-defence and could expect some leniency.

The two were taken before the Lieutenant of the Tower, who had them marched across the City to Newgate, which had one of the worst reputations of all fourteen London prisons. Their names were inscribed in Newgate's Black Book – Tom Watson entered as 'gentleman', Kit (to his chagrin) as 'yeoman' – then they were manacled and shoved through a hatch into a stinking hold called Limbo, a 'dark Opace wild room' that appeared to be a dungeon but was in reality the space between the top and the bottom of the arch under Newgate. It was lit by a single candle on a large black rock, known as the Black Dog of Newgate, against which a prisoner had once dashed out his brains.

Rats writhed about their ankles, leaping and snatching anything edible from their hands. Starved, diseased fellow inmates pressed in on them from the gloom, piteously pleading for pennies. For, as with all prisons of the time, Newgate was more tolerable if you were rich. Prisoners had to pay for everything: for one of three grades of accommodation, for food, to have manacles removed and doors opened or locked. And they had to pay again and again, not just an official fee, but considerable 'garnish'.

As he was fairly sure he would be there only a short time, and had friends who could pay for him, Kit was soon free of his chains and able to move to the Master's Side (the privileged realm of master felons), rather than the Middle Ward or subterranean Stone Hold, described by the prisoner Luke Hutton, who had arrived in Newgate just a few months before, as 'a foul kennel' where men lay worse than dogs 'on boards as hard as chennell [hard coal]'. For a weekly charge of ten shillings Kit might enjoy a daily repast of:

> Bone of meat with broth
> Bone beef, a piece
> Veal roasted a loin or breast or else one capon
> Bread, as much as [he] will eat
> Small beer and wine claret, a quart

while poorer prisoners cooked for themselves, filling the chambers with fumes and steam, or surviving off beer and bread soaked in broth. Around them there were, in the words of the playwright Thomas Dekker (who also did a stretch), 'jailors hoarsely and harshly bawling for prisoners to their bed, and prisoners reviling and cursing jailers for making such a hellish din . . . some in their chamber singing and dancing, being half drunk; others breaking open doors to get more drink to be whole drunk. Some roaring for tobacco; others raging and bidding hell's plague on all tobacco . . .'.

Kit, who had not even wounded Bradley, was released on recognisance of £40 after just thirteen days. At a trial at the Old Bailey in December, the judges accepted the claim of self-defence. There is no record of any further punishment for Kit, but Tom Watson was sent back to Newgate to await royal pardon, and it was only in February that he was set free. On the bench was Sir Roger Manwood, Kit's scurrilous childhood patron, who no doubt earned himself another line or two of the flattering Latin epitaph Kit would one day compose for him. Sir Roger was related to the Walsinghams by marriage, and was a neighbour to Thomas, who might have also been influential in Kit's favour. Of the two men who had stood surety for Kit for the hefty sum of £40, one, Richard Kitchen, was a gentleman and frequenter of the Mermaid, though the other was a lowly 'horn-breaker', a maker of lantern horns, Humphrey Rowland. Just how he and Kit knew each other becomes clearer on closer examination. Curiously, despite his humble profession, Rowland was considered financially sound enough to stand surety for people on at least two other occasions. What is more, his admission to the freedom of the City and entry into the (entirely inappropriate) Guild of Cutlers was effected by a personal letter from none other than the mighty Lord Burghley, despite protestations by the Lord Mayor that this was against City ordinances, and that cutlery was an 'art he doth not occupie'. Rowland was also rich enough to have a number of servants, including one Andrew Vandepeare and a 'Jn° Cornelis' of Antwerp. The Low Countries, conspicuous wealth, Lord Burghley, and high favour – once again we find elements of the alchemy of espionage in Kit's life. His powerful friends were apparently still at work on his behalf. He needed them.

Following his extended stay in Italy, hasty retreat from Padua, long journey home after shipwreck – and then a spell in jail – Kit had no money in his purse. His first solution to this was to dig out, rework and speedily sell plays he had written before. In this he found a useful assistant in the ever-willing Will Shakespere, who while Kit had been away had made no progress at all in his attempts to relinquish acting and theatrical odd-jobbing for the heady world of writing plays.[*]

Using his old foul papers of *The Tragedy of the Duke of Guise* – a blood-and-bombast piece, written largely from news pamphlets and his recollection of Oliver Laurens's account of the St Bartholomew's Day Massacre, and originally performed on the Continent by Bradstriet's men – Kit hastily reworked the play as *The Massacre at Paris*, giving shades of Machiavellian subtlety to the character of Guise, and closing the action with the death of Henry III (which had occurred while he was in Italy). He was taking a chance that distance, rewriting and a name change would prevent any objection from Bradstriet, and none seems to have been forthcoming, though curiously Henslowe in his diary refers to the play first as 'gvyes' and 'Gwies' before using the title 'masacer'. The play comes down to us in a fragmented and butchered form, but even so, it is clear that it has been quickly cobbled together.

More care appears to have been taken over that other guts-and-gore piece (also originally written for English comedians on the Continent), *Titus Andronicus*. Despite its violence and spectacle it has moments of fine verse, and could very well belong to a later period. We can only surmise that Kit was reworking it along with other early pieces at the beginning of the 1590s. Like most of his plays from this time, its first performance is hard to date – first records of some of the dramas occur up to forty years after we know they must have been performed. It

---

[*] Boyd, *Two's Company* p. 42.

would also appear that he worked again briefly with Tom Nashe on *Dido, Queen of Carthage*, a play they had begun years before while together at Cambridge. The poets embroider their source, Virgil's *Aeneid*, considerably, with moments of love interest and gratuitous violence. Kit's relish for his Paduan Bardasso is evident in the opening lines as Jupiter woos the boy Ganymede with 'Come gentle Ganymede, and play with me,/I love thee well, say Juno what she will', and a Bardasso's acquisitive petulance is discernible in 'I would have a jewel for mine ear,/And a fine brooch to put in my hat,/And then I'll hug with you an hundred times' (*Dido* I i 1–2 and 46–8). The brutality with which the King of Troy's hands are amputated in *Dido* provides a prototype for the even more sensational string of amputations in *Titus*.

A number of new plays appear, too, with a rapidity which indicates the assistance of his *Johannes factotum*. It would also appear that at least some of the scripts belong to the time Kit spent in Italy, and that he had somehow managed to rescue his belongings from Padua. There is *The Two Gentlemen of Verona*, and the *commedia dell'arte*-inspired *The Comedy of Errors*, as well as *The Jew of Malta* and *The Taming of a Shrew* – though none of these can be accurately dated: the first recorded performance of *Two Gentlemen*, for example, is nearly a hundred years later, in 1672. '*A Shrew*' is a possible precursor to the better-known *The Taming of the Shrew*, itself a slipshod piece (at least in the version we have now), which begins with the drunken Sly, of whom we never hear again after Act One Scene I, and where the 'taming' of Kate is subordinate to a limp story of the love of Lucentio and Bianca. The heavy hand of Will Shakespere is certainly evident here. The august critic Sir Arthur Quiller-Couch, who harrumphed that to call *The Taming of the Shrew* a masterpiece was to bend criticism into sycophancy and fawning, has spotted in its elaborate stage directions another hand (he calls it Hand B), that of 'an actor of some kind', who is also to be found at work in *The Comedy of Errors*. Admittedly, it is a matter of speculation as to whether Will Shakespere also had a hand in *The Two Gentlemen of Verona*. The primary source for the story of Julia in the play is Jorge de Montemayor's romance *Diana Enamorada*, which at the time the play was written was available only in the original Spanish and in a French version, neither of which languages Shakespere knew.

Kit was living at a furious pace and increasingly summoning the help of 'Hand B' to ease his workload. It was not just the need to turn plays into money that drove him; he cannily cultivated new friendships and was on a constant look-out for patrons. One such carefully nurtured benefactor was Ferdinando Stanley, Lord Strange, whose company of players performed many of Kit's early tragedies, including *The Jew of Malta* and *Titus Andronicus*, and which, incidentally, boasted in its number the clown Will Kempe, with whom Kit had worked in the Low Countries. Possibly it was Kemp who effected Kit's introduction to Strange's milieu, though it was more likely to have been Tom Nashe, who was intimate enough with the young nobleman to dedicate to him his obscene poem *The Choice of Valentines* (also known as 'Nashe's Dildo'). By 1592 Kit could claim that he was 'very well known to both the Earl of Northumberland and my Lord Strange'.

These two cultured, intelligent Catholic peers shared a number of young poet friends. With 'unmuzzled thoughts', and bristling with dangerous ideas gathered at debates in Padua, Kit was enthusiastically welcomed back into the mystic, intellectual circle of the 'Wizard Earl' Northumberland and Sir Walter Ralegh. At the same time he also sparkled in the set that surrounded Ralegh's glamorous rival, the Earl of Essex – or, more specifically, that of his brilliant and witty sister Penelope Devereux, who, exploiting Elizabethan celebrity culture, used her brother's fame to establish a small court of wanton poets, pleasant wits and musicians around him. It says something for Kit's charm and social dexterity that he flirted successfully with both bitter rivals. This was something that did not go unnoticed by Sir Robert Cecil. Nor did Kit's extravagant tastes and need for money. In the tug between Cecil and Essex to control the spy network after Walsingham's death, Cecil secured Kit as an informer not only in Essex's court, but in the cultured circles of the Catholic Lords Strange and Northumberland, who were both high in the order of succession and (whether or not they welcomed it) were looked to as figureheads by Catholic rebels.

Just how Kit justified this betrayal is hard to know – though perhaps he thought he could get away with supplying what a modern spy would call 'chicken feed', apparently useful but actually harmless information, which would fill his purse without unduly endangering his friends. He may have realised that it was Cecil and not Essex who would eventually triumph – or maybe Sir Robert simply paid more. Whatever Kit's justification for the deception, it is clear from subsequent events that his conscience supplied a threshold to duplicity, beyond which he would not go. And that reluctance was to prove very dangerous.

Of course, not every step Kit took was tainted by treachery. Oliver Laurens's descriptions of visits to Thomas Walsingham at Scadbury, of singing 'melodious madrigals' together, and of Kit's near worship of Tom Watson, tell of a capacity for truer friendship. And Kit was passionately in love. The rumours Will Shakespere heard soon after he arrived in London that 'Marloe had tumbled on the bed of my Lord Hunsdon's mistress', told only part of the tale. Kit had met the love of his life, a feisty woman who could match him in conversation and parry his sharp wit, Emilia Bassano.

The illegitimate daughter of Baptiste Bassano, one of family of Italian musicians who had served at Court since the time of Henry VIII, Emilia was proud to the point of tyranny, exotic, temperamental, musical and extremely clever. She was Bianca, the beautiful Venetian courtesan whose rosary of sucked olive pits Kit still carried, but Bianca with brains. Her eyes and hair were raven black; her dark beauty threw men off balance. In 1587, when she was just seventeen, Lord Hunsdon took her as a mistress, but the old Lord Chamberlain was in his sixties, and nimble Kit Marloe deftly out-manoeuvred the 'crooked-pated old cuckoldy ram' behind his back. But loving Emilia was no simple business: 'Alas that love, so gentle in his view,/Should be so tyrannous and rough in proof!' (*Romeo and Juliet* I i 167–8). Toyed with, spurned and ultimately rejected, Kit wrote some of his finest sonnets to her – poems not intended for publication, but, like his other sonnets, compact verse letters which were read by a few friends and collected and printed only in 1609.

Soon after returning from Italy, he was firing off sonnets in quite another direction. The object of these passionate (and often quite suggestive) missives was the pretty young Earl of Southampton, Henry Wriothesley – known as 'Rose' to those who dared. (Martin Green convincingly argues that the family name was pronounced 'Rose-ly', and points out the use of heraldic roses decorating the Southampton seat, and the allusion in Sonnet 95 to 'thy budding name'.) A locket miniature by Nicholas Hillyard shows the earl, who was just sixteen when Kit met him, as a 'beauteous and lovely youth' (Sonnet 54), more lovely and more temperate than a summer's day, unripe, 'the world's fresh ornament' (Sonnet 1). 'Small show of man was yet upon his chin;/His phoenix-down began but to appear/Like unshorn velvet on that termless skin' (*A Lover's Complaint*). His bouffant hair curls into a long lovelock that drapes down over his left shoulder; his eyebrows, thin and arched, appear delicately plucked; his 'tempting lip' petulantly pursed, his alabaster complexion tinged with the faintest of flushes. The long lovelock was something of a Southampton trademark. We see it again in a later portrait of him as gallant knight, posing with sucked-in cheeks in an 'I'm a teapot' stance, beside an outrageously ornamented suit of armour, complete with burgeoning panache of ostrich plumes. Ambrose Willoughby, an Esquire of the Body, once pulled a large chunk of the lord's locks out during a huffy scuffle that ensued when he interrupted a card game between Wriothesley and Ralegh.

We know now that 'Rose' Wriothesley liked to dress as a woman. A recently identified portrait at Hatchlands Park in Surrey shows him with his familiar long tresses of hair and pouting lower lip, but this time with lipstick, rouge and elaborate, looping double earrings. He is wearing a dress with a very expensive Venetian lace collar (which helps date the portrait to between 1590 and 1593), and his hand is draped camply over his heart. Perhaps the oddest thing about the portrait is that it was painted at all. The earl seems to desire a permanent record of his transgression – rather like Kit, who, while at Cambridge, had had his own portrait painted in clothing that flouted current social rules. Rose's transvestism did not bother Kit, who was, after all, friends with many a boy actor that played women's roles. On the contrary, he appears rather to have liked it:

> A woman's face, with Nature's own hand painted,
> Hast thou, the Master-Mistress of my passion;
> A woman's gentle heart, but not acquainted
> With shifting change, as is false woman's fashion . . .
> (Sonnet 20)

He does go on to acknowledge that Nature 'has pricked thee out for women's pleasure' with a 'thing to my purpose nothing', but this may be read simply as a statement of Kit's sexual preferences – his 'purpose' with this Rose is not 'love's prick', but what he once termed 'the melting buttock'.

Kit's passion for the dainty earl inspired other poems than the sonnets. Three in particular are a public profession of what the sonnets confessed in private. In *Venus and Adonis* (which is dedicated to Southampton) he departs from Ovid in making Adonis almost a child, of 'hairless face'; and in focusing on

Venus's desire for him opens the myth to a strong homoerotic reading. In the far superior *Hero and Leander* the astonishingly beautiful boy Leander fires lust and confusion in gods and men, from a frisky Neptune to a Thracian soldier who simply cannot resist him. Kit describes Leander's 'dangling tresses that were never shorn' and notes 'Some swore he was a maid in man's attire,/For in his looks were all that men desire'. And we again sense Wriothesley's androgynous appeal in *A Lover's Complaint* when we encounter a youth who reigns 'in the general bosom ... Of young, of old, and sexes both enchanted', and in the beauty 'Which steals men's eyes and women's souls amazeth' (Sonnet 20).

It was, we may surmise, love at first sight – instantaneous, without reason:

> The reason no man knows; let it suffice,
> What we behold is censured by our eyes.
> Where both deliberate, the love is slight;
> Who ever loved, that loved not at first sight?
> *(Hero and Leander)*

Kit would repeat that famous last line word for word in *As You Like It* (III v 81). But although the relationship was a lasting one, in which Southampton (albeit indirectly) became patron as well as lover, yet again Kit found he could not command constancy. Southampton was passionately attached to the Earl of Essex, another devotee of same-sex relationships, and both enjoyed the attentions of minions. The soldier William Reynolds writes in a letter to Robert Cecil, during Essex's Irish campaign, how Southampton (who more than once followed Essex abroad) lavished favours on one Piers Edmonds, whom he invited to sleep in his tent and would 'clip [embrace] and hug him in his arms and play wantonly with him'. (We can perhaps compare the affection Southampton lavishes on Piers Edmonds with the king's doting on Piers Gaveston in *Edward II* – 'He claps his cheeks and hangs about his neck,/ Smiles in his face and whispers in his ears' (*Edward II* I ii 51–2). But then Kit was no stranger himself to frolic thoughts and lusty deeds. He may not have been one of those men who loitered too long in Pissing Lane, fumbling furtively with his codpiece – the ones that arrived singly and left in pairs. Nor was he party to the secret, sweaty trysts that took place in walled gardens on the edge of town, though he did perhaps take his pleasure (in John Donne's words) with the 'plump muddy whore, or prostitute boy' in busy taverns near the theatres, where ingles (rent boys) could be seduced with hard coin and trinkets. By the early eighteenth century such taverns had grown into 'molly houses' – public inns or private homes like the famous one run by Margaret Clap, where men could be found 'fiddling and dancing and singing bawdy songs, kissing and using their hands in a very unseemly manner', or going out 'by couples into another room on the same floor to be married, as they call it'. A scandalised observer gives us a glimpse of a party at a molly tavern that (though it took place in a very different cultural milieu) one can imagine appealing to Rose Wriothseley:

> The men [called] one another 'my dear' and [were] hugging, kissing, and tickling each other as if they were a mixture of wanton males and females, and assuming effeminate voices and airs; some telling others that they ought to be whipped for not coming to school more frequently ... Some were completely rigged in gowns, petticoats, headcloths, fine laced shoes, furbelowed scarves, and masks; some had riding hoods; some were dressed like milkmaids, others like shepherdesses ...

There is no direct evidence that such places existed in Kit's London, but Margaret Clap's house did not fall from heaven.

Alan Bray detects a 'line of continuity' between the eighteenth-century molly houses and the male brothel-taverns of Eliza-bethan Southwark, where boy actors and Master-Mistresses, married merchants and Bacchanalian blades, catamites and men like Kit, frolicked with their friends, sported upstairs or toyed in the inglenooks. This was not yet a distinct subculture, but a fellowship of outsiders, a zone for mixed predilections, where nothing was declared, still less admitted, but the world was permitted.

Not Essex, Southampton nor Kit Marloe would have identified themselves as 'homosexual'. That, as Bruce Smith points out, 'is a clinical, scientific coinage of the clinical, scientific nineteenth century'. Nor did 'bugger' or 'sodomite' quite fit the bill. 'Bug-gery' was also used to refer to bestiality, and 'sodomy' included heterosexual acts. The Elizabethans saw both practices not as indicators of exclusive sexual preference, or a lifestyle, but as vices from the darker end of a continuum of debauchery, sins (according to the Puritan writer John Rainolds) to which 'men's natural corruption and viciousness is prone'. As Alan Bray puts it: 'The temptation to debauchery, from which homosexuality was not clearly distinguished, was accepted as part of the com-mon lot, be it never so abhorred.' Buggery and 'sodometrie' formed part of a package of wickednesses, with sorcery, atheism and treason swept up into the bag. Dally with one, and you might find yourself accused of the lot. Excess, promiscuity and rebelliousness were also likely to set Elizabethan tongues tutting with accusations of sodomy, which marked one out as a wanton sinner but did not imply a separate homosexual identity.

Even 'bedfellow' was a common term in an age when beds, at home and in inns, were frequently shared, and does not imply (though nor did it preclude) romping between the sheets. Bray argues that in homes where rooms casually led into each other and masters mingled with their servants, whom one shared one's bed with became a public fact, and a meaningful one, as 'beds are not only places where people sleep: they are also places where people talk. To be someone's "bedfellow" suggested that one had influence and could be the making of a fortune.' He sees Anne Bacon's letter to her son Anthony complaining 'your brother . . . keepeth that bloody Pérez, as I told him then, yea as a coach-companion and bed-companion' in that light, and he views as sexually innocent Archbishop Laud's dream of his patron, the Duke of Buckingham, ascending into his bed 'where he carried himself with much love towards me, after such rest wherein wearied men are wont exceedingly to rejoice; and likewise many seemed to me to enter the chamber who did see this'. But beds are not only places where people sleep and talk, they are, of course, also places where people have sex, and we can safely consider this to be true even of Elizabethan times. To strip 'bedfellow' of any association of rumpus is to deprive it of an important layer of meaning. It would make nonsense, for example, of the accusation later levelled at Kit that he said that 'St John the Evangelist was bedfellow to C[hrist] and leaned alwaies on his bosom, that he used him as the sinners of Sodama.' Suggesting that St John 'had influence' with Christ is no scandal at all.

Likewise, interpreting the Earl of Southampton's wanton playing with Piers Edmonds on the battlefield as merely an expression of the 'daily conventions of friendship', part of a 'placid orderliness' which is 'set a world away from the wild sin of Sodom', runs the risk of being disingenuous. The image of the masculine friend, *sans* overtones of buggery, is indeed a common one in Elizabethan literature, and intense male bonding of course took place without sexual correlates – we have an example of this in the relationship between Kit and Tom Watson, and perhaps even more so in his friendship with Thomas Walsingham. Men did kiss in public and use the word 'love' without sexual import, but the reverse was also true, and we should not allow literary fastidiousness to blind us to the fact.

The law against sodomy, which had been repealed under Mary, was reinstated in Elizabeth's second Parliament (at the instigation of indignant Parliamentarians rather than of the Crown). But, as Bruce Smith points out, the law was seldom put into effect. During the forty-five years of Elizabeth's reign, and the twenty-three of James I's, only six men are recorded as indicted for sodomy in the Home Counties assizes, and only one was convicted. Indictments for bestiality outnumber those for sodomy six to one. Convictions generally involved rape, under-age sex, or were the result of a shady political agenda. 'Unless one were famous and had powerful enemies,' Smith argues, 'one could be indicted for sodomy only by forcing another male (more likely than not a minor) to be the passive partner in anal sex.' In other words, not much different from the situation in many Western countries today. Sexual relations between masters and minions – their pages, 'Ganymedes', 'catamites' or 'ingles' – were openly talked about. Male stews and taverns where ingles plied their trade were rife; and players especially had the reputation of being promiscuous and predatory, seducing stage-struck young men to the ways of Sodom.

But it is a disrespect to the hearts and minds of men to presume that all this stopped at lust, and that desire and love between same-sex couples did not exist, simply because no-one had given it a name. It existed, the world knew it existed, but in a society where marriage was both a business and the grist of social status, it had acquired no label of its own. As Smith puts it: 'The question confronting a young man in [Elizabethan times] was not, am I heterosexual or am I homosexual, but where do my greater loyalties lie, with other men or with women.' The answer for Kit was 'with both'. The torque of turning loyalties impelled his life; the tensions and conflicts this presented played themselves out in his dramas.

Bruce Smith sees Kit's examination of master and minion in *Edward II*, which was written at this time, as showing the beginnings of 'a specifically homosexual subjectivity', and the Sonnets as moving beyond this expression of desire into previously unmapped artistic and emotional territory. This reflects a wider and more far-reaching shift in Kit's dramatic technique and aesthetic perspective. In the words of the biographer Anthony Holden: 'Marlowe [was] breaking free of the plodding, one-dimensional archetypes of the medieval tradition'. For the first time in English theatre, the figures in dramas became more than symbol-laden cut-outs, and can rightly be called 'characters'. As the players' acting style changed from declamation to 'personation', they found the material they were offered to work with more subtle and more realistic. The making of a play was a two-way process. In *Faustus* Kit is at a half-way point – a Good Angel and an Evil Angel are external representations of the Doctor's warring conscience. Flawed though the rest of the *Shrew* is, Kate (at least) shows some sign of internal conflict and resolution. The manipulative streak evident in the character of the Duke of Guise in *The Massacre at Paris* burgeons in *The Jew of Malta* into a full-blown Machiavellian protagonist, the prototype for later villains in Elizabethan and Jacobean drama. Though Kit's astute theatrical instinct drove him to create a stereotypical stage Jew, a deeper dramatic integrity tempered this with real knowledge of Jews from Padua (there were so few Jews in London at the time it is highly unlikely he would have gained his insights there). Though the villain of the piece, the Jew Barabus does to some extent engage our sympathy, as his plight is caused by Christians who are hardly more morally attractive than he is.

Even in the frenzy of writing for quick money, Kit was strengthening the foundations for a whole new superstructure of Elizabethan drama. He was beginning to respond to the advice given him years before by Montaigne in the baths at Plombières, that he should examine the 'movement of the mind' and 'pierce and usurp the senses of other men', so that 'the sacred inspiration that stirs thee as Poet unto a choler, unto griefe, unto fury and beyond thyself, shoulde by thee strike and enter into the Actor and thus the multitude'. In the new amphitheatres in London, where the minds of multitudes could be moved by actors' speeches, Montaigne's words came to life. 'Poets had never before been able to grasp the opportunity of moving the "affections" of three thousand packed and willing hearers at one time,' writes the theatre historian Andrew Gurr. 'Marlowe was the first poet to grasp that chance.' Together with the players with whom he was working, he was looking at character in an entirely new way, one that involved not just morality, but the bumps, ditches and unexpected turns of a personal psychology. His blank verse had already given Elizabethan theatre its rhythm; his new perspective now gave it depth.

Edward II was the first play in which Kit used as a source Raphael Holinshed's *Chronicles*, which included a complete history of England, published in 1577. Thomas Walsingham had given him the rather expensive second edition, which came out a decade later, the year he graduated with his MA. Holinshed was to form the background to a radical new direction for Kit, 'a theatrical feat never previously attempted . . . assigning character and motives, thoughts and feelings to historical figures still fresh in the national mind . . . holding them (rather than divine will) responsible for the consequences of their own actions . . .'. Starting with *Edward II* he embarked on a series of history plays which, though not written in chronological order, covered events in the reigns of Henries IV, V and VI and Richards II and III. (Titles were never Kit's forte. In an age that produced such snappy box-office draws as *Gammer Gurton's Needle* and *The Roaring Girl*, he – to the end of his career – often opted simply to name his play after its leading character.)

After *Edward II* came the *Henry VI* trilogy, in which Kit possibly still collaborated with Tom Nashe. He certainly made use of the services of Will Shakespere to transcribe his foul copy and, given Will's eager persistence, allowed him to pen the more workaday scenes. Norlet Boyd maintains that Shakespere's contribution to the plays was more than as a mere scribe, and that the lad from Stratford brought an earthiness to the shepherds, huntsmen and other more rumbustious country characters that the university-educated, city-loving Marloe disdained.* This does tally with Shakespere's own strutting as a writer around this time. And Kit needed the help as much as ever. Poetry and spying, mistress and inamorato, grubbing for money and glittering in grand households, all combined to make 1591 a very busy year. Yet he could not have foreseen how essential this help was to become as 1591 led in to 1592, which from the outset was for Kit an *annus horribilis.* The year began with his arrest in Flushing.

---

* Boyd, *Two's Company,* p. 45.

CHAPTER NINE

Theatre of Blood

Flushing (or Vlissingen) was a small, overburdened port, controlled by the English, at the mouth of the Schelde river – a 'cautionary town' ceded by the Dutch as security for loans and military support against the Spanish invaders. It was astir with the business of war, infested with profiteers, overrun by soldiers and refugees, and seething with spies. Bright young men marched through on their way to the wars; damaged, rotting, soured ones were spewed back home. Food was scarce and rents were astronomical. Fresh salt breezes from the open seas were soon swallowed up in the sullen stink of an insanitary, overcrowded, angry town. Locals resented the English governor; the English garrison pushed up prices and wreaked havoc in the streets. 'We beginne,' wrote one Englishman, 'to grow as hatefull to the people as the Spaniard himself who governeth his townes of conquest with a milder hand than we doe our frends and allyes.' Treachery mushroomed in this dung of discontent. Strangers spoke secretly in the darker recesses of St Jacob's Church; men left small packages with Elisabeth Brandt, who ran a letter-drop at the sign of De Gheit [the Goat]; seditious books found their way past the 'watchers' and into ship's holds; traitors slipped off to join renegade armies inland.

Kit was swimming deep in all this by Christmas of 1591. Sir

Robert Cecil, who already had him marked as an informer in the retinue of Lord Strange, had sent him as a 'projector' to sniff out conspiracy around Strange's cousin Sir William Stanley, who was camped with his rebel force near Nijmegen. Stanley, who had originally fought under Leicester but then gone over to the Spanish, was at the heart of Catholic intrigues to persuade Strange to exercise his claim to the throne. Strange himself may very well have been innocent of subversion, but Lord Burghley was aware of pro-Strange plotting as early as the summer of 1591, and Sir Robert was set on infiltrating and sabotaging the intrigue. Exploding a Catholic conspiracy would stand him in good stead in his ambitions to be Secretary of State.

Kit materialises in Flushing when he is arrested for 'coining' (counterfeiting) in January 1592. For centuries nothing was known of this incident, until in 1976 Professor Robert B. Wernham extracted a single letter from deep within the maw of the Public Record Office at Kew. It was to Lord Burghley from the Governor of Flushing, Sir Robert Sidney (a younger brother of the soldier-poet Sir Philip, recently killed in fighting in the Low Countries), and was written to explain the dispatch back to England of two prisoners, 'Christofer Marly, by his profession a scholar' and Gilbert Gifford, a goldsmith. Sir Robert also sent their erstwhile 'chamber-fellow', who had reported them for coining. His name was Richard Baines.

The antagonism between Kit and the wheezing, sybaritic Baines, in the cramped room they shared with Gilbert, crackled beneath a fragile shell of civility. Baines had loathed Kit for more than a decade, but had no proof of his suspicion that it was Kit who had betrayed him at Rheims. Kit knew it was Baines who had tried to scupper his Cambridge career, but to give voice to this would bring Rheims to the fore and imply his guilt. Besides, he had just lampooned Baines's attempt to do away with the seminarists by poisoning their well water, in a parallel incident in *The Jew of Malta*. Baines had seen this, and it rekindled his fury for revenge. Claiming Sir Robert Cecil's authority, the former Walsingham spy had wheedled his way into sharing the chamber with Gilbert and Kit, and at this distance from England Kit could not counter him. But both could smile and smile and yet play the villain. We can be sure that Kit had some revenge in mind, but it was Baines who pounced first.

He waited until the counterfeiters' first coin was 'uttered' – issued in public – then calmly walked down to the governor's residence beside the inner haven and accused Kit not only of 'inducing' the goldsmith to forgery, but of being an avid student of the craft, and also intending 'to go to the enemy, or to Rome'. Bundled off to the governor for questioning, Kit admitted the crime, protesting that it was done 'only to see the goldsmith's cunning'. Kit's panic and venom is evident in Sir Robert's letter to Lord Burghley, as a spat develops with Baines, and 'they do one accuse another to have been the inducers' of the hapless goldsmith, and 'do also accuse one another of intent to go to the enemy, or to Rome, both as they say of malice to one another'. Sir Robert appears to wish to distance himself from the whole difficult affair. He seems to believe the goldsmith, but remains sceptical about Kit and his accuser. Wisely, he decided not to 'deliver them into the town's hands' as in that rather hostile environment 'I know not how it would have been liked', but instead sends all three (with Kit and Gilbert under guard) to the higher authority of Burghley. He does wryly remark that their efforts were somewhat inept, that the Dutch shilling they uttered would not convince many 'for the metal is plain pewter and with half an eye to be discovered'.

What Kit was up to (no doubt with Baines at first playing along) was preparing his access to Sir William Stanley. As Charles Nicholl points out, the one thing that the Catholic exiles lacked – conspirators and soldiers alike – was money. A chest of assorted coins was the perfect passport to Sir William's inner circle. And if beneath the glittering gold and silver at the top of the chest, things were bulked up a little with pewter, so much the better for Kit – especially if Sir Robert Cecil had provided him with a full coffer.

On the surface, everything Baines said to the governor was true. Kit chose to risk the consequences of arrest rather than reveal his status as an agent, mainly because that would have blown his cover back home with Lord Strange (who was, after all, the patron of the company that at the time was performing his plays). On the contrary, arrest as a Catholic coiner would reinforce his position in Strange's household. It is significant that in his statement to Sir Robert Sidney he 'says himself to be very well known both to the Earl of Northumberland and my Lord Strange' – Catholic nobles both – rather than claiming the protection of Lord Burghley, who had come to his aid before, and would have been a less risky option in the situation Kit found himself in. It is also curious that Kit gave himself over as a 'scholar', rather than a playwright, but that might have been further to obscure his tracks. Intriguingly, Robert Browne and John Bradstriet, with whose company of players he had travelled before while on missions on the Continent, were granted a passport to travel to the Low Countries that February. It is highly possible that Kit was planning to join them. They journeyed through the war zone to Arnhem (just a few miles from Sir William Stanley's camp at Nijmegen) with a licence granted by the Dutch commander Prince Maurice of Orange, and were later at the book fair in Frankfurt, where they gave *Gammer Gurton's Needle*, and plays by the 'celebrated Herr Christopher Marlowe'.

Besides, the surfeit of spies was giving the Flushing authorities dangerous indigestion – later in 1592 a Burghley informer, Ralph Birkenshaw, was denounced as a double agent, held close prisoner and later taken 'fast bound like a thief' to the marketplace, where his ears were nailed to a gibbet, and then sliced off. Far rather that Kit take his chances and hope for deportation, so that Cecil and Burghley could quietly intervene. His bluff paid off. Although coining was a capital offence – it was classed as petty treason – once back in England, Kit was discreetly released. Apart from an entry in Chamber accounts of payment to Sir Robert Sidney's ensign for delivering the coiners to Burghley's charge, there is no record anywhere of Kit's punishment or imprisonment, and by May 1592 he is on the streets of London once more. Yet again Richard Baines had to fume and bide his time.

In May 1592, two Shoreditch constables, Allen Nicholas and his ageing sidekick Nicholas Helliott, appealed to Sir Owen Hopton at the Middlesex sessions that 'Christopherus Marle' of London, 'gener*osus*' (gentleman) be bound over to keep the peace towards the Queen's subjects in general, and themselves in particular (Kit must have been pleased by the 'gentleman', having had to suffer the 'yeoman' label in Newgate). As with the Hog Lane affray, biographers have been quick to point to this as proof of Kit's violent nature. But such an injunction was nothing out of the ordinary in the lively quarter of Shoreditch, where the tearaway antics of actors and poets often riled stodgy official-dom. Being jailed for debt, for 'rude brawling', or for other minor misdemeanours was so common that far from having any social stigma attached, it seemed a positive recommendation for a poet. Tom Nashe opined that there was no place on earth like jail to make a man wise, and that 'a gentleman is never thoroughly entered into credit till he hath been there; that poet or novice, be he what he will, ought to suspect his wit, and remain half in doubt that it is not authentical, till it hath been seen and allowed in [jail]'. Nearly every popular playwright of the time – including Thomas Dekker, Philip Massinger and Ben Jonson did a stretch inside. Complaints like that made by con-

stables Nichols and Helliot were commonplace – Kit's neighbours were bound over a few months later – and this one points
to no more than Kit's boisterousness and untamed temper. His
own Quip Modest (or perhaps Reply Churlish) to the affair was
to lampoon the blusteringly inefficient Nicholas and his inept
assistant in the characters of Dogberry and Verges in *Much Ado
About Nothing.*

But the Dogberries of Shoreditch were the least of Kit's
worries in 1592. Despite his careful machinations in Flushing
to disguise his role as an informer, he found when he returned
to London that he was slipping from Lord Strange's favour.
The dramatist Thomas Kyd (who was by now 'wrytinge in one
chamber' with Kit in Shoreditch) puts this down to Kit's 'repro-
bate' ideas. In a letter to Lord Strange he hastens to acknowledge
that 'never could my Lord endure [Kit's] name or sight when
he had heard of his conditions' and assures the noblemen that,
as for himself, he 'left & did refrain' from Kit's company, not
only out of aversion to Kit's life and thought, but 'as well by
my Lord's commandment'. But Kyd wrote this the following
year, when he was trying cravenly to distance himself from Kit
and ingratiate himself with Strange. Lord Strange would have
known of Kit's views and behaviour. The reason for his cooling
towards him was that he began to suspect he had a spy in his
midst.*

Warily, Kit began to draw back a little. He did not want to
endanger a good source of income – Lord Strange's Men were
by far the leading theatre company of the day. Doubly cautious
of the effect his tainted name might have, he stepped behind
Will Shakespere, whom we may remember was working with
him on the simpler scenes of the *Henry VI* plays, allowing him
momentarily to move forward in the players' (and patron's) eyes
as the chief author. This was easily done in the collaborative

---

* Zelle, *Bare Truth*, p. 119.

blur that characterised the way theatre was made. Indeed, in *Pierce Penilesse* Tom Nashe appears not to know who the dominant dramatist behind *Henry VI* is, even though he may well have had a hand in it himself.

Will grabbed the opportunity. This was the moment he had been working and waiting for, and he made great show of his 'arrival' as a poet. His strutting did not go unnoticed. Within months, the sarcastic pamphlet *Groats-worth of Witte, bought with a million of Repentance* was in the stationers' stalls in St Paul's Churchyard, bearing the now famous passage:

> ... there is an upstart Crow, beautified with our feathers, that with his *Tyger's hart wrapt in a Player's hide* supposes he is well able to bombast out a blanke verse as the best of you: and beeing an absolute *Iohannes fac totum*, is in his owne conceit the onely Shake-scene in the countrey.

The 'Tyger's hart wrapt in a Player's hide' is a direct echo of a line from the most recent work in which this 'upstart Crow' of a do-it-all actor was posturing in the brighter plumage of a poet, the play now known as *3 Henry VI*. After the Battle of Wakefield, as Queen Margaret taunts the Duke of York with a handkerchief dripping with his dead son's blood, he berates her with; 'O tiger's heart wrapp'd in a woman's hide!' (*3 Henry VI* I iv 137). The player-tiger showed its claws. Puffed by his own conceit, Will Shakespere complained to the printer of the pamphlet, Henry Chettle, and seems, rather unpleasantly, to have found a powerful friend to twist the thumbscrews. Under pressure from 'divers of worship' (we do not know whom) Chettle, in an exaggerated apology, praises Shakespere's *acting* skills, and though he admits no first-hand experience, says he has been told of the man's honesty and his 'facetious grace in writing'. The *Oxford English Dictionary* cites the Chettle phrase to illustrate the meaning of 'facetious' as 'polished and agreeable, urbane' in style. Norlet Boyd argues that Chettle is not referring to Shakespere's work as a dramatist (which in *Henry VI* can hardly be termed 'agreeable' or 'urbane'), but is side-stepping cleverly into ambiguity as the 'writing' he praises is instead Shakespere's polished, graceful Secretary Hand.* But this is purely conjecture, since the only certain examples of Will's handwriting to have survived are a few shaky signatures.

Kit had deeper concerns in the summer of 1592 than Will Shakespere's bumptiousness and Lord Strange's suspicion. While he was in Flushing, something had happened that put him 'past cure ... past care,/And frantic-mad with evermore unrest' (Sonnet 147). His 'fairest and most precious jewel', the ravenous, raven-haired Emilia Bassano (who apparently had a taste for older men) had secretly seduced Tom Watson, his closest friend and poetic mentor, his 'next self'. The betrayal that bored through so much else of Kit's life had infected the friendship he held most dear. A pang of despair pierces the Sonnets, as he addresses the rival poet ('by spirits taught to write'), who outdoes him in artistry and now in love. He changes the story of de Montemayor's *Diana Enamorada,* the romance that is the primary source of *The Two Gentlemen of Verona,* to introduce the hero's most intimate friend as his rival in love. We can still hear blank resignation years later in:

> Friendship is constant in all other things
> Save in the office and affairs of love;
> Therefore all hearts in love use their own tongues.
> Let every eye negotiate for itself,
> And trust no agent; for beauty is a witch
> Against whose charms faith melteth into blood.
> (*Much Ado About Nothing* II i 154–9)

---

* Boyd, *Two's Company,* p. 53.

Loath to admit disloyalty on Tom Watson's part, Kit quite squarely blames Emilia for the affair:

> Two loves I have of comfort and despair,
> Which like two spirits do suggest me still:
> The better angel is a man right fair,
> The worser spirit a woman coloured ill . . .
> [who] would corrupt my saint to be a devil,
> Wooing his purity with her foul pride.
> (Sonnet 144)

Tom Watson is exonerated, he is the 'gentle thief' whose robbery can be forgiven; what agonises Kit is the strain it puts on their friendship, and for that Emilia is the culprit:

> Beshrew that heart that makes my heart to groan
> For that deep wound it gives my friend and me!
> Is't not enough to torture me alone
> But slave to slavery my sweet'st friend must be?
> Me from myself thy cruel eye hath taken,
> And my next self thou harder hast engrossed:
> Of him, myself, and thee I am forsaken,
> A torment thrice threefold thus to be crossed.
> (Sonnet 133)

To some extent Kit could console himself with his 'fragrant Rose', the clever, coquettish Lord Southampton, whose burst of petulance at Kit's long absence in Flushing and his devotion to Emilia Kit had allayed with a sonnet: 'O, never say that I was false of heart,/Though absence seem'd my flame to qualify!', assuring the beauteous and lovely youth that 'If I have rang'd [been unfaithful],/Like him that travels, I return again . . . For nothing this wide universe I call/Save thou my [R]ose; in it thou art my all' (Sonnet 109). But Wriothesley was not only 'fair

friend', he was also rich patron, and he liked to pull rank –
something that irked and humiliated Kit, who knew that 'Being
your vassal [I am] bound to stay your leisure.' He had to accept
the complicated position, within a rigid Elizabethan class system,
of being a lover who was also a suppliant, an older man in the
role of an ingle – for in harsh social terms, he was barely a step
up from one of the young nobleman's many minions and had
to endure Wriothesley's dalliances without complaint:

> Being your slave, what should I do but tend
> Upon the hours and times of your desire?
> I have no precious time at all to spend,
> Nor services to do, till you require . . .
> Nor dare I question with my jealous thought
> Where you may be, or your affairs suppose,
> But like a sad slave stay and think of naught
> Save, where you are, how happy you make those.
> (Sonnet 57)

As for Emilia Bassano, she was still (in as far as such things
are ever official) the mistress of Lord Hunsdon. Within a few
months it was discovered she was pregnant by the ancient peer,
and she was married off for good form to Alphonso Lanier, a
member of another family of court musicians. She continued
an energetic and interesting love life (her conquests included
the astrologer and physician Simon Forman), and later underwent a religious conversion, which inspired her to pen a long
though not unpraiseworthy poem, *Salve Deus Rex Judaeorum*. To
Kit she remained an ideal, albeit a tarnished one, and continued
to colour his sonnets, and to emerge in his plays. But she was
lost to him.

Worse was to come. By the autumn, Tom Watson was dead.
'Witty Tom Watson', dramatist, philosopher, scholar of science,
'dearly loved and honoured' by the literary set and one of the

most admired poets of his time, had never really recovered from his spell in Newgate. Though just seven or eight years older than Kit, he had played a fatherly role to the young poet, nurturing Kit's art and introducing him to the London literary world. Even Emilia Bassano had not wrenched this bond apart; but 'Death's ebon dart' had done what Cupid's arrow could not.

Kit did not write an elegy for his 'gentle thief'. Instead, he wrote a dedication to the Countess of Pembroke for Watson's posthumously published *Amintæ Gaudia*, acknowledging the poet as his 'dying father' and speaking of the 'breathings of lofty rage' of his own rude pen. Interestingly, he also implies that the countess (who was the cultured and generous sister of Sir Philip Sidney) had become his patron, referring to himself as 'thine adoptive son'. Perhaps he was seeking alternatives to income from Lord Strange's troupe. The countess certainly seems to have had a word with her husband. In the winter of that year, the short-lived 'Earl of Pembroke's Men' (of whom nothing is heard before the early 1590s) performed not only *Edward II*, but also *Titus Andronicus, The Taming of the Shrew* and two parts of *Henry VI* – though it is not certain that Kit would have derived any financial benefit from this. Money was still a problem. In June plague had broken out – one of the worst ever to hit London, causing 15,000 deaths in the city that year alone. Those who could afford it, or who had the right connections, left for the safety of the countryside. Apart from two short winter seasons, the theatres were closed for a ruining twenty-month stretch. Theatre companies dispersed, some breaking into smaller groups to tour the provinces (the Earl of Pembroke's Men appear to have gone bankrupt).

Kit was becoming increasingly reliant on support from Southampton, and, bereft of a theatre, seems to have devoted his time to writing longer poems, two of which would later be dedicated to the earl. Fleeing the perils of pestilence in Shoreditch, he spent considerable periods in Kent – at Scadbury, the family home of Thomas Walsingham. They had long been friends, and before he retreated to the life of a gentleman at Scadbury, Walsingham had been Kit's superior at the London spy head-quarters at the house in Seething Lane. But Kit's presence at Scadbury also owed something to the late Tom Watson. Like Kit, Tom had been a part-time spy, reporting to his friend the younger Walsingham at Seething Lane. It was he who wrote Sir Francis Walsingham's elegy. His knowledge of the dangers of this secret life, as well as remorse over the affair with Emilia, led him before he died to enjoin Thomas to safeguard Kit. It was a request he repeated to his brother-in-law – a man who was rapidly rising in the secret service – 'Sweet Robyn' Poley.*

Robert Poley lived near Kit in Shoreditch. His Catholic cover had been blown during the Babington affair, but he had moved from being a spy into a supervisory role, reporting directly to the Cecils. He had taken over some of Thomas Walsingham's agents and was now running a network in the Low Countries. He had been in charge of Kit's activities in Flushing, and in September 1592 he can be found together with Kit in Canterbury.

It is known for certain Kit was in Canterbury in 1592 because he was involved in a scuffle with the tailor William Corkine, a fellow former cathedral choirboy. On 10 September Corkine had launched an assault on Kit and 'did there and then beat, wound and maltreat' him, inflicting other atrocities [*enormia*]. Yet again, biographers cite this incident as proof of Kit's violent nature. But when Kit takes his revenge five days later, though armed with staff and dagger, he does not injure Corkine in any way, merely causes him to 'suffer loss and incur damages' amounting to £5. Walter Hoochspier is still on his mind. Prob-ably – like the skilled duellist Tybalt, who was the 'very butcher of a silk button' (*Romeo and Juliet* II iv 23), or like Cutpurse who

---

* Gertrud Zelle, *Bare Truth*, p. 140.

snips the gold buttons from Mugeroun's cloak in *The Massacre at Paris* – Kit effected nothing more than sartorial outrage, as a cheeky symbolic revenge on the bullying tailor. There followed a flurry of suing and counter-suing, but in the end the case was dropped by mutual consent. And far from thoughts of violence or malice, Kit even persuaded the town serjeant to press the bud of a late-summer rose between the leaves of the appeal book where the case is recorded, perhaps as a symbol of reconciliation. It can still be seen in the library of Canterbury Cathedral.

It is all too easy to cast Kit in the role of perpetual rebel and malcontent. The young man who had made a tumultuous transition from Puritanism to Catholicism, whose aspiring mind 'climbing after knowledge infinite' had then toyed with atheism and danced with the strangest ideas of science, who cut a fashionable dash and mixed with the most glittering of friends, who tore through Italy and revelled in Shoreditch, was nearly thirty. By Elizabethan standards that was a time for the follies of youth to fall into sharper focus, under the more penetrating beam of contemplative late adulthood. He had killed a man, and it produced remorse of conscience in him. The minor deceptions that Sir Francis Walsingham had amply rewarded in the 1580s had grown by degree into more serious betrayals, each somehow easing the duplicity of the next. And the agony of the affair between Emilia and Tom Watson had given him a keener view on loyalty. An unease creeps into his dealings with Sir Robert Cecil. It would lead to a crisis of conscience. We can hear an echo of this in a speech he wrote not long afterwards:

> What do I fear? Myself? There's none else by,
> Richard loves Richard; that is, I am I.
> Is there a murderer here? No – yes, I am.
> Then fly. What, from myself? Great reason why –
> Lest I revenge. What, myself upon myself?
> O, no! Alas, I rather hate myself

For hateful deeds committed by myself!
I am a villain: yet I lie, I am not.
Fool, of thyself speak well. Fool, do not flatter.
My conscience hath a thousand several tongues,
And every tongue brings in a several tale,
And every tale condemns me for a villain.
(*Richard III* V iii 182–95)

Like the stage characters to which he was giving an unprecedented inner life, Kit was wakening to new self-awareness. He uses the word 'myself' more frequently in this play than in any other. (For those who like to count these things, the word occurs eighteen times in *Richard III*, seventeen in the almost contemporaneous *The Jew of Malta*, and eight times in *The Two Gentlemen of Verona*, which he wrote during the affair between Tom Watson and Emilia. Subsequently he used the word just twice in *Much Ado About Nothing*, then once each in only three other plays.) The sneer that threatens in the Cambridge portrait slides from his face. The sardonic distance he once kept from the figures that peopled his plays is replaced by a penetrating psychology, as he grows up and questions his own integrity. Worse was to happen to trouble his conscience.

Kit's visits home were rare. There is only one other record of a return to Canterbury – in November 1585, while still a student at Cambridge, he was in town for a fortnight, and one Sunday morning 'plainely and distinckly' read the will of his father's neighbour, Widow Katherine Benchkin of Stour Street. Perhaps, though, there is more subtle evidence of another visit, in that it was a taste of his sister Anne, 'a scowlde' and 'comon swearer', who was known 'for a malicious contencious uncharitable person, seeking the unjust vexacion of her neighbours' that inspired his depiction of Kate in *The Taming of the Shrew*.

But Kit was not in Canterbury in September 1592 to visit his family. Not only was Robert Poley in town, so was Paul Ive, the young engineer and spy whose military know-how had helped with technical details for the second *Tamburlaine*. And Oliver Laurens – shipwreck survivor, former stationer's apprentice and budding spy – was there too. After making his way back to England with Kit, he had resumed his old position at the stationer's in St Paul's Churchyard but, using the name William Hall, began increasingly to work as a secret courier. The first glimpse of him in this role is in June 1592, when 'Will Hall' is paid a handsome £10 for services to the Archbishop of Canterbury's pursuivant Anthony Munday. A former boy actor and also once a stationer's apprentice, Munday was a writer and a spy, and had been an *agent provocateur* at the English College in Rome before turning his attention to anti-Anglican Puritans. At the time he was operating against the clandestine authors of the extreme-Puritan 'Martin Marprelate' tracts. He later wrote plays for the Admiral's Men. Once Oliver's credentials had been established, missions to the Low Countries and Denmark, and more importantly to Prague for the Cecils, followed.

The very presence of these men in the same place at the same time is enough to raise an eyebrow. Canterbury was a convenient contact point for agents crossing the Channel to liaise on their way to or from elsewhere in the country. This little group gives a glimpse of the tangled interconnections of an Elizabethan spy network. Paul Ive, who was working on the Canterbury canal, ran a letter-drop. Robert Poley had just been in the Low Countries and was on his way to Scotland. He had been north of the border four times in the previous year, and had carried letters there as early as 1586, when he was recommended as a man who 'knoweth the best ways to pass into Scotland'. Catholic lords in Scotland played a major role in Sir William Stanley's deliberations to place his cousin Ferdinando Stanley, Lord Strange, on the throne, which brings Kit (one of Lord Strange's protégés) into the picture, and also one Matthew Roydon. A fellow poet and spy, Roydon, too, was in Lord Strange's circle, a friend of Kit's ('such as he conversed withal'), and had known Tom Watson (he wrote a poem in praise of Watson's sonnets). Like Poley, Roydon had dealings in Scotland – and not only because of the Stanley connection. Elizabeth had still not named a successor, and political tension over the question was agonising. She was already sixty, and there was every probability she would soon die. Sir Robert Cecil was particularly interested in having a peephole on the Scottish court, where James VI was a legitimate heir, especially as Cecil's rival Essex favoured the Scottish king and relations between the two were warming daily.

Kit's missions to Scotland possibly went as far back as his last long absence from Cambridge in 1586, and went on through the 1590s, probably as a double agent in Cecil's employ. Karl Elze points to the similarity between the incantation of the First Witch: 'But in a sieve I'll thither sail/ And, like a rat without a tail,/ I'll do, I'll do, and I'll do.' (*Macbeth* I iii 8–10) and the witches who bore witness against one Dr Fian in Edinburgh in 1591, who said among other things 'that they all went to sea, each one in a riddle or sieve'. Thomas Kyd, in his toadying letter to Lord Strange the following year, accused Kit of persuading 'men of quality to go unto the K of Scots, whither I hear Roydon is gone'.

In addition to missions in Scotland, the Cecils employed Roydon to carry letters to Prague, a task also assigned to Oliver Laurens, alias William Hall. The recipient of many of these missives was the alchemist Edward Kelley, former assistant to the great Dr Dee – which takes us directly back to the intrigues surrounding Ferdinando Stanley. Kelley was at the heart of a Prague group of English Catholics that included one Richard Hesketh, who was very soon to be associated with a plot to place Stanley on the throne. This plot is as tangled and perplexing an affair as only Elizabethan politicking can create. At its heart, albeit unwittingly, was Ferdinando Stanley, also known as Lord Strange, eventually to become the 5th Earl of Derby. Its chief dupe was Hesketh, not to be confused with Hickman, a peripheral protagonist. Edward Kelley played a part also, Cecil pulled the strings, and Lord Strange's father, the fourth Earl of Derby, never quite made it out of the wings. (Appendix IV lays out the relationship between the main players.)

This criss-crossing complexity was a legacy of Sir Francis Walsingham's checks and counter-checks, his spies who spied on spies, confidants who kept secrets from each other, bit players who knew only their roles and never comprehended the whole drama. In the clandestine world, information was power. It was the agent's currency, secrets were his armoury. But stolen knowledge, or knowledge mishandled, was perilous – and conscience, far from making cowards of us all, can sometimes incite recklessness. From his privileged position linking the realms of spies, players and aristocrats, Kit caught a glimpse of three separate currents of a winding intrigue set in motion by Sir Robert Cecil. He had tumbled to something that would put him in mortal danger.

CHAPTER TEN

The Mousetrap

Sir Robert Cecil was becoming desperate. In 1593, the climb to the secretaryship was still looking slippery. His bitter rival, the Earl of Essex, was now also a member of the Privy Council, and Sir Walter Ralegh, who might have put a check on Essex's rise as the Queen's favourite, had dramatically fallen from grace. Lord Burghley was old and ill, and so 'decayed in strength' that he at times could not write and was too weak to go to court. If he died before Sir Robert gained power, the battle would be half lost. If the Queen died without either appointing him Secretary or naming her successor, the path upwards would become even more perilous. Cecil needed to overcome her reservations, while at the same time keeping a hook on the belt of every possible contender for the succession. Considerable prowess would be needed, but this was, as Bacon had noted, the 'excellent wherryman, who, you know, looketh toward the bridge when he pulleth toward Westminster'.

If Cecil could prove his worth by uncovering a pretender to the throne, or an intrigue to kill the Queen, his way up would be assured. When he raided the Walsingham archives after Sir Francis's death, he had uncovered the structures of scheming behind the Babington plot. Could he similarly create a conspiracy to suit his purposes? It would have to be firmly based in fact, thoroughly feasible, with elements of undeniable evidence, but with an artificial twist in the tail to serve his ends.* Catholic conspirators were the obvious vehicles for such a scheme, and they had a ready-made, if reluctant, figurehead. Cecil decided to frame Ferdinando Stanley, Lord Strange. Such a plan had the added value of giving him a grip on the Stanleys, who were legitimate heirs to the throne. Just how he could effect this plan is suggested in an often overlooked series of articles by Christopher Devlin, in the Jesuit journal *The Month*. Lord Strange, Devlin argues, was a difficult customer, 'very aloof, very cautious, not giving anything away':

> Supposing you had a mind like Cecil's, confronted with a man like Ferdinando, what would you do to bring him to heel? You cannot sift him openly, for – out of loyalty or malice – he may expose you. Yet sift him you must. Your only chance is to approach him by indirections and anonymously, in a way that can never be proved against you, and to get a hold over him by something very like blackmail.

Cecil needed someone to do his dirty work. His calculating gaze fell on Richard Hesketh in Prague. Hesketh's landlord there gives us a picture of him as 'a stout man, fifty years of age, clothed in yellow fustian with lace after the English manner'. He is 'yellow-haired', jovial and, it would seem, good-naturedly gullible, a canary-coloured satellite orbiting the alchemist Edward Kelley, one-time assistant to Dr Dee. (He is, though, no Osric or Malvolio. Yellow was a widely worn colour at the time, and lace here means braid – as in shoe lace – which was used as a trimming.) Hesketh's original contact with Kelley would have been through Dee. In 1581, when Hesketh was Agent (a half-diplomatic, half-commercial post) at Antwerp, Dee men-

---

* For Cecil's motives see Troy Blonde's *Scheming Cecil.*

tions him in his diary as 'my friend Richard Hesketh', commending him for his 'diligence in my affairs'.

Hesketh was possibly in Cecil's sights as early as August 1592, when Dee – who until then had appeared no great favourite of Lord Burghley – was suddenly sent a haunch of venison as a gift, and asked two nights in a row to dine with the aged Lord Treasurer, only to find himself badgered by Sir Robert over the buttered crawfish (simmered with white wine, mace, nutmeg and a little lemon peel, then tossed with butter – a Cecil favourite) about exiles in Bohemia. But Cecil is more likely to have heard the sort of information he was looking for direct from Edward Kelley.

Kelley, Cecil had discovered after his raid on the late Sir Francis Walsingham's archive, was a useful source of intelligence on the court at Prague. He was, according to an English visitor to Bohemia, 'fat and merry', with a limp, and long hair grown to cover the fact that his ears had been cropped as punishment for coining. Soon after arriving in Bohemia, Kelley achieved independent renown as a transmuter of metals – the appearance of gold in his crucible spread his fame throughout Europe. Stories were soon rife of the transmutation of coins, flagons and even a bedpan to gold (an example of the latter was reputedly presented to Elizabeth). There were rumours of a magic powder, one ounce of which would yield 272,330 ounces of gold. Kelley soon acquired a castle, two houses in Prague and country estates. Emperor Rudolph made him a baron of Bohemia, and Lord Burghley wrote regularly, begging him to return home 'to honour Her Majesty . . . with the fruits of such great knowledge as God hath given him' or at least to slip enough gold-making powder 'in some secret box' and send it to the Queen to help her 'defer her charges for this summer for her navy'. But Kelley would not budge, nor, of course, could the charlatan co-operate. He was enjoying himself and, as Devlin puts it, had no ears left to tingle. His celebrity grew. Devotees of Dr Dee deserted master for disciple, and in 1589 it was Dee who came limping home.

In the same year, Richard Hesketh was involved in a fracas in his native Lancashire which ended in the death of a local landowner. He fled before being arrested, and joined Edward Kelley in Prague – along with a rush of other English gold-diggers who hoped to profit from Kelley's magical powers, and certainly benefited from the glow of his international celebrity. But in 1591 Kelley fell foul of the Emperor Rudolph, and (even as Matthew Roydon was bringing him another letter from Lord Burghley) was thrown into jail. Deprived of his patron, Hesketh turned to the protection of an English Jesuit, Father Thomas Stephenson, and began to long for Lancashire and his com-forting wife in Over Darwen.

Cecil, who was in secret correspondence with Kelley even while he was in jail, had found his man. Hesketh was, Devlin suggests, a carefully chosen dupe: 'A guilty man on other grounds he was simple and ignorant of political tensions in England, but he had connections both with occult circles in Prague and with Catholic exiles' – and, apart from his wife, no-one in England gave a straw about him. Cecil communicated that Hesketh should be allowed home to Lancashire, and pro-vided with a passport that made clear he was freed from any charge of murder. Such pardons were not given *gratis* – though payment may be made unwittingly. Hesketh would be obliged to show this passport to the Lord Lieutenant of Lancashire, who was none other than the Earl of Derby, Lord Strange's father. On the way a letter would be planted on him which implicated Strange in a plan to depose the Queen. Addressed to Derby, the letter would purport to come from Prague, but would be drawn up by one Bartholomew Hickman (another fraud, and Dee's current skryer). It would be couched as a cryptic astrologi-cal prediction of the old order being eclipsed by the new – of the rise of the House of Stanley over the House of Tudor, of 'the bond cracked betwixt son and father'. Cecil's idea was that the old earl, who was an upright but timid man, would, as Devlin has it, be thrown 'into a mixture of the terrible plights of Gloucester in *King Lear,* I.ii, and York in *Richard the Second,* V.iii. He would be led to suspect his son, perhaps of designs against himself, certainly of designs against the throne.' Cautious and law-abiding he would then most likely consult the wise old counsellor Lord Burghley, and play into Sir Robert Cecil's hands; or he would trust his son, destroy the letter and say nothing. In either event, Cecil had fresh evidence carefully tucked away to produce at the opportune moment. In 1591 two renegade priests had revealed to him that they had been sent to England by the Jesuit Robert Parsons to 'seek entrance with my Lord Strange and cause Catholics to cast their eyes upon him'. They handed over a letter from Parsons, couched in the oblique terms of conspiracy, instructing them to reply to him thus:

> Your cousin the baker is well inclined and glad to hear of you, and meaneth not to give over his pretence to the old bakehouse you know of, but rather to put the same in suit when his ability shall serve.

The informer-priests glossed this as: 'by baker and bakehouse is understood my Lord Strange and the title they would have him pretend when her Majesty dieth'. There is some doubt as to whether this letter was genuine, but whether or not it was a forgery, it served Cecil's purpose. At the time he had done nothing about it, but subtly kept it back for an occasion when it would be most useful to him – and that moment had presented itself. 'Beyond a doubt,' writes Devlin, 'the old Earl would have been scared rigid. From that time on, the heir of the house of Stanley would have been as wax under the Cecilian thumb.' And, one might add, a grateful monarch would have been more likely, if Strange were exposed, to reward Sir Robert's diligence with fitting promotion. Essex might finally be seen off, and the coveted secretaryship would at last be his.

Two impediments appeared that threatened Cecil's plans. One was Christofer Marlow (as he was now sometimes known), the other was the result of a curious twist of fate. The complex plot is more clearly viewed if we jump ahead a few months to see how it eventually worked out. Once Christofer Marlow was out of the way.

Some time in August 1593, three months after the incident in Eleanor Bull's house on Deptford Strand, 'William Hall' was dispatched to Prague, with a letter to Kelley from Lord Burghley. He was also carrying a message for Richard Hesketh, instructing him to leave for England. He may, too, have handed over Hesketh's passport, though it seems more likely that Hesketh picked up the document from Sir Robert Cecil, or from the Warden of Ports, Lord Cobham, when he arrived at one of the Cinque Ports in September. Hesketh made his way on foot to Canterbury, where at The Bell he engaged a former soldier, one Trumpeter Baylie, as fellow traveller and servant. Baylie's account of subsequent events chimes well with other evidence, and gives a reliable view of what happened over the next three weeks. The two followed the usual route through Rochester and Gravesend, then up river to London, where they spent two nights at St Paul's Wharf. Fearful of plague in London, they spent a further night in Hampstead, then another in The White Lion in Islington, where the reason for their dallying becomes evident. On the morning of their departure from The White Lion, Hesketh was given a letter to take 'from one Mr Hickman' to the Earl of Derby.

But Hesketh's first thoughts were for his wife – 'a painful housewife' with 'many children' – and on reaching Lancashire he crossed the high fells to Over Darwen to spend the weekend with his family. He set off the following Tuesday to deliver the letter and show his passport to Derby. By a sharp turn of fate, the old earl died that very day. The Earl is dead, long live the

Earl. The letter Hickman had given Hesketh was handed over, as addressed, to the Earl of Derby – Ferdinando Stanley, Lord Strange. Unlike his cautious father, the bold Ferdinando took it straight to the Queen, claiming conspiracy against her in which he had no part. Hesketh was arrested, and was immediately visited in jail by Sir Robert Cecil.

Cecil was in danger of being hoist with his own petard, and needed to act quickly. It was essential that the Hickman letter should not come to light. He had a contingency plan. Hesketh had, some months before, been set up (perhaps thinking he was acting as Cecil's agent provocateur) through correspondence with the rebel Sir William Stanley and Cardinal Allen, the head of the Jesuit English College. The declarations he made there could now be turned against him. Cecil also had a copy of a letter to Hesketh from his former protector, Father Thomas Stephenson, mentioning the overthrow of the Queen. And indeed, Hesketh as instrument of Sir William Stanley, instructed to offer 'a hallowed crown' to Lord Strange, would become one of the official versions of the incident, in a (now discredited) report written by Lord Burghley six months after Hesketh's death.

Hesketh was artless, had a guilty conscience because of his involvement with Stanley and Cardinal Allen, and had no idea that the Hickman letter, not his link with Stanley, was the cause of his woes. Devlin portrays Hesketh as 'a dupe in a complicated scheme who had to suffer because the scheme had misfired', and shows how Cecil effectively kept the Hickman letter out of play, and excluded Ferdinando from proceedings. The new earl was 'really a witness in Hesketh's favour, since the only tangible evidence of Hesketh's communication with him was the Hickman letter'. There was no trial – a 'confession' was extracted from Hesketh, which meant he could speedily be executed without further inconvenience.

But knowledge of the Hickman connection meant the young

earl remained a menace to Cecil even after Hesketh's death. Ferdinando, Earl of Derby, died just a few months later in April 1594 in mysterious circumstances (some blamed witchcraft, others said it was poison), spewing 'vomits . . . like soot or rusty iron, the substance gross and fatty, the quantity about seven pints, the smell not without some offence'. Just two weeks before the earl's illness, Bartholomew Hickman and his brother William had ridden north on a nag given them by their employer, Dr Dee.

So, in the end, Cecil's scheme ran horribly aground. It would be another two years before he was finally made Secretary. But in early 1593, as he deftly twined the strands of intrigue into a knotty plot, exposure of his perfidy would have been devastating. He kept his machinations hidden even from Lord Burghley. In the same way as Sir Francis Walsingham had quietly lifted his hands from the workings of the Babington plot, Cecil set about making himself invisible. Careful to avoid suspicion, he made sure his messages to Prague went under another guise. It was easy enough to slip secret letters to one of the couriers that Lord Burghley was regularly dispatching to beg Kelley to come home – Cecil was by now dealing with most of his ailing father's business. Like the book-keeper to a troupe of players he divided the 'parts' between his men, making sure no-one but himself knew the whole drama. Roydon carried his letters to Kelley, but he chose Oliver Laurens to communicate with Hesketh. Not wanting to be associated with a direct approach to Dr Dee, he asked Christofer Marlow, who was trusted in occult circles, to arrange the cryptic astrological prediction with Dee's scurrilous assistant Bartholomew Hickman. Robert Poley was involved in the contingency plan to implicate Hesketh as an instrument of Sir William Stanley and Cardinal Allen. Each role was kept meticulously separate.

But Kit, whose job as a dramatist was daily to 'devise fictions and knaveries', whose mind was adept at contriving a plot as the sum of its bit parts, could turn that process on its head, view the roles of the separate players in the affair and assemble them into a disturbing whole. The odd task Cecil had assigned him, to approach Hickman for an astrological chart, first aroused his curiosity. Perhaps, while visiting the 'Wizard Earl' Northumberland, he had heard of Dr Dee's summer dinners with the Cecils, when Dee was prodded for information on Prague. Kit remembered Roydon's quip that Cecil was looking for 'an empty purse with an empty purse', a simple gull with no money, among the exiles there. A chance remark of Oliver's, that Hesketh was a 'foolish mild man', led Kit to probe into what message his friend had carried to Bohemia. He had noticed the quick narrowing of Poley's eyes when Hesketh's name was mentioned. Separately, these moments were nothing but dust, spindrift. But like ink spray from a scratchy quill, once settled they seeped together to make a blot. Kit began to form an idea of what Cecil was up to, and it pushed him beyond the threshold of his good conscience.

Ferdinando Stanley, a friend and patron, was noble in the broadest sense: intelligent, cultured, generous and, Kit knew, innocent. Some critics see him as the model for the philosophical Ferdinand, King of Navarre in *Love's Labour's Lost*, with the Earl of Essex (whose opposition to the occult circles of Ralegh, Strange and Northumberland was well known) as the more sceptical Berowne. It was one thing to be a low-grade informer in his milieu, quite another to condone a scheme that would send him to the chopping-block, purely for another man's self-advancement. Kit had no hard proof, nor did he know if there was any real urgency in the affair. He did not even have a clear idea of what Cecil was plotting – though like Eleanor Bull he had an instinctive dislike of the man, and (as is evident in his plays) an astute sense of Machiavellian politicking, which focused his suspicions. It could all be pure fancy, but his misgivings were strong enough for him to decide to warn Lord Strange.

On 28 April Kit wrote to Ferdinando from Scadbury, where he was staying with Thomas Walsingham, safe from plague in London.* The letter contained a sonnet (a common enough communication to a patron of poets), indirectly alerting Strange to 'deep plots and delicate stratagems' practised against him in high places. Kit was cautious enough not to sign it, but included the olive-pit rosary that Bianca the Venetian courtesan had once made him, which Strange would have recognised as his talisman.

Cecil intercepted the letter. He did not recognise Bianca's well-sucked beads, though he had his suspicions about the author of the sonnet – and had them confirmed when someone more closely acquainted with Kit, possibly Dr Dee himself, identified the rosary. Few but Kit's trusted friends would have known of it, as carrying a rosary was illegal at the time. Just how the 'necklace of beads made of olive stones with a cross' then found its way into Dr Dee's cedar chest, to be discovered sixty years later by Robert Jones, a confectioner in Lombard Street, remains a mystery.

Cecil acted quickly. While Kit was staying at Scadbury he was unassailable. He had to be brought back to London. Cecil had him arrested. On 18 May the Privy Council issued 'A warrant to Henry Maunder, one of the Messengers of her Majesty's Chamber, to repair to the house of Mr Thomas Walsingham in Kent, or to anie other place where he shall understand Christofer Marlow to be remayning, and by vertue thereof to apprehend and bring him to the Court in his companie.'

The arrest was not difficult to arrange. Kit's reputation as a wild malcontent, and his presence among the magi and blasphemers of what we now call the 'School of Night' – the doubters and questioners around Northumberland and Sir Walter Ralegh – made him an easy target. Cecil called in Richard Cholmeley, an unpleasant, vitriolic braggart, skilled at libel and entrapment,

---

* The letter is quoted in Blonde, *Scheming Cecil*, p. 72.

who seems at times to have been both pseudo-Catholic and fake atheist, skilled at inciting those about him to treason and blasphemy. Cecil had previously employed Cholmeley to pen 'certen libellious verses in commendation of papists and seminary priests', pro-Catholic 'libels' that could be used to provoke and entrap rebels. Cecil had even given him a copy of a Jesuit tract – Robert Southwell's *Epistle of Comfort* to direct his muse. He now set Cholmeley a similar task, based on the work of the most popular playwright of the day.

On the evening of 5 May, fifty-three lines of verse signed with the pseudonym 'Tamburlaine' mysteriously appeared fixed to the wall of the Dutch Churchyard in London. For centuries the full text was lost to us, but resurfaced in 1971 among a bundle of 'residual manuscripts' in the collection of Sir Thomas Phillips. The poem, written in Kit's trademark iambic pentameter, is a clumsy racist deprecation of foreigners and the economic ills they bring. Londoners at the time resented immigrants – mainly Protestant refugees from the Low Countries – who, they said, the Queen allowed to live in England 'in better case and more freedom than her own people'. The poem on the Dutch Church-yard wall complains that these are not refugees at all, but economic migrants 'counterfeiting religion for [their] flight', who are 'living far better than at [their] native home'. A vote in the House of Commons on 21 March to further extend immigrant merchants' privileges led to threats of militant action, and a flurry of 'libels' similar to the one on the wall of the Dutch Church. Sir Walter Ralegh demanded that rather than receiving government relief, immigrants should be sent home: 'Whereas it is pretended that for strangers it is against charity, against honour, against profit to expel them, in my opinion it is no matter of charity to relieve them ... I see no reason that so much respect should be given unto them.' The mood on the streets was violent, and the Privy Council was growing edgy. On 22 April, just a week before Cecil intercepted Kit's letter to Lord

Strange, the Council set up a special commission to investigate the authors of the inflammatory 'libels'. On 30 April, when Cecil was urgently casting around for a pretext to have Kit arrested, and thus extracted from the safety of Scadbury, he seized on the opportunity this commotion and paranoia afforded. Within five days the writing was, quite literally, on the wall.

The 'Dutch Church libel', secretly penned by Cholmeley, was not only more vituperative than the rest, but it threatened violence and ended with the dangerous claim that government officials were enriching themselves by their protection of foreign merchants, at the expense of Englishmen:

> With Spanish gold, you all are infected
> And with that gold our Nobles wink at feats.
> Nobles, say I? Nay, men to be rejected,
> Upstarts that enjoy the noblest seats
> That wound their Country's breast for lucre's sake
> And wrong our gracious Queen & Subjects good
> By letting strangers make our hearts to ache
> For which our swords are whet, to shed their blood . . .

That alone was enough to have the pursuivants banging on the door. Apart from the signature 'Tamburlaine', there were other clues to point a finger in Kit's direction, threads that connected to plays Londoners had recently seen – mention of Machiavelli and Jews that recall the opening of *The Jew of Malta*; a reference to the massacre at Paris; an allusion to such scenes of bloodletting as were famous from *Titus Andronicus*; and in the line 'We'll cut your throats, in your temples praying' an echo of *I Henry VI*: 'Within their chiefest temple I'll erect/A tomb' (II ii 12).

This was perhaps a little heavy-handed on Cecil's part. One would hardly have expected the author of such a libel to signal his identity so literally. But it at least turned minds in the direction Cecil required, and as always Cecil was working subtly, with a full quiver of contingencies. He was having to move quickly, yet at the same time keep his distance. There should be nothing directly to connect him to Kit's arrest. He engaged a minor agent, the fretful, querulous Thomas Drury, to draw up a report of 'Remembrances of Words & Matter against Ric: Cholmeley', which could in turn be used if necessary to incriminate Cholmeley (easy enough to do, given his loudmouthing among atheists). This move proved doubly effective, as one of the paragraphs of the 'Remembrances' alleges:

> he saith & verily believeth that one Marlowe is able to show more sound reasons for atheism than any divine in England is able to give to prove divinity, & that Marlowe told him he hath read the atheist lecture to Sr Walter Ralegh & others.

Cecil, agonising in the Star Chamber as the Privy Council met *in camera*, subtly nudged the old men's deliberations towards the proclamation that of all the libels, it was the one 'set upon the wall of the Dutch Churchyard, that doth exceed the rest in lewdness'. On 11 May the Council issued a directive ordering officers to arrest all suspects, to 'search in any the chambers, studies, chests, or other like places, for all manner of writing and papers that may give you light for the discovery of the libellers', authorising them to torture their captives and 'by the extremity thereof draw them to discover their knowledge'. Here was a smack of the cold terror of the *Regnum Cecilianum*, a glimpse of what Charles Nicholl terms 'the raw tones of the Elizabethan police-state'.

That night the officers were in Shoreditch, hammering on the door not of Kit's lodgings, but to arrest his fellow writer and former chamber mate, Thomas Kyd. This was perhaps not quite what Cecil had planned – or possibly, as Nicholl suggests, the purpose of arresting Kyd was all along to incriminate Kit. In either event, while poor Kyd was suffering 'pains and undeserved tortures', all the time protesting his innocence, the officers began to rifle through some of the 'waste and idle papers' from the accumulated debris of his writer's lair. Cecil and Cholmeley had already been at work. The officers came across 'a fragment of a disputation', in neither Kyd's nor Kit's hand – a passage copied from an old theological text, *The Fall of the Late Arian*, which contained 'Vile heretical conceits denying the deity of Jesus Christ our Saviour'. Terrified at this sudden turn in events, and genuinely ignorant of the document, Kyd denied all knowledge of it and, as can be gathered from his later recounting of the incident, blurted to his interrogators that such an opinion had been 'affirmed by Marlowe to be his' and that the paper must have been 'shuffled with some of mine, unknown to me, by some occasion of our writing in one chamber two years since'. We must reserve judgement on a man who had not tidied up in two years. But Kyd's panicked accusations tallied with Kit's reputation. Cecil had his man. Within a few days Henry Maunder was on his way to Scadbury with the Privy Council warrant.

Ever careful, Cecil prepared yet another arrow to skewer the hapless Marlowe. He simply could not be too thorough. The man had to be silenced without the slightest hint of Cecil's involvement, and Kit's boisterous Shoreditch lifestyle provided the perfect material he needed to build up evidence against him. In conjunction with the peevish Thomas Drury, Cecil commissioned a former agent – one who had worked with Kit and known him for years – secretly to draw up a 'Note' similar to the 'Remembrances' Drury was penning about Cholmeley. It was to be an incriminating list of Kit's blasphemies, crimes and outrages. That task went to a delighted, vengeful Richard Baines.

On 20 May, two days after his arrest, Kit appeared briefly before the Privy Council, who recorded that: 'This daie Christofer Marley of London, gentleman, being sent for by warrant from their Lordships, hath entered his apparance accordinglie for his indemnity therein, and is commaunded to give his daily attendaunce on their Lordships untill he shalbe lycensed to the contrary.' This was the equivalent of a brief appearance in court to be granted bail. Kit was to report daily to the Council, but was otherwise free to go – in stark contrast to his erstwhile chamber-fellow Thomas Kyd, who had been imprisoned and tortured. As Nicholl writes: 'In the realities of Elizabethan politics, it was not innocence that kept a man out of jail, but influence.' As had happened after his arrest at Flushing, and years earlier when his Cambridge degree was threatened, someone very powerful had intervened on Kit's behalf. Kit's coercive protector on this occasion was none other than Sir Robert Cecil himself, acting with a subtleness that could 'set the murderous Machiavel to school'.

Cecil had arranged Kit's arrest purely to draw him out from under Walsingham's wing. On no account could he allow Kit voice to reveal his suspicions about the plot to frame Lord Strange, either under torture, or to the Council. Instead, he appeared to intercede on Kit's behalf – thus cleverly distancing himself from involvement in the arrest, and perhaps even blurring in Kit's mind the true reason he had been plucked from Scadbury. Kit, after all, did not know that his letter to Strange had been intercepted, and may not even have fully divined the nature of the plot. His arrest had come as a surprise.

Cecil kept Kit as far from Council members as he could. There is no record of 'Christofer Marley' even once giving 'his daily attendaunce on their Lordships', instead, he was required each morning at ten to make his presence known at the 'safe house' run by Eleanor Bull on Deptford Strand. The plague still ravaged London, so the village of Deptford – safe from disease, yet still within call of the Council at either Greenwich or Westminster – was a suitable location for Kit to keep his bond. Widow Bull, a 'cousin' of the Cecils, had been trusted with similar responsibilities before, and aroused no suspicion.

Cecil had long since decided that Kit would not be interrogated at all. His initial move, after engineering his arrest, had been to keep him out of the way of the Privy Council. The next, should he prove to know too much, was to put him out of the way entirely. Cecil was doubtless driven by a consuming fear that Kit might uncover his plot – but he seems also to have borne fierce malice against Marlowe, a deep hatred, spurred perhaps by Kit's popularity with Essex and his associaties.

Cecil needed to find out just how much Kit had worked out about the Strange plot, and whom he had told. To do that he had briefly to become more visible and find an interrogator (and if necessary an assassin) that he could rely on, and one whom Kit would trust. There was only one real candidate – Robert Poley, a man who had proved his worth at the heart of the Babington plot, one who was ruthless, who had risen under Cecil to the position of an operational chief, and who would be enticed by possibilities of advancement in the next phase of the *Regnum Cecilianum*. However, on 8 May, ten days before Kit's arrest, Lord Burghley had sent Poley with 'letters of great importance for Her Majesty's special service' to The Hague. Cecil had him recalled as quickly as he could, but it was not until late May that Poley returned. Cecil was waiting to brief him at Dover.

A corner was lifted on the Strange plot – just enough for Poley to see that although it was a set-up, it was, like the Babington affair and the ensnaring of Mary Queen of Scots, one obviously conducted for the national good (not, of course, anything to do with Sir Robert's personal advancement). Absolute discretion would be required of him. But Poley, Cecil knew, had been down this sort of road before, and proved himself a worthy fellow traveller. His co-operation, naturally, would find fit reward – not only gold, but high favour in Cecil's network. The poet Marlowe, Cecil pointed out, was proving an impediment that had to be eliminated. He was to die in a fight, after Poley had, under guise of friendship, divined the depth of his knowledge of the Strange plot. Poley would be a purger, not a murderer (and of course could himself easily be dispatched if he came to know too much). Besides, the death of a dramatist was of no great consequence. The debriefing and the death would take place at Eleanor Bull's house in Deptford. Widow Bull lived 'within the Verge', so Poley would be justified in calling the Queen's Coroner, rather than local constables or the district man, and was assured there would be no inconvenient questions at the inquest. There would be a brief spell in jail (but Poley had been there before, and the sojourn could be made comfortable enough) before a guaranteed royal pardon, on the grounds of self-defence.

It is tempting, in retrospect, for history to attach far greater significance to the murder in Deptford than is warranted. In the world of Elizabethan politicking and espionage such deaths, while not perhaps commonplace, were from the assassin's point of view perfunctory, and the violent end of a theatre man was (given the low-life milieu of the play-houses) unsurprising. To Sir Robert Cecil the bother at Deptford was just another snarl in the intricate imbroglio of politics. At this point in his life, Kit had written only a handful of plays, albeit ones that had given the companies that performed them some renown. Outside of a small circle of connoisseurs, his death would not have been seen as particularly important. As with film today, it was the actors and the titles of the dramas that attracted public fame. As a writer, Kit's celebrity was on a lower rung, and any ripples his removal caused could be easily managed.

Poley was wily enough not to turn Sir Robert down, but secretly he hesitated to see Marlowe's murder through. There are any number of reasons for this. It may be quite simply that he was honouring his promise to the dying Tom Watson to protect Kit. He certainly had a long working relationship with Thomas Walsingham, who had made a similar vow, and as he lived in the bohemian quarter of Shoreditch he may well have had friends and loyalties in Kit's milieu. Some biographers even posit that Kit and 'Sweet Robyn' were lovers. But the slippery Poley was a man of many faces and conflicting allegiances, who was quite possibly working to an agenda of his very own.

Quick-witted Robyn pointed out to Cecil that he would need assistance. He was no smooth assassin, and Marlowe was a younger man. He was familiar with Widow Bull's house – it would be possible to hold chat in private with the poet in the garden, or set the assassins to play at tables and pass the business about Strange out of their earshot. He knew men who would ask no questions. After leaving Sir Robert, Poley followed the usual route towards London, via Canterbury, and through Rochester and Gravesend. Then, instead of taking a boat up river, he slipped south to Scadbury, where he spent an afternoon 'in private conference' with Thomas Walsingham.

Three days later, just before ten o'clock in the morning on Wednesday, 30 May, he was in Deptford, at the house of Eleanor Bull, waiting for the poet Marlowe to arrive.

CHAPTER ELEVEN

The Reckoning

Sweet Robyn passed the time on that mild May morning gently buffeting Widow Bull with his customary banter, though perhaps his smile was more forced than usual. With him was the man Skeres, who skulked, watchful and sullen, in the background. He had lurked on the periphery of events before: in Paris when Kit first met Thomas Walsingham and Tom Watson; as a Walsingham man in Robert Poley's garden as the Babington plot worked its way to a nasty end; and more recently as a tout for money-lenders, which brought him into contact with Matthew Roydon and others of Kit's circle. Mrs Bull was correct in thinking him not quite a gentleman. His father, who had died when he was three, was a merchant tailor and had left him lands in Yorkshire and Surrey, but twenty-seven years on, Nicholas Skeres was neither craftsman nor gent. He haunted a shadier world. In his teens he had taken up with a man he met in a tavern, one Richard Parradine, as an accomplice in a money-lending racket; at twenty-two he appeared alongside rogues known only by underworld tags like 'Staring Robyn' and 'Welsh Dick' on a list of 'masterless men & cut-purses, whose practice is to rob gentlemen's chambers and artificers' shops in and about London'; he was a fixer and a fence, a rakehell, a friend of thieves and a catcher of gullible conies. A man with contacts and an eye for profit, he slipped easily from the shadows of the criminal world into secret alcoves of espionage – a useful conduit to be used when spying spilled over into the murkier areas of murder, theft and violence.

Kit arrived with Ingram Frizer, just after ten o'clock. The two had the taut, tired look of men who had been locked in difficult discussion. Like Skeres, Frizer had connections with Thomas Walsingham, but while Skeres was a low-life lackey serving Walsingham in his work as a spy, Frizer was more respectable, a small-time businessman whom Thomas used as a steward and property agent – though he was not averse to a little scurrilous dealing, and had already been involved in loan-shark trickery with Skeres. Frizer was unknown to Sir Robert, but the name 'Skeres' on the inquest report would carry an authentic whiff of the underworld upstream to Westminster.

Upstairs, in the room apart he had asked for, while Ingram Frizer and Skeres indeed played 'tables' – backgammon (you had to believe that Cecil had eyes everywhere), Robert Poley pursued the discussion that Frizer had begun with Kit that morning, outlining what he and Thomas Walsingham had planned in their long private parley three days earlier: that it was 'bootless to fly' [useless to flee], as Kit would be pursued, and Poley would be compromised; that the securest way to escape Cecil was to let him think his plot had gone forward and that Kit was dead. Walsingham, he continued, had already sent word to Oliver Laurens, who waited at the river with gold, books and the means to help Kit disappear across the Channel. Walsingham would send more money, and perhaps seek help from Southampton – though for his own safety, Kit's 'sweet rosy lad' (like Poley and Frizer) would be kept in ignorance of his whereabouts. If Kit wrote any more plays, Oliver, who was now going on frequent missions abroad, would bring them back for sale to London theatres. Overreaching Will Shakespere was easily bought, and was sure to seize the chance to masquerade them as his own –

as the upstart crow had already been doing with the Henry tragedies. Skeres had found a ruffler (a superior sort of vagabond and trickster) outside The Crown at Bishopsgate (a known 'harbouring house' of thieves and cozeners), a man who 'in face, in gait, in outward form somewhat did resemble [Kit]', and who, as they spoke, was waiting, as instructed, at the end of Mistress Bull's garden, ready to change habits and places with him. Lured by promises of gold, he thought he was playing a part in one of Skeres's schemes to gull a gentleman, and had no idea that his only chance of reward would be in heaven. Skeres, of course, knew Kit, and so was able to make a reasonable match.*

But Kit would have none of it. He would send no man to death for his sake, thinking it 'full lamentable that the skin of another be made parchment for [his] own life to be scribbled on'. The point of his warning to Lord Strange had been to prevent an innocent man dying in order to favour a corrupt one, and he could not, with any sort of conscience, live out a parallel course.

At around eleven o'clock, Eleanor Bull came in with the meal. The four ate in silence. Poley had ordered a feast of neat's-tongue, capon, lamb and stag, knowing that Kit would be eating poorly for a while, but Kit barely touched it. When the dishes and trenchers had been cleared, he and Poley continued to talk 'in quiet sort' but deadly earnest, while the other two – waspish and bored by now – went back to playing tables. Skeres threw hard glances across to Kit, with eyes that 'could drop a man's heart into a sink of fear'. He did not care to whom he did the deed, so long as he got his money. He knew that by the evening there was going to have to be a corpse. The four walked out into Widow Bull's garden.

---

* For a careful reconstruction of events behind the scenes in Deptford, see Philip White, *Innocent Blood*, pp. 56–63, which uses papers that appear to be a recollection written by Ingram Frizer.

Some may argue that Kit was a coward finally to succumb to Poley's scheme, that he acted simply from self-preservation. Whatever his motivations, he certainly never forgave himself. The death of the ruffler in Deptford (as that of Walter Hoochspier) would haunt him, like the ghosts that afflicted Richard III. We can hear his agony in Richard's speech of self-hate and stricken conscience; we can spot the stain in countless plays in the years to come. In the history plays, writes biographer Katherine Duncan-Jones, 'one man's sudden death is very often the occasion of another man's sudden promotion'. In *Measure for Measure* the parallel is even more telling. The Duke of Vienna (in the guise of a friar), in order to save the young nobleman Claudio from execution, persuades the prison Provost to disguise one Barnadine, a dissolute murderer, as Claudio and send him to the block instead. He dismisses the Provost's concern that the swap will be noticed with 'O, death's a great disguiser, and you may add to it' (IV ii 166). In the event, a third prisoner dies of fever – 'A man of Claudio's years; his beard and head/ Just of his colour' (IV iii 68) – so Barnadine momentarily escapes execution and Claudio is unburdened of a guilty conscience.

No such providence intervened to relieve Kit. It is clear that at some point during that walk in the garden, he agreed to go along with the plan. They found Skeres's ruffler, and behind high hedges Kit handed over his fine hose and doublet in exchange for 'stinking clothes that fretted in their own grease' and, quite alone, slipped away to find Oliver at the river.

Skeres, Poley, Frizer and the ruffler went back to the house, where Mistress Bull had laid out a supper. Poley took her aside to discuss 'the reckoning' so she would not see the others come in. When he returned to the room, he brought up a pitcher of ale, into which he had dropped a measure of potion sold him by the 'notorious physician' Simon Forman (he who would one day be seduced by Emilia Bassano). Directions for the potion are given in one of Forman's compendia under 'Somnes

or Slepe' as a method 'to make on slepe whille he is cut', and
read:

> 'Take iii sponfulls of the galle of a swine and of the Joice
> of hemloke. of wine viniger iii sponfulls. mix them all and
> put yt in a glasse. & when youe will cut or burn a man, put
> on sponfulle therof in a gallon of alle or wine. Yf youe will
> make it strong put 2 sponfulls therof to a gallon of wine or
> alle. and giue the partie on sponfulle ther of to droincke
> and he will slepe soundly, whill youe cut him or burne him
> . . . To make him to a wake – Rub the palmes of his handes
> and soulles of his feet with wine viniger.'

By the end of the meal, the ruffler was asleep. They laid him
on the bed behind the table, with his back to the room, while
Poley and Frizer played backgammon, and Skeres drank ale –
the scene remembered by a servant who cleared the supper
dishes. Philip White maintains that Kit never acquiesced to the
plan, and that some of Forman's potion was used on him, so
that the swap-over could be made without his knowing it. While
this neatly excuses Kit of any moral blame in the affair, and
raises interesting questions about how far friends may intervene in one's life for (in their perception) one's own good, it
is a scenario of excuses. Kit's expressions of guilt and his subsequent behaviour indicate that he was quite aware of what was
going on.

It was Skeres that delivered the fatal cut. Cold Skeres knew
exactly where the blade should go to strike out their victim with
one hard stab – above the eye, so the spurt of blood covered
his face and matted his hair. Two gashes to Frizer's head added
to the gore, and to the realism. Frizer's dagger was used. He,
not Skeres, was to take the blame. As the more respectable of
the two, he would earn an easier pardon – but he drew back
from an actual act of murder. The sleeping ruffler co-operated

perfectly. The deed done, they created the sounds of a scuffle, and called in Eleanor Bull. She did not linger. Ever heedful, Sweet Robyn hastened to calm her, and took control. It was too late for a surgeon, and he did not call the watch. Instead, they waited for the coroner – the Queen's man, William Danby. The inquest was held thirty-six hours later. Neither the coroner nor any one of the jury had known Christopher Marlowe personally, and they were none the wiser as to the identity of the corpse. They accepted the story of the argument over the 'payment of a sum of pence, that is, *le recknynge*', and that Marlowe had 'moved in anger' against Frizer. They found that Frizer (as Poley had assured him they would) had acted 'in the defence and saving of his own life, against the peace of our said lady the Queen, her now crown & dignity'. The body was carried that day along the Common to St Nicholas's Church, and buried in an unmarked grave.

But by this time the real Christopher Marlowe was on his way to the coast where, despite his terror of the open seas, he would board the *Expedition* for Flushing. Or Vlissingen, as he would now have to call it. For together with the copy of Holinshed's *Chronicles* that Walsingham had given him (in a cedar chest with some other books), and a purse of gold, Oliver had provided him with 'a suit of apparel in the Flemish guise'. An Englishman abroad would be easily spotted, as different nationalities adhered to quite distinct fashions. There was, as Philip Stubbes put it in his *Anatomie of Abuses*, 'one manner of cut called the French cut, another the Spanish cut; one the Dutch cut, another the Italian'. It would not do to be like Falconbridge, the young baron of England in *The Merchant of Venice* who is so 'oddly suited' that it appears 'he bought his doublet in Italy, his round hose in France, his bonnet in Germany', a tasteless mix-and-match for which the English were notorious – like Thomas Nashe's young hero in *The Unfortunate Traveller*, who 'being a youth of the English cut, w[o]re my hair long, went apparelled in light colours, and imitated foure or five sundry nations in my attire at once', and found on arriving in Rome that he 'had all the boies of the citie in a swarme wondering about me'.

In his Flanders guise, Kit could live in the Low Countries until such time as he might safely return. His Flemish was good enough, so was his French, and he could find work with printers safe from Cecil behind enemy lines in Antwerp. Oliver had noted for him the names of two people who might help, and (from one of those houses in Gravesend known to men who had occasion for such things) had secured a forged passport to Vlissingen. The alias used on the passport throws a sudden light on Kit's distressed state of mind. It was 'Walter Hoochspier', the first man he had killed, and in whose name hid an anagram of his own. This name – with its variants Walter Hooche, Walter de Hoogh, and later Gualtiero Stangone – would travel with Kit for the next sixteen years.

Interlude

Sir Robert Cecil noted a job well done. Ingram Frizer was duly arrested, but obtained the Queen's pardon a mere four weeks later, on 28 June 1593. We may compare this with Tom Watson, who, on exactly the same charge after the Bradley affray, languished in Newgate for a full five months before pardon. Frizer immediately went back to working for the Walsinghams, with whom he enjoyed a lucrative relationship for the next twenty years. Nicholas Skeres slipped back into the underworld and disappeared into its shadows – 'Nicholas Kyrse, alias Skeers' is arrested in 1595, one of 'a very dangerous company, and very well provided of weapons', and he is again in Newgate in 1601, after which we hear of him no more. Robert Poley went on to run a network of agents in the Low Countries, Scotland and France, in Sir Robert Cecil's close employ, retiring at the age of fifty, when a last payment appears in the Chamber accounts to 'our well-beloved subject R. P.'. The death of a fairly famous playwright caused hardly a ripple.

Cecil himself had, following events at Deptford, a few loose ends to tie. Richard Cholmeley was quickly dispatched. He was arrested the very day that Frizer was pardoned, and indicted as a violent atheist – an easy enough charge to conjure given his provocateur's rantings. The list of 'Remembrances' that Thomas Drury had compiled against him was enough to ensure an energetic interrogation. Cholmeley appeared not particularly concerned, shouting as he was bundled away: 'I do know the law, and when it comes to pass I can shift well enough.' He was never heard of again.

A triumphant Richard Baines delivered his 'Note' to Cecil on Sunday, 27 May, three days before the death at Deptford. It was a malicious hotchpotch of contemporary atheist clichés, tavern gossip, examples of Kit's wicked wit, and sheer fantasy. Lazy Baines even drew some inspiration from his own 'confession' made a decade earlier in Rheims, and a significant section of the Note repeats almost word for word Drury's accusations against Cholmeley. He entitled his work 'A note Containing the opinion of one Christopher Marly Concerning his Damnable Judgement of Religion, and scorn of gods word'. He accused Kit, amongst other blasphemies, of claiming: 'That the first beginning of Religioun was only to keep men in awe', and 'That Christ was a bastard and his mother dishonest'. But he veers from his brief with unrelated accusations of coining (he had still not quite got over Kit's easy release after Flushing), and by repeating Kit's quip 'That all they that love not Tobacco & Boies were fooles'. Other elements of Kit's audacious tavern patter find their way into the Note – his claim that the Sacrament would have been 'much better being administred in a Tobacco pipe', and that he could improve on the style of the New Testament, which was 'filthily written'. Baines rounded off with the unsolicited recommendation that 'the mouth of so dangerous a member may be stopped'. Perhaps, given the events of three days later, Baines thought he had finally got his way. In any event, he did in a sense wreak his revenge, as some of the tags in the Note still stick to Kit today.

While Baines thus reaped personal as well as financial reward, poor, peevish Thomas Drury was ignored. Cecil did not even bother to pay him – and later in the year received two whinging letters, one complaining that he had neither 'shirt, doublet, nor hose, that scant will cover my nakedness', and the other ending melodramatically on a wail of eternal misery with 'Banish me forever as my lord thinketh meet . . . farewell country, life and all.'

After 30 May, Cecil no longer needed Baines's gleefully constructed evidence. Marlowe was dead, so a back-up plan to indict him for atheism was no longer necessary. But he nevertheless had a fair copy made of the Note to send to the Queen, carefully timed to arrive a day after the inquest. This may have been Cecil with his usual meticulous diligence making sure no strands of his plot were left loose to arouse suspicion. Or possibly a rumour had flashed through the Court that Kit had been assassinated, and he needed to direct royal indignation to the man's criminal atheism, rather than the nature of his death. The scribe's neat copy of the Note has been edited by a wilder, panicked hand. Three paragraphs are deleted: Baines's off-the-point meanderings about coining, tobacco and boys, and the final paragraph where he promises witnesses, and suggests Marlowe's mouth be stopped. This leaves the Note as a pure indictment of Marlowe's 'Damnable Judgement of Religion, and scorn of gods word'. But the title is also changed, to acknowledge that Marlowe has died 'a soden & vyolent deathe'; and this is again altered to the safer, more neutral statement that he had met a 'soden & fearfull end of his life'.

Cecil had managed Kit's arrest so quietly that it made little impact at all. Even Kit's arch enemy Gabriel Harvey, who would have leapt at the chance to issue a gloating pamphlet on the errant atheist, appears not to have known about it. Similarly, news of the death spread slowly, and then through a filter of disinformation. Harvey, writing in September 1593, appears to think Kit died of the plague. In Canterbury, Kit's sister Anne was married just twelve days after events in Deptford. Friends and associates pay passing tribute to 'Marley, the Muses darling', or 'poor deceased Kit Marlowe', but it is not until 1597 that the first independent account of the nature of his death emerges. Thomas Beard in *The Theatre of God's Judgements* sums up current rumour in having '*Marlin* . . . a Poet of scurrilitie' and vile atheist die in a street fight, cursing and blaspheming 'to his last gaspe'. Francis Meres, writing a year later, adds a prurient detail that was to prevail for centuries, blaming homosexual jealousy for the fray, as 'Christopher Marlow was stabd to death by a bawdy Servingman, a rival of his in his lewde love'. Other accounts make that a spat over a harlot in Smithfield. By the turn of the century, in William Vaughan's *Golden Grove*, this becomes a brawl at 'a feast' in Deptford. Subsequent tradition turns Eleanor Bull's house into a tavern, or even a brothel.

The poem *Venus and Adonis*, which Kit had entered in the Stationers' Register on 18 April 1593 (anonymously, as was common practice) was published in early June. It was dedicated to the beautiful young Earl of Southampton. No name appeared on the title page, but the dedication is signed by William Shakespere, who calls the poem 'the first heir of my invention' – his first noticeable appearance in the public arena. *Hero and Leander*, which Kit was working on at the time of his arrest, was left unfinished. It was published as such in 1598, dedicated to Walsingham, with a second version, completed by Kit's friend, George Chapman, and dedicated to Walshingham's wife Audrey, brought out the same year.

Only Oliver and Walsingham knew where Kit was. Every-

one else he had been close to, with the exception of Southampton, thought him dead. That was to prove one of the
most agonising aspects of his exile. But odd ripples of doubt
do surface. His old friend Thomas Nashe, perhaps sensing
something amiss and hurt at not being trusted with the
secret, appears to have turned against him, maligning him
as an atheist in his religious diatribe: *Christ's Tears over Jerusalem*. Another old friend and fellow spy, Roger Walton (he
who had lent Kit the sumptuous doublet for the Cambridge
portrait), seems to have scented foul play, and not quite
arriving at the correct scenario, blamed Poley for Kit's
death. In September 1593, he turned tattler on Poley, who
was on government business in the Low Countries, launch-
ing accusations that had him arrested by the Dutch authorities. But as so often in this secret world, we sense the
pressure of a powerful hidden thumb. Poley was released
within weeks, and Walton himself ended up in jail for nearly
two years.

Thomas Walsingham, who had orchestrated Kit's escape
at considerable risk to his own safety, did not endanger
himself further. He kept quiet about whatever he had
gleaned about the plot to frame Lord Strange, perhaps
reasoning that it would be easier to expose the perfidy once
the scheme had played itself out a little further. But as we
now know, when the intrigue went awry the hapless Richard
Hesketh was so swiftly and quietly dealt with that not even
Strange was aware of the proceedings – and the young earl
himself died soon afterwards. Under the rule of terror,
torture and surveillance that Cecil was perfecting, Walsingham's discretion is quite understandable: he had
already been brave enough.

Walsingham had conceived his plan in haste, and did
not dream that it would ensnare him for nearly two decades.
Strange's death and Cecil's tightening grip on power meant,

as the years went by, that there was scant chance of Kit's ever returning to England. And although it may have been Kit's compulsion to write that moved him to agree to the plan, an instinctive urge to survive and create, neither he nor Walsingham could have known the scale and importance of the works he would produce. Nor had they any idea of the perplexities they began to wind by knotting Kit's life with that of William Shakespere.

PART III

CHAPTER TWELVE

His Exits and His Entrances

Oliver had waited at the river for Kit to leave Widow Bull's house from mid-morning through to late afternoon, in trepidation that churned more violently as each hour passed. By the time the figure in stinking rags walked down the lane that bent behind Great Dock to the shore, Oliver's tension had whipped up into panic. He saw Sir Robert's men everywhere: the wherryman who seemed to linger too long without a passenger; the labourer who went nowhere with a bundle of hemp; the naval cadet who passed by too often. And then Kit came – distracted, distraught, eyes wet, muttering 'base, base . . .', making to turn back, then sitting very still, staring blankly at Oliver in the boat, whispering words Oliver could barely catch, about guilt, cold conscience, and 'invisible disgrace'. Furtive, tense, the pair had slunk away like two thievish dogs, downstream to Gravesend.*

Kit brooded, dull, sporadically jumping to his feet; simply to stand still as his thoughts seemed to stupefy him. It was up to Oliver (disturbed by Kit's insistence on taking the name Walter Hoochspier) to visit the passport forger, and to arrange passage to Vlissingen. But as he watched Kit's half-hearted attempts to put on his sombre Flemish garb – doublet unbuttoned, hose

---

* The image is Oliver's: Laurens box, folder 12 (journal, folio 122).

ungartered, face as pale as his shirt – he decided to travel with his friend, at least across the Channel.

They were lucky to be able to leave quickly. Even a short Channel crossing could involve days of studying ships' bills to get a berth, and finding a boat by no means meant immediate departure, as the captain had to wait for sailing conditions to be favourable. But by a fortuitous combination of tide and good winds (together perhaps with a little string-pulling on Oliver's part), shortly after midnight of the day they arrived in Gravesend they were aboard the *Expedition*, bound for Vlissingen. There had been just enough time to fill the phobic Kit with sufficient sack at the Golden Bull either to overcome his fear of sea travel, or to blur his perceptions of where he was being taken to pass out.

They were below deck, which though abetting secrecy, was far from easy on the stomach. It was airless, stinking, and they were constantly stepped on by sailors. Kit was barely conscious, and Oliver was cornered by 'one Chatwynne', apparently a hardened traveller, who went on at length about how he had once spent fourteen days at Calais before the ship could leave; how, on another occasion, he had waited seven hours at Rye for the tide, and then the bark, after managing just a league or two, had been becalmed for half a day, and how they had had to return to shore by rowing boat and then take post horses to Dover, where it was another two days before they found a berth – but then winds had blown them off course and carried them along the coast back to Rye.

Chatwynne was the first to vomit. He 'waxed wonderful sick with the cruel surges of the water and the unsavoury stench of the ship', despite his much-boasted remedy of eating quince marmalade and drinking sea water mixed with wine to 'dry cold humours and shut the Orifices of the belly'.* The three had

---

* Quoted in Rosine, *Oliver Laurens*, p. 213.

just one bucket between them, and were seasick all the way to Vlissingen.

On the second night, the ship was almost capsized by a strong gust; and the following morning as the fog cleared and they approached Vlissingen, they were chased by Spanish pirates in small boats – a common enough occurrence, smartly ended by a great discharge of cannon fire. The *Expedition*, which was bound for the Delft haven near Rotterdam, anchored some distance off the coast while a boatman came out to collect the Vlissingen passengers, charging an exorbitant amount to convey them back to shore.

Vlissingen was dangerous. Kit might easily be recognised. But it was also tumultuously busy – when Thomas Coryate passed through a few years later he marvelled that he saw more ships in Vlissingen than in any other port of his travels, some two hundred at one time, exceeding traffic even in Venice. There would certainly be spies from all quarters waiting to note who disembarked from an English ship, but the melancholic Fleming and his English manservant seem to have slipped unnoticed through the dockside throngs and on to a tavern called Den Eenhooren. With Kit out of sight in an upstairs room, Oliver could move more freely. Once again, espionage contacts were useful. One Hans Wouters at the sign of Den Radijs could arrange secret passage behind enemy lines. ('Den Radijs' translates as 'The Radish', which had sexual connotations in both French and local Dutch dialect, so Wouters probably ran a bordello rather than a tavern.)

Kit had long experience in the Low Countries, and had picked up the language as a child. Through Flanders, Holland, Brabant and Limburg (and arguably much of Germany too) people spoke in a tongue that was almost generally comprehensible, but which was engulfed by a fog of different dialects – a haze of accents and wayward grammar that all travellers had to penetrate. Fynes Moryson notes that '[t]he language of the

Netherlanders is a Dialect of the German toung, but sweetened with the levity of the French toung' (not an observation that would be well received today). He goes on to observe that Netherlanders 'delight more to speake the French toung' anyway, because of its 'sweetness and alacrity' in comparison with their own language. This *mélange* was even more common in the south. Oddities of pronunciation or mistakes on Kit's part would simply have been taken as a curious regional variation. A year earlier, Sir Henry Wotton, one day to be English ambassador to Venice, had spent a month in Rome (where Englishmen were unwelcome) disguised as a dashing young German, 'drinking deep, in the German fashion, with mad German priests' and clinching his disguise by wearing 'a mighty blue feather in a black hat', which no Englishman would ever do. He managed not only to fool the priests, but also convinced one Baron Berloc of Cleves that he was almost a neighbour of his, from Cologne. By comparison, Kit's task was easy. Besides, he also had good French and Latin, and could 'add colours to the chameleon, Change shapes with Proteus'; he was a wizard when it came to disguise.

A week after the pair had arrived in Vlissingen, Oliver Laurens walked the four miles to the Dutch-held town of Middelburg alone. He needed to fabricate an excuse to explain his sudden absence from London. Middelburg was known as a source of many of the 'books of sedition' that were smuggled across the Channel, and Oliver had made this journey before, when he was sent by Robert Poley to crack a book-smuggling ring, using the cover of a stationer and book-buyer. His slothful employer, the 'Puddinge of St Paul's', was resigned to such forays, and would be placated with a batch of new titles on which he could make a fat profit.

'Walter Hoogh' had quit Vlissingen a few nights previously, past a bribed watch, along the river bank then with muffled oars across the Scheldt. After that he had to negotiate inland waterways and a treacherous, roundabout route to Antwerp on his own.

Antwerp was in a forlorn condition. In the first part of the six-teenth century it had been one of the busiest and richest trading cities in the world. It was where the pepper and cloves of the Portuguese spice trade were exchanged for copper and silver from the north; where fine English cloth was dressed and finished; where rough diamonds were turned into glittering gems; where Baltic grain, French wine, Italian silks, sugar from the Canaries, cheese from Gouda, beer from Haarlem converged, to be shipped out again to other parts of Europe, or to Africa, Asia and America. It was where the economies of Europe, for the first time in history, linked with a world market. A Venetian envoy once said that Antwerp was 'Venice outdone', and at its peak it did more trade in a fortnight than Venice did in a year. The money-men were quick to spot opportunities, speculating in pepper futures or foreign exchange rates, dealing in credit, making loans. Mer-chants became bankers, and grew immensely rich. In the wake of wealth came tapestry workshops, makers of musical instruments and publishers of lavish books, and magnificent architecture.

But it was not to last. Occupation by the Spanish and the revolt of the Dutch led to the disruption of trade and economic collapse. Long years of war left Antwerp a gaunt town of ghosts and dim promise. When, after a lengthy siege, the city had again fallen to the Spanish in 1585, the Dutch responded by closing the River Scheldt, its main artery to the oceans. As sea trade dwindled to a trickle, so industry imploded. Merchants took their mer-chandise elsewhere, the money men no longer met at the Bourse, shopkeepers struggled to stock their shelves. Thousands moved north – the Jews who had been the heart of the diamond-cutting industry fled to Amsterdam; Protestants who refused to convert to Catholicism took advantage of a dispensation granted by Philip II of Spain to sell their property and depart. In four years the population dropped from 80,000 to just over half that number. Some critics see the gloomy opening to *The Merchant of Venice*, where a melancholic trader Antonio bewails his 'want-wit sadness', as a reflection of the mood in Antwerp.* There was a parallel to draw: Venice was also by now in an economic decline.

The countryside became a wilderness. Spanish soldiers robbed and ravaged. Whole villages were abandoned, fields were left fallow, grass grew over the roads, dykes crumbled and houses collapsed. Wolves moved in. One hundred men were devoured by the creatures within a two-mile radius of Ghent in one year; a quarter of an hour's walk from Antwerp, the woods were so wolf-infested that you had to go armed against them; the historian Hooft cites an eyewitness account of a woman who had her breasts devoured by rogue dogs.

Kit's progress was sporadic; his journey terrifying. And his destination held no attraction for him – the farther he went, the farther behind him lay familiarity and friendship. Exhausted one night, at an isolated inn (which he had apparently reached on the back of an old, slow horse) Kit wrote, probably to Southampton:

> How heavy do I journey on the way,
> When what I seek – my weary travel's end –
> Doth teach that ease and that repose to say
> 'Thus far the miles are measur'd from thy friend!'
> The beast that bears me, tired with my woe,
> Plods dully on, to bear that weight in me,
> As if by some instinct the wretch did know
> His rider lov'd not speed being made from thee.
> (Sonnet 50)

---

* Carol Heasman, *Hate and Redemption in* A Winter's Tale, *and Other Essays*, p. 432.

He ends his poem with the mournful realisation that 'My grief lies onward, and my joy behind.' When Kit had been on the Continent as a spy there had been moments when he had felt utterly set asunder, knowing that if he were caught his controllers would deny his existence. But there was always the sense of a covert network of support, the possibility of refuge. Nothing measured up to this extremity of loneliness in exile. He was a single dot in a land of strangers. And if he saw a face he recognised, he would have to hide.

Still shaken by the sudden nature of his flight, morbidly guilty that a man had been killed in exchange for his life, Kit started to blame Tom Walsingham for his predicament, complaining in a verse letter: 'Why didst thou promise such a beauteous day/ And make me travel forth without my cloak,/ To let base clouds o'ertake me in my way,/ Hiding thy bravery in their rotten smoke' (Sonnet 34). The courage of Walsingham's action is clouded over by Kit's loneliness and guilt, and while Walsingham may shrug it off, Kit is stuck with the consequences: 'Though thou repent, yet I still have the loss'. He feels morally stained, and however Walsingham and Oliver may try to explain away what has happened ('To dry the rain on my storm-beaten face'), this is a salve 'That heals the wound, and cures not the disgrace.'

He entered Antwerp towards the end of June (continental reckoning of dates being ten days later than in England), taking a ferry across the near-deserted Scheldt to one of the *hoofden* – piers that gave access to gates in the riverside city wall. His passport (this one bought from a forger in Vlissingen) was penned in the hand of the Count of Brabant, and would appear not to have been questioned. Knowing he should avoid De Roy Lelie inn, which had belonged to the English Nation (a merchant's fellowship) and might still harbour the odd spy, he followed directions Oliver had given him to Het Gulden Cruys, a tavern among the bordellos and bathhouses of Stoofstraat (the 'Street of Stews'), just a few minutes from the Sandersgat, where he had alighted. The big, wooden communal tub of steaming water at the 'stew' next door, the table alongside laid with bread and Hoegaerden beer, and perhaps the attentions of a resident 'vrouwken van occasie' ('woman of opportunity'), were welcome respite to a weary and traumatised traveller.

There were places in the city that Kit knew he had to avoid. Zwartzustersstraat on the other side of town, where the city postmaster Adrian de Langhe, a notable passport forger, had his home, was a meeting point for banished English priests who were about to slip back across the Channel; and Den Gulden Hoorn tavern was also a rendezvous for English recusants and a mailing depot – one Jacques Ghibbes (or Gibels) had for years been running letters to England, and smuggling human cargo for forty shillings a head. At either of these places Kit could have run into one of Cecil's secret 'watchers'. Cecil had two resident agents in Antwerp, a Welshman who lived in De Langhe's house and a man variously known as Sterrell, Robert Robinson and H. Saint Main – though neither of these men knew Kit. Tom Walsingham had suggested Antwerp as a haven precisely because it was behind enemy lines and was therefore relatively free of Englishmen. And Oliver, of course, knew clandestine means of reaching the city to keep communication running.

Oliver's earlier contacts seem to have been useful to Kit. Within a few weeks of arriving he was lodging in chambers (near Stoofstraat) owned by Diego Lopez Alleman, a Marrano merchant who had fallen on hard times. By mid-July a 'Wter. de Hooch' is mentioned in the accounts of the printer and bookseller Pieter Bellerus, where some years earlier an 'o lourens' was paid as a temporary proof-reader.*

The steam and smoke from the chimneys of the stews in

---

* Copies of the accounts are held in Bernhardt Institute, Laurens box, folder 14.

Stoofstraat acted as a beacon to Kit, as he walked back home each day after work at the Bellerus printing shop. He may also have dropped in on the bookshop of Bellerus's rival, the renowned publisher Christophe Plantin, who operated from a large establishment on the Vrijdagmarkt at the sign of the 'Gulden Passer' ('Golden Compasses', the name by which Plantin's firm had long been known, after its colophon). Antwerp was a safe distance from the battlefront, and intellectual activity was still vigorous (though perhaps of a more Catholic bent than before), centred on the surviving book trade. The streets were deserted, but the city held on to its beauty, like a grandly dressed widow waiting quietly for something to happen (or, as one visitor put it, 'a superannuated Virgin that hath lost her Lover').

Writing in 1616, a traveller called Dudley Carleton noted: 'Antwerp I own surpasses all the towns I have seen in the magnificence of its buildings, the breadth of its streets, the strength and beauty of its fortifications', but goes on to say that grass grew between the paving stones, that Jesuits were giving lessons in the former English Factory, and that '[f]or all the time I was there, I never could count in the whole length of any street more than forty persons at once. I saw neither carriages nor horsemen, and though it was a week-day, not one of us saw a pennyworth sold in the shops'. By the time Kit arrived, the Dominicans and Jesuits were already working to restore fine churches smashed by Protestants, and the Spanish had renovated the star-shaped citadel, which now housed a crack Castilian regiment – tall, dark men whom the locals thought 'proud and magnificull', and who sported enviable neckware. 'Their hose and their ruffs are nothing less than comely!' was one admiring opinion – quite an admission in a city that was renowned for the lily-whiteness of its linen, and which had given England the ruff.

Isolated from any contact with players, Kit turned again to writing narrative poetry. The antics in the bordello next door appear to have set the tone. To this period belongs *The Rape of Lucrece*, a poem of Ovidian sensuality (like the *Amores* Kit had translated years before, which would be banned as 'unseemly' in England in 1599), in which the rapist Tarquin is caught between 'frozen conscience and hot-burning will' – a similar dilemma, perhaps, to the one that faced Kit in Deptford, where his will to survive and ambition to create had to be balanced against another man's life. He would explore similar territory in *Macbeth*. Like *Tamburlaine* and *Titus Andronicus*, the poem is preoccupied with bloodshed, and a description of the Battle of Troy matches the detail of Guilio Romano's fresco in Mantua with extraordinary fervour – but this was more likely the result of a vivid impression made during an earlier visit than proof that Kit somehow made a trip to Italy at this point. He dedicated *Lucrece* to Southampton with the words 'The love I dedicate to your Lordship is without end', wishing him 'long life still lengthned with all hapinesse', a poignant acknowledgement perhaps that they would never see each other again.

Kit appears not to have waited for a visit from Oliver, but to have taken the risk of sending *Lucrece* with the ordinary post. The spy 'Sterrell' who bribed one of De Langhe's letter clerks with twenty-eight ducats a month, was able briefly to delay and scan all mail weighed in Antwerp. On 26 August 1593 he records 'a verse of Lucr. & Tarquin' that is 'too long for suspicion of cipher'. Curiously, he also notes a 'tragedie *Ric tert*', which may indicate that Kit was making changes to the *Richard III* he had been working on in England. (One wonders whether Sir Robert Cecil would have been riled by the portrayal of a hunchbacked, Machiavellian power-seeker who would stop at nothing, in the same way that Queen Elizabeth, on seeing *Richard II*, is alleged to have exclaimed angrily: 'I am Richard II, know ye not that?)

Kit was certainly by this time writing *Love's Labour's Lost*, a comedy which has no literary source but which was possibly based on a visit he made to Navarre in the early 1580s. In unfamiliar surrounds Kit drew on his past for inspiration and on people he had known in England for his characters – Thomas Nashe can be seen in Moth, a cheeky child who lays verbal traps and makes pert phrases; his rival Gabriel Harvey in the linguistic fop Armado, and a compliment to Lord Strange in naming the king Ferdinand. He wickedly satirised Sir Walter Ralegh and his intellectual circle (this play is the source of the phrase 'the School of Night'), lending fuel to the argument that before leaving England Kit had fallen out with Ralegh and associated more with the rival grouping around Essex and Southampton – yet another reason for incurring Cecil's loathing. There is further evidence of a souring in his relationship with Sir Walter. Kit's ballad 'Come live with me and be my love', which was wildly popular at the time (even more so when it was given a new tune by William Corkine, eponymous son of the man whose buttons Kit had sliced off in Canterbury), became the subject of Ralegh's tart satire. Some critics even detect the sulky petulance of a cuckolded lover in Ralegh's reply:

> If all the world and love were young,
> And truth in every shepherd's tongue,
> These pretty pleasures might me move,
> To live with thee and be thy love . . .

Love's Labour's Lost represents the first time that Kit had attempted writing drama in the absence of a group of players. But soon after he had begun, fortune delivered him a theatre troupe – or rather transported him to the foot of their stage. His employer Pieter Bellerus sent him to Frankfurt, as the firm's representative at the September book fair. Performing there, as it often did, was the travelling company of Robert Browne.

Kit travelled with two of Bellerus's colleagues, the book-sellers Jan van Keerbergen and Martin Nutius. It is through Van

Keerbergen's account of the journey that we can follow the progress of 'Walter de Hoogh'.*

The Frankfurt book fair was crucial to trade, especially in such tumultuous times, when reaching customers was difficult. Despite the war the fair remained important for meeting German and Parisian clients, and had become Christendom's foremost book mart. Bellerus was probably reluctant to undertake the dangerous journey himself. Not only wolves, but brigands and deserters terrorised small parties of travellers, and the safest option was to move in large convoys under military escort. Or to send an assistant. Kit and his colleagues joined a group of merchants who, accompanied by Spanish soldiers, journeyed first to Brussels to wait for more to join the train, then on through Liège and up to Cologne – a few travellers on horseback, and twenty covered wagons juddering on large spoked wheels along awful roads, pursued by dogs, splattered by mud and from time to time drenched by rain, the precious cargo of books taking priority over bodies and clothes in the struggle to keep things dry.

At Cologne they rested a few days, ostensibly to do business but primarily for 'een schale goeden Rijnsch wijn' ('a bowl of good Rhenish wine') with local bookseller friends, in a tavern near the river. Cologne was the main German metropolis of the time, and nearly as important as Antwerp as a centre of publishing. According to Thomas Coryate, it had a 'very delectable' situation 'in a pleasant and fruitful plaine' hard by the Rhine, and was so vast that 'a man can hardly goe round about it under the space of foure houres'. The size, energy and prosperity of the city must have set Kit longing for life in London – though the cathedral could hardly compare with St Paul's, having just one rather dumpy unfinished tower.

---

* See the recently published *Het Reisjournaal van Jan van Keerbergen*, edited by Eduard Dekker.

After '*dri daghe verblivinge*' ('three daies aboad') they took a boat up the Rhine to Frankfurt. Booksellers, publishers and their agents, printers and scholars descended on Frankfurt for what one visitor, Henri Estienne (known as 'Stephanus'), called an 'Academy-Fair', likening it to classical Athens. It was a meeting place for scholars, a chance for famed academics to exchange views, air new ideas, find publishers and buy books. 'For here all may enjoy the living voice of many honoured persons, who gather here from many different academies,' wrote Estienne. 'Here very often right in the shops of the book-sellers you can hear them discussing philosophy no less seriously than once the Socrateses and the Platos discussed it in the Lyceum.' It was a cosmopolitan crossing point for what Dr Dee once called the 'intertraffique of the mind'. The visiting booksellers put up their stalls in the Buchgasse, hanging boards in front that announced the names of their publishing houses, and plastering posters about heralding new publications. They came from all over Europe, as varied in dress and appearance as in the languages they spoke. In the streets, as a fringe to this more respectable trade, were women and children selling songs and calendars, and beyond that, the general fair with arms merchants and jugglers, English comedians, elephants and ostriches, dentists, quacks and (in the year that Kit was there) a troupe of Russian maskers '*gecleet in wonderlijck garnement ende bonte mutse*' ('in fantastical garb and hats of fur'). It was frantically busy. A young visitor called Josias Maler, who (like Kit) spoke French and Latin and so was much in demand, worked during one fair for his stepbrother Christoph Froschauer and 'had an evil time in carrying books back and forth and could not escape any time to see the city' (though he did eventually manage a jug or two of 'a good class of beer' on a boat on the Main).

Frankfurt was surrounded by fertile land that 'cheere[d] the tables of the Fair with many sorts of wine, especially the Rhenish'. Eating, drinking, socialising and entertainment were a crucial part of the fair's activities. The tavern where the Antwerp party stayed, the Nuernberger Hof, never had fewer than 125 extra 'strangers' eating there on fair days and Robert Browne's English comedians performed two or three plays a day.

Kit, of course, had to avoid any direct contact with Browne's men, many of whom had worked with him before, but he did approach them circuitously. Van Keerbergen records that: '*here de Hoogh mochte geerne spelen schriven, ende oock in die Engelendische tale, maer hi es seer verlegen ende swigelijc daerover. Hi hevet sine spelen met ene bootschapper aen het Engelendische Comoedianten gestuurt ende si hebben slechts twee talers daervoor betaelt, ende nochtans woude hi niet hen spreecken*' ('de Hoogh would fain write plaies, and in English, but is very shy with it and keeps close, and has sent it with a messenger to the English Comedians and was paid but two thalers yet would not speake with them withal'). He mentions Kit at the back of the crowd that pressed around the players' platform, fingertips on lips, brow slightly knit – perhaps watching his own *Jew of Malta* or *Tamburlaine,* then one day seeing what they could do with *Love's Labour's Lost* before a non-English-speaking audience. This performance pedigree probably explains why the play uses every conceivable farce convention in the book, from mistaken identity and straying letters, to drunk scenes and impersonation – as well as an appearance by elaborately dressed Russian maskers. Kit saw the work acted and knew what changes he had to make. The play was taken to England some weeks later by Oliver (who was in Frankfurt on behalf of the Puddinge). It was printed in 1598 'as it was presented before her Highness this last Christmas, *Newly corrected and augmented by W. Shakespeare*' – the first time Will's name appeared on a title page (even if not yet as an author). Will himself had a go at an imitative sequel, *Love's Labour's Won,* a dismal piece that flopped immediately and was soon lost, though it is mentioned by the playgoer Francis Meres in his *Wit's Treasury* of 1598. Neither Oliver nor Tom Walsingham paid much attention to the appearance of a *Love's Labour's Won*. Had they known what it augured, they might very well have cut all contact with Will Shakespere 'incontinently'.

Kit had had no time to make a copy of *Love's Labour's Lost* – but he knew the drinking habits of Browne's men, and more importantly, the secret of the complicated lock on the old coffer in which Robert Browne stored the players' parts and a few heavy prompt-books. He also knew that given the inflated inn prices at fair time, the men would be sleeping in their wagon, and that it would be empty in the hour following their afternoon performance.

Browne had been agreeably surprised to have been offered a play of such quality, albeit anonymously. He was quite astounded to find the manuscript missing the morning after the first performance, and the paltry two thalers he had paid for it left *inside* his safe box. The astonishment turned to anger when he discovered that also missing was his long-held manuscript of *Hamlet, Prince of Denmark* – the play Marlin had written for Essex's men in Elsinore (that elusive work that the modern world refers to as the *Ur-Hamlet*).

By mid-autumn, Kit was back in Antwerp, his own meagre library now extended by a clutch of books he had picked up at Frankfurt – volumes not so easy to come by in Antwerp, and (given the price of books, and his unstable finances) probably traded in lieu of wages. He had indulged his taste for things Italian with a used copy of Dante's *Divina Commedia*, novellas by Bandello, and a brand new history of Verona by Corte, which told the tale of the mindless feud between the Montecchi and Capelletti. This no doubt reminded Kit of the poem by Arthur Brooke, *The Tragicall Historye of Romeus and Iuilet*, which he had lightly drawn on in *Venus and Adonis*. Curiously the names of the Montecchi and Capelletti families are also to be found in the *Purgatorio*.

He returned to find his landlord Diego Lopez Alleman in some trouble, having been accused of practising Judaism. Marranos like the Allemans were Jews who had ostensibly converted to Christianity, though behind a veil of Catholicism many kept the old religion. We have here (if we are to follow Heasman's reasoning that *The Merchant of Venice* is partially based on Kit's experiences in Antwerp) a possible clue to what Antonio is asking when he makes the odd demand of Shylock that as a condition of his pardon he 'presently become a Christian' (IV i 382), and why (given the ambiguity of Marrano religious practice) Shylock so readily agrees. Diego Alleman had let his Marrano façade slip. Antwerp under the Spanish had become less tolerant, and a spy had reported to the authorities that, though the weather was icy, no smoke was seen from the chimneys of the Alleman household on Friday nights or Saturdays. Although Jewish law forbade the lighting of fires on the Sabbath, many Marrano families employed trustworthy gentiles to light fires for them, and it is unclear why the Allemans had stopped doing this. Kit's rooms were near the Alleman house, and it would appear that soon after coming back from Frankfurt he took over this fire-lighting role, perhaps for a reduction in his rent but quite possibly simply as a kindness. Closer contact with the Alleman family gave him an unexpected insight into events in England.

Jews had been expelled from England by King Edward I in 1290, and were not legally to return until 1652, under Cromwell. A very few had remained, preferring conversion to banishment and taking shelter in a *Domus conversorum*, a House of Converts initially run by Dominicans in what is now Chancery Lane. There were also tiny settlements of Marranos, escapees from the Inquisition, in London and Bristol. One of these refugees was Roderigo Lopez, who had fled Portugal in 1579 and set up in London as a doctor. By 1586 his reputation was so strong that he had been appointed chief physician to Queen Elizabeth. Lopez frequently sent money to poor Marranos in Antwerp, and was in correspondence with Diego Lopez Alleman. In January 1594 he was accused by the Earl of Essex of conspiring to poison the Queen. Evidence for this was scanty, and it seems most likely that Lopez was set up by the earl, a victim of personal politicking. Confessions were wrested from servants under torture, and some enigmatically worded letters from the Spanish Netherlands were intercepted and held up as proof of Lopez's involvement in anti-English activities. An unsigned letter from Antwerp (which turned out to be from Diego Lopez Alleman) was one of these, and was used in Lopez's conviction in February. Elizabeth remained unconvinced and put a hold on the matter for three months, but on 7 June 1594 Lopez was castrated, hanged, cut down while still alive, disembowelled, and quartered at Tyburn.

The Alleman family were considerably shaken, and felt some responsibility for Lopez's death – even though Diego's letter had nothing to do with a conspiracy, and most probably referred to arrangements Lopez was making to leave London for Antwerp, en route to Italy or Constantinople, where Jews were tolerated. As news filtered back from London, to be discussed at the Alleman's Sabbath family gatherings, Kit picked up fragments of talk about the welling of anti-Jewish sentiment in London, and the consequent enormous popularity of a play called *The Jew of Malta*, which was performed no fewer than fifteen times during the Lopez trial and in the months before his execution.

That news must have been disturbing to Kit. Although the wicked Barabas in *The Jew of Malta* has all the trappings of a stock stage Jew, the Christians in his milieu are hardly models of virtue either, and their treatment of Barabas in part accounts for his crimes. To hear that his play (with who knows what coarse amendments incorporated by the players) was thus abused, angered Kit. He had known Jews in Padua, where there was a large and erudite community, and had become close to the Allemans and other Marranos in Antwerp. While his views were possibly still clouded by standard Elizabethan prejudice, he had a keener, more sophisticated perception of Jews than many of his contemporaries. It was as a counterblast to the surge of unpleasant interest in *The Jew of Malta* that he set about writing *The Merchant of Venice*, with its now famous plea:

> I am a Jew. Hath not a Jew eyes? Hath not a Jew hands, organs, dimensions, senses, affections, passions, fed with the same food, hurt with the same weapons, subject to the same diseases, healed by the same means, warmed and cooled by the same winter and summer, as a Christian is? If you prick us, do we not bleed? If you tickle us, do we not laugh? If you poison us, do we not die? And if you wrong us, shall we not revenge?
>
> (III i 51ff)

Critics have noted strong similarities between the plays, but Kit was careful this time around to open a gateway of sympathy for his main character – though of course we have no way of knowing how much was altered or added by the company in performance, and now comes down to us set in stone. Kit's main source for the story was Ser Giovanni's collection of prose romances *Il Pecorone*, a rather ill-considered move if he was to pass the work off as Will Shakespere's, as *Il Pecorone* was at the time available only in Italian, and anybody detecting the source might know that Will could not read or speak that language.

One of the changes the players instituted was, no doubt, the transformation of Shylock's costume from one including a yellow beret or turban (which all Jews in Venice, with the exception of some bankers, were required to wear) to one involving a 'Jewish gaberdine' (*The Merchant of Venice* I iii 107; a gaberdine was a full, loose-fitting cloak). There is no historical justification for this, not among Italian Jews nor London or Flanders Marranos, and no-one has satisfactorily explained what it means. Some commentators point out that Thomas Coryate noted on his travels that all Venetian Jews wore 'a kinde of light yellowish vaile, made of Linsie Woolsie (as I take it) over [their] shoulders, something worse than our courser Holland, which reacheth a little beneath the middle of their backes'. But perhaps the explanation is simply that the Lord Chamberlain's Men, who performed it first, had a gaberdine cloak but no yellow beret in their costume box. Or that 'gaberdine' scans better than 'vaile' or 'flatte hatte' in the context. This is, after all, a play, and there is a danger in being too literal-minded about its historical references.

Although Kit chose to set his new play in Venice – an alluringly exotic location to an Elizabethan audience, a city of unfettered passions and immense riches – he drew on his experiences among Jews in Padua, Antwerp, and possibly Mantua, in creating Shylock. He had, of course, visited Venice during the time he and Oliver had spent in Padua, and he incorporated his recollections and impressions in the play: the bustle on the Rialto, the ferry between the two cities, moonrise over Villa Barbaro (which he transforms into Belmont). Perhaps, like Thomas Coryate did in 1608, he visited the Ghetto and argued religion with a rabbi:

> For when as walking in the Court of the Ghetto, I casually met with a certaine learned Jewish Rabbin that spake good Latin, I insinuated my selfe after some few termes of complement into conference with him, and asked him his opinion of Christ, and why he did not receive him for his Messias . . . after there had passed many vehement speeches to and fro betwixt us, it happened that some forty or fifty Jewes more flocked about me, and some of them beganne very insolently to swagger with me, because I durst reprehend

their religion: Whereupon fearing least they would have offered me some violence, I with drew my selfe by little and little towards the bridge at the entrance into the Ghetto, with an intent to flie from the[re], but by good fortune our noble Ambassador Sir *Henry Wotton* passing under the bridge in his Gondola at that very time, espyed me some-what earnestly bickering with them, and so incontinently sent unto me out of his boate one of his principall Gentle-men . . . who conveighed mee safely from these unchristian miscreants, which perhaps would have given mee just occasion to forsweare any more coming to the Ghetto.

We can perhaps take the gathering of the crowd of 'forty or fifty' with a pinch of salt. These Jews, and those he had encountered a few days earlier in Padua, were the first Coryate had ever seen, and he was inclined to marvel, and to exaggerate – for instance he puts the number of Jews in Venice at the time at five or six thousand, when more conservative estimates hold the figure to be nearer one or two thousand.

Curiously Kit does not mention the Ghetto. The Ghetto in Venice, set up in 1516, was the first of its kind, and derives its name from the old public foundry (*geto* in Venetian dialect) formerly sited on the island. Jews in Padua and Mantua were not at this time subject to such strict confinement, and Marranos in Antwerp were free to live anywhere in the city. Kit's dramatic world is an amalgam of Venice and of Jewish communities in Padua and Mantua, with something of the gloomy air of contemporary Antwerp. He anchored many of his plays in real places yet bent facts to suit his dramatic purposes, such as, notoriously, giving Bohemia a coastline in *The Winter's Tale.**

---

* This is what Lord Yentob calls the Ambridge Effect, after the village in a long-running BBC radio soap opera. Ambridge is said to be near Birmingham, yet has residents with a curious range of romantic rustic dialects, and neighbouring towns with entirely made-up names. (*cont* . . .)

Though seemingly settled in Antwerp, Kit was stirred by a deep restlessness. He still believed he might one day return to England, so all about him felt inescapably temporary. Nothing held a history, all friends were new friends, the ground was thin beneath his feet. So, like the wind, he was drawn to wander. He is not always easy to track down – but he does not completely disappear. It is possible to spot him from time to time, flitting through cities as an itinerant actor, perched on a printing house stool arguing with scholars, or as a stranger shining for a moment among a court's intelligentsia.

A poet may change his name, but not his plumage.

Characters travel via fictional 'Borchester' on to real-life events in London; people from the outside world make appearances in Ambridge in their own persona. The audience is quite happy to let fantasy and reality mingle (see K. Yentob, *Borchester Chronicles*, p. 6). Technically, though, it may be argued that Bohemia *did* have a coastline in the sixteenth and early seventeenth centuries, as it was incorporated in Hapsburg territory, and so the King of Bohemia (who also happened to be the Holy Roman Emperor) held sovereignty all the way to the coast.

CHAPTER THIRTEEN

In the Bleak Midwinter

Kit laid low for much of 1594, outcast, guilt-ridden and home-sick. He could not even find consolation in his pipe-smoking as tobacco was hard to come by and cripplingly expensive in Antwerp. Hints of his mood over this period can be traced in sonnets of loneliness and exile, through the outsiders and cast-aways of his plays, in scenes of fated parting. Falstaff's reluctant leave-taking of a tearful Doll Tearsheet and Mistress Quickly in *Henry IV Part Two* springs to mind. As he leaves, Mistress Quickly notes mournfully: 'Well, fare thee well. I have known thee these twenty-nine years . . .' – (II iv 369–70, Kit's age when he fled England).

In his guise as Walter de Hoogh, sparkling Kit Marlowe had lost one of his greatest delights: the curl and energy of spoken English, the easy wit and wilful waywardness of a mother-tongue conversation. Like Mowbray in *Richard II*, he realised sadly that: 'My native English, now I must forgo;/ And now my tongue's use is to me no more/ Than an unstringed viol or harp' (I iii 160–62). Though he was adept at other languages, none fired him like his own tongue. English may have disappeared from his day-to-day life, but in private he clung to it, wrote in it, disrupted, expanded and re-invented it – for the rest of his life. He continued writing plays because he needed the money, but the underlying impetus – and the one that is most evident to us today – was his passion for the language. He simply could not leave it alone. The language was all he had left.

Kit's yearning for home, and for the friends and lover he was separated from found expression in John of Gaunt's aching lament in *Richard II* for an idealised England, viewed from a distance – a 'scept'red isle', a 'demi-paradise', a 'precious stone set in the silver sea', inhabited by a happy breed of men, a 'land of such dear souls, this dear, dear land' (II i 30ff). Kit even continued to write sonnets to his lost Emilia Bassano, and while his feelings for the young Southampton somehow sustained him, at the same time the hopelessness of the passion consumed him. The motto on his 1585 portrait '*Quod me nutrit me destruit*' (What nourishes me, destroys me) seems oddly prescient here; it recurs as 'Consum'd with that which it was nourish'd by' in Sonnet 73, a poem of regret and parting. He hears, too, that his 'posthumous' reputation is being blackened – probably by rumours spread by Cecil. He is sinking into public disgrace, and feels cheated by Fortune. All this culminates in a howl of isolation:

> When in disgrace with Fortune and men's eyes,
> I all alone beweep my outcast state,
> And trouble deaf heaven with my bootless [useless] cries,
> And look upon myself and curse my fate . . .
> (Sonnet 29)

Disgrace and loss of reputation become a recurrent theme in Kit's writings hereon, from Mowbray's concern with his 'fair name' through Cassio's 'Reputation, reputation, reputation! O, I have lost my reputation!' (*Othello* II iii 255). Part of Kit's shame was a secret one, the 'invisible disgrace' of the death of the ruffler in Deptford; but as rumours about a 'brawl' began to circulate, there was also the public infamy of a name linked with violence and debauchery. He was absolutely powerless to do anything about that, and the slur has stuck.

In the autumn of 1594, Kit suddenly disappeared from Antwerp. Payments made to 'de Hooch' in the Bellerus account book stop abruptly in September – so it is possible that he again went to Frankfurt, but did not come back.* Oliver Laurens mentions just one visit to Kit in 1594, and it is not improbable that they once more met at the book fair. No part of Oliver's journal for this year survives, but in a later table he records collecting three plays from Kit in 1594. Unfortunately, he does not record what they were, though *Richard II*, *Romeo and Juliet* and *The Merchant of Venice* are the most likely candidates, as all appear to have been performed in 1595/6. By 1594 Oliver had at last left the sticky employ of the Puddinge of St Paul's, and was working with Thomas Thorpe, a young man of around his own age, who, after a nine-year apprenticeship, had in 1594 become a freeman of the Stationers' Company. 'Odd' Thorpe, as he was known, did not have a press or stall of his own – his books were printed by the publisher George Eld, and sold in the shop of John Wright at Christ Church Gate. At a time when printing, publishing and bookselling were only just beginning to untwine into distinct professions, 'Odd' Thorpe was probably one of the first ever packagers. His was a fluid, almost freelance life, and the arrangement between them suited Oliver perfectly, as it gave him even more flexibility to travel abroad.

Oliver no doubt brought Kit news of changes in London. He told of how the theatre companies had reorganised, that the recently amalgamated troupes of Lord Strange's and the Admiral's Men had once again split – Alleyn and Henslowe hiving off to the Rose with most of the Admiral's Men, while the remainder joined Strange's troupe to form a strong new

---

* Laurens box, folder 14.

company, the Lord Chamberlain's Men. He had to reveal that Will Shakespere was demanding a larger cut than had originally been agreed of the payments for Kit's plays. This was bad news for Kit, who needed the money. Hope for further financial help from Walsingham or Southampton receded, as they were already putting out large amounts in Kit's cause. Shakespere had implied blackmail to Tom Walsingham and had been bought off with a lump sum of £1,000. This huge amount (the equivalent of £500,000 today) had been in part met by the Earl of Southampton, who, enraged by Will Shakespere's greed, had severed all ties with him, and was no longer willing to pose as his patron. Will had used the money to become a shareholder of the Lord Chamberlain's Men, a shrewd business move, but hard to explain away on the salary of a humble bit-part actor and budding author. To make matters worse, Will was beginning to pen his own rather inept plays (such as *Love's Labour's Won*) and trivial verse, like that accompanying the rather mean wedding gift of gloves from his father's shop to Alexander Aspinall, an old Stratford friend:

> The gift is small,
> The will is all:
> Alexander Aspinall.

This doggerel is surpassed in awfulness only by the verses he would one day compose for his tombstone.

Kit had probably already heard of the gruesome death of the new Earl of Derby. An unsigned letter (in English) found among the Bellerus company correspondence tells of a 'loyal Derby hound poisoned by biting on a bunchback toad'.* With Derby's

---

* Laurens box, folder 14; This does seem to refer to Lord Strange, who, it will be remembered, suffered a revolting and mysterious death by apparent poisoning soon after becoming the fifth Earl of Derby.

death and Sir Robert Cecil's continuing ascent, any last hope of Kit's return to England was extinguished. Now that the Strange plot had misfired, were Cecil ever to discover that Kit was still alive and able to link him to events, it would mean instant death not only for Kit, but for his closest and most loyal friends – and Cecil was increasingly reaching a position from which he could effect that with ease.

It is little wonder that it was at this time, when Kit was faced with the realities of permanent exile, that he decided to leave the gloom of Antwerp and seek out pleasure and adventure.

Kit's first move was to attach himself to one of the troupes of players performing at the Frankfurt fair. This would not have been Robert Browne's company, as not even Kit would be so audacious as to assume his new persona was effective enough to fool, for any protracted time, people he had once known. Besides, it would appear from records that 1594 was one year that Browne did not travel to Germany, as he had just lost his wife and children to the plague.

There were, however, other companies to choose from. The last few years of the sixteenth century were a high point of the English comedians' activity on the Continent, especially after 1594 when the Lord Admiral's and the Lord Chamberlain's Men held a virtual monopoly in London, forcing smaller troupes to tour. Ad hoc companies of five or six men would form in London, and pick up foreign players when necessary along the way. After the spring and summer fairs many troupes returned to England, though a lucky few managed to secure winter patronage in the court of a local aristocrat. The Duke of Brunswick and Landgrave Maurice of Hesse-Kassel were especially enthusiastic about the English comedians. They were the first princes in Germany to establish permanent theatres, and maintained resident companies of English players and musicians throughout the winter (although casts changed frequently). In 1594, the star lutenist and songwriter John Dowland was amply rewarded by both:

> When I came to the Duke of Brunswick he used me kindly & gave me a rich chain of gold, £23 in money with velvet and satin and gold lace to make apparel, with promise that if I would serve him he would give me as much as any prince in the world. From thence I went to the Lantgrave of Hessen, who gave me the greatest welcome that might be for one of my quality who sent a ring into England to my wife valued at £20 sterling, and gave me a great standing cup with a cover gilt, full of dollars, with many great offers for my service.

These were courts that sparkled with intellect as much as they glistered with gold, where brains were valued as well as background, where winters were spent in a fizz of plays and song, in poetry, debate and witty conversation. It was all Kit could hope for, and more – Kassel also had hot, healing mineral springs, where you could steam and stew, though the snow came to the very water's edge.

A 'Walter Hooghspier' appears on the payroll of a small company led by Harry Brodribb, which, after giving the rather old-fashioned but ever popular *Gammer Gurton's Needle* at the Frankfurt fair, travelled north to spend at least part of the winter in the court at Kassel.* Brodribb was 'a good, portly soul', 'a tun of a man' who was 'full of jests, and gipes, and knaveries, and mocks', a white-bearded old trouper who warmed Kit's heart. He was a good comic actor, perfectly suited to the role of Bottom in an early version of *A Midsummer Night's Dream*, and was the

---

* Keaton, *Luvvies' Labours*, p. 385ff.

prototype for the ebullient character of Falstaff. It is said that his rich turn of phrase awakened Kit's genius for living vernacular prose, which blossomed for the first time in the *Henry* plays and *The Merry Wives of Windsor*. Brodribb was no friend of Robert Browne, having once said that he 'wouldn't trust his arse with a fart', and slipped quickly and happily into his absent rival's place on the winter circuit.

Once again, Kit's fine singing voice was his passport – as it had been a decade earlier, when as a student he had slipped away with travelling players to France. He travelled with Brodribb's company as a singer and interpreter, providing a running scene-by-scene commentary at indoor performances. Like other strolling troupes, Brodribb's band travelled light, with few props and costumes and much of their repertoire already committed to memory. They had been given a wagon at Arnhem by Ernest Casimir, the Count of Nassau, but because of the appalling condition of the roads, wheels impeded rather than speeded their progress.

They are probably the players given leave to perform for a week in the market-place at Fulda in mid-October; and the '*Engelendische Comoedianten*' with such '*herliche, guette musicha*' ('wonderful good music') reported by one Balthasar Hofgartner in a letter to his wife in early November, from Marburg – a precariously steep university town beside the river Lahn, where the players would have had temporarily to abandon their wagon to tackle the narrow stairways that twisted up the mountain towards the Schloss, between high stone walls and half-timbered houses. They are almost certainly the troupe in Wilhelmsburg Castle in the tiny town of Schmalkalden earlier in the summer. A company of English comedians would not normally visit such a poor town, well away from the trade routes, but Landgrave Maurice was there between June and August each year for the annual *Hirschessen* (a great feast of venison), and this is most likely when the arrangements for their winter visit to Kassel were made. By the end of November they were in Kassel performing at Maurice's court, possibly arriving in time to see the pillars of fire, mountains of flame and thousands of 'firespitting rockets' that made up a pyrotechnic display in celebration of his son Otto's christening.

This was the first time we have a record of Landgrave Maurice hosting English players, though his kinsman the Duke of Brunswick had hired Browne's men as early as 1592, and as Kassel was on the way from Frankfurt to Brunswick's seat, comedians may have stopped over before. Unlike the Duke, who penned plays that were 'beyond measure obscene and full of the lowest terms of abuse', Maurice 'the Learned' of Hesse was a paragon among princes, renowned for his learning and high culture. Edward Monings, arriving in the train of Lord Hunsdon, who was sent as ambassador to the court of Hesse in 1596, describes him as 'a goodly personage, of stature tall and stra[i]ght for his proportion, of a good presence and a gallant countenance, manly visaged, with a faire big blacke eye, deepe aburne haire, comlie in behaviour, gratious and persuasive in speach'. He was a hearty drinker (getting so mightily intoxicated on a visit to Spandau, that he and his servants could barely find the city gate), with an arched brow and lips that seemed constantly at work suppressing an explosion of laughter. Yet he was also known for his gravity and wide knowledge, was a good composer in his own right, played the organ well, and (rare among his contemporaries) spoke fluent English, as well as French and Italian.

Maurice the Learned had a five-storey castle, 'like the Louvre in Paris, hie and statelie', with a large upper hall, 'a very curious roome, made no doubt of purpose to entertaine strange Princes, all of marble, the doores, the flower [floor], the sides, windowes, roofe, and all things pertinent, being of carved gray marble'. In winter, the marble had to be kept continuously hot, to prevent it from cracking and loosening, and the hall made a warm, convivial indoor theatre. Playing indoors seems to have alerted Kit to the power of night scenes, which begin to be a feature of his plays (though in the open-air London theatres, where performances took place in the afternoon, they would have lacked impact). The players seem to have inspired Maurice in turn – within a few years he would have his own theatre, on the English model, the first purpose-built theatre in Germany.

By the time Brodribb's troupe arrived in Kassel, John Dowland was already 'plying marvellous eloquent music to feast the ears' of Maurice's court. Meeting Dowland would give Kit's thinking, and his work, a new direction. The musician was a melancholy man – a 'humour' much in vogue with artists and intellectuals at the time, but in his case it was a genuine and at times intense depression. Later, Kit would affectionately make light of him in the character of Jaques in *As You Like It*, a man who can 'suck melancholy out of a song, as a weasel sucks eggs', and who has 'a melancholy of [his] own compounded of many simples, extracted from many objects', one of these being 'the sundry contemplation of [his] travels' – ruminations that wrap him in sadness (II iv 13; IV i 15–18).

When they first met, Dowland's mood was a match for Kit's own despair. His music offered a means of expressing it. John Dowland was beginning to write highly innovative 'ayres', which occupied a middle ground between recitative and Italian aria (essentially the same word). He took the twangs and scrapes of the background accompaniment to recitative, and transformed them into music that fused so singly with the words of his songs that the shades and shapes and colours became one, like burnished walnut wood. His airs were not narrative, but poised moments of contemplation, solo musings that perfectly crystallised a mood, or enfolded a thought. They are the difference between the long bombastic speeches in Kit's earlier plays and the complex, sophisticated soliloquies of *Hamlet*.

Kit's voice enchanted Dowland, and the pair worked closely

that winter. One of the songs they wrote together, perhaps the most famous, encapsulates (like Sonnet 29) Kit's sense of exile and shame:

> Flow, my tears, fall from your springs!
>   Exiled for ever let me mourn;
> Where night's black bird her sad infamy sings,
>   There let me live forlorn.

> Down, vain lights, shine you no more!
>   No nights are dark enough for those
> That in despair their lost fortunes deplore.
>   Light doth but shame disclose.

In one verse, Kit appears to pun rather sadly on his new name: 'From the *highest spire* of contentment/My fortune is thrown'. The biographer Diana Poulton detects the same hand in the lyrics of 'Flow, my tears' as in some other Dowland songs, such as 'In darknesse let me dwell', pointing to a number of verbal parallels, and to the idea of hell as not so much a place of fire and torment, but of blackness and perpetual night. That idea runs through many of Kit's other works – 'That his soul may be as damn'd and black/As hell . . .' (*Hamlet* III iii 94–5); 'though ignorance were as dark as hell' (*Twelfth Night* IV ii 45); 'In hell-black night endured' (*Lear* III vii 59); 'as black as hell, as dark as night' (Sonnet 147), and so on. Poulton also points out that the song 'Farewell unkind farewell', which expresses the sentiments of a young girl who has eloped from home taking her father's fortune, parallels perfectly the situation in *The Merchant of Venice*, down to the apposite line; 'Love, not in the blood [i.e. her Jewish blood], but in the spirit doth lie'.

Before the winter's end, Kit had disappeared off Brodribb's payroll, and from the court at Kassel. Exactly why he did this, or where he went, is not clear. The most likely explanation is that someone arrived in Kassel who might recognise him – there was significant traffic between Maurice's court and London. A sadder possibility is that he feared John Dowland might betray him to Sir Robert Cecil. It is hard to imagine Kit's working so intensely with someone, and not feeling tempted to reveal who he was, and it is not improbable that Dowland was in contact with Cecil during his stay at Kassel – Cecil had signed Dowland's passport, and a year later Dowland felt the need to write a contradictory, panic-stricken letter to the privy councillor, dis-associating himself from the treasonable activities of English Catholics in Italy.

There is a further, more intriguing, possibility – that Kit tem-porarily resumed his former profession of spying. Germany was a welter of petty principalities that were already beginning to polarise into a largely western Protestant Union and a Catholic League, centred on Bavaria in the south. Landgrave Maurice, despite his merry-making and fondness for theatre, was moving from Lutheranism towards a stricter Calvinism. By 1604, the people of Hesse would be smashing 'dumb idols' and graven images, with Germany edging closer to the internecine destruc-tion of the Thirty Years War. Even in the mid-1590s, it is not unlikely that Maurice needed an ear in the courts of some of his southern neighbours.

Early in 1595, there are reports of 'Walter, a Fleming', who is 'a melancholic singer and bitter foole', dispensing verbal birchings to delighted aristocrats all the way from Würzburg to Vienna.* It would have been quite possible for such an itinerant entertainer also to dispatch coded letters back to Landgrave Maurice. A jester's motley would not have settled easily on proud

---

* Zelle, *Bare Truth*, pp. 232–6.

Kit, and if this is him, it perhaps explains the acid streak that runs through many of his stage fools. Touchstone, Feste, the Fool in *King Lear* and Lavatch in *All's Well That Ends Well*, all have the bitterness of the scholar reduced to earning his bread by clowning.

Walter, the 'bitter foole', quickly disappears from gossip and court records, and within a month one 'Hooghius' arrives to lodge with the librarian of the Imperial Library in Vienna, the ageing Doctor Hugo Blotz.* 'Blotius', as he was known, was a scholarly and amiable Dutchman (though perhaps he and Hooghius spoke Latin) not averse to taking in financially straitened, intelligent travellers as lodgers. The roving, and at times blue-plumed, soon-to-be-ambassador to Venice, Sir Henry Wotton, had spent some time under Blotius's roof four years earlier. Hooghius occupied the same comfortable chambers, adjoining the former Minorite monastery where the library was housed. His private study opened directly into the library, and he had access not only to its 9,000 volumes, but also to Dr Blotius's personal collection, which included a copy of Holinshed's chronicles of England (a similar edition to the one Kit had had to leave behind in Antwerp). The rent was the same as Wotton had paid – two florins a week for chamber, stove, table and lights, with ample wine. Hooghius and Blotius spent many a convivial evening discussing Ovid and the Greeks, and arguing about war, rebellion and the rights of kings. (Blotius was an ardent advocate of unity and peace in the civil strife that was beginning to tear apart the German states.)

Hooghius's abrupt departure from Vienna is perhaps explained by a reference in the city magistrate's records in September of 1595 to a 'Walter de Hooch . . . charged to have attempted to bugger one Heinrich Engelbert and for other unlawful entry', who later escaped over the Alps to Italy, where (at least

---

* William H. Pratt, *The Doctor's Men*, p. 82.

so Protestant foreigners believed) such activities were viewed as
a something of a national pastime.* ('*Bugeria* is an Italian word',
opined the learned Justice Coke in his *Laws of England.*) Kit's dis-
taste for the attitude of minor Viennese officials towards sexual
licence is evident in *Measure for Measure*. He was never to return.

In Italy, a possible false trail appears. In the late 1890s, a
Scots Jesuit called Father Hugh MacLennan, while research-
ing the life of the eccentric and sometimes extravagantly men-
dacious seventeenth-century poet, essayist and biographer Sir
Thomas Urquhart, uncovered mention of 'a second Admirable
Crichton', active in Italy in 1596 and 1597.[†] This, of course,
refers not to the castaway manservant of J. M. Barrie's 1902 play,
but to a successor to the original Admirable Crichton, James
Crichton of Cluny, whose multifarious talents astonished courtiers and learned men all over northern Italy, before his death
in a brawl in Mantua in 1582, at the age of twenty-two. Sir
Thomas Urquhart was this Admirable Crichton's first biographer, but between Crichton's own self-invention, the legend that
grew around him, and Urquhart's less than strict adherence to
the tiresome strictures of truth (he once claimed to have traced
his own family tree back to Adam) the facts of his life are sometimes hard to discern.

Born into a good Scottish family, young James Crichton nevertheless found himself penniless, so set about earning handsome
reward in Genoa, Venice, Padua and Mantua by flashy displays
of swordsmanship, excellent dancing and acrobatics, champion
jousting, and dangerous feats of horse-breaking. He conversed
in ten languages, debated theology, science and philosophy with
the best minds of the time (and won), and produced 'unpre-
meditated and beautiful' extempore Latin poetry, which he

---

* Quoted in Pratt, *Doctor's Men*, p. 95.
† Fr Hugh MacLennan, *A Roman in the Gloamin': Sir Thomas Urquhart
and the Decline of Scottish Catholicism*, p. 23 ff.

would then proceed to recite backwards, just for effect. His sudden death – most likely at the hands of the Duke of Mantua himself, in jealousy over a shared mistress – fanned the flames of an already blazing fame. Poems in his name continued to appear for two or three years after his 'death' in Mantua, and there was talk of 'Crichton, The Survivor'. Father MacLennan seems to have stumbled upon a revival of this myth of a revenant, recurring some ten years later – or simply on an impostor. This 'Second Admirable Crichton' not only extemporised 'silver-tongued' verses, but improvised on stage, wrote comedies for courtiers, seduced ladies, was 'audacious and nimble' and a 'roguish mimick'. He is sometimes known as Gualtiero l'Alto (a literal translation of Walter de Hoogh). So it is tempting to see him as Kit. He certainly had Kit's style (or that of a much reinvigorated Kit), and the feats of the original Admirable Crichton would surely have been known to Kit, who was in Padua with Oliver Laurens just a few years after Crichton's well-publicised Mantua brawl. But this resurrected Crichton is heard of as far away as Sicily, and continues to appear well into 1597, by which time Kit was back in Antwerp.

In London, meanwhile, Oliver Laurens was beginning to fret. Harry Brodribb had brought back a letter in the spring of 1595, and also the news that Walter Hooghspier had left Kassel months earlier. There had been some sonnets from Vienna, then silence. As the supply of plays dried up, Will Shakespere became increasingly difficult to deal with. Through the winter and into 1595, Oliver had passed on, one by one, the three plays he had received from Kit in 1594. Will wrote them out in his familiar hand, for sale to the Chamberlain's Men. Although he incorporated the changes that emerged in rehearsal (mainly ad-libbing by star clowns and topical spice, but also practical changes made by the players themselves), Will made no attempt to foul these papers with the scratchings and stirrings of a restive muse, but presented them with scarcely a blot. According to John Heminges and Henry Condell in their preface to the First Folio: 'His mind and hand went together, and what he thought he uttered with that easiness that we have scarce received from him a blot in his papers.' Far from permitting this to arouse suspicion, Will used it to promote the reputation of his extraordinary talent. In a passage 'concerning our Shakespeare' in his literary notebook, the playwright Ben Jonson wrote: 'I remember the Players have often mentioned it as an honour to Shakespeare that in his writing, whatsoever he penned, he never blotted out a line.' Jonson went on to say 'Would he had blotted out a thousand,' but then, as Jonathan Bate notes, the tone of most of Jonson's allusions to Will Shakespere during his lifetime was one of 'affectionate mockery'. (However, at times it was more vicious than that, as when in a rancorous epigram he labelled Shakespere a 'Poet-Ape'.) It was only after Will's death, seven years after, when he was paid to contribute an elegy to the First Folio – that Jonson wrote a poem praising him as 'Sweet Swan of Avon' and 'Soul of the Age'.

Given the swift turnaround in London theatres, the three plays Oliver had received in 1594 did not go far, and although verse-letter sonnets continued to come, Kit had stipulated that these be kept private. (Rumours of their existence did surface, perhaps through Will's conniving – Francis Meres seems to have had an inkling of something when he wrote in his *Wit's Treasury*, 1598, of Shakespere's 'sugared sonnets among his private friends'.) The drying up of the source meant that from early 1595, Will Shakespere's promising new career as a writer appeared threatened, and he was once again becoming difficult and unpleasant. His revealing the truth about Kit would not have much effect on Kit himself, but would have nasty consequences for the friends he had left behind. Oliver would have to persuade Kit to keep writing, and decided to use the opportunity of a 1595 visit to the Frankfurt book fair to travel to Vienna and speak to him. He appears also to have used a little espionage work to help finance the trip, under his old alias of William Hall – in March 1596, the Chamber Treasurer paid £15 to 'Hall and Wayte' for messages brought from the Low Countries. A surviving fragment of Oliver's journal, which appears to date from the preceding January, describes a winter crossing of the Alps, from Italy into Switzerland. Kit was with him.

Either Blotius had been at the Frankfurt fair, and knew of Kit's departure from Vienna, or Oliver travelled to Vienna after the fair, only to find his friend had flown. Given the lapse of time between the fair and the Alps crossing, the latter seems the most likely case. Oliver may well have suspected that Kit would be in Padua or the nearby spa town of Àbano, where he could indulge his weakness for the waters and where he stood less chance of meeting someone he knew. What remains of Oliver's journal picks up the journey farther west, on Lake Como – but this does not necessarily provide a clue to Kit's earlier whereabouts, as this was en route to a pass that was good for a winter crossing, and one not much frequented by English travellers. The pair travelled as Netherlanders from the Spanish-occupied south. Oliver's sometime guise as a Frenchman (one also favoured by Fynes Moryson) would have been inadvisable, as by now France was at war with Spain, and the Duke of Milan, through whose territory they were passing, was sympathetic to the Spanish. They appear to have had a rough passage across Lake Como, and to have been forced ashore during a storm, onto the island of Comacina – a wild, forested, rocky isle that had the reputation of being haunted. Some see Comacina as inspiring the setting for Prospero's enchanted island in *The Tempest*. In the Middle Ages it had indeed been a refuge for the occasional dethroned monarch or misunderstood holy man; its nine churches were later sacked and the island depopulated.

From Lake Como they took a stagecoach into thick forest and up the Bregaglia valley, through villages where houses were painted in splendid patterns, their bright colours glinting in the hard winter light, past frozen waterfalls and a creaking glacier to Casaccia, at the foot of the Septimer pass. The Septimer had been built by the Romans, was at a fairly low altitude, and was not quite as treacherous as some other routes, where sometimes stakes were set in the snow, a spear's length apart, 'to guide the Passinger his dangerous way, of the which stoopes if hee faile, he is lost for ever', and where wayside mortuaries were set up to preserve the more hapless wayfarers in snow. Fynes Moryson had heard of people being conveyed on sleds, when 'sometimes it happens, that in a turning or winding way, the sledge whereon the passenger sits, is cast out of the way, and hangs downe into a most deepe valley, with the passengers head downewards and heeles upward'.

Oliver and Kit had no such terrors ahead. Contrary to what one might expect, current travel advice was that 'the fittest time to passe the Alpes, are the Winter moneths, when no snow is newly fallen, and the old snow is hard congealed'. They set out with two guides and a small party from Casaccia, wearing boots studded with nails, and each with a mule which they sometimes led, and otherwise rode, one hand on the mane, the other on the saddle, face bent low over its neck. The first part of the pass was rocky, and extraordinarily steep: 'a Staircase!' wrote Oliver, 'slippery and Excessive cold, a smart hill and every inch as surly as we had expected from its rugged brow'. At the top they were enveloped in mist, but then the mountains changed from 'rough great Text [capitals] to a faire running hand', and the descent was much easier. They emerged from the cloud, 'and fell as it were out of the skyes on a place called Bivio'.* From here, Kit began the long, cold journey back to Antwerp.

---

* Rosine, *Oliver Laurens*, p. 322. The traveller Richard Lassels had a similar crossing in the 1660s.

CHAPTER FOURTEEN

Renaissance Man

Oliver slipped back into the United Provinces, no doubt to meet up with his fellow courier William Wayte and collect whatever correspondence it was that the pair carried to London in order to receive their £15 payment in March. Curiously, in November that year William Wayte petitioned in a suit for sureties of the peace against Will Shakespere, '*ob metum mortis*' – 'for fear of death' – an unsolved riddle which appears to indicate that he, too, was exposed to the poseur's unpleasantness.

Oliver took with him to England Kit's sole output for the previous two years, the play we now know as *King Henry IV Part I*, and *The Merry Wives of Windsor*, a farce of some gusto that shows every sign of being based on a piece written for Brodribb and his company. The play refers to the knighting of a 'Duke de Jarmany' [Germany] (IV 3 and IV 5), in reality Maurice's neighbour, the Duke of Württemberg, who was petitioning Queen Elizabeth to be admitted to the Order of the Garter at the time. The story that Queen Elizabeth so enjoyed a performance of *Henry IV* that she requested a play 'showing Falstaff in love', which Shakespere produced in ten days, is pure myth. There is absolutely no evidence to support the tradition. (Nor, incidentally, is Falstaff really in love in the play.) Though if the story were true, Will would have had no difficulty in speedily producing a play that had already been written. In the event, Kit's timing was unwittingly bad, as this knockabout comedy appeared as the first play Shakespere wrote after the death of his infant son Hamnet.

Very little of *The Merry Wives* is in verse, which perhaps reflects the influence of the tubby old trouper Brodribb's pithy prose. Although Kit had been the first, in *Tamburlaine,* to popularise drama in blank verse, he was also an innovator in mingling prose with poetry in his plays. Up until his time, drama had been almost entirely in verse. A manuscript in prose is easier to alter, and this is the first play in which Will Shakespere dared insert his own lines – a practice that was to so enrage Kit as time went on, but one that he was powerless to stop. The indefatigable scholar Leslie Hotson has argued that the foolish character of Justice Shallow in *The Merry Wives* is based on William Wayte's stepfather, who was also embroiled in the suit against Shakespere, which if true would indicate Will's vengeful hand in the first scene of the play.

Will Shakespere was intent, as the biographer Katherine Duncan-Jones puts it, on seeking 'worldly recognition on the world's terms'. He wanted not merely fame as a poet, but irrefutable social status, and had 'a larger plan to turn himself into a gentleman'. This quest became more urgent when it appeared that the supply of plays from Kit was drying up. Will set about acquiring a coat of arms, then securing (with the purchase of New Place in Stratford in 1597) a suitable residence on which to display it. Both these moves were expensive – especially buying the patent for a coat of arms on absurdly fragile grounds, from a distinctly dubious official – raising the suspicion that some sort of blackmail of Tom Walsingham was again involved. Income from the plays at this point would not have been sufficient, though Will did display a coldly astute business sense in managing the money he had, purchasing shares in the Chamberlain's Men and later in the Globe theatre, dodging taxes, and hoarding grain at a time of famine in Stratford. His 10 percent share of takings at the Globe would alone eventually earn him several hundred pounds a year, a considerable fortune.

The coat of arms he designed was supremely tacky, wildly over-detailed (including a falcon shaking a spear) and almost entirely covered in gold and silver, itself a considerable expense, as ordinary colours were much cheaper when it came to making the escutcheon. The motto – in medieval French, to imply ancient lineage – was *'Non sanz droict'* ('not without right'), which Ben Jonson wickedly sent up as 'Not without Mustard' in *Every Man out of his Humour*, in which Sogliardo, a country bumpkin, is ludicrously proud of his new, highly coloured coat of arms with a crest depicting 'a boar without a head, rampant' and silly motto – the 'mustard' was probably a reference to the excess of gold leaf in Shakespere's arms. Kit, too, could not resist a stab at Will's pomposity, in the character of the foolish, socially over-weening Malvolio, who is so enjoyably humiliated in *Twelfth Night*. As Duncan-Jones demonstrates, Malvolio's cross-gartered yellow stockings visibly mimicked the Shakespere coat of arms, an effect that must have been 'exquisitely ridiculous' as Malvolio, a firm believer that 'Some are born great, some achieve great-ness, and some have greatness thrust upon 'em' (II v 158), gets his comeuppance – and especially so if (as is quite possible) Will himself had to play the part.

Kit's journeys had purged him of his melancholy (unlike Jaques, or John Dowland), and his return to Antwerp was effected with ease. The Alleman family seem to have held no hard feelings against him, and to have kept his possessions safe, and within a month or two he was settled back in his old chambers. Pieter Bellerus, his former employer, was less forgiving, however. There is no record of Kit's having rejoined the firm. Oliver notes that

Kit instead took up work as a proofreader with Bellerus's rivals at the 'Gulden Passer', the famed publishing house of Christophe Plantin. This is quite feasible, though difficult to verify. Plantin was dead, and the company was now in the hands of his son-in-law, Jan Moretus. Both Moretus and Plantin are known to have employed freelance workers to help translate or rewrite texts, and to assist in some of the tasks of proofreading; but, unlike his predecessor, Jan Moretus did not record their names in his *livres des ouvriers* unless their work or pay was for some reason out of the ordinary. Kit may also have received books in lieu of pay – Plantin remunerated some authors in this way.

Proofreading was a high-status job, done by top scholars and graduates. At the Plantin-Moretus press readers had to be competent in a range of languages to cope with multilingual texts, so Kit certainly had the required skills – and he did develop a detailed knowledge of printing. At a lecture at the Stationers' Hall in 1933, Captain W. Jaggard (a descendant of the printers of the First Folio) presented some 500 quotations, from *All's Well* through to *The Winter's Tale*, as evidence of the author's specialist knowledge of printers' trade expressions, technical words and workshop habits.

At the Gulden Passer, each permanent proofreader was assigned to check the output of three presses, though at busy times even family members helped out. Plantin's daughters are known to have done so, and his grandson Christophe (in a letter describing his 'occupations for this day', written one icy winter as punishment for being 'proud, stubborn and wilful') reveals he was sulky about having to read proofs of *Libellus Sodalitus* with his cousin Raphelingius. Young Christophe was probably acting as a *lector*, reading aloud while his cousin was *corrector*. The proof-readers usually worked in tandem, and the mood in their room (which was kept warm, but not so as to cause drowsiness, with sloping desks hard up against the windows) was convivial, and enlivened by educated banter – perhaps at times a little too jolly. Strict rules, written in Latin in Jan Moretus's hand, demanded of proof-readers that 'they do not laugh when in very large type, not only letters but entire phrases have been omitted', and warn that 'drunkenness must be carefully avoided; it is like a shameful illness, and very bad for the body and for the eyes'.

Kit would surely have enjoyed working with the proof-readers, and he was certainly in the Moretus milieu. This is evident from a fragment of a letter, recently discovered on the reverse side of a pen sketch (attributed to the young Rubens) when it was removed from the frame it had occupied since the late seventeenth century.* Dated November 1597, the letter identifies the figures in the drawing as 'Hooghius, Lipsius and his dog Mopsus', and begins to quote part of a public dialogue between Hooghius and Lipsius. Mopsus was indeed the much-loved pet of the humanist philosopher Justus Lipsius (Joest Lips). Peter Paul Rubens, who turned twenty that year, was a boyhood friend of Jan Moretus's son Balthazar, and did sometimes illustrate his letters with sketches. Balthazar had once been Lipsius's amanuensis. The scholar's books were published by the Plantin-Moretus press, where he was often resident. And Hooghius and Lipsius had much to talk about.

Lipsius was the world expert on Seneca and Tacitus. In 1591, he had left his long-held post at the University of Leiden to move back to the Spanish Netherlands, taking up a professorship in Leuven (Louvain) near Antwerp, where he took in a number of 'contubernales' (live-in students). His relationship with his publisher went beyond a simple business arrangement. He had been close friends with Christophe Plantin, and after Plantin died, became increasingly friendly with Jan Moretus, becoming in a sense resident author at the Gulden Passer, with his own study. When Plantin's widow died in August of 1596, Moretus moved from his house on the Kammerstraat into larger premises

---

* Now held in a private collection.

at the Gulden Passer, and very soon invited Lipsius to visit. Lipsius had reluctantly declined as he had six contubernales to look after (his reply exists, though not Moretus's original invitation). It would appear from Rubens's sketch and letter fragment that Lipsius later took up the offer, and a gap in his correspondence with Moretus between October 1597 and January 1598 indicates he was in situ at the Gulden Passer.

His study was an intimate room on an inner courtyard, hung with a tapestry depicting 'Proud Cleopatra when she met her Roman on the swelling river Cyndus', and lined with embossed leather (though not the priceless sixteenth-century *guadamacil* – gilt leather from Cordoba – that is there today. This was moved from another room in the late seventeenth century). 'Hooghius' and Lipsius, perhaps with Mopsus at their feet in his collar with gold stitching, talked long of Tacitus, Plutarch and Seneca. Kit had read Plutarch in both Greek and in English (in Sir Thomas North's influential 1579 translation, one of the books he had brought from England), but knew Seneca in Latin. *Tamburlaine* and *Titus Andronicus*, and to some extent *Richard III* all bear the stamp of Seneca's bloodthirsty, ghost-ridden tragedies, and the power of Kit's blank verse owes much to what T. S. Eliot called 'the solemnity and weight of the Senecan iambic'.

Lipsius reawakened Kit's interest in classical Rome. *Julius Caesar* was one of two plays Oliver took back with him after a visit in late 1598.* The other was *Much Ado About Nothing* (the second part of *Henry IV* had probably been sent through Jacques Ghibbes's illicit courier service, though no record exists). Kit relied heavily on Sir Thomas North's translation of Plutarch as a source for *Julius Caesar*, at times rather lazily taking over entire passages, much as he would do with his later Roman plays. On that visit Oliver brought Kit a copy of *Hero and Leander*, published 'posthumously' under Kit's own name by their mutual

---

* Rosine, *Oliver Laurens*, p. 354.

friend Edward Blount, with a dedication (addressed to Tom Walsingham) that mentions Kit as a 'man that hath been dear to us, living an after-life in our memory'. Blount himself would feature in a more curious dedication a year later, in Kit's new translation of Lucan's *Pharsalia*, which was published by Oliver's employer in London, Thomas Thorpe:

> Blount, I purpose to be blunt with you, and out of my dullness to encounter you with a dedication in the memory of that pure elemental wit, Christopher Marlow, whose ghost or genius is to be seen walking in the Churchyard in at least three or four sheets.
>
> Methinks you should presently look wild now, and grow humourously frantic upon the test of it.

Thorpe's reference is to the Stationers of St Paul's Churchyard, with a pun on ghostly winding sheets and sheets of paper, but there is here perhaps the first clue that he knew (or at least suspected) the truth, in the hint that Blount (to be blunt) if he 'tested' this ghost would 'grow humourously frantic' (become wildly excited) by what he found.

Kit's revival of interest in Lucan (who was Seneca's nephew) and the epic *Pharsalia* may well have been a result of his friendship with Lipsius, or simply an exercise to keep his working Latin up to scratch. As it was well known that Will Shakespere had 'small Latin and less Greek', the work obviously could not be passed off as his, so it became another 'posthumous' publication. A number of early works already known to a wider public as Kit's were published around this time, but there is no record of who benefited financially. It is to be hoped that Kit did see some of the money, as he was in sore need of it. He was scraping by in economically depressed Antwerp, and producing little in the way of English plays to supplement his income.

Although Kit was beginning to write again by the end of

1598, his first two years back in Antwerp had been relatively unproductive, perhaps because of the unfamiliarity of working without a theatre company at hand. He had bombarded Southampton with sonnets, urging him to take his guardian Lord Burghley's advice and marry, and had come up with a sequel to *Henry IV*, but very little else. In an attempt to consolidate his position, Will Shakespere had not only made himself into a gentleman, but was continuing (despite the flop of *Love's Labour's Won*) to put out his own work – a second-rate city-comedy called *The London Prodigal*, which was registered in 1598, and an anthology of stolen poems (including one or two of Kit's sonnets) published as *The Passionate Pilgrim* in 1599, with his name on the title page. Even more cheekily it included Kit's poem 'The Passionate Shepherd to His Love', which had been popular as a song (though not published) long before 1593.

News of this irked Kit less than the knowledge that Shakespere was altering the plays he sent over to London without truly comprehending them. Kit felt impotent, anonymous and ill understood. Later he would accuse Will of 'dulling my lines, doing me disgrace' (Sonnet 103). He wryly alludes to the situation (and to his 'death' in Deptford) in *As You Like It* (III iii 9): 'When a man's verses cannot be understood . . . it strikes a man more dead than a great reckoning in a little room.' This would have been very much an in-joke as, it may be remembered, '*le recknynge*' formed no part of contemporary accounts of Kit's 'death' at Deptford and was only to be found in the inquest report (rediscovered by Leslie Hotson in 1925), so the allusion would have meant little to those not in the know. It is spoken by the court fool Touchstone, who later thoroughly confuses a poor yokel called William, from the Forest of Arden (which was in Warwickshire, near Stratford). Touchstone is married to Audrey, a country girl, by a vicar called Sir Oliver Mar-text whose shortened name (Ol Mar) can be turned into Marlo. Calvin

Hoffman sees the marriage as an allegory: Mar-text (Marlowe's text) marries Touchstone (Marlowe) to Audrey (the Elizabethan audience), dismissing William the rustic from Arden. That would perhaps be wishful thinking on Kit's part, but whatever the interpretation of this intricate set of references, it is clear that Kit is rather acidly making a point.

In addition to their interest in classical culture, Kit and Lipsius shared a passion (and perhaps a need) for healing waters. On at least on occasion, in July of 1599, they travelled together to the baths at Spa, a few days journey south-east of Antwerp. Pliny the Elder had known of the medicinal properties of the mineral springs there, and in the course of the sixteenth century, Spa had become a fashionable resort (subsequently contributing its name generically to thermal baths the world over). King Henry VIII was an early visitor, and the baths were much frequented by aristocrats and intellectuals. Vincenzo Gonzaga, the Duke of Mantua, was there that summer, ostensibly to heal a sore on his leg, but mainly to cock a diplomatic snook at the Spanish, who had refused him the Governorship of Flanders, partly on a pleasure tour, and – it transpired – also on something of a culture-raid. By the time he left for Italy in the autumn (having also visited Brussels and Antwerp) he had recruited to his court in Mantua the man reputed to be the best portrait painter in Europe, Franz Pourbus; he had also lured south Peter Paul Rubens (a promising but obscure young artist whose only known work hung in his mother's house); and one of the musicians travelling in his retinue, Claudio Monteverdi, had (according to his brother Giulio Cesare Monteverdi) picked up a new style of song, 'canto alla francese', for Mantuan import. At the end of 1599 Pourbus and Rubens were preparing to leave Antwerp, Peter Paul's brother Philip Rubens was already at the University of Padua, and Lipsius was planning to travel to Rome. (He had been invited there for Holy Year 1600, though later abruptly changed his mind.) Kit decided to join this migration south. He was thirty-five (in full Elizabethan middle-age), had always loved Italy, and had himself been given an invitation by the duke to join his court, as a singer. What is more, his artistic life had reached a crux.

When Oliver Laurens visited Antwerp one last time, to try to dissuade Kit from leaving, Kit had given him a play that he had been working on and reworking for years. It was a tragedy, one that would mark him as 'the alchemist of eloquence' – a transmuter of thought and emotion into verbal gold, who had distilled his isolation and despair, his own confrontation with killing, into purest poetry and brilliant theatre. The play was *Hamlet*. His old script, written in Elsinore and stolen back from Robert Browne, had been transformed by the lessons in prose he had learned from Harry Brodribb and the perceptions into soliloquy he had been given by John Dowland and lifted to another level entirely by the trauma of Deptford, and the anguish of the years that followed. Anthony Holden writes:

> The dizzying display of poetry and philosophy, wit and insight, finds its central focus in one man, one very mortal man, perhaps the most complex creation in literary history, in whom every subsequent generation has found multiple reflections of itself . . . As [*Hamlet*] lurches from comedy to tragedy, high art to low, violence to stillness, love to hatred, confusion to redemption, it tells the story of Everyman as never before or since, distilling as much individual and collective experience as can be contained in one frail, confused man of action, a poet-philosopher confronting all our own everyday problems while trying to solve one none of us will ever have to face.

Hamlet marked a shift in Kit's psychological and aesthetic bedrock, and sent out the tremors that made new ground for the creation of *Macbeth, Othello* and *King Lear*. The critic Frank Kermode writes of 'a new inwardness, almost independent of dramatic necessity', noting that the years 1599–1600 marked a time when a poet who was already the author of several masterpieces 'moved up to a new level of achievement and difficulty'. With *Hamlet* something fundamental had changed. Kit's earlier plays had been closely interrelated – the structure of *Richard II* and *Edward II* is identical; *The Merchant of Venice* grew out of *The Jew of Malta,* and at times he even quotes himself in subsequent works. Compare 'Holla ye pamper'd jades of Asia!/ What, can ye draw but twenty miles a day' (2 *Tamburlaine* IV iii 1–2) and 'hollow pamper'd jades of Asia,/ Which cannot go but thirty miles a day' (2 *Henry IV* II iv 155–6); or Sir Hugh Evans singing 'To shallow rivers, to whose falls/Melodious birds sing madrigals; There will we make our beds of roses,/ And a thousand fragrant posies', which (excuses made for the odd mistake and his Welsh pronunciation of 'beds') is from Kit's earlier poem *The Passionate Shepherd to his Love* (*Merry Wives* II i 15–18, and *Passionate Shepherd* 7–10).

Now, on the eve of his move over the Alps, the only play he ever set in northern Europe heralded a departure on more than one level.

~⚬~

Since 1593, life for Kit had been purely a matter of survival; now it was something he valued. Completing *Hamlet* had made him acutely aware of his own mortality – or ephemerality. To his peers and posterity, he was voiceless and invisible. Will Shakespere's posturing was risible, the changes he made to Kit's work infuriating, but it was he whose name would live on, while 'Chrisopher Marlowe' would forever be associated with a brawl at Deptford, and a few early works. After *Hamlet*, Kit valued his art, and his abilities, quite differently. Attached to the manuscript was a sonnet for Will Shakespere. It was a moving admission that whichever of them died first ('Or [whether] I shall live your epitaph to make,/Or you survive when I in earth am rotten'), Kit's pen would make the name Shakespere immortal, *his* verse would be Shakespere's monument, and as spoken drama it would even live on 'in the mouths of men', while all Kit could expect was to be forgotten in 'a common grave':

> Or I shall live your epitaph to make,
> Or you survive when I in earth am rotten;
> From hence your memory death cannot take,
> Although in me each part will be forgotten.
> *Your* name from hence immortal life shall have,
> Though I, once gone, to all the world must die;
> The earth can yield me but a common grave,
> When you entombed in men's eyes shall live.
> Your monument shall be *my* gentle verse,
> Which eyes not yet created shall o'er-read;
> And tongues to be, your being shall rehearse,
> When all the breathers of this world are dead,
>   *You* still shall live (such virtue hath my pen)
>   Where breath most breathes, even in the mouths of men.
> (Sonnet 81) [my italics]

On 8 May 1600, after the burgomaster of Antwerp had issued documents certifying that the travellers were in good health and the city was free of plague, Kit joined the party of Peter Paul Rubens to set off across the Alps, on horseback to Mantua.

CHAPTER FIFTEEN

Under the Mask

The band that left Antwerp in May travelled first to Cologne, then up the Rhine. At Strasbourg, Rubens inexplicably branched off to Paris, a loss which did not leave Kit particularly crestfallen. The young painter had displayed a monstrous arrogance, and had proved to be a taxing travelling companion. Although he was but a bright-eyed unknown, initially employed merely as a copyist, he boasted that he had himself 'chosen my Lord the Duke as patron'. He was full of the superior wonders of Italy (a country he had not yet visited), disdained his fellow Flemings, and kept correcting Kit's Italian. Kit had, anyway, always been friendlier with the Brueghels. Perhaps, also, Rubens's pride and ambition was a little too close a reminder of the callow Kit Marlin who had roistered through Cambridge two decades earlier. Rubens's posturing was made even more irksome by a smug urbanity, a facile social grace that he had honed while a pageboy to the Countess de Lalaing. The rest of the party pushed on to the Alps without him. He finally deigned to appear in Mantua nearly a year later.

In a letter back to Antwerp, one of the travellers records his delight and astonishment at his first view of Italy, which seemed to happen in an instant, as they rounded a corner at the top of a pass. The light seemed sharper, the sky higher. Before them lay 'the paradise to gain which we have suffered the purgatory

of these uncouth mountains, fair Italy, the fount of learning'.*
Sunlight soaked the plains of Lombardy. The way ahead looked
daunting, dramatic and alluring. They rode down through the
foothills, some to Venice, others towards Mantua.

The ducal city of Mantua was an island, flanked by four glittering lakes that reflected its towers and spires and the pinkish
yellow of its sandstone and brick. Bending reeds and perfumed
lily-beds crowded the marshes on the lakes' far edges, beyond
which lay 'whole *Forests* of *Olive-trees*, whole woods of *Lemmons*,
and *Oranges*, whole fields of *Rice, Turky wheat* and *Muskmillions*'.
The seasoned traveller Thomas Coryate was enraptured by the
'abundance of goodly meadows, pastures, orchards and gardens'
around the lakes, which supplied Mantua's markets with a profusion of 'delectable fruites' and 'odoriferous flowers'. He
enthused that 'this most sweet Paradise . . . did even so ravish
my senses, and tickle my spirits with such inward delight that I
said unto my selfe, this is the Citie which of all other places in
the world, I would wish to make my habitation in, and spend
the remainder of my dayes . . .' (were it not, of course, for the
unfortunate presence of grossly idolatrous Catholics).

Mantua was reached through what Kit had once called 'fruitful Lombardy,/The pleasant garden of great Italy' (*The Taming
of the Shrew* I i 3–4), or by sailboat along waterways that led as
far as Venice and Milan. In a sense, the entire duchy was an
island – independent of the Spanish, not subservient to Venice,
uncowed by the Pope, and protected by politic marriages against
unfriendly inroads from its neighbours. Though strategically
important, Mantua was not particularly powerful; and though
prosperous, it stood economically in Venice's shadow. Duke
Vincenzo smarted a little at his lack of military might and dwin-
dling financial influence, and compensated by making Mantua
pre-eminent in the arts.

---

* Quoted in Roy Delbont, *Travellers' Tales*, p. 212.

Vincenzo's Gonzaga forebears had been tasteful and pro-
digious builders, and had amassed a magnificent collection of
some of the leading painters of the Renaissance. In 1588 the
Venetian ambassador Francesco Contarini had marvelled at
Mantua's 'wealth of many beautiful and great palaces' and (with
a Venetian's envy) at its spacious streets, which were 'long and
wondrously straight'; and the sixteenth-century art historian
Giorgio Vasari was full of praise for the city's adornments.
Vincenzo added to the artworks, buying startling new paintings
by the young Caravaggio, cornering the services of Pourbus, and
spotting the talent of Peter Paul Rubens. A Raphael Madonna
belonging to the Count of Canossa had so bewitched him that
he handed over an entire estate – land, castle, title, rent, and
all – in exchange. He collected intaglios and cameos, and commissioned jewellers, goldsmiths and silversmiths from across
the world. His beneficence was not confined to the plastic arts.
In 1586 he had rescued the poet Tasso from a madhouse in
Ferrara, and offered him succour for the rest of his life. Claudio
Monteverdi played in his private orchestra, and in 1601 became
his *maestro di cappella.*

Most of all, Vincenzo loved the theatre. The court troupe
was renowned throughout Italy, and its chief actor Tristano
Martinelli was the greatest Arlecchino (Harlequin) of his day.
So jealous was Vincenzo of his performers' talent, that he rarely
gave permission for wandering companies to perform in
Mantua. (This was lucky for Kit, as his former colleague Will
Kempe had left the Lord Chamberlain's Men, and after morris
dancing from London to Norwich, had embarked on a tour of
Germany and Italy.) The duke adored old-fashioned spectacle
and pastorals, yet he was adventurous in his tastes and enthusiastic about new forms, especially appreciating combinations of
music and drama. Barely a day passed without a concert or
theatrical performance of some kind.

Kit could hardly have chosen a more stimulating refuge.

Padua was out of the question, as it contained too many people he knew, and by the turn of the century was swarming with Sir Robert Cecil's spies. Venice was similarly risky. Mantua was gratifyingly cosmopolitan, yet more popular among Flemings, Germans and the nations south of the Alps, than with the English – though the loss of the Scotsman, the Admirable Crichton, was still 'heavily bemoaned' two decades after his death.

It would appear that Kit was not directly connected with the court, but did move in its milieu. The most likely scenario is that he had taken up with the duke's musicians at Spa, and had some promise of future employment. At times he used the name Walter de Hooch, though this later became Gualtiero Stangone – an Italianisation of 'Walter Hoochspier' ('Stangone' means high pole). His Antwerp landlord, Diego Lopez Alleman, had provided him with a letter of introduction to a Mantuan Jewish family, who arranged lodgings for him near the ducal palace, on the edge of the San Pietro district – a quarter popular at the time with the Jewish community.

Mantuan Jews made up 7 percent of the city's population, and in contrast to those in Venice, were not forced to live in a ghetto. The Gonzagas had held out against three successive anti-Semitic papal bulls in the course of the sixteenth century, and Mantua became a haven for Jews fleeing from elsewhere in Europe. The contemporary annalist Joseph Hacohen says of Vincenzo that 'he favoured the Jews and spoke kindly to them', and the duke sent officials on horseback, armed with clubs, to protect Jews after a Franciscan monk named Bartholomew da Solutio had been rousing the rabble against them, demanding that Vincenzo institute a ghetto and the wearing of yellow badges. Vincenzo would finally give in to papal demands, but delayed the creation of a ghetto by drawing out negotiations with the Jewish community from 1602 to 1610. The Mantuan Jews were the last in Italy to be confined to a ghetto. Kit's experience of Mantuan Jewry would lead to his play *Jehuda*, a

development of the *Merchant of Venice.* The play is mentioned
by Oliver in 1608, but no record of a performance exists. It was
either suppressed, lost, considered too eccentric for the time,
or was a casualty of an incident in 1607 when Laurens was a
victim of a highway robbery. Aspects of *The Merchant of Venice* –
the absence of a ghetto, the fact that Jews and gentiles can social-
ise together – indicate that it was based on knowledge of the
state of affairs in Mantua rather than Venice, and hint at an
earlier visit.

The Jewish community was very much part of daily city life,
and made a strong contribution to music and theatre at court.
By the time Kit arrived in Mantua, Leone de' Sommi, the Jewish
court poet who was famed for his comedies and the lighting
effects in his productions, had died, but his plays were still popular – and some say form the basis of modern Italian comedy.
The Jewish composer Salomone Rossi, who was just a few years
younger than Kit and had been a pupil of Palestrina, had long
held a court appointment, and was an innovator in choral music
and a prolific writer of madrigals. Kit was soon singing madrigals
for Rossi, and through him re-established ties he had made at
Spa with Claudio Monteverdi.

As gaunt as if he had stepped out of a painting by El Greco,
with a thin, straying beard and a deeply melancholic air, Monteverdi was, oddly enough, almost the double of the great Arlecchino, Tristano Martinelli. They had been mistaken for each other
on at least one occasion. He was still fresh with the ideas of the
'*canto alla francese*' he had picked up in Flanders, and Kit further
inspired him by singing songs by John Dowland. Indeed, one
of the airs that Kit had worked on together with Dowland, *In
darkness let me dwell,* is strangely similar to Monteverdi's *Lament
of Arianna* (see Appendix V). A cautious working relationship
grew into close friendship, and Kit sang frequently in court
concerts. He appears in some measure to have slipped into the
hollow left by the Admirable Crichton, not only singing but

improvising verse, displaying phenomenal feats of memory, holding exuberant public disputes and writing short comedies in Italian for courtiers to play in.* Despite his obscure background, he moved into the duke's favoured circle, and could be found not only in the main Gonzaga court, but at Palazzo Te, Vincenzo's intimate pleasure-palace on its own island in the lake; and also some miles from Mantua at Sabbioneta, where Vespasiano Gonzaga, a minor scion of the family, had created a *'città ideale'*, an ideal city modelled on ancient Athens and Rome.

A legend of terror had grown around Vespasiano, who as a soldier had carried off the beautiful Diana de Cardona, but on later returning from the wars had been informed of her unfaithfulness and had murdered her gruesomely. Some critics see in this a parallel to *Othello*. In 1590, shortly before his death, Vespasiano had completed in Sabbioneta the Teatro Olimpico, an indoor theatre copied from Palladio's playhouse in Vicenza, and well ahead of its time in terms of stage design. Permanent pillars, arches and working windows receded in a contrived perspective on the playing area, and there were facilities for all manner of special effects, such as storms, magical disappearances and moving statues. At the other end of the auditorium, a loggia of Corinthian columns was crowned with sculptures of Olympian gods, which looked startlingly realistic by rushlight. The classical design of the theatre, indeed the air of ancient Athens and Rome that pervaded the whole of Sabbioneta, fed a fire in Kit's imagination that had been rekindled by Lipsius in Antwerp. His great Greek and Roman plays – *Coriolanus, Troilus and Cressida* and *Antony and Cleopatra*, as well as *Pericles* and *Timon of Athens*, were to follow. During his frequent visits to the Teatro Olimpico, he became even more powerfully aware

---

* Mentioned by Oliver Laurens in his journal, Laurens box, folder 12. Sadly, none of the comedies has survived, though it seems they were slight affairs. Kit retained his chief passion for writing in English.

of the dramatic potential of darkness, which performing indoors allowed. His first real experience of this, in Kassel, had led to the ghost scenes in *Hamlet*. Now his theatrical use of night became more subtle and sophisticated – for Duncan's murder in *Macbeth*, in the opening scenes of *Othello*, and most supremely on the stormy heath in *King Lear*.

At the Palazzo Te, Duke Vincenzo held his more private entertainments. The palace, built by Vincenzo's grandfather as a hideaway for his mistress, had been designed and covered in extraordinary frescos by Giulio Romano, the man Kit was to call 'that rare Italian master' in *The Winter's Tale*, selecting him as an artist who could feasibly fashion a statue that was so realistic one could almost believe it lived:

> . . . a piece many years in doing and now newly perform'd by that rare Italian master Julio Romano, who, had he himself eternity and could put breath into his work, would beguile nature of her custom, so perfectly he is her ape. He so near to Hermione hath done Hermione that they say one would speak to her and stand in hope of answer . . .
>
> (*The Winter's Tale* V ii 93–100)

In the play, the 'statue' of Hermione is, of course, Hermione herself. But the point of Romano's consummate artistry is made. Critics of the snickering sort are quick to point out Kit's 'mistake' in taking Romano (who is now known as a painter) for a maker of statues, but in Mantua, Romano was equally famed as architect, painter and creator of theatrical effects. His tombstone in the church of San Barbara referred to him as a master of three arts: painting, architecture and sculpture. Kit's favourite part of the Palazzo Te (he once managed to smuggle Oliver in for a look at it) was the extraordinary *Sala dei Giganti*, which depicted Jupiter's battle with the Giants. The room was round and domed, its floor covered with pebbles that made a crashing noise underfoot, which echoed in the cupola to give thunderous sound effect to the frescos. Real fires in the fireplaces appeared to burn the Giants; in the curved space perspective was completely distorted, so that the world seemed to be collapsing in on top of the spectator. The Giants themselves were terrifying. An impressed Giorgio Vasari wrote of it in 1541 that 'no one thought ever to see work of brush more horrible and frightening or more natural than this; and whoever enters in that room, seeing the windows, doors, and other such things twisted, and as if about to collapse, and the buildings falling, cannot but fear that everything will crash down upon him . . .'. The *Sala dei Giganti* shows a skilled mingling of art and reality that would have made Giulio Romano the perfect choice as the supposed sculptor of a living statue of Hermione. (The room still exists. It is one of the unsung wonders of Italy.)

Art and life melded in the Palazzo Te; so did aesthetic appreciation and lechery. Duke Vincenzo loved not only the arts, but the artistes. And with some success. As a young man he had been alluringly handsome, with fine bones, features that seemed cut in alabaster, and strong auburn hair that offset his delicate complexion. He dressed with extreme elegance, in silks, jewels and rich brocades. Now nearly forty (he was just two years older than Kit) he had grown florid with luxurious living, but he maintained his attraction to women. Though fickle, he had the reputation of being tender. Musicians and performers were drawn to him not through sycophancy, but because he showed taste and practical understanding of their art. Hurt by the failure of his military campaigns against the Turks, he threw himself with fervour into a series of extravagant passions, usually with singers and actresses, and gave himself over to good living. One Mantuan chronicler, Ludovico Muratori, described him in 1612 as a 'great gambler, a spendthrift, much taken with luxury and women, for ever engaged in new love affairs, happy pastimes, fêtes, balls, music and plays'. He was squandering his huge inheritance, and was forever losing himself in sincere but distracting amours, a man 'that loved not wisely, but too well' (*Othello* V ii 347), and perhaps a little too often. It was against this backdrop of music, generosity, longing, discovery and romance that Kit wrote his energetic, optimistic *Twelfth Night*, with perhaps more than a passing wink at Vincenzo in the infatuated Duke Orsino, with the famous opening lines: 'If music be the food of love, play on . . .'.

Kit was settled and content. A portrait from this period (of unknown origin, though not, as one might have hoped, by Rubens) shows a milder, more pensive man than the petulant rebel of the Corpus Christi painting. There is a touch of world-weariness about his eyes; the lips do not quite make it as far as a smile, but he has an air of guarded happiness. The fine, bouffant hair of his youth has thinned completely on top (he was already balding in London), but it is still long, and frizzes slightly over his ears. A gold earring in his left lobe adds a somewhat rakish dash.*

Yet Kit's new life in Italy was not all froth and spectacle. Duke Vincenzo was also at the centre of Mantuan academic circles. Although Tasso had died in 1595, Vincenzo kept up a serious literary tradition, and gave strong support to Mantua's academies. There are at least three records of a 'Gualtiero Stangone' contributing to scholarly debates.† The duke was also fascinated by discovery, and in the cellars of the ducal palace and in special apartments at the Palazzo Te, he housed a band of alchemists. In addition to their normal alchemical duties (including making gold and coming up with a potency powder for the forty-year-old duke), they were engaged in experimenting

---

* The portrait is in the private collection of Comtessa Luigina la Lollo, and bears a strong resemblance to the second image produced by the computer-ageing programme applied to the Corpus portrait (see Appendix II).
† Maria Servaes, *Cum Grano Salis*, p. 32.

with forms of early chemical weapons. Vincenzo had instructed them to make cannonballs which would release clouds of poisonous gas that would kill the enemy Turk, or at least make him fall asleep or lose his memory. Kit, who had moved through Puritanism and Catholicism, who had been accused of atheism, and had mixed with magicians, was drawn to the alchemists. His thought in this period took an interesting turn towards paganism and sorcery, an extension of the interest he had shown years earlier in the shadowy circle of the Earl of Northumberland and Sir Walter Ralegh, and one that would be reflected in plays like *King Lear, Cymbeline* and *Macbeth*.

Another shadow from Kit's past was to sharpen into reality, in the late winter of 1600/1601, when he risked a visit to Venice.

Kit's ventures to Venice were rare – though his patchy knowledge of the city did not stop him from using it as a setting for his plays. To an English audience Venice was associated with riches, greed, beauty and debauchery. Kit had the theatrical sense to exploit this, but was, at times, prepared to use the Venetian backdrop loosely – the Doge, for instance, in *Othello* and *The Merchant of Venice* is wrongly ascribed with the power of a prince. Mantua could not be used with quite the same dramatic shorthand as Venice, and setting a play in his new hometown also ran the risk of giving the game away.

But there was one time of year when Kit could walk through the city without much danger of being recognised by spies or wandering Englishmen – during the masked revels of Carnevale. Masks were worn at other festivals, but never so generally as during the days of pre-Lenten excess. Although he was writing in 1688, the traveller Maximilian Misson gives some idea of the carnival licence Kit would have encountered:

... you shall see sometimes ten or twelve Rooms on a floor, with Gaming-tables in all of 'em, crowded with Gamesters mask'd, with Courtesans and Ladies of Quality, who under this disguise have the privilege of enjoying all the Diversions of the Carnival, provided they [the ladies of quality] can get a little out of the way of their Spies or jealous Husbands. They have also certain Rooms, where they sell Liquors, Sweetmeats and suchlike things.

Everyone thus mask'd, provided he be in good Apparel, has the liberty of talking to the Ladies even of the highest Quality, no body, not even the Husband himself, taking notice at that time what is said to his Wife, because the Mask is sacred, tho' this sometimes gives occasion to an Intrigue, in a place where scarcity of Opportunity prompts them to do more with the wink of an Eye, than in other countries with long Courtship.

Gondoliers knew secret byways to the 'Waiting-women' and 'for a good Reward will furnish ladders of Cords for an Intrigue'. At this time of the year St Mark's Square was filled with puppet-players, rope-dancers and fortune tellers, and hundreds of revellers. Social barriers crumbled and Priapus rcigncd. Thc renowned Venetian courtesans had a busy time of it. Thomas Coryate estimated there were twenty thousand of them, 'whereof many are esteemed so loose, that they are said to open their quivers to every arrow'. Others were 'fragrantly perfumed', decked in gowns of damask and stockings of carnation silk, adorned with jewels and costly stones, with 'chaines of gold and orient pearle like a second *Cleopatra*'. They lived in rich palaces, and in a cultured role similar to Japanese geisha, could sing, compose sonnets and discuss Boccaccio. Kit always did have a weakness for clever women.

'Gualtiero Stangone' was one of a group of men (which could very well have included the duke, incognito) who travelled to

Venice for Carnevale in 1601.* They spent days and nights in dubious *palazzi*, gaming, singing and being sung to, eating sweet mincemeats and marzipan cakes and drinking muscat wine. It was on one of these nights that Kit noticed a woman standing apart. She was a little older than he, yet (in his words) hers was not the 'carcase of a beauty spent and done./Time had not scythed all that youth had begun,/ Nor youth all quit; but, spite of heaven's fell rage,/Some beauty peep'd through lattice of sear'd age.' (*A Lover's Complaint* 8–14). It was not until he heard her voice, and noticed her fingering a rosary of olive pips, that he realised who she was.

Venetians were renowned for their youthfulness and longevity, and though in her mid-fifties Bianca was still a striking beauty. Coryate remarked that many courtesans, having dedicated the flower of their youth to the devil, consecrated 'the dregs of their olde age to God by going into a Nunnery', while a rare few, those who had been most successful, lived out their old age in riches. Bianca was evidently of the latter sort. The woman who had relieved Kit of his virginity two decades earlier had been the djinni that incited his love for his 'Dark Lady', Emilia Bassano. Now Emilia returned to inhabit an older Bianca. She appeared wiser, wittier than Kit remembered her (though that was possibly because he understood more Italian), and the befuddled lust of his youth returned as a deep, clear passion. What followed is not entirely clear. An engraving exists, in one of the catalogues of courtesans and their pleasures that were common at the time, of '*Il Signior Gualtiero Stangone*' and '*Bianca Emiliana bella Cortesana di Venetia*'.† Both are masked. He wears characteristic Venetian black, a slender doublet and simple hose; she is in a rich damask gown with a high lace collar, her breasts bare, as was the custom. One of her hands is on his shoulder,

---

* Roy Delbont, *Travellers' Tales*, p. 154.
† Julius Marx Collection.

the other beckons him closer. The presence of the engraving in the book is curious. Although portraits of courtesans were displayed around the city, and bawds kept miniatures for advertising purposes, the appearance of a picture of courtesan and client in a catalogue, especially as she is masked, is odd. The engraving is on a different paper from the rest of the catalogue, and was likely bound with it at a later date, which may mean that it was specifically aimed at a Mantuan market, or that there is a personal history involved.*

A fragmented account in Oliver Laurens's journal, written a year or so later, gives clues that the love was unrequited, or that the affair was corrupted by betrayal and ridden with jealousy. Two of Kit's poems date from this period – *A Lover's Complaint*, and the cryptic fragment now called *The Phoenix and the Turtle*, which proclaims 'Love and constancy is dead', and in which passion ends in ashes from which the phoenix does not rise. In *A Lover's Complaint*, it is the woman who is abandoned by an enchanting boy – a perplexing inversion, especially as the description of the seducer mingles a nostalgia for the young Henry Wriothesley into the poem. Kit had no doubt heard news of the Essex rebellion against Elizabeth in February, and rumours of Southampton's execution. In the end, Southampton's mother had intervened on his behalf, and he was reprieved and imprisoned in the Tower until after James I's accession, but the shock of hearing about the arrest seems to have re-awakened a fervour in Kit for a man whom he perhaps loved more in retrospect than he had in reality.

Kit would lay bare the corrosive powers of suspicion, mistrust and jealousy a few years later, in *Othello*, but before that he vented his bile in *Troilus and Cressida*, dipping deep into the pit of war and potato-fingered lechery, and bemoaning the fickleness

---

* That the volume is unique, and is owned by the same collector as *First suckes* opens interesting ground for speculation.

of women. (*Troilus and Cressida* is also riddled with references to bone-ache and other symptoms then ascribed to venereal disease, which may indicate that an inflammation of old problems was adding to Kit's woes.) The play is cynical and misogynous, and as it moves back and forth between Troy and the Greek enemy encampment it so effectively recreates the stasis and boredom of two armies in a stand-off situation – the constant sense of waiting, punctuated with displays of pointless machismo – that it has the tang of first-hand experience. This could well have been the case.

From July to December 1601, Duke Vincenzo once again attempted to flaunt his military prowess in battle against the Turks, who were moving through Croatia towards Vienna. Like his earlier expeditions, this would bring him little glory. During his 1595 campaign, he had taken along a small *cappella* of four musicians, headed (probably because of his versatility) by the young Monteverdi. In 1601, however, Monteverdi stayed in Mantua, and so, it appears, did Kit. There is no indication that he accompanied Vincenzo, apart from the uncannily realistic battleground atmosphere of *Troilus and Cressida*. On the contrary, there is strong evidence that he remained in Mantua.

Duke Vincenzo handed the reins of state to his wife Leonora dei Medici. She gripped them firmly, and relished the ride. A glance at her papers of the time shows she had every bit of the Medici political wit, and savoured the powers of command. She brought with her the more subdued tastes of Florence. In contrast to Vicenzo's extravagant costume and the bejewelled ladies about her, she developed a studied simplicity in dress, offsetting her gowns with just one or two adornments, sometimes just a single string of pearls. She took violently against Vincenzo's alchemists, and even more so against her husband's profligate behaviour. Together with her eldest son Francesco – a watery, rather dull youth – she formed a moral faction against the duke. She was determined to curb any tendency to voluptuousness or excess in the upcoming generation. When Francesco had incurred his first debt to a moneylender, at the age of seven, she called for a whip and was stopped from publicly flaying him only by the sight of her other children kneeling in a row, in tears.

There is an echo of the situation that reigned in Mantua in late 1601 in *Measure for Measure,* where the Duke of Vienna (who in the play is called Vincentio), though not himself a libertine, thinks the city has grown morally lax and, under pretence of going on a pilgrimage, hands over to the puritanical Angelo. As with *Othello,* part of the plot of *Measure for Measure* comes from a story by the Ferrara-born writer Giraldi Cinthio, whose collection the *Hecatommithi* ('Hundred Tales') was favourite reading of the better sort of Venetian courtesan, and had apparently been passed on to Kit. His examination of the ethics of public office perhaps owes a debt to his long political discussions with Blotius in Vienna.

In Mantua, the political scene was further complicated by the appearance of Duke Vincenzo's sister, Margherita Gonzaga, who after the death of her husband, Alfonso d'Este II of Ferrara, had withdrawn into a nunnery, but returned shortly before Vincenzo's departure for battle, intent on wresting some power for herself. The venom that developed between the sisters-in-law widely infected an already dysfunctional family, creating an adders' nest of entangled hatreds worthy of *King Lear.*

Oliver Laurens did not manage to visit Kit in 1601. His use of espionage work as a cover for journeys to the Continent had backfired and he had been sent on a long mission north. On 2 October 1601, a 'Willm Halle' is mentioned by the Secretary of State's clerk as having returned with intelligence from Denmark. After this, Oliver either abandoned his usual alias, or stopped spy work, as there are no further references in the records to William Hall. He was not able to see Kit again until late summer of the next year, when Kit was dangerously ill with malaria. Stagnant pools after summer floods had brought the 'chilling, trembling sweat', as well as swamp fever, to Mantua.

The only works that had reached London since Kit left Antwerp were *Troilus and Cressida, Twelfth Night, The Phoenix and the Turtle,* and *A Lover's Complaint.* It is not known how these were sent, though Kit possibly made indirect use of the frequent traffic between England and Padua, where Tom Walsingham still had contacts. Kit's first years in Mantua had been enjoyable but not overly productive, and Oliver was to return in 1602 almost empty-handed. He brought back *Measure for Measure* and *All's Well that Ends Well,* another rather bitter comedy of unrequited love. The play is based on a story by Boccaccio (also a favourite author of the courtesans), though the difference in wealth between the two main characters is Kit's invention, and creates the opportunity for a long speech about the value of virtue over high breeding, an issue which still troubled Kit. Although he had penetrated the circle of the duke's favourites (as had Rubens, with even greater success), he was still very aware of the strictures of rank.

Will Shakespere's reaction to the slow supply of plays was characteristically opportunistic – he attempted to pass off one of his own pieces as of equal quality to the work he was getting from Kit. *The True Chronicle History of Thomas Lord Cromwell,* written by 'W. S.' was published by William Jones in 1602. It was not a success. Blackmail had ceased to be an effective ploy as (especially since *Hamlet*) the scales had tipped, and Shakespere had more to lose by exposing Tom Walsingham than he stood to gain by extortion. His own loss of face would be considerable, and besides, he no longer needed the money as shrewd early investments, particularly in the Globe, were making him a rich man. In May 1602 he paid the enormous sum of £320 for seven acres of farmland near Stratford, and entered into what would be a long business and personal relationship with William and John Combe, members of one of the most unpleasant, acquisitive and least-liked families in the town.

Whatever excuses Shakespere was inventing for his slow production, he found he had to continue making them long after Laurens's return from Italy with just two comedies. The play drought extended well into 1603, as Kit was unreachable for much of that year. Will Shakespere (in the eyes of the nation, now one of its leading poets) had to endure the embarrassment, if not the scandal, of coming up with no suitable eulogy when Queen Elizabeth died in March, nor any ode for the coronation of King James in the summer. In spite of his burgeoning fame, as the dry period of 1603 drew on, he stooped to collaborate with the relatively unknown Thomas Dekker and Henry Chettle on a rewrite of a play that was already a decade old, *Sir Thomas More.*

CHAPTER SIXTEEN

Themes and Variations

The clue to Kit's inaccessibility in 1603 can be found in three letters written from Florence and Pisa by Pietro Paulo Rubens (as he now styled himself) in March of that year. Although he had been in Mantua only two years, the high-stepping young painter had been entrusted with an ambassadorial mission to Spain. He had been quick to use his charm, as well as the courtly finesse he had learned from the Countess de Lalaing, to his advantage in Vincenzo's household, rapidly winning the very useful intimacy of Annibale Chieppio, the intendant of the duchy and one of Vincenzo's most trusted advisers. He made his mark with a flourish, taking care during a 'surprise' visit by the duke to his studio to be discovered reciting Virgil in Latin while simultaneously painting. The ensuing Latin conversation convinced the duke that here was a young man who could hold his own with aristocrats, yet knew his place. When Chieppio put forward the name of his foreign, twenty-six-year-old new friend for an important diplomatic mission, the duke readily accepted but, unbeknown to either Rubens or Chieppio, he made sure that the party included an observer who could keep a quiet check on the young man, one who could follow conversations in Italian, Latin or Flemish: Rubens's older compatriot Gualtiero Stangone.

Despite his inglorious Turkish campaign, Vincenzo hoped that Philip III, the flabby, undistinguished new King of Spain, would grant him the courtesy title of Admiral, an honour usually given to a member of the Doria family in Genoa. He sent a convoy of gifts to sweeten the king and leading courtiers, including an exuberantly decorated silver coach with six bay horses, and copies (not by Rubens) of paintings by Titian, Raphael and other Italian Masters. The gifts – coach included – were carefully boxed, and Rubens was dispatched to present them to the king and charged with the utmost secrecy about what was in his care.

The most logical route would have been to Genoa and then by sea to Spain, but Rubens was sent on a puzzlingly difficult detour, over the Appenines and through Florence and Pisa, to find a ship at Livorno. This may have been planned as a test of his ingenuity and skills of improvisation, but it seems more likely an attempt to pluck a few of the poseur's feathers in public. Someone in the corridors and whispering corners of the Mantuan court had become irritated by this strutting young man's ascent and his growing friendship with Chieppio. He, or she, was most likely an ally of Annibale Iberti, Vincenzo's official legate in Spain, who was indeed to receive the upstart very coolly. Hearing that Gualtiero Stangone was to accompany Rubens, and knowing that the young painter's posturing riled the older man, this canny courtier saw the opportunity for a little mischief.

On 18 March 1603, Rubens wrote to Chieppio from Florence, having endured the derision of muleteers at his attempt to cart a coach-sized box over the mountains, and the suppressed snorts of local merchants at the route he had taken – 'they almost crossed themselves in astonishment at such a mistake,' he wrote, 'saying we should have gone to Genoa to embark, instead of risking the roundabout route to Livorno without first being assured of a passage'. He seems already to suspect some sort of sabotage, pleading to Chieppio: 'I know that in the vast sea of your many important affairs, you will not refuse to care for this poor little boat of mine, badly guided until now by the incompetent advice of I know not whom.' The funds he had been allocated would appear to have been for the shorter, easier route, something he complains about with characteristic self-assurance, writing: 'If [the duke] mistrusts me, he has given me a great deal of money; but if he trusts me, then he has given me very little.' Worse was to follow. After delays caused by 'floods and other unforeseen circumstances' he managed to reach Livorno, and even to secure immediate passage to Spain, only to find his ship requisitioned at the last minute for apparently paltry reasons by the Grand Duke of Tuscany.

Kit's role in this rather elaborate prank was to create subtle disruption along the way to tarnish the young man's sheen – the business with the Grand Duke being part of it. Kit had a contact in the Tuscan court – an old acquaintance from Antwerp – and the two set to work. No sooner had Rubens secured a second ship, than he received a request from the grand duke, 'through a Flemish gentleman in his service, to take one of his own palfreys along with the other horses, and to give it to someone in Cartagena'. Compared with his earlier tribulations, this was a slight inconvenience, but it caused him to remark, in a letter from Pisa on 26 March, that the grand duke 'was kept very well informed by others' of everything he was up to. Three days later, he was summoned before the grand duke, who astonished him utterly by not only knowing who he was, his country, profession and rank, but in being minutely informed 'in every detail as to the quantity and quality of the gifts destined for this person and that'. Hastening to disassociate himself from any indiscretion, a flustered Rubens immediately wrote another letter to Chieppio, assuring his patron that the boxes had not been opened and that 'I have not specified my baggage, either at the customs or elsewhere', pleading his simplicity and naïveté in the world of diplomacy, and reiterating his belief that he was being undermined by spies.

Kit and the Mantuan legate, Annibale Iberti, would have had ample time to laugh over tales of Rubens's bewilderment and mishaps, for when the party finally arrived in Madrid they found the Spanish court had moved to Valladolid, and when they got to Valladolid on 13 May they were told that King Philip was hunting rabbits in Aranjuez and would not be back for weeks. (As it transpired, that came as a relief to the Mantuans, as when they unpacked the paintings it became evident that the canvases had been damaged during the voyage from Livorno and by heavy rain en route.)

Iberti proposed that Rubens, together with some Spanish artists, restore the paintings. Rubens's swagger seems hardly to have faltered, despite the tribulations of his journey. In a letter to Chieppio he sniffily stated that even though 'it has pleased His Most Serene Highness to make me guardian and bearer of the works of others, without including a brushstroke of my own', he would indeed do the work, but drew the line at any Spanish collaboration, as local artists did not measure up to his standards: 'God keep me from resembling them in any way!'. However, obey Iberti he must, although working with another artist was something 'which I will not tolerate, for I have always guarded against being confused with anyone, however great a man', and what was more, 'I shall be disgraced unduly by an inferior production unworthy of my reputation, which is not unknown here'. This from the man whose renown to date rested (apart from the canvasses to be admired in his mother's drawing room) on a single painting, the triptych for the church of Santa Croce in Gerusalemme in Rome, for which he had been paid a pittance, and perhaps on early studies done for *The Gonzaga family worshipping the Holy Trinity*.

King Philip did not return to Valladolid until early July, when Iberti, exercising his official powers, excluded Rubens from a long-desired royal audience. Rubens could witness the presentation of the troublesome coach to the monarch only from some distance, although he was permitted to hand over the retouched paintings to the royal favourite and Chief Minister, the Duke of Lerma. Lerma was a powerful, vain and tempestuous man, ever thirsty for flattery. This was ground Rubens was adept at tilling. He made a good impression and was quick to secure a number of lucrative commissions from Lerma, staying on in Spain until the spring of 1604. With the ceremonies over, Kit's work was done, though he too remained in Spain until the early autumn.

Kit had participated in one of the peripheral presentations, during which the Countess of Lemos received a cross made of rock crystal and two chandeliers. They were appropriate gifts. Her husband the Count of Lemos burned a light of shining intellect in an otherwise dull court. He wrote poetry and took a true interest in letters, fostering friendship with a wide circle of artists and authors. Lope de Vega, the playwright whom many consider a genius of Kit's calibre, had been his secretary from 1598 to 1599, and the count was known among writers for his unstinting largesse. In his friendships he was flexible with the rigid rules of rank, and seems to have rather taken to Gualtiero Stangone (whose status was anyway enhanced by being a member of the Mantuan mission).

The foreigners were, of course, discreetly watched. The historian Loryn de Bot has uncovered reports by the spies assigned to tail the less senior members of the Mantuan delegation.* One of these dossiers, compiled by a dull incompetent named Sanchez, recorded a visit by Lemos and 'Estangon' (surely Stangone) to the shop of the bookseller Francesco de Robles, where 'with a group of like men' they listened to an elderly reader outlining the life of 'one Quixada, or Quesada, or Quixana, he seemed to know not which, but yet promised to keep to the

---

* See Loryn de Bot, doctoral thesis 'Secondary Espionage in the court of Philip III 1601–1604'.

truth in every point of his history'.* The reader was of course the former playwright and disgraced tax collector Miguel de Cervantes Saavedra, a protégé of the Count of Lemos.

Cervantes had recently followed the royal court to Valladolid (his niece, sisters and daughter, who as seamstresses depended on proximity to court for their living, would join him the following summer in rooms above a noisy tavern). As had been his custom in Robles's shop in Madrid, he was nervously reading from his manuscript of *The Ingenious Gentleman Don Quixote of La Mancha*, which had long been in preparation, and which Robles would publish in 1605. The reading affected Kit profoundly. Sanchez noted that Lemos made clear in Italian what he could not follow in Spanish, and that the foreigner seemed quite shaken. '*Don Quixote,*' writes one of Cervantes's biographers, William Byron, is 'a magic book, as close to being a living object as any work of art has ever been. It has a life of its own which is like our lives, if we think about it, a game of mirrors, an impression of receding depths, of truths just beyond our grasp, of planes of reality shifting and blurring. In all the garrulous annals of human expression, only a handful of characters – Quixote, Hamlet, Faust, Don Juan, perhaps Oedipus – have so perfectly summarised areas of the human condition as to embed themselves as symbols in humanity's unconscious.' Madame Bovary and Hannibal Lecter may be added to this list.

Kit had long ago begun the journey of 'personation', transforming his characters from ciphers into living beings, penetrating crevices of human psychology. He had already created a clutch of characters that would not only transcend his time, but would escape his own work, fixing themselves in the minds of people who had never read his plays. In Cervantes's Don Quixote he recognised another such figure.

Over the next few weeks, the want-wit spy Sanchez transcribed

---

* De Bot, 'Secondary Espionage'.

a number of conversations between Kit and Cervantes about this 'Don Quixote' (which he seems to think is a coded reference to a real knight), before growing tired, becoming distracted by some other task, or being sacked, and leaving posterity with a frustrating silence. His obsession with the idea that he was eavesdropping on a plot means that the fragments and phrases he reports are chosen with an arcane logic, one certainly at a frustrating tangent to that of literary scholars, making the true content of these exchanges troublesome to discern, and their meaning difficult to interpret. Two names do emerge clearly, early on in the conversations: those of the Englishmen Marlowe and Shakespere – but it is quite apparent that Cervantes had heard of neither (though the mention of England, the enemy power, thrilled Sanchez, particularly as there was a Christopher Marlor, or Marlowe, a Cambridge man, in the English seminary in Valladolid at the time).

The fifty-five-year-old Cervantes had led a punishing life, much of it spent in sour poverty, and part of it spent in jail. In 1603 he was at an especially low point, though his lot was to improve with the publication and immediate success of *Don Quixote*. It was a position Kit identified with, and a path he perhaps foresaw. Sanchez records him as remarking: 'Things at the worst will cease, or else climb upward to what they were before', a sentiment he repeats in *Macbeth* IV ii 24–5, and which Cervantes used in a later book, *Trabajos de Persiles y Sigismunda*: '*cuando en el extremo de los trabajos no sucede el de la muerte, ques es el último de todos, ha de seguirse la mudanza, no de mal a mal sino de mal a bien y de bien a más bien*' (when at the very end of all trials that of death does not follow – death being the ultimate trial – then the process has to be not from bad to bad, but from bad to good and good to better). In the 1580s, Cervantes had written twenty or thirty dramas which, he remarked, were received 'without cucumbers or other missiles' and earned him some renown; but for nearly twenty years he had maintained literary silence. Part of the reason for this (it emerges through Sanchez's fog) was disillusion with play-writing. He believed the drama had failed his muse, and in a consumer market that demanded an even quicker turnover than in London, he was probably right. At a conservative count, Lope de Vega quick-fed voracious audiences with some five hundred plays in his lifetime (some estimates reach over fifteen hundred). The Italian story of the Capulets and Montagues, which Kit laboured over for months, producing *Romeo and Juliet*, was made over in a few days by Lope into his *Castelvines y Monteses*, which has since slipped into the abyss of collective amnesia. Cervantes had publicly condemned Lope for trivialising his high calling and debasing Spanish theatre with the quantity of his output, an accusation that Lope met with justifiable outrage – a handful of his surviving plays are valued for their dark comedy, technical mastery and trenchant imagery. It is tempting to speculate that Kit met Lope as well, either through Lemos or Cervantes, but it is unlikely since Lope had long since bitterly fallen out with Cervantes, and had lately been making too greedy a demand on the count's generosity.

Kit listened in silence, as the ageing Cervantes grew vehement on the question of control, on the need to have his own fingers on the details, on wresting power from the players, as it was only by escaping their tastes and casting off the millstone of live staging that his art could fly to perfection. *Don Quixote*, he said, could never have emerged from the theatre. (A confused Sanchez gleefully pounced on the talk of casting off millstones, interpreting it in terms of riot, assassination and rebellion.)

Kit must have seen some truth in Cervantes's argument. He knew from Oliver how clowns ad libbed in his comedy scenes; he was angered when Will Shakespere botched and bungled his lines; and, detached from the company that was performing his works, he was powerless against the players' pragmatic warps and changes. But while he was clearly aware of the fundamental difference between the Italian novellas he had plundered for some of his plays, and Cervantes's psychologically searching, detailed, densely knitted work, he still argued with the Spaniard for the power of poetry and the immediacy of theatre. He would later try to write his own theatrical version of one of the incidents in *Don Quixote* (the love-madness of Cardenio), but for some reason could never finish it. The play, called *Cardenio* (and later *Double Falsehood*), ended up in Will Shakespere's hands, who gave it to John Fletcher to complete under the guise of a collaboration (Fletcher was tipped to be Shakespere's successor as playwright to the King's Men, and Will easily recognised bold ambition). It disappeared from the theatres and was rediscovered in 1727 by the lawyer turned scholar Lewis Theobald, who claimed to have unearthed not just one but three manuscripts, though it is still not part of the accepted canon.

Sanchez repeatedly stressed in his reports that the stranger Estangon was argumentative, yet often silent and troubled by what he heard. It is evident that Don Quixote and his creator discomposed Kit. (The two were not always easy to distinguish. Cervantes is said to have somewhat resembled his knight errant, and sometimes used the date and place he was composing a story as its time and location. As Flaubert wrote, '*Madame Bovary, c'est moi!*'.) The lanky knight had issued a challenge that jolted the core of Kit's thinking. Yet the result was an eruption of some of the best drama he had ever written, plays that had been rumbling beneath the surface for years. Detached from the strictures and demands of working directly with a company of players, he was able to indulge in a poetic density that astonished – perhaps even dumbfounded – audiences back in London. Over the next eighteen months, Kit wrote *Othello, Macbeth* and *King Lear.*

Sanchez's last report dates from September of 1603, and although the next mention of Kit in Mantua is early the following May (when he attended the baptism of Monteverdi's second son), it seems likely that he made the journey back from Spain before winter gripped the sierra and thrust its icy fingers through the plains. Travelling in Spain was uncomfortable, difficult and expensive, even in good weather. Humanity was gathered in a few large cities, interspersed by unprofitable wastelands of 'antres [caves] vast and deserts idle,/ Rough quarries, rocks, and hills whose heads touch heaven' (*Othello* I iii 140–41); lodging was in *ventas* beside the way, but tired and travel-stained wanderers often found they had to sleep on the floor, and unless they had brought their own provisions, went supperless. Nicolaus Clenardus on his way to the University of Salamanca had to make do with a thin meal of rabbit, and to bed down on the earth in a hovel with nothing but his groom to pillow his head. The Comtesse d'Aunoy grumbled that she was crowded in a smoky room, full of men and women 'clad like Beggars ... always some of 'em impudently grating on a sorry guitar'. Predatory customs officers who issued dues on the very clothes travellers stood up in, bands of less legitimate robbers, and a population that showed no solicitude to strangers were further complaints. Kit must dearly have welcomed the return to his warm chambers near the Palazzo Ducale, where he heartily enjoyed a thick Mantuan beef-and-chicken *brodo*.

Claudio and Claudia Monteverdi now also lived in the San Pietro district, in a large house appropriate to the composer's new standing as Vincenzo's maestro di cappella. Kit found the household in a state of excitement. Not only was Claudia Monteverdi again pregnant (with the ancient midwife predicting a son), but a new pupil and lodger had taken up residence – the magical, thirteen-year-old soprano Caterina Martinelli, who became known as 'La Romanina'. She was the pride of the court, and most particularly of its prince. Duke Vincenzo's singers, not without wry reason, were dubbed his 'musical harem'. Mindful of this, Caterina's parents had not only driven a hard bargain, but had suggested to the duke's ambassador in Rome that a doctor and midwife ascertain the girl's virginity before she travelled to the court at Mantua. Vincenzo had searched the country for such a singer, and was not going to lose her to his reputation for lechery, so he suggested to the Martinellis that she lodge with 'our Director of Music, who has a wife and other relatives'. Caterina arrived in the autumn, and though Monteverdi at first confined her to religious music, by the time Kit was back in town she already had the court transfixed.

La Romanina flashed another pulse into an already radiant environment. Duke Vincenzo's riotous appetites may have given his court sensation, but his judgement gave it tone, and his eye for talent ensured brilliance. He combined a taste for the secular, an enthusiasm for the new style of solo singing, and a passion for theatre in a way that sparked experiment and was a catalyst to creative daring. From the alchemists in the cellar to artists in the attic, through chambers where music was being played the like of which had never been heard before, came a pervading sense of adventure, a quest for the new. Poets wrote for composers, painters were startled by strange music, and actors learned to sing.

Claudio Monteverdi was an inspired choice for maestro di cappella in this milieu. He was one of the most progressive composers of his day. His books of madrigals had shocked the musical establishment. There seemed no need for such innovation – polyphony had barely been invented, yet he was experimenting with harmonics in ways that were quite alarming, and now began to toy with the new fashion for solo voice in place of choral singing. In 1600, both Monteverdi and Duke Vincenzo had heard Jacopo Peri's *Euridice*, the work often named as the first ever opera, when the Mantuan court had visited Florence for Maria dei Medici's wedding to the King of France. Vincenzo

quickly commissioned something similar from Monteverdi, who
– ever a slow and painstaking composer – came up with *Orfeo*
in 1607. It is a piece of immense sophistication, pathos and
delicacy, far more deserving of the 'first opera' tag than its
predecessors. Vincenzo was entranced, not only attending rehearsals but having the opera repeated three times. The excitement at the news of this novel combination of music and drama
spread even before the first performance. One Carlo Magni,
writing from Mantua to his brother Giovanni in Rome, enthused:
'It should be most unusual, as all the actors are to sing their
parts; it is said on all sides it will be a great success. No doubt
I shall be driven to attend out of sheer curiosity, unless I am
prevented from getting in by lack of space.' At its premiere on
24 February, *Orfeo* was indeed a huge success. Members of the
audience were given printed copies of the play so they could
follow the words as the performance went along, and though
no contemporary account of the event exists, later reports
described the Mantuan singers as refined actors:

> They accompanied the music and the sentiments with
> appropriate facial expressions, glances and gestures, with
> no awkward movements of the mouth or hands or body
> which might not express the feeling of the song. They made
> the words clear in such a way that one could hear even the
> last syllable of every word, which was never interrupted or
> suppressed by passages and other embellishments.

It was as if they had heeded Hamlet's advice to the players to
pronounce their speeches 'trippingly on the tongue', not to 'saw
the air too much' with their hands and to: 'Suit the action to
the word, the word to the action, with this special observance,
that you not o'erstep the modesty of nature' (*Hamlet* III ii
1–20). It is not known whether La Romanina performed at the
premiere of *Orfeo*, though she does appear to have sung in later

performances. Monteverdi prepared her for the title role of his next opera, the now lost *Arianna*, but she died tragically, of smallpox or scarlet fever, shortly before the first performance in 1608.

Kit could not help being drawn into this creative vortex. He had long used music in his plays not merely as incidental entertainment, but as an integral means of expression in some of his most powerful and moving scenes – for Ophelia in her madness, or Desdemona, prescient of her death, sadly singing the willow song. He had already conceived staging that drew together words, action and music – as Jonathan Bate reveals: 'When Romeo and Juliet first speak to each other as they are dancing at the ball, they do so in the form of a sonnet . . . They weave a verbal dance to match their musical motion: Romeo speaks the first quatrain, Juliet the second . . . the third quatrain is divided between them, then each delivers one line of the closing rhyming couple.' Back in his Crichtonesque role in court, Kit may well have had a hand in the production of *Orfeo*.

A glancing reference to the new art form, in a letter of complaint written to Duke Vincenzo early in 1606, quite possibly throws light on one aspect of Kit's thought about the opera.* *Orfeo* was sponsored in Mantua by the Academia degli Invaghiti, a courtly society devoted to chivalry, the arts and learning, which was modelled on the Florentine confraternity that had given rise to Peri's *Euridice*. Across the way from the *palazzo* where the Academy met, was a shop renowned for its fine cakes, monstrous sausages and salami – and for the allures of its female staff. The shop provided popular respite from the athletics of the mind, and as early as 1565 complaints were being made that the wicked waitresses were behaving '*in maniera che a poco a poco la sua Academia andarà in bordello*' ('in ways that little by little are turning the Academy into a bordello'). In addition to food and

---

* Servaes, *Cum Grano Salis*, p. 48.

frolics, the establishment also offered opportunity for members of the Invaghiti to engage in conversation with interested non-academicians. Five decades later, it maintained both traditions, and was still provoking letters of complaint to the authorities. One of these mentioned talk of 'a play that shall be sung', and (by way of illustrating the dreadful impropriety of this alternative academy) expressed outrage that 'a quaint-talking Fleming often seen in Your Highness's service' dared propose that this sung drama should not pay honour to the classics, but instead involve the tale of a 'mad Moor'.* One of the few conservative aspects of *Orfeo* is the use of the myth of Orpheus and Euridice for its narrative. The Florentine Academies were infatuated with the Greeks, and much of the reasoning behind creating sung theatre was that it was thought to reflect classical practice. In using the same story for his opera as had Peri, Monteverdi was showing a rare conformity to an established idea. If this 'quaint-talking Fleming' is indeed Kit, proposing Cinthio's (or his own) story of Othello as fit subject for an opera, then he was skidding way ahead of his time. It was not until 280 years later that Monteverdi's near namesake composed *Otello*; and it was only in 1901 that George Bernard Shaw would write: 'The truth is that instead of *Otello* being an Italian opera written in the style of Shakespeare, *Othello* is a play written ... in the style of an Italian opera.'

After the full-sail creative surge immediately following his visit to Spain, Kit seems to have run into the doldrums. He wrote nothing at all in 1606, a year in which there is also scant record of Gualtiero Stangone in Mantua, raising the possibility that he was once again ill with malaria or the 'Neapolitan bone-ache'.

---

* Servaes, *Cum Grano Salis*, p. 35.

In the following two years he produced, possibly after a sojourn in Sabbioneta, *Antony and Cleopatra* and *Coriolanus*, the first about a fine mind devoured by fatal attraction to a woman (Bianca perhaps still hovers here), the second also dealing with self-obsession. Both fell back into Kit's Roman mould, and he seems to have had trouble completing *Antony and Cleopatra*, lifting much of the fifth act from an earlier play. To this period, too, belong the less satisfactory *Pericles* and *Timon of Athens* – plays which he left unfinished. Maybe his muse had faltered, distracted by the new paths offered by *Don Quixote* and *Orfeo*, or perhaps illness had indeed incapacitated him. The increasing frequency of his bouts of fever and aching joints may very well indicate advancing syphilis – in which case his misspent youth was being played out both in body and mind, as *Pericles* is his only play to contain a sustained scene in a brothel.

Will Shakespere was again forced to find collaborators – Thomas Middleton for *Timon*, and a London friend of his, one George Wilkins, for *Pericles*. Wilkins was a second-rate writer who owned a house at the corner of Turnmill Street and Cow Cross that he ran as part tavern, part brothel. His violent nature led to frequent clashes with the law, on one occasion kicking a pregnant woman in the belly, on another trampling on a woman he had already so severely beaten that she had to be carried away in a chair. The company Will Shakespere kept – Wilkins in London, the Combes in Stratford – was causing Oliver Laurens and Tom Walsingham some concern.

Shakespere worked with Wilkins again (probably also together with Middleton) on a drama called *A Yorkshire Tragedy*, which was published as 'Written by W. Shakespeare' in 1608. The play seems to have been largely the work of Wilkins and Middleton, however, by copying Kit's style, Shakespere was now coming up with work independently, albeit of a quality which led later compilers to drop it from the canon. *A Yorkshire Tragedy* lifts images from *King Lear*, including the epithet 'marble-hearted' (which appears to be used nowhere else in contemporary literature). Far from employing his collaborators, Will Shakespere made them pay for the privilege of using his now weighty name. The wily merchant was also apparently milking money from other sources. In 1605 he had purchased a half-interest in a lease of 'Tythes of Corne grayne blade & heye' as well as other tithes in hamlets around Stratford, which ensured him a fat income from the toil of farm labourers, not only from grain and grass, but also through levies on mutton and wool profits. His share cost £440, the kind of sum, Katherine Duncan-Jones points out, 'that prodigal aristocrats squandered, or borrowed – not the sort of money naturally associated with a mere player and poet' – especially in a period of long theatre closures. He was profiting heartily not only from his arrangement with Kit Marlowe, but from his other investments, and was well on the way to achieving his aim of establishing himself as a learned gentleman. The only difficulty was the slow drip of plays from Mantua.

CHAPTER SEVENTEEN

Prospero's Books

Oliver Laurens visited Mantua once in 1604, and again in 1607 – on the second occasion being attacked by bandits near Bergamo while on his way back to England. They stole his cloak, as well as 'what small gold was not in my boots or sewn in my jerkin', and broke open the chest containing Kit's manuscripts. This may be another reason for the texts of *Timon* and *Pericles* arriving incomplete in London, and was possibly the occasion on which Kit's third Jewish play *Jehuda* disappeared. Bernard Rosine suggests that Kit was so ill that he appeared near death, which is why Oliver took the incomplete plays with him; but it seems unlikely that Oliver would leave his friend in such circumstances.* In 1608 Oliver returned for a sustained visit, which lasted until the spring of the following year. This may indicate that Kit was again ill and needed close care. If he was overheard muttering in English while delirious, it could lead to complications.

At some point during this visit, the two old friends brewed up an extraordinary idea. They became determined to see the wonders of the New World. The provenance of this apparent madness is not clear. Kit had doubtless heard the fantastical

---

* Rosine, *Oliver Laurens*, p. 392.

tales told by Spanish explorers who had returned to Valladolid, and he had sipped bitter chocolate from Mexico. Oliver was fired up by talk of new colonies, big visions expounded in London taverns now that the Spanish sea power had been checked. Their imaginations were captured by voyagers' reports of an Eden of free love, with natives devoid of guile and treason. Kit had been engrossed by Antonio Pigafetta's account of Magellan's circumnavigation, and, long ago, he had read Montaigne and spoken to the great essayist about a Utopia beyond the seas. This New World was also the source of tobacco, which Kit missed sorely, and rumours were wild of a rare root or bark that was a cure for cupid's burn, so if not a land of milk and honey, at the very least the Americas offered a good smoke and relief from the clap.

In Mantua, life was growing more difficult. A dishonest and unpleasant court treasurer, Ottavio Benintendi (whom Monteverdi caustically nicknamed 'Belintento') diverted Duke Vincenzo's good intentions, as well as his money, and artists went unpaid. Even the maestro di cappella had to write letters to the duke begging for his dues, and Kit knew that Vincenzo's dull heir, Francesco, bore no love for the Monteverdis. (He was right. When Vincenzo died in 1612, the new duke dismissed Monteverdi within weeks.) Kit was forty-five, a ripe age for retreat and retirement – but his enquiring spirit saw in such a move a chance for transformation. Like Proteus, he was once again changing shape, and the first twitches and writhings already showed in his weakening desire to write. Perhaps he had indeed been seriously ill, and had felt the imminence of death, so discovery became an antidote to dying, a voyage into the wondrously unknown new world being an earthly substitute for the more fearful journey to 'the undiscover'd country, from whose bourn/No traveller returns', a shadow-play of death that removed its dread by ensuring that he left the world he knew on his own terms.

The plans that the pair made, with the same boyish fervour as they had once played together in Canterbury, were not impracticable. Kit's old paramour the Earl of Southampton was a major 'adventurer' in the Virginia Company, the leading force in England's move to colonise the Americas. 'Adventurer' at the time meant one who undertook commercial enterprises, or adventures – as in the Society of Merchant Adventurers – but the word already had connotations of personal daring, or venturing off on something risky, as in 'then will they adventure upon the exploit themselves' (*I Henry IV* I ii 165). As early as 1602, while he was still in the Tower, Southampton had backed an expedition to the New World. When the Virginia Company was granted a new charter in 1609, with powers to govern and regulate the American colony, Southampton was one of the first subscribers. It was easy for him discreetly to arrange passage for Kit and Oliver, and perhaps he was even inclined to secure them some land and invest in their adventure.* Oliver's journal simply notes that they left Mantua in April 'to meet with Sir Thomas in Plimouth'. This may refer to Tom Walsingham, who had been knighted in 1597, or possibly Sir Thomas Gates – a Netherlander and friend of Southampton's – who was going out as temporary governor of the colony. Southampton used his own influence, or this Low Countries connection, to gain the pair berths on the flagship the *Sea Venture.* They travelled as Flemings.

Kit arrived back in England as he had left sixteen years earlier, using the alias Walter Hoochspier. He still had to be extremely cautious. Sir Robert Cecil had long grasped his coveted secretaryship, and other high offices, but was now the Earl of Salisbury, far more powerful than he had been in 1593, and doubtless just as vengeful. The Walsinghams had risen socially

---

* The ever-prurient Seb Melmoth in *The Ring of Rose's* argues that Southampton himself was planning to go to Virginia with Kit, and was merely using Oliver as a pander, but this seems unlikely.

under King James – Sir Thomas's wife Audrey was now a friend of Queen Anne, and one of the Keepers of the Queen's Wardrobe. Dark scandal was no way to repay him for his years of loyalty. Oliver records an emotional reunion between Kit and Tom Walsingham, and also a meeting with his own former employer Thomas Thorpe, but it is not clear whether these took place in London. The rendezvous were most likely held within the privacy of Scadbury, or in the anonymity of Gravesend or Plymouth. They did not meet Will Shakespere.

Two plays were sent on to Shakespere with the clear message that they would be the last. Both have a mysterious, fairy-tale quality and offer curious parallels to Kit's brief return to England and venture out into the brave New World. The first part of *The Winter's Tale* is set indoors, and is dark and fraught; the second part takes place sixteen years later (exactly the time Kit had been away from England), but occurs largely outdoors and is bright and forward-looking. *Cymbeline* (based in part on an anonymous Dutch story) moves from a decaying old world towards a new (albeit not quite ideal) order, along the way affirming passion, integrity and initiative over high breeding.

As part of his attempt to raise as much money as possible for the venture, Kit sold Thomas Thorpe the right to publish the sonnets he had written as verse letters, which had been circulating 'among his private friends'. As Will Shakespere had already put five in the public domain (in *The Passionate Pilgrim* in 1599), and had claimed others as his own, and as the style was by now so recognisable, even these had to come out under Shakespere's name. Thorpe, who a decade earlier had written the curious dedication in Kit's translation of Lucan's *Pharsalia*, hinting that Marlowe was still alive, brought out the *Sonnets* later in 1609, and himself penned their dedication – an affectionate, if enigmatic, tribute to Kit himself, which is worth examining in full:

TO.THE.ONLIE.BEGETTER.OF.
THESE.INSUING.SONNETS.
Mr W.H. ALL.HAPPINESSE.
AND.THAT.ETERNETIE.
PROMISED.
BY.
OUR.EVER-LIVING.POET.
WISHETH.
THE.WELL-WISHING.
ADVENTURER.IN.
SETTING.
FORTH.

T. T.

Once again, Thomas Thorpe carefully places his clues. 'Mr W. H.' refers to the name that Kit had borne (in various mutations) for the past sixteen years: Walter Hoochspier. The 'Mr' completes the near anagram that had so disturbed Kit when he killed the original Hoochspier in Italy – 'Mr Walter Hoochspier' is an exact anagram of Christopher Marlowe. Mr W. H. is, of course, the 'only begetter' – the only creator – of the ensuing sonnets (a wry prod at Shakespere). The purity of the logic that Mr W. H. as 'onlie begetter' refers to the single *author* of the *Sonnets*, and not the Beautiful Young Man, the Dark Lady in Disguise, the Patron, or any of the other alleged *recipients* of the poems, eludes many commentators. Their perplexity has led to centuries of squabbling. Thomas Thorpe wishes him – this optimistic ('well-wishing') 'adventurer' setting forth into the New World, the secretly 'ever-living poet' – all happiness, and through the publication of the sonnets, that eternity he himself promises in the poems.

Among other papers relating to Oliver Laurens held at the Bernhardt Institute are two receipts signed by Thomas Thorpe, one for a portrait and the second attached to an inventory of books received from 'W-H' (reproduced in Appendix VI). It would appear that Kit had either sold his books to Thorpe to raise money for the venture, or had left them as a deposit – as other travellers of the time would leave money with London goldsmiths – to be drawn on in case of financial need. The list provides a helpful clue to the sources of some of Kit's plays. The portrait is most likely one that Kit had painted by a Flemish artist in Mantua, in the week of his fortieth birthday, soon after arriving back from Spain. It later passed from Thorpe's possession, possibly in settlement of a debt, to one John Taylor, the 'Water Poet'. (This John Taylor, 1580–1653, a Thames waterman, eccentric poet and early travel writer, has often been confused with the Joseph Taylor, ?1586–1652, who took over from Richard Burbage as an actor with the King's Men.)

By the mid-seventeenth century, the portrait was owned by Shakespere's scurrilous godson Sir William Davenant, an acquisitive old fraud who exploited the faint resemblance to Shakespere to pass it off as a likeness of his godfather. It is possible that Davenant (who was only ten when Shakespere died) was himself duped, but far more likely that the invention was his own. He notoriously made every possible gainful use of his Shakespere connection (even claiming he was Will's bastard son). A comparison of the portrait with the only two images made of Shakespere under the auspices of people who knew him – the bust in Holy Trinity Church, Stratford, commissioned by his son-in-law and the engraving by Martin Droeshout used as a frontispiece for the First Folio – makes it quite clear that apart from baldness and a similar domed forehead, these and the Davenant portrait are of different people; whereas the application of computer face-ageing software to the Corpus Christi painting of Kit, shows equally clearly that the Davenant portrait is the same man twenty years on (see Appendix II). Davenant died bankrupt and intestate in 1668 and the picture was claimed by his principal creditor John Otway, who was only too happy to perpetuate Davenant's claim in order to raise the value of the goods he had managed to seize. As 'A Portrait of William Shakespeare' the painting passed through a succession of hands, eventually coming into the possession of the dukes of Chandos, and it is as the 'Chandos portrait' that it now hangs in the National Portrait Gallery in London.

Having raised as much money as they could from Thomas Thorpe, Kit and Oliver retreated into hiding – either at Scadbury or in Plymouth – to await the departure of the *Sea Venture*. A fleet of nine vessels, with some six hundred colonists on board, left Plymouth in early June. In October, report reached London that although the rest of the fleet had reached the Chesapeake, the flagship *Sea Venture* had been lost in a terrifying storm.

Will Shakespere had *Cymbeline* and *The Winter's Tale* to get by on, but was alarmed by a royal command from King James in 1613 to write a play to celebrate the marriage of the Princess Elizabeth to Frederick, the Elector Palatine of the Rhine. Shakespere hastened to his earlier 'collaborator' John Fletcher, and together they came up with *Henry VIII*, a play the biographer Anthony Holden calls 'a pallid, pompous, prettified version of events from 1520 to 1533'. Their sorry effort was cancelled on the day of the wedding in favour of the 'greater pleasures' of a masque and was later presented at the Globe, where with deft dramatic irony the firing of a cannon in one of the scenes set fire to the thatch and burned the theatre down. Undeterred, Shakespere hazarded a further unfortunate collaboration with Fletcher, *The Two Noble Kinsmen*, before making a politic withdrawal to retirement in Stratford, to tend his famous mulberry tree, lord it like a local gentleman, and live off the fat of his rents and tithes. He made one more venture into the world of verse – the appalling piece of doggerel that now defends his tomb:

GOOD FREND FOR JESUS SAKE FORBEARE,
TO DIGG THE DUST ENCLOSED HEARE:
BLESTE BE YE MAN THAT SPARES THESE STONES,
AND CURST BE HE THAT MOVES MY BONES.

Before his retreat to Stratford, before, even, the difficult epi-
sode of the royal command, one other play had come his way.
It arrived without any letter of explanation, in a package bearing
the seal of the Earl of Southampton. It was entitled *The Tempest*.
In October 1610 a confidential report had reached the Council
of the Virginia Company revealing that the *Sea Venture* had not
been lost, but had been driven on to the uninhabited island of
Bermuda – 'the still-vex'd Bcrmoothes' (*The Tempest* I ii 229) –
and had broken up. This letter, or *True Reportory*, was compiled
by the company's secretary, William Strachey, and recounts how
all lives on the *Sea Venture* had been spared, how the castaways
found the forests of the island rich in swine and fowl, and the
seas full of fish, and how they had spent the winter and spring
after the wreck building boats that would take them on to Virginia. The *True Reportory* also contained damaging information
on the misgovernment of Jamestown, and so was kept secret.
With the letter came a sealed parcel personally addressed to one
of the company's leading shareholders, the Earl of Southampton. It was the contents of this package that Southampton
forwarded, without comment, to Will Shakespere. The play the
package contained showed striking similarities with some of the
events described in the *True Reportory*. Both the *Sea Venture* and
the ship in *The Tempest* are wrecked without any loss of life;
and the crews of both are frightened by the phenomenon of
St Elmo's fire: 'Sometime I'd divide,/And burn in many places;
on the topmast,/The yards and bowsprit, would I flame distinctly,/Then meet and join' (*The Tempest* I ii 198–200). The
colonists (like Prospero's islanders) were convinced their island
was haunted, full of spirits and strange noises; and there were

two or three attempts at mutiny, including a plot to kill Sir Thomas Gates, that are reflected in events in *The Tempest*.

It is in *The Tempest* that Kit finally bows out from his work as a dramatist. He pays homage to the *commedia dell' arte* – the story of Pantalone and Pulcinella trying to steal an Enchanter's book, the subsequent buffoonery of mishandled magic, and the setting of a magic island visited by strangers, was a popular one in *commedia*, and informs the structure of *The Tempest*. Kit's play is the counter-image of one of his earliest successes, *Doctor Faustus*. Faustus is a black magician, whereas Prospero in *The Tempest* uses white magic. Their names both signify 'one who is lucky, prosperous' (Faustus in Latin, Prospero in Italian), but in *The Tempest* Kit substitutes the dangerous, youthful fire of *Faustus* with the softening waters of a sea change into wiser old age. Faustus yells dramatically as he is taken off to Hell: 'I'll burn my books', Prospero promises 'deeper than did ever plummet sound/I'll drown my book' (*Tempest* V i 56–7). He abjures his 'rough magic', renounces his attempts to control those who have collaborated with him in his art (Ariel the actor and Caliban the clown), and turns to rely on his own faint strength.

The Tempest was staged in 1611, many months before the Virginia Company made the contents of Strachey's report public.

In the years that followed, London, ever hungry for the young and the new, effortlessly shifted its gaze from the man who had slipped away to Stratford. Will Shakespere played his final role – as squire of New Place – to an entirely local audience. On 23 April 1616, sated and swine-drunk after a night spent swilling with his merchant cronies, he collapsed on his second-best bed, belched, then muttering the figures that were swirling in his head, spat once and was seized by a fatal apoplexy. There were no eulogies. On the same date, in Madrid, wiry old Cervantes, who had sweated to produce a second part to *Don Quixote* and found it even more rapturously received than the first, but who had lately been suffering from dropsy, lapsed into a coma from which he never recovered.

And on an island near Bermuda, Kit Marlowe picked up a quill (plucked from the wing of an albatross), dipped it in deep red ink that Oliver had made from the gum of a dragon's-blood palm, and began his first novel.

Afterword

Mark Twain likened writing the biography of Shakespeare to reconstructing the skeleton of a brontosaurus – using 'nine bones and six hundred barrels of plaster of Paris'. We work with a handful of facts and a pile of conjecture. Very soon the 'might have beens' and 'we have reason to believes' build up into 'as tradition instructs us' and harden into 'unquestionablys'. All biographies of Shakespeare, from the wayward to the academic, use the same few-score hard facts kneaded together with legend, then leavened by a dash of *Zeitgeist* and a large dollop of author's imagination. Poems and plays are plundered for biographical booty, even by those who profess scepticism as to the inferences that can be drawn about the life from the work. A river current in *The Rape of Lucrece* is likened to one in the Avon; all references in the plays to dolphins are lined up to suggest that, maybe, as a boy Shakespeare travelled twelve miles to see a water pageant staged by the Earl of Leicester in his castle grounds at Kenilworth. And so a story is stitched together. But like statistics, quotations in isolation can be turned to very different ends.

This book has not been an attempt to prove that Christopher Marlowe staged his own death, fled to the Continent, and went on to write the works attributed to Shakespeare. It assumes that as its starting point. It swings the old bones around, viewing them from another angle to build a different brontosaurus. By assuming the seemingly preposterous I have hoped to shake up our notions of the possible, or at the very least to look a little more sharply at how we construct truth. I have done this in a spirit of fun, and with the intention of a little saucy iconoclasm. Shakespeare's works are unassailable, and will survive any amount of subversion, but the quasi-religious idol that the man has become is perhaps in need of the efforts of a wicked wood-worm. Purists who do not relish the breezes of disruption blowing around sensible ideas will perhaps be displeased, but those who are willing to keep a literary tongue firmly in an historical cheek might enjoy seeing all the familiar bones thrown in the air, and watching them land in a different pattern. It is useful, as T. S. Eliot put it, from time to time to change our way of being wrong. Taking a fresh look at something we have grown used to – be it an historical fact or a Shakespearean sonnet – can sometimes yield unexpected rewards.

This book is, of course, an exercise of purest (or most impure) conjecture. But then so is the work of countless other writers of lives of Shakespeare and Marlowe. This story differs only in the degree to which invention has played a role in the outcome, and in the method by which it was told. Other writers have looked at the evidence and deduced a story; I have imagined a story, then supported it with the same sparse evidence. At this distance, the difference between deduction and speculation is paper thin. The book may very well have been called *The Impossibility of Biography*. It might be placed at a point of convergence of several different strands: of the historical novel that blurs fact with fantasy and doesn't admit the difference; of autobiographies that are so imaginatively written that some readers think they are novels; of novels that are so autobiographical that they approach the same point from the opposite direction; and of Shakespearean biography that carries an unsloughable burden of rumour and tradition.

Admittedly, in building this different brontosaurus, I have fashioned a few bones of my own. The book is grounded in fact, but has the courage of its own (con-)fictions. In the tradition of Shakespearean biography, made-up bits and might-have-beens gradually meld with what we know, to make a story of their own. In doing this I have played with Marlowe's history, but not with real history – though sometimes in the spirit of the fiction I have accepted one person's interpretation of history as fact.

Truth is never easily come by. Like Don Quixote, we can be perplexed by the intertwining of the credible and the fantastic. So for those who enjoy unravelling, I have followed a general rule. The footnotes at the bottoms of pages signal my broader inventions. For many this may be enough – but for those who like to delve, I have combed out the fiction from facts, as other writers have presented them, in the source notes that follow.

Part of the point of the tale has been to observe how people travelled, how cultures crossed, and how theatre got made. As he ruffled the ruffs of a post-Calvinist society, Kit Marlowe travelled through an extraordinarily cosmopolitan Europe, curling his tongue around different languages, accustoming his palate to new cuisines, quickly taking on new customs. He travels in a world tinged with panic, beset with secrets, yet delighting in erudition, catching the Continent at a fascinating moment in its history, one in which our contemporary culture is clearly being forged.

Rodney Bolt
Amsterdam 2004

315

Appendix I

Passport issued to players led by Will Ireland
written by the Lord Chamberlain, 14 June 1581
[Translated from the French]

Gentlemen, as the present bearers William Ireland, Thomas Jones, William Peeters, Jack Gielgaffe, Gordon Bene't, and Ben Frankson, have determined on making a journey in Germany and France with the intention of passing through the cities of Paris and Strasbourg, and while going on their said journey, of practising their profession by performing of music, feats of agility, and games of comedies, tragedies and histories for maintaining themselves and providing for their expenses on the said journey. These presents are therefore to request you to show and afford them every favour in your countries and jurisdictions, and to grant them in my favour your full passport under the seal of the states, to the end that the Burgomasters of the towns being under your jurisdiction, do not hinder them in passing from practising their said profession everywhere. In your doing which I shall remain obliged to all, and you will find me very ready to return your courtesy in greater instances. Given from my Chamber at the Court of England this fourteenth day of June, 1581.

> Your most devoted
> > to doing you pleasure and service
> > > C. Howard

Appendix II

Computer face-ageing technology applied to the Corpus Christi portrait of Christopher Marlowe. Marlowe's face is aged from the original 21 years old to 28 years old, and subsequently to 36 and 40.

Appendix III

Transcription of letter from William Larkin to
Dr Norgate (Master of Bene't College 1573–97),
circulated among the Fellows of Corpus Christi College
by Dr Mara Kalnins and Dr Linne Mooney on 1 April 1996,
after being found behind a skirting board
during renovations in Old Court.

Righte worshipful ande goode maister dr. norgate, I comende me vnto
yow Ande I Sende vnto yow by this Bearer the portraiture of maister
marley, a scoler wythin yowre colege wich he hath contracted wyth me
to performe ande for the wich I can in no wayes receyve of him payment.
for that he Sayth yt ys noo goode lykenes, but al men Sayth yt ys, for
wych cause I Sende the Same to yow that yowre grete auctorite wyth
hym maye induce hym to paye me what he hath promysed, to wyt vij
[pounds] × [shillings], wych Sum yf yow may receve of hym I praye
yow Sende vnto me. for wych Servyce yow Shal evir fynde me, Sir,

Yowre humble ande obediente etc.
Wm. Larkin

Appendix IV

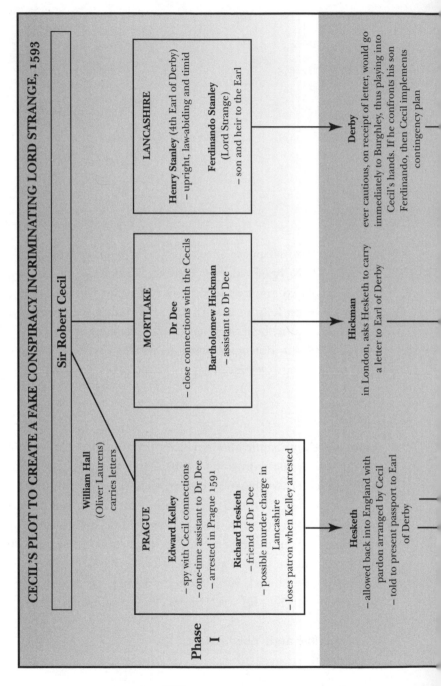

CECIL'S PLOT TO CREATE A FAKE CONSPIRACY INCRIMINATING LORD STRANGE, 1593

Sir Robert Cecil

William Hall
(Oliver Laurens)
carries letters

Phase I

PRAGUE

Edward Kelley
– spy with Cecil connections
– one-time assistant to Dr Dee
– arrested in Prague 1591

Richard Hesketh
– friend of Dr Dee
– possible murder charge in Lancashire
– loses patron when Kelley arrested

MORTLAKE

Dr Dee
– close connections with the Cecils

Bartholomew Hickman
– assistant to Dr Dee

LANCASHIRE

Henry Stanley (4th Earl of Derby)
– upright, law-abiding and timid

Ferdinando Stanley
(Lord Strange)
– son and heir to the Earl

Hesketh
– allowed back into England with pardon arranged by Cecil
– told to present passport to Earl of Derby

Hickman
in London, asks Hesketh to carry a letter to Earl of Derby

Derby
ever cautious, on receipt of letter, would go immediately to Burghley, thus playing into Cecil's hands. If he confronts his son Ferdinando, then Cecil implements contingency plan

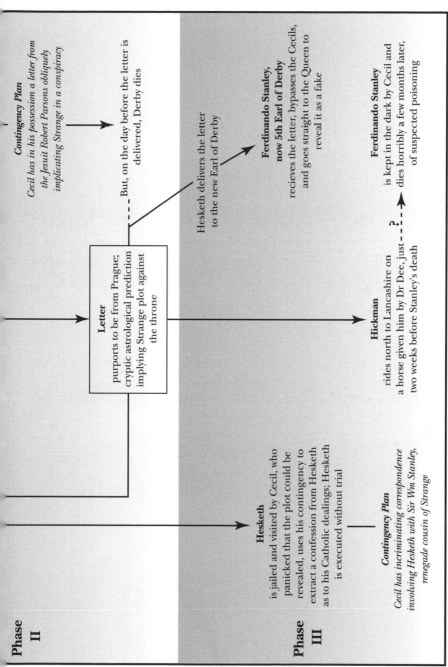

Phase II

Contingency Plan
Cecil has in his possession a letter from the Jesuit Robert Parsons obliquely implicating Strange in a conspiracy

But, on the day before the letter is delivered, Derby dies

Letter
purports to be from Prague; cryptic astrological prediction implying Strange plot against the throne

Hesketh delivers the letter to the new Earl of Derby

Ferdinando Stanley, now 5th Earl of Derby
recieves the letter, bypasses the Cecils, and goes straight to the Queen to reveal it as a fake

Hickman
rides north to Lancashire on a horse given him by Dr Dee, just two weeks before Stanley's death

Ferdinando Stanley
is kept in the dark by Cecil and dies horribly a few months later, of suspected poisoning

Hesketh
is jailed and visited by Cecil, who panicked that the plot could be revealed, uses his contingency to extract a confession from Hesketh as to his Catholic dealings; Hesketh is executed without trial

Phase III

Contingency Plan
Cecil has incriminating correspondence involving Hesketh with Sir Wm Stanley, renegade cousin of Strange

Appendix V

Lament of Arianna

in co-sì du – ra sor-te, in co-sì gran mar – ti-re, la – scia – te-

-mi mo-ri – re, la – scia – te – mi mo – ri – re.

In darkness let me dwell

Thus wed - ded to my woes, And bed - ded to my tomb,___

O let me liv - ing die,

O let me liv-ing, let me liv - ing, liv-ing die

Appendix VI

*A full and perfit Catalogue of W-H his books both got in England and acquired and bought in forraine parts.**

> Holinsheds Chronicles, best edition
> The Tragicall Historye of Romeus and Iuliet
> The Lives of Plutarch of North
> Hero and Leander
> A great Bible
> Essais de Montaigne
> Brounes method of the Italian tongue
> Cinthio Hekatommithi
> Saauedra Quixote
> Boccacio Decameron
> Manasseh ben Israel de termino vitae
> Cleopatra of daniels
> New jestes or witty Reparties
> Rosalynde
> Frederyke van Jennen
> Ammirati politica and Tacitum
> Fiorentino Il Pecorone
> Gesta romanorum bad edition
> Bandello novelles iii
> Gower Confessio
> Greenes Pandosto
> A historie of verona Corte

T. T. 1609

---

* Some of these books were no doubt the ones that Kit Marlowe took with him when he fled England in 1593.

Notes and References

EPIGRAPH

The T. S. Eliot quotation is from his essay 'Shakespeare and the Stoicism of Seneca', in *Selected Essays*, Faber and Faber, New York, 1932, p. 126.

FOREWORD

Sam Clemens' Foreword is a reproduction, with slight adaptation, of chapter three of Mark Twain's *Is Shakespeare Dead?*. Though written nearly a century ago it still offers a reasonable sketch of our verifiable knowledge of Shakespeare. Decades of subsequent research by tens of thousands of scholars and academics have added a little to Twain's store of facts: Robert Bearman in *Shakespeare in the Stratford Records* (Alan Sutton Press, Stroud, 1994), pp. 79–81, lists thirty-five Shakespeare-related items in the Stratford records, and Jonathan Bate, *The Genius of Shakespeare* (Picador, London, 1997), p. 4, points out that there are some fifty documents relating to Shakespeare, his family and his acting company in the Public Record Office at Kew. But many of these are repetitious (multiple references to the same incident), or tangential (lists of jurors at a court

case), and most by their very nature speak only of the bare facts of birth, marriage and death, of taxes, petty debt and the accumulation of property. They tell us little of nothing of Shakespeare's character or of his work – some people even dispute that the Stratford and London Shakespeares were the same man. Yet these are the dry bones that all biographers have to work with. Samuel Langhorne Clemens was, of course, Mark Twain's real name.

PROLOGUE *A Dead Man in Deptford*

Eleanor Bull was indeed a 'cousin' of one Blanche Parry, who in turn was 'cousin' to both Lord Burghley and the conjuror Dr Dee – see Charles Nicholl, *The Reckoning* (University of Chicago Press, Chicago, 1992), p. 35 ff. Although in Elizabethan times the term 'cousin' could encompass fairly distant relatives, it did imply bonds of obligation. And it does appear that if she ran anything at all, Widow Bull had some sort of gentleman's victualling house, not a seedy inn.

Recent research suggests. Most notably Nicholl, *Reckoning*, and

M. J. Trow, *Who Killed Kit Marlowe?* (Sutton Publishing, Stroud, 2001). **Deptford, in 1593**. Nicholl, *Reckoning*, pp. 13–15 provides much of this background on Deptford, though my turning Eleanor Bull's home into a safe house is a surmise, and I've elaborated on her relationship with Poley and Cecil.
'the tenth hour before noon'. Alan Haynes, *The Elizabethan Secret Services*, (Sutton Publishing, Stroud, 2000), p. 119, claims that Marlowe was reporting to Widow Bull's house on Cecil's orders.
'Sweet Robyn'. At least one person (Anthony Babington of the Babington plot) called Poley 'Sweet Robyn'. I've turned it into a nickname.
severed the internal carotid artery. Haynes, *Secret Services*, p. 120; Nicholl, *Reckoning*, p. 18.
William Danby. Details are as mentioned in the coroner's report. See Leslie Hotson, *The Death of Christopher Marlowe* (Nonesuch Press, London, 1925) for a full reproduction and translation from Latin of the document.
a friend of her kinsman Lord Burghley. Trow, *Marlowe?*, p. 244.

PART I

CHAPTER ONE *Prefaces to Shakespeare*
his beautiful singing voice. Sheer surmise – though as will be seen, Marlowe would have to have been able to sing well in order to win his scholarship to Cambridge.
John Marlowe . . . an immigrant to Canterbury. I owe much in this chapter to William Urry's painstaking examination of the Canterbury archives as revealed in his *Christopher Marlowe and Canterbury* (Faber and Faber, London, 1988).
a short cut to citizenship. Urry, *Marlowe*, p. 13; John Bakeless, *The Tragicall History of Christopher Marlowe*, Vol. 1 (Archon Books, Connecticut, 1964), p. 21.
'a scowlde, comon swearer'. Urry, *Marlowe*, pp. 27 and 34.
bellow and scream. Urry, *Marlowe*, p. 3, places the Marlowe household between the butchers' shambles, cattle market and clanging bells.
how far cheverel will stretch. Anthony Holden makes similar points about blood and leather in *William Shakespeare, His Life and Work* (Abacus, London, 1999), pp. 16 and 40–41.
'the small boy Shakespeare'. Urry, *Marlowe*, p. 2.
visiting his maternal grandparents in Dover. Marlowe's mother came from Dover, A. D. Wraight (who does believe Marlowe wrote the works attributed to Shakespeare) makes the *King Lear* connection in *The Story that the Sonnets Tell* (Adam Hart, London, 1994), pp. 327–9, and posits the existence of a tanner named Best in Wingham, ('Best's son, the tanner of Wingham' is mentioned in *Henry VI Part 2*).
A court case of 1565. Related in Bakeless, *Tragicall History*, Vol. I, p. 24; Urry, *Marlowe*, p. 29.
the tale of Dorothy Hocking. The story was uncovered in Canterbury archives by William Urry, and is

cited in Andrew Butcher's introduction to Urry's *Marlowe*, pp. xxxii–xxxiv, and by Wraight, *The Story*, pp. 321–4.

Clemence Ward, a notorious harlot. See Urry, *Marlowe*, pp. xxxiv–xxxv, and Wraight, *The Story*, pp. 325–7.

the Marlowes' only son. Christopher already had a younger sister, Margaret (b. 1565). Katherine was to give birth to another daughter, Jane, in 1569, lost another infant son in 1570, had her fiery daughter Anne in 1571, then Dorothy in 1573, and finally a surviving son named Thomas, in 1576.

Richard Umbarffeld and his fellow apprentices are mentioned in Bakeless, *Tragicall History*, Vol. 1, p. 23. Stephen Gosson's shopping spree is invented, though he lived in the same small parish as the Marlowes and did go to the King's School that year.

the private tutelage of Thomas Bull. Thomas Bull lived near the Marlowes in St George's parish and did take in pupils (see Urry, *Marlowe*, p. 9), but I have expanded on his relationship with Christopher.

'The midle sort of parentes'. Quoted in Daryll Grantley and Peter Roberts (eds), *Christopher Marlowe and English Renaissance Culture*, (Scolar Press, Aldershot, 1996), p. vii.

'The Master Downhale'. R. Willis (b. 1564), *Mount Tabor* (1639), quoted in John Dover Wilson, *Life in Shakespeare's England*, (Cambridge University Press, Cambridge, 1911), p. 53.

Sir Roger Manwood's history and character are revealed in Mark Eccles, *Christopher Marlowe in London* (Harvard University Press, Cambridge, Mass., 1934), pp. 20–21; and Trow, *Marlowe?*, pp. 23–4. Sir Roger did take an interest in the young Christopher, though it is not clear how far his support went. Kit would later appear before him in court and write his epitaph.

£1 a quarter. Bakeless, *Tragicall History*, Vol. 1, pp. 41–2.

Oliver Laurens is of such stuff as dreams are made on.

'On Sunday, Saint Bartholomew's Day'. Report of Juan de Olaegui, 1572, quoted in Trow, *Marlowe?*, p. 60.

Some 4,000 Huguenots were slaughtered. S. T. Bindoff, *Tudor England* (Penguin, London, 1987), p. 249. Trow, *Marlowe?*, p. 60, has 40,000 dead.

made their way to Canterbury. Urry, *Marlowe*, p. 3, also J. B. Black, *The Reign of Elizabeth* (Clarendon Press, Oxford, 1992), pp. 157–60.

a family of Gossons. Urry mentions a Huguenot Gosson, *Marlowe*, p. 3, and Stephen's father's foreign origins, p. 10.

Claudius Hollyband's language book, together with another by Peter Erondell are reproduced in M. St Clare Byrne (ed.), *The Elizabethan Home* (Cobden-Sanderson, London, 1930). The taut definition of language teaching is quoted in the introduction (p. ix), and young Francis's wail comes on p. 2.

in Canterbury to meet the Queen.

Description of the progress and
the preparations are from J.
Nichols, *Progresses and Processions of
Queen Elizabeth* (London, 1823,
reprinted Burt Franklin, New York,
1966), p. 336 ff.
travelling troupes. Urry, *Marlowe*,
p. 6.
'Lord of Leycester his players'.
Bakeless, *Tragicall History*, Vol. 1,
p. 33.
'between his leggs'. Quoted by
Andrew Butcher in his essay '*onleye
a boye called Christopher Mowle*' in
Grantley and Roberts (eds),
*Marlowe and English Renaissance
Culture*, p. 10.
**'harborowe[r] of the Devill and
the Pope'**. William Lambarde in
his *Perambulation of Kent* (1576),
quoted in Peter Roberts's essay
'*The "Studious Artizan"'*, in
Grantley and Roberts, *Marlowe
and English Renaissance Culture*,
p. 17.
the Red Lion. The history of the
first commercial playhouses and
what went on in them is based on
Andrew Gurr, *Playgoing in
Shakespeare's London* (Cambridge
University Press, Cambridge,
2000), pp. 10–12 and 119–24.
'the best for pastoral'. Francis
Meres mentions Gosson in his
survey of English authors, *Palladis
Tamia, 'Wit's Treasury'* (1598),
edited by Don Cameron Allen
(Scholar's Facsimiles and Reprints,
New York, 1938).
'marvellously ragingly'. The sky at
night is described by Urry in
Marlowe, p. 4.
'a problem of discipline'. This
point is made by Peter Roberts, in
Grantley and Roberts (eds),

*Marlowe and English Renaissance
Culture*, p. 19.
£14 6s 8d Christmas plays. Bakeless,
Tragicall History, Vol. 1, p. 34.
'dyd anymate the boyes'. The men
on both occasions were one
Edwards and one William Symcox;
the quotes are from Roberts in
Grantley and Roberts (eds),
*Marlowe and English Renaissance
Culture*, p. 19.
**'History [is] the treasure of times
past'**. Quoted in John Morrill,
Tudor and Stuart Britain (Oxford
University Press, Oxford, 1996),
p. 184.
**Christopher read the poets and
the historians**. Details of Marlowe's
school studies are based on M. H.
Curtis, 'Education and
Apprenticeship' in Allardyce Nicoll
(ed.), *Shakespeare in His Own Age*,
Shakespeare Survey No. 17
(Cambridge University Press,
Cambridge, 1964).
peas and prunes. Details of the
school diet are from Urry, *Marlowe*,
p. 43.
standard-bearer to Henry V. Urry,
Marlowe p. 49.
his manners. For young Francis's
lesson in table manners see
St Clare Byrne (ed.), *Elizabethan
Home*, p. 17. No doubt the young
Marlowe had to learn much the
same.
'schollers shal and must'. Quoted
in Trow, *Marlowe?*, p. 28.

CHAPTER TWO *Une Histoire Inventée*
'a sharp maintainer'. Camden is
quoted in C. R. N. Routh, *Who's
Who in Tudor England* (Shepheard-
Walwyn, London, 1990), pp. 217,
218.

a certificate signed by the vicar of Wimbledon. Burghley's caution is mentioned by Conrad Russell in 'The Reformation and the Church of England', in Morrill, *Tudor and Stuart Britain*, p. 280.

Jesuits from abroad. Nicholl, *Reckoning*, pp. 95–7, mentions the Jesuit network; other details of Protestant politicking are from Bindoff, *Tudor England*, pp. 247–51; Nicholl, *Reckoning* pp. 102–6; Morrill, *Tudor and Stuart Britain*, pp. 335–7 and 409–13.

he immediately spent 1*d* on a meal. Marlowe's initial expenditure, recorded in the Corpus Christi buttery book and college accounts is mentioned in Urry, *Marlowe*, pp. 55–6. Information on his scholarship and first days at Cambridge is from G. C. Moore Smith, 'Marlowe at Cambridge', *Modern Language Review*, 4, (1909), pp. 167 ff; and Roberts, in Grantley and Roberts (eds), *Marlowe and English Renaissance Culture*, pp. 22–4.

a Puritan college. The college's Puritan credentials are discussed in Austin K. Gray, 'Some Observations on Christopher Marlowe, Government Agent', *Modern Language Association of America*, 43 (1928), pp. 685–6.

'plain, simple, sullen, young, contemptuous'. Quoted in Nicholl, *Reckoning*, p. 95.

rebels was Thomas Nashe. Urry in *Marlowe*, p. 60, says that Kit 'may well have known' Nashe; Trow, *Marlowe?*, p. 44, states their friendship as a fact; Nicholl, *Reckoning*, p. 53 ff, notes that

Nashe once recalled Marlowe as one who 'used me as a friend' and says that the two men undoubtedly knew one another, and traces a decline in their intimacy. They did mix in the same circles, and Nashe's name appears as a collaborator on the title page of *Dido*. I have embroidered a little on their friendship.

conferrers of gentlemanly virtues. John Adamson in 'The Aristocracy and their Mental World', in Morrill, *Tudor and Stuart Britain*, pp. 176–7.

'Consort yourself with gentlemen'. Henry Peachem's *The Compleate Gentleman* (1622), quoted by Rosemary O'Day, in 'An Educated Society', in Morrill, *Tudor and Stuart Britain*, p. 136.

'a thinne Chest'. The impecunious student is mentioned by Bakeless in *Tragicall History*, Vol. 1, p. 55; and the ranking of his associates by Elisabeth Leedham-Green in *A Concise History of the University of Cambridge* (Cambridge University Press, Cambridge, 1996), p. 62.

Hero and Leander. Bakeless, *Tragicall History*, Vol. 1, p. 55.

3*s* 1½*d*. Urry, *Marlowe*, p. 56.

'one William Peeters'. Urry, *Marlowe*, p. 59. Apart from this brief mention, nothing seems to have been written about Peeters, so I have invented a history.

'dissoluteness in playes'. Quoted in Roberts in Grantley and Roberts (eds), *Marlowe and English Renaissance Culture*, p. 23.

'ridd theim cleane away'. Roberts in Grantley and Roberts (eds), *Marlowe and English Renaissance Culture*, p. 23.

Gammer Gurton's Needle. Record of the performance of this old favourite together with *Tarrarantantara* and other plays at Cambridge, as well as descriptions of the drama and its audience at the university, can be found in Bakeless, *Tragicall History*, Vol. 1, pp. 62–3.

'with vizors and lights'. Quoted in Roberts in Grantley and Roberts (eds), *Marlowe and English Renaissance Culture*, p. 35.

Bene't college accounts for 1581. These payments are mentioned in Roberts in Grantley and Roberts (eds), *Marlowe and English Renaissance Culture*, p. 24.

English players did indeed tour the Continent, as has been amply documented by Albert Cohn in *Shakespeare in Germany in the Sixteenth and Seventeenth Centuries* (Asher and Co., London, 1865), and Jerzy Limon in *Gentlemen of a Company* (Cambridge University Press, Cambridge, 1985). The earliest players are mentioned in Cohn, pp. xxi–xxiv and Limon, pp. 28–30. The troupe William Peeters joins is a fiction, though squarely based on a number of real strolling companies of the time.

'a filthy play'. Quoted in Trow, *Marlowe?*, p. 92.

the famous university at Padua. Jonathan Woolfson, *Padua and the Tudors* (James Clarke and Co., Cambridge, 1998), p. 15, mentions these informally registered students.

strictures on visiting Rome. E. S. Bates, *Touring in 1600* (Constable and Co., London, 1911), p. 55, gives the conditions under which passports were issued.

a letter from one J. Beaulieu. Quoted in Limon, *Gentlemen of a Company*, p. 161 (fn 26).

'Skeggs'. Nicholl, *Reckoning*, p. 116.

'by the banks of the Seine'. Watson does dedicate the elegy *Meliboeus* to Thomas Walsingham and recalls their trip to Paris. Nicholl, *Reckoning*, p. 182 ff, holds that the friendship between them was a warm one, and dates the visit to Paris as between the summer of 1581 and the spring of 1583. That Marlowe joins the fun is certainly not impossible, but is unverified.

Measure for Measure. Georges Lambin's comments on the play are given in Joseph Sobran, *Alias Shakespeare* (The Free Press, New York, 1997), p. 186.

a honeypot for converts. Gray, 'Some Observations . . .', pp. 687–9, writes of the 'perpetual leakage' of students from Cambridge to Douai and Rheims that increased after 1580; and Marlowe would a few years later be accused of going to Rheims – but this early mission to collect a 'note' from Baines (who was indeed there at the time) is my creation.

'insinuated a certain priest'. Quoted in Gray, 'Some Observations . . .', p. 689. Acquavivia is a real name.

poisoning the well water. Baines did indeed have such a plan; Nicholl, *Reckoning*, pp. 122–4.

'a delight rather to fill [his] mouth'. Part of Baines's confession, quoted in Nicholl,

Reckoning, p. 128, though Nicholl does point out that it should be viewed with caution as 'public writing' written in exchange for his release.

'carnal delights'. Quoted in Nicholl, *Reckoning*, p. 128, though Baines's penchant for a 'well-looked boy' is my addition.

'Henry Baily, a young youth'. Quoted in Nicholl, *Reckoning*, p. 126.

letter to the Jesuit . . . Agazzari. Nicholl, *Reckoning*, p. 124.

CHAPTER THREE *Catch My Soul*

'There be divers there'. Thomas Lever, *A Sermon Preached at Pauls Crosse* (*c.*1550), quoted in Bakeless, *Tragicall History*, Vol. 1, p. 58; here with spelling slightly modernised.

'amongst wags as lewd as myself'. Quoted in Bakeless, *Tragicall History*, Vol. 1, p. 50.

'initiated in a tavern by the way'. This final phrase comes from John Earle's *Micro-cosmographie*, 1628 (Scolar Press Facsimile, Leeds, 1966), p. 81. His description of students provides a partial model for the invention of Marlowe's Babylonical friends.

the rigid Cambridge curriculum. Details of Cambridge studies are from M. H. Curtis, 'Education and Apprenticeship' in Nicoll (ed.), *Shakespeare in His Own Age*, pp. 64–6, though I speculate on Marlowe's personal passions.

dubbed as *homo memorabilis*. By the musical scribe John Baldwin in *My Ladye Nevells Book*; see Edmund Fellowes, *William Byrd* (Oxford University Press, London, 1948), p. 237.

a university wait. The entry in college accounts is mentioned by Roberts in Grantley and Roberts (eds), *Marlowe and English Renaissance Culture*, p. 24.

the name was a common one. Fellowes, *Byrd*, p. 34.

William Byrd (alias Borne). Fellowes, *Byrd*, p. 34.

Ricardus Tertius, written by Thomas Legge, was performed in 1579 and on other occasions, including in 1582, and William Byrd did compose the music – see Fellowes, *Byrd*, pp. 167–9 and John Harley, *William Byrd, Gentleman of the Chapel Royal* (Scolar Press, Aldershot, 1997), p. 278. Bakeless, *Tragicall History*, Vol. 1, p. 62, suggests it is probable Marlowe saw the play and others claim that it influenced Greene, Marlowe, and perhaps Shakespeare (Alan and Veronica Palmer, *Who's Who in Shakespeare* (Methuen, London, 2000), p. 150). Like Legge, Byrd was a Catholic, and Tom Watson probably was too. Watson certainly collaborated with Byrd (see Harley, pp. 103, 275 and 281) and was friendly with Marlowe – but that he introduced the two is my surmise, as is Marlowe's meeting with Essex at a performance of *Ricardus Tertius*.

Bene't accounts and buttery books. Urry interprets entries as indicating a five-week absence in the three months before Michaelmas (Urry, *Marlowe*, p. 56); Moore-Smith ('Marlowe at Cambridge', p. 173), says six or seven weeks over the summer.

St Helen's, Bishopsgate. Harley, *William Byrd, Gentleman*, p. 103,

mentions Watson's return from the Continent to life in St Helen's ('where there was a strong Catholic presence'). Though it is clear Watson and Marlowe knew each other, I have expanded on the relationship – and this summer visit to London is conjecture.
'strangers who go not to church'. Quoted in Harley, *William Byrd, Gentleman*, p. 103.
'no want of young ruffins'. The rumbustious high jinks surrounding play-going are described by Gurr, *Playgoing*, pp. 123–5; and my description of the styles of plays is based both on Gurr and on Stephen Gosson's *Playes Confuted*, quoted in Gurr, p. 214.
Richard Tarlton. Gurr connects Tarlton with the rise in popularity of the word 'clown' (*Playgoing*, p. 276 fn. 14), quotes Henry Peacham's verses on Tarlton (p. 129), and highlights Tarlton's old-fashioned style (pp. 132–3).
'a Stationer that I knowe'. Nashe's description comes from his *Pierce Penilesse, His Supplication to the Divell*, reprint of 1592 edition (Bodley Head Quartos, London, 1924), p. 82, though Oliver's connection with this man, and subsequently with Thomas Thorpe (who did exist), is of course invention.
Sam Kennet, Marlowe's school-mate, did convert and go to Rheims, see Urry, *Marlowe*, p. 49.
something seductive about Catholicism. Nicholl, *Reckoning*, p. 95.
'places where certaine Recusantes remaine'. PRO SP12/151/11, quoted in Harley, *William Byrd,*

Gentleman, p. 73. The Catholic connections are all verifiable (see Harley, pp. 58–9, 74, 103), but the house party at Harlington is my invention. Poley did marry one Miss Watson, who probably was Thomas Watson's sister, though was later estranged from her (see Nicholl, *Reckoning*, p. 182).
'voluptuous music'. William Prynne, *Histriomastix*, quoted in F. W. Sternfeld, 'Music and Ballads' in Nicoll (ed.), *Shakespeare in His Own Age*, p. 217.
'lute, cittern, and virginals'. William Chappell, *Popular Music of the Olden Time* (Cramer, Beale and Chappell, London, 1853), Vol. 1, p. 78.
'But supper being ended'. Quoted in Sternfeld in Nicoll (ed.), *Shakespeare in his Own Age*, p. 214.
'Since singing is so good a thing'. Fellowes, *Byrd*, pp. 149–50.
The first sett, of Italian madrigalls Englished was indeed published in 1590 and dedicated to Essex (see Harley, *William Byrd, Gentleman*, p. 103), though the merry madrigal singing at Harlington, with the earl joining in, is speculation.
***Love's Labour's Lost*.** Lefranc's theory, and further parallels in *Love's Labour's Lost* and *Hamlet*, can be found in John Michell's *Who Wrote Shakespeare?* (Thames and Hudson, London, 1999), pp. 197–204.
'Mr Marlin'. Mentioned in Bakeless, *Tragicall History*, Vol. 1, p. 84.
'gorgeous attire'. Marlowe's penchant for flashy dressing is conjecture – though university attitudes to fashion are not (see

Bakeless, *Tragicall History*, Vol. 1, pp. 50–3). The description of Marlowe's clothing is based on Thomas Middleton's portrait of a dandy in *Father Hubbards Tales*, and is used with a little poetic licence, as Middleton was writing in 1604.
an absence of six or seven weeks. Urry, *Marlowe*, p. 56; Moore-Smith, 'Marlowe at Cambridge', p. 173.
'mak'st waste in niggarding'. Alan Haynes, *Sex in Elizabethan England* (Sutton Publishing, Stroud, 1997), p. 79) is not alone in providing an autoerotic reading of the sonnet.
I modi, with engravings by Romano and text by Aretino exists. See Lynne Lawner (ed. and trans.) *I modi, the sixteen pleasures* (Peter Owen, London, 1988).
'one of the wittiest knaves that ever God made'. Thomas Nashe, *The Unfortunate Traveller* (reprint of 1594 edition, Percy Reprints, Basil Blackwell, Oxford, 1927), p. 61.
Jean-Frédéric-Maximilien de Waldeck. For the full, extraordinary tale of chance and adventure behind the resurfacing of *I modi*, from Toulon to Toscanini, see Lawner (trans.), *I modi*, pp. 15–17. The *First suckes* is my creation.
'Che per mia fé' questo é, miglior boccone'. The lines from *I modi* can be found in Lawner (trans.), p. 64 – though she rather anachronistically translates '*il pan unto*' as 'garlic bread'.
'La signora Bianca' and her transgressions are mentioned in David C. McPherson, *Shakespeare, Jonson and the Myth of Venice* (Associated University Presses, New Jersey, 1990), p. 86.

Ponte delle Tette. Too true.
frisky young men. Thomas Cogan's hints for healthy living are cited in Haynes, *Sex in Elizabethan England*, p. 78.
Andrew Badoer is quoted in J. W. Thompson and S. K. Padover, *Secret Diplomacy* (Jarrolds, London, 1937), pp. 31–2; Roger Ascham's remark can be found in Richard Lassels, *The Voyage of Italy* (sold by John Starkey, Fleet Street, 1670), p. 1; and Henry Cavendish's journey is recorded by his servant Fox, in 'Mr. Harrie Cavendish His Journey to and from Constantynople', in *Camden Miscellany XVII*, 1940, *passim*.
a secret drawer of a cedar chest. Benjamin Woolley, *The Queen's Conjuror* (HarperCollins, London, 2001), pp. xv–xvi, tells the story of the discovery of the secret drawer, which contained books and papers by the great astrologer Dr John Dee, together with 'a necklace of beads made of olive stones, from which dangled a wooden cross'. The Marlowe/rosary idea is my creation.
'Our regret has no real claim on him'. Nicholl, *Reckoning*, p. 266.
'Treason begets spies'. Quoted in Haynes, *Elizabethan Secret Services*, p. xi.
'You teach them to cheat'. John le Carré, *The Spy Who Came in from the Cold* (Coronet Books, London, 1963), p. 10.
'There is less danger in fearing too much than too little'. Letter of 1568, quoted in Richard Deacon, *A History of the British Secret Service* (Grafton, London, 1991), p. 17.
the case of one Richard Foley is

mentioned in Deacon, *British Secret Service*, p. 45.

'They knew the international language, Latin'. See Nicholl, *Reckoning*, p. 171, whose analysis of the nature of Elizabethan intelligence work has been invaluable to me.

a discrepancy in the records. Urry, *Marlowe*, p. 56; Moore-Smith, 'Marlowe at Cambridge', p. 174. That these periods of absence represent a period of probation for spy Marlowe is conjecture.

for Her Majesty's special and secret affairs. These methods of payment are outlined by Nicholl, *Reckoning*, p. 109.

the people he is beginning to mix with. Percy, Hariot and Ralegh were all friends with shared intellectual interests. The Paget incident is true, and it appears Walsingham and Burghley were keeping Percy under surveillance. Marlowe and Walsingham were friends, and he and Ralegh certainly knew one another, but I have speculated as to how well, and have expanded on his friendships with the others (also see Nicholl, *Reckoning*, pp. 193–9; Trow, *Marlowe?*, pp. 167–73).

Sir Walter's personal intervention. A distinct possibility, though not a corroborated fact (Trow, *Marlowe?*, p. 168).

Thomas Walsingham was indeed at Seething Lane, apparently with some sort of senior position, and Poley did apply to him for 'secret recourse' to Sir Francis (Nicholl, *Reckoning*, pp. 116–17).

'go out at midnight into a wood'. Quoted in Nicholl, *Reckoning*, p. 205.

CHAPTER FOUR *Gentlemen of a Company*

three men reporting from Paris. The increase in espionage activity is outlined in Haynes, *Elizabethan Secret Services*, pp. 16–17.

the Low Countries. For the historical background to the situation in the Low Countries I am indebted to Jonathan I. Israel, *The Dutch Republic* (Clarendon Press, Oxford, 1998), and Susan Doran, *Elizabeth I and Foreign Policy* (Routledge, London, 2000).

English players. This discussion of the English comedians is based on Albert Cohn, *Shakespeare in Germany in the Sixteenth and Seventeenth Centuries* (Asher & Co., London, 1865); Limon, *Gentlemen of a Company*; Simon Williams (*Shakespeare on the German Stage*, Cambridge University Press, Cambridge, 1990); E. Brennecke, *Shakespeare in Germany 1590–1700* (University of Chicago Press, Chicago, 1964); Willem Schrickx's article: 'English Actors at the Courts of Wolfenbüttel, Brussels and Graz during the Lifetime of Shakespeare', *Shakespeare Survey*, No. 33, 1980; and maps in E. Herz, *Englische Schauspieler und Englisches Schauspiel zur Zeit Shakespeares in Deutschland* (L. Voss, Hamburg, 1903). That the companies were a cover for spies, and that Marlowe was of their ilk, is purely speculation.

In court, a simultaneous translator. Fynes Moryson, supplementary to *Itinerary* in Charles Hughes (ed.) *Shakespeare's Europe* (Sherratt & Hughes, London, 1903), p. 304; Limon, *Gentlemen of a Company* p. 12.

'their pretty inventions'. From the preface of the first collection of works performed by the English comedians (1620), quoted in Cohn, *Shakespeare in Germany*, p. xciv.

'We can be bankrupts on this side'. Quoted in Cohn, *Shakespeare in Germany*, p. xcvi.

Kit's absences from college. Urry, *Marlowe*, p. 56.

O crudelis hyena. These anagrams are given in Grantley and Roberts (eds), *Marlowe and English Renaissance Culture*, p. 70.

a passport for a number of players. Schrickx, 'English Actors . . .', pp. 153–5. The text of this passport is given in English in Cohn, *Shakespeare in Germany*, p. xxix, and in a more complete version in French in Schrickx, p. 153. Bradstriet does appear on the passport, and though a John Breadstreet/Bradstriet is mentioned in other groups of travelling players, there is no mention of him in London (see Cohn, p. xxxiii). In the pages that follow I have given him an independent existence, and his own troupe. Details on Robert Browne are true.

'chose to steer towards Genoa'. Lassels, *Voyage of Italy*, p. 74.

'leaving both armies barking'. William Lithgow, *A Total Discourse of Rare Adventures and Painefull Peregrinations of Long Ninteene Yeares of Travayles* (I. Okes, London, 1640), p. 412.

one Wychegerde. Haynes, *Elizabethan Secret Services*, p. 102.

'The tumbler also did us please'. Translated by Brennecke,

Shakespeare in Germany 1590–1700, p. 8.

Pyramus and Thisbe. A slight fudge here, though another group of players was performing a play called *Pyramus and Thisbe* in 1604 (Schrickx, 'English Actors . . .', p. 167).

Marlin, Marlen, Malyn or Marlyn. Moore-Smith, 'Marlowe at Cambridge', p. 176.

the shadow of a Tudor portrait. The story of the discovery is true, though the college is always very careful to state that it is a putative portrait of Marlowe. Calvin Hoffman's sleuth work is chronicled in his *The Man Who Was Shakespeare* (M. Parrish, London, 1955, p. 65ff). The ageing of the Corpus face into the Chandos portrait is a digital sleight of hand.

conspirators posed for portraits. Roberts, in Grantley and Roberts, *Marlowe and English Renaissance Culture*, pp. 28–9.

a fashionable melancholy. Strong is cited in Roberts, in Grantley and Roberts (eds), *Marlowe and English Renaissance Culture*, p. 28.

'I am one who is entrusted to keep secrets'. Wraight, *The Story*, p. 92.

18*d* and 21*d* extravagances. Nicholl, *Reckoning*, p. 100.

'a doublet of black carke, cut upon a dark reddish velvet'. Letter from Sir Edward Stafford to Sir Francis Walsingham, 10 July 1588, quoted in Gray, 'Some Observations . . .', p. 693. That Marlowe borrowed the doublet from Roger Walton is guesswork.

'All prostitutes and immodest girls'. Montaigne was amused enough by the rules to note them

335

in his journal: E. J. Trechmann (trans.), *The Diary of Montaigne's Journey to Italy in 1580 and 1581* (Hogarth Press, London, 1929), p. 13.

a dose of the clap. Wraight, *The Story*, p. 233–5, discusses gonorrhoea and the Sonnets; Haynes, *Sex in Elizabethan England*, p. 152, writes about syphilis and the plays. The details of Marlowe's sexual health are a matter for speculation.

visit to Plombières. Montaigne had indeed visited Plombières in 1580, and records the event in his travel journal (*Diary*, p. 9 ff), but this subsequent visit and meeting with Marlowe is my invention. (Montaigne was travelling through Europe at this time, but it is not certain where exactly.) My description of the baths is informed by Montaigne.

a troupe that followed the Earl of Leicester. Leicester did have a company of players with him. I've slipped Marlowe in among them.

Claudio Monteverdi travelled as *maestro di cappella*. Paolo Fabbri, *Monteverdi*, translated by Tim Carter (Cambridge University Press, Cambridge, 1994), pp. 30–1 and Denis Arnold, *Monteverdi* (Oxford University Press, Oxford, 2000), p. 10.

'commended unto him by the honourable the Earl of Leicester'. The players in Elsinore in 1586 do appear to have been from Leicester's own troupe – see E. K. Chambers, *The Elizabethan Stage* (Oxford University Press, Oxford, 1923) Vol. 2, pp. 271–2; Cohn, *Shakespeare in Germany* p. xxxix.

snippet of tactical know-how. The parallel between the passages in *2 Tamburlaine* and Paul Ive's book is pointed out by Nicholl, *Reckoning*, p. 120.

Will Kempe, the clown was with the company – see Chambers, *Elizabethan Stage*, p. 272, and Jon Stefansson, 'Shakespeare at Elsinore' in *Contemporary Review*, LXIX, 1896, p. 35: both cite Court records; and 'Will, the Lord of Lester's jesting plaier' did carry a letter from Sydney to Walsingham – see Karl Elze, 'The Supposed Travels of Shakespeare', in *Essays on Shakespeare* (Macmillan, London, 1874), p. 256.

'spent his life in mad Jigges'. Will Kemp, *Kemps nine daies wonder*, edited by Susan Yaxley (The Larks Press, Norfolk, 1985), p. 1.

Kronborg Castle had just been completed, and the players were probably there as part of inaugural celebrations. The possibility of Kronborg as a setting for *Hamlet*, and other parallels, is based on discussions in Kenneth Kirkwood, *Did Shakespeare Visit Denmark?* (privately published, Karachi, 1953), p. 26 ff, and Jon Stefansson, 'Shakespeare at Elsinore'.

forbade them to make noise with their drums. Limon, *Gentlemen of a Company*, p. 29.

'vastly fond of great noises'. Paul Hentzner, 'A Journey into England in the Year MDXCVIII' in *Paul Hentzner's Travels in England during the Reign of Queen Elizabeth*, translated by Richard Bentley, London, 1797, p. 89.

'It would make a man sick'.

Quoted in Stefansson, 'Shakespeare at Elsinore', p. 31.

dumb-show prologues were a special feature of the English comedians' performances (Limon, *Gentlemen of a Company*, p. 19).

'very black, heavy and windy'. Fynes Moryson, *Itinerary*, Vol. 4 (1617 edition, James MacLehose and Sons, Glasgow, 1906), p. 67.

a knowledge of Danish words. These observations are made by Stefansson, 'Shakespeare at Elsinore', pp. 32–3.

'. . . it is hanged with Tapistary'. Quoted in Stefansson, 'Shakespeare at Elsinore', p. 28.

the *Ur-Hamlet*. Cohn points out both an English *Hamlet* and an early version of *Der Bestrafte Brudermord* were in the repertoire of bands of English comedians, *Shakespeare in Germany*, p. cxx. Brennecke, *Shakespeare in Germany 1590–1700*, pp. 247–8 cites Henslowe's and Lodge's early references to such a play. Marlowe's time in Denmark is, however, my invention.

Rosencrance . . . and Guildenstiene, students from Denmark, did indeed register at the University of Padua (see Kirkwood, *Did Shakespeare Visit Denmark?*, p. 20 and Stefansson, 'Shakespeare at Elsinore', p. 32).

the Babington plot. For my account of the plot I am indebted to Nicholl, *Reckoning*, pp. 147–65, and Christopher Haigh, 'Politics in an Age of Peace and War' in Morrill, *Tudor and Stuart Britain*, pp. 337–9.

'I am the same I always pretended'. Quoted in Nicholl, *Reckoning*, pp. 158–9.

'handled so circumspectly'. Quoted in Nicholl, *Reckoning*, p. 158.

Raptus Helenae. Watson did paraphrase the poem in 1586, and there are contemporary references to a (now lost) version by Marlowe published in 1587, but the relation between the two is uncertain (Bakeless, *Tragicall History*, Vol. 1, pp. 293–4).

The *Faustbuch* was introduced at the 1587 Frankfurt Book Fair, and the annotated Aquinas is in the Parker Library at Corpus Christi College, Cambridge.

'Witty Tom Watson'. The various contemporary references to Watson are from Mark Eccles, *Christopher Marlowe in London* (Harvard University Press, Cambridge, Mass., 1934), pp. 7–8. It was Eccles who first showed that Marlowe and Watson were friends. Thomas Walsingham was friendly with both (I have, as pointed out earlier, elaborated on the friendships). Shakespeare was labelled 'Watson's heir' for *Venus and Adonis*.

the 'flower-strewn world'. Alan Bray, 'Homosexuality and the Signs of Male Friendship in Elizabethan England' in *History Workshop Journal*, 29 (1990), p. 16.

'Whereas it was reported that Christopher Morley'. From *Acts of the Privy Council*, Vol. 4, 29 June 1587, quoted in Bakeless, *Tragicall History*, Vol. 1, p. 77 (spelling modernised). Baines's role in the affair is invented, though his Cambridge connections are not.

INTERLUDE

strolling troupes visited Stratford.
Holden, *William Shakespeare*, p. 78,
lists the companies that visited
Stratford.

to repair a broken bench. Holden,
William Shakespeare, p. 79.

Will stepped into the breach. My
account of the Thame affray is
based on Katherine Duncan-
Jones's, *Ungentle Shakespeare* (The
Arden Shakespeare, London,
2001), p. 29. A number of
biographers, including Holden
(*William Shakespeare*) and Mark
Eccles (*Shakespeare in Warwickshire*),
surmise that this is when
Shakespeare was recruited by the
Queen's Men, though there is no
evidence to support this.

PART II

CHAPTER FIVE *West Side Story*

London. The following have been
helpful to me in creating a picture
of London at this time: John Stow,
Survey of London (1598, reprinted
by Everyman, London, 1929); Paul
Hentzner, 'A Journey into
England. . .', (1598); Peter
Ackroyd, *London, The Biography*
(Chatto & Windus, London,
2000); Roy Porter, *London, A Social
History* (Penguin, London, 1994);
Gāmini Salgādo, *The Elizabethan
Underworld* (Sutton Publishing,
Stroud, 1995); T. F. Reddaway,
'London and the Court' in Nicoll,
(ed.), *Shakespeare in His Own Age*.

100,000 people. A conservative
estimate. There were no censuses,
so numbers for this time are a
matter of guesswork. Roy Porter

traces a population growth from
85,000 in 1565 to 140,000 in
1603, with a further 40,000 in the
burgeoning suburbs (*London, A
Social History*, p. 42). Others prefer
a figure going on for 200,000
within the city walls by 1600.

barely a handful of Jews. The
number of foreigners in London is
discussed in G. K. Hunter,
'Elizabethans and Foreigners' in
Nicoll (ed.), *Shakespeare in His Own
Age*, pp. 45 and 49.

'handsome and clean'. Hentzner,
'A Journey into England . . .',
p. 33.

scoured with paste of almonds.
St Clare Byrne (ed.), *The
Elizabethan Home*, p. 59ff.

'building of filthy Cottages'. Stow,
The Survey of London, p. 376.

**'her Eyes small, yet black and
pleasant'**. Hentzner, 'A Journey
into England . . .', p. 48.

'All manners of attire'. Moryson,
Itinerary, I, p. 428.

**'dressed most exquisitely and
elegantly'**. Quoted in S.
Schoenbaum, *William Shakespeare, a
Compact Documentary Life* (Oxford
University Press, Oxford, 1975),
pp. 134–5.

'uncomely to be used'. Moryson,
Itinerary, I, p. 428.

**'No 1 Little Crown St
Westminster'**. Cited by various
biographers, including Holden,
William Shakespeare, p. 90.

**fifty-seven documented varieties of
the family name**. These are listed
in Michell, *Who Wrote Shakespeare?*,
pp. 13–16.

**lodging . . . with his friend Thomas
Watson**. Watson was living in
St Helen's, and later moved to

Norton Folgate, and certainly by
1589 his friend Kit Marlowe was
also living in Norton Folgate,
Eccles, *Marlowe in London*,
pp. 159 and 114 respectively. That
they lodged together is my
invention. Eccles posits that
Shakespeare was also in
Shoreditch/Norton Folgate at the
time (pp. 122–4). Robert Poley
was there too (see Bakeless,
Tragicall History, Vol. 1, p. 104).

John Heminges did marry Rebecca
Knell, and many believe also acted
with the Queen's Men before
moving on (see Duncan-Jones,
Ungentle Shakespeare, p. 31); and he
was left money in Shakspeare's will
(see Schoenbaum, *William
Shakespeare*, p. 300).

book-keeper and stage-keeper.
Duncan-Jones, *Ungentle Shakespeare*,
p. 43.

'an absolute *Johannes factotum*'. As
quoted in Duncan-Jones, *Ungentle
Shakespeare*, pp. 43–5; the *Johannes
fac totum* label comes from the
famous 'upstart Crow' passage of
Robert Greene's *Groats-worth of
Witte, bought with a million of
Repentance* (reprint of 1592
edition, Bodley Head Quartos,
London, 1923), which (this
passage at least) Duncan-Jones
convincingly argues is by
Nashe.

**no proven examples of his
handwriting**. His will was not in his
own hand, but dictated to his
lawyer Francis Collins (see Holden,
William Shakespeare, p. 320). The
only other handwriting argued to
be Shakespeare's is 'Hand D' –
147 lines written as an
amendment to Anthony Munday's

play about Sir Thomas More – but
this is a typical example of an early
surmise becoming tradition and
then hardening into a form of
fact. Apart from some eccentric
spellings, no proof exists.

**'upstart Crow, beautified with our
feathers'**. Greene, *Groats-worth of
Witte*, p. 45.

**the sensational young Christopher
Marley**. I've elaborated a little on
Marlowe's personal (though not
his theatrical) reputation. There is
no absolute proof that Shakespeare
and Marlowe ever met, though they
did both have connections with
Lord Strange's Men. Their working
relationship is an invention –
though many have posited collaboration (for example on *Henry VI*),
quite possibly work that an ambitious *Johannes factotum* might do.

creation of the Romantic era.
Jonathan Bate makes a similar
point in *The Genius of Shakespeare*
(Picador, London, 1997), p. 99
and *passim*.

'presiding personality'. Cited in
Frank Kermode, *Shakespeare's
Language* (Penguin, London,
2000), p. 18.

'self-satisfied pork-butcher'.
Quoted in Holden, *William
Shakespeare*, p. 327.

the 'Chandos portrait'. All shall be
revealed.

'the precisest man in England'.
That the proprietor saw to it that
the Mermaid was a quiet and
respectable tavern is noted in
Eccles, *Marlowe in London*, p. 88,
while Trow points out that
Marlowe and Nashe also drank at
the Nag's Head (Trow, *Marlowe?*,
p. 97). Shakespeare's local

remains a mystery, and the tavern
tattler is invented.

CHAPTER SIX *Gypsy Soul*
Colloquia et Dictionariolum. The
publication is mentioned in
Francine De Nave and Leon Voet,
Museum Plantin-Moretus (Ludion,
Brussels, 1989), p. 99.
**'many lands and speaking many
tongues'**. Bindoff, *Tudor England*,
p. 274.
an Esperanto of War. De Somogyi,
in 'Maps of War' in Grantley and
Roberts (eds), *Marlowe and English
Renaissance Culture*, pp. 104–5.
'franco piccolo'. Mentioned in
Bates, *Touring in 1600*, p. 48.
Dictionorium Teutonico-Latinum.
Listed in Leon Voet, *The Plantin
Press, 1555–1589* (Van Hoeve,
Amsterdam, 1983), pp. 1300–03.
Oliver's involvement is of course
fictitious.
Plantin's allegiances and various
clients are discussed in Leon Voet,
The Golden Compasses (A. L.
Vangendt & Co., Amsterdam,
1969), pp. 94–8 and 113–15.
a broadside 'Declaration'. Haynes,
Elizabethan Secret Services, p. 103,
mentions this broadside, stolen for
Walsingham.
**Jasper Himselroy, who traded in
passports**. Haynes, *Elizabethan Secret
Services*, p. 3, mentions Himselroy's
activities in this field.
**Stephen Powle, who had probably
recruited Wroth**. Jonathan
Woolfson, *Padua and the Tudors*
(James Clarke & Co., Cambridge,
1998), pp. 265 and 287–8,
establishes the connection between
the two and that they were both
intelligencers. I surmise that the

older Powle recruited Wroth
before he left.
the 'best listening post in Europe'.
Deacon, *British Secret Service*, p. 41.
a subtle psychological warfare.
Deacon, *British Secret Service*,
pp. 35–9.
coded espionage messages. Edward
Kelley is a most mysterious
character. Woolley, *Queen's
Conjuror*, pp. 218–23, examines
the possibility that he had been
lured into the Walsingham spy
network. I treat a Walsingham/
Dee/Kelley espionage link – a
distinct possibility – as fact.
Steganographia. Both Haynes,
Elizabethan Secret Services, p. 22 and
Woolley, *Queen's Conjuror*,
pp. 72–81, discuss Dee's discovery
of the *Steganographia* and his
excitement at the idea of occult
communication.
The occult was taken seriously.
Gareth Roberts in 'Necromantic
Books' in Grantley and Roberts
(eds), *Marlowe and English
Renaissance Culture*, p. 162,
mentions the wax dolls; Bruno's
plans are outlined in John Bossy,
*Giordano Bruno and the Embassy
Affair* (Yale University Press, New
Haven, 1991), p. 154.
**The Jesuit scholar Christopher
Parkins**. Woolfson, *Padua and the
Tudors*, p. 262, notes Parkins's
presence in Padua; and Woolley,
Queen's Conjuror, p. 300, mentions
his letters about Kelley from
Prague.
**daring young gentlemen like
Harrie Cavendish**. Fox, his
manservant, gives an account of
the trip undertaken in 1589 in
'Mr. Harrie Cavendish His Journey

to and from Constantynople . . .',
edited by A. C. Wood, *Camden
Miscellany*, XVII, 1940.
**Nashe found himself embraced
and fêted**. Elze, 'Supposed
Travels . . .', p. 267, relates this
experience and dates Nashe's visit
to Italy as ending in the summer
of 1588 – though many hold that
Nashe's accounts of Italy are pure
fiction, and that he never went
there at all. Nashe's travelling with
Marlowe is my invention.
commedia dell'arte. The various
parallels between the plays and
those of *commedia* are based on
discussions in K. M. Lea, *Italian
Popular Comedy* (Russell & Russell,
New York, 1962), Vol. 2,
pp. 431–47, and Andrew Grewar,
'The Clowning Zanies:
Shakespeare and the Actors of the
Commedia dell' Arte' in
Shakespeare in Southern Africa, 3,
1989. Allardyce Nicoll is cited in
Grewar, pp. 17–18, and Edward
Gordon Craig on p. 9.
'the Academie of man-slaughter'.
Thomas Nashe, *Pierce Penilesse*,
p. 48.
'the art of atheisme'. Thomas
Nashe, *The Unfortunate Traveller*,
p. 96.
**'a sort of squirting baudie
Comedians'**. Thomas Nashe, *Pierce
Penilesse*, p. 90.
*'with as good a grace, action,
gesture'*. Thomas Coryate, *Coryats
Crudities 1611* (Scolar Press,
London, 1978), p. 15.
Savore sauce. The recipe is given
in Moryson, *Itinerary*, Vol. 4,
p. 100. The meal at Bergamo is
based on Moryson's descriptions of
Italian food, pp. 95–100.

'wrapt up in cleane paper'.
Perhaps the first ever mention of a
doggy bag. The take-away, as well
as the effects of *Lachrimae Christi*,
are mentioned in Lithgow, *Total
Discourse*, p. 15.
**students from Illyria, from
Bohemia and from Cyprus**. The
various nationalities that made up
the university's cosmopolitan
student body are listed in
Woolfson, *Padua and the Tudors*,
p. 280, and Lucia Rossetti, *The
University of Padua* (Erredici,
Padua, 1999), pp. 37–8.
**'More students of forraine and
remote nations'**. Coryate, *Coryats
Crudities*, p. 154.
Oliver – on his first visit to Italy.
This fictional visit echoes that of
Fynes Moryson (Moryson, *Itinerary*,
Vol. 1, p. 147 ff).
**'a man may lie down in the
exhalations'**. Montaigne describes
the visit to Àbano in his *Diary of
Montaigne's Journey to Italy*, p. 95.
'A monstrous filthinesse'.
Lithgow's musings on buggery and
the gloominess of Padua are in his
Total Discourse, p. 43.
'punished with banishment'.
Moryson, *Itinerary*, Vol. 1, p. 156.
Richard Willoughby. True:
Woolfson, *Padua and the Tudors*,
pp. 283–4.
cushions strewn about for comfort.
A number of travellers have left
records of their journeys – see, for
instance, Francis Mortoft, 'Francis
Mortoft: His Book', *Hakluyt Society*,
LVII (London, 1925), p. 186 and
note 2. I *know* that multitudes of
examples of inaccuracies about
Italy and Venice can also be
quoted in retort. This is partially

the point. We could ping-pong details back and forth without any certainty of how or why they got there in the first place. Who knows what bits of information or misinformation actors may have contributed in rehearsals; or how an author may bend reality to create a stage Verona or a conceptual Venice that suits his dramatic purposes? Should we care whether the writer went there or not? As Geoffrey Braithwaite, Julian Barnes's narrator in *Flaubert's Parrot*, puts it: 'Why does writing make us chase the writer? Why can't we leave well alone? Why aren't the books enough?' (Barnes, *Flaubert's Parrot* p. 2.) (Incidentally, of all his contemporaries, Ben Jonson seems to have had the fullest idea of Venice.)

candidates for Belmont. The various theories are expounded in Elze, 'Supposed Travels . . .', pp. 278–81; Ernesto Grillo, *Shakespeare and Italy* (The University Press, Glasgow, 1949), p. 138; and J. R. Mulryne, 'History and myth in *The Merchant of Venice*', in Michele Marrapodi et al. (eds), *Shakespeare's Italy* (Manchester University Press, Manchester, 1997), pp. 93–8.

below the Belvedere, is a chapel. It's there.

depiction of Rome. A. J. Hoenselaars, 'Italy staged in English Renaissance drama', in Marrapodi et al., *Shakespeare's Italy*, p. 34; and A. D. Wraight, *New Evidence* (Adam Hart, London, 1996), pp. 251–2.

Correggio's *Io and Jupiter*. Elze,

'Supposed Travels . . .', p. 291, and Michell, *Who Wrote Shakespeare?*, p. 225, are among those who point out the link between the play and the painting.

'This signior Julio's gyant dwarf'. The gloss is made by Elze, 'Supposed Travels . . .', p. 290.

described . . . in *The Rape of Lucrece*. Lines 1366–456, mentioned in Michell, *Who Wrote Shakespeare?*, p. 225.

Muzio Giustinopolitano's *Il Duello*. Sergio Rossi, in 'Duelling in the Italian manner' in Marrapodi et al. (eds) *Shakespeare in Italy*, p. 114, points out that Saviolo's book is almost a direct translation from the Italian.

rules gave way to dirty tricks. Sydney Anglo, in *The Martial Arts of Renaissance Europe* (Yale University Press, New Haven, 2000), pp. 273–4, points out the anarchic nature of street combat, despite the rules.

the 200-ton *Tiger* under Captain John Bostocke. W. B. Whall, *Shakespeare's Sea Terms Explained* (J. W. Arrowsmith, Bristol, 1910), pp. 13–14, lists this ship as being part of the fleet in 1588. Captain Barnestrawe, his 'copernose' and his *Tiger* are real enough (see D. B. Quinn, 'Sailors and the Sea', in Nicoll (ed.), *Shakespeare in His Own Age*, p. 29), but their presence in Venice is hopeful thinking.

'Master had no compasse'. Lithgow, *Total Discourse*, p. 44.

'stamp of death in his pale visage'. Lithgow, *Total Discourse*, p. 99.

use correct professional language. The mariners' expertise is pointed

out by A. F. Falconer, in
Shakespeare and the Sea (Constable,
London, 1964), pp. 38–9.

CHAPTER SEVEN *Men of Respect*
as lonely as an owl. Lord Burghley
bewails his loneliness in David
Cecil, *The Cecils of Hatfield House*
(Cardinal, London, 1973), p. 57.
Also see Curtis Breight, *Surveillance
Militarism and Drama in the
Elizabethan Era* (Macmillan,
London, 1996); Conyers Read,
Lord Burghley and Queen Elizabeth
(Jonathan Cape, London, 1960).
Regnum Cecilianum. A position
outlined in Breight, *Surveillance
Militarism*, pp. 1–42.
**'Suffer not [your] sons to pass the
Alps'**. Quoted in Cecil, *The Cecils of
Hatfield House*, p. 180.
**Robert Devereux, the young Earl
of Essex**. His entry into the Cecil
household is described in Read,
Burghley and Queen Elizabeth,
p. 467. The antagonism between
the two Roberts became quite
clear in later years, but I have
speculated as to its source and
driving force.
'godly vigilance'. Cecil's
impeccable public behaviour is
chronicled in Cecil, *The Cecils of
Hatfield House*, p. 93.
**'a man likely to trust much to his
art and finesse'**. Quoted in Read,
Burghley and Queen Elizabeth,
p. 496. Read holds that the
remark could apply either to
Burghley or Cecil.
pits of blackest depression. Cecil,
The Cecils of Hatfield House, p. 91.
**'Towards thy superiors be
humble'**. Quoted in Cecil, *The
Cecils of Hatfield House*, p. 82.

'bringinge lettres in post'. From
government accounts, quoted in
Bakeless, *Tragicall History*, Vol. 1,
p. 84.
**the battle between Ralegh and
Essex**. The tumult and violence of
this rivalry is highlighted by
Nicholl, *Reckoning*, pp. 295–6.
**a clandestine raid on Walsingham's
house**. Haynes points out that
there 'are no other candidates for
the organizer of the raid'
(*Elizabethan Secret Services*, p. 156). I
have turned surmise into fact, and
later come up with some credible
(though invented) discoveries
Cecil made.
**'Sir Robert Cecil, as you may have
heard'**. Quoted in Read, *Burghley
and Queen Elizabeth*, p. 477, who
also dates Essex's efforts to
countercheck the Cecils' influence
from his return to England from
France.

CHAPTER EIGHT *Shakespeare in Love*
The Hog Lane affray. The
following were useful to my
account of the Hog Lane affray:
Bakeless, *Tragicall History*, Vol. 1,
pp. 98–103; Eccles, *Marlowe in
London*, p. 38 ff; Trow, *Marlowe?*,
pp. 129–30. I've kept to the facts
as we know them, but interpret
Marlowe's role more leniently than
others do.
'kynde Kit Marlowe'. Bakeless
quotes these and other mild
epithets, Bakeless, *Tragicall History*,
Vol. 1, pp. 186–7.
a known thug and scoundrel.
Eccles, *Marlowe in London*,
pp. 43–68 and Trow, *Marlowe?*,
pp. 129–30, convincingly argue
the case for Bradley's ill nature

and the existence of a feud over money.

Newgate. Accounts of Newgate and Elizabethan prison life are drawn from Salgãdo, *Elizabethan Underworld*, pp. 165–86 and Eccles, *Marlowe in London*, pp. 39–41.

'a foul kennel'. From Luke Hutton's prison poem *The Black Dog of Newgate* (1596), quoted in Salgãdo, *Elizabethan Underworld*, p. 184.

'jailors hoarsely and harshly bawling'. Quoted in Salgãdo, *Elizabethan Underworld*, p. 184.

Sir Roger Manwood was indeed on the bench, and his connections with the Walsinghams are elaborated in Bakeless, *Tragicall History*, Vol. 2, p. 162. Richard Kitchen and Humphrey Rowland were Marlowe's sureties (see Eccles, *Marlowe in London*, p. 66 ff), and the Burghley and Antwerp connections are true (Eccles, p. 91 ff).

'gvyes' and 'Gwies'. Bakeless, *Tragicall History*, Vol. 2, p. 89, lists the relevant entries in Henslowe's diaries, pertaining to performances by Strange's Men at the Rose – though these performances date from 1593 (or 1594) onwards. This flurry of activity on Marlowe's part is an invention – there is no certainty about first performances of any of the plays mentioned.

worked . . . with Tom Nashe. Duncan-Jones, *Ungentle Shakespeare*, pp. 50–3, writes on the collaboration with Nashe, on the departures from the *Aeneid*, and on the embellishment in *Titus* of the gore of *Dido*.

'an actor of some kind'. Quiller-Couch writes in the introduction and notes to the 1928 Cambridge University Press edition of the play. *Diana Enamorada* is the generally accepted source of much of the plot, and was not translated into English until 1598. *The Decameron* also appears to be a source, but was not translated from the Italian until 1620. There is no performance recorded of *Two Gentlemen* until after the Restoration, though most commentators date it before 1592 (Holden, *William Shakespeare*, p. 330, for example, places it some time between 1587 and 1592).

'very well known to . . . my Lord Strange'. Marlowe made this claim in 1592 (see Nicholl, *Reckoning*, p. 235). I have embellished on his relationship with Lord Strange, though Nashe did dedicate his *Dildo* to Strange, and Strange's Men did perform both Marlowe and early Shakespeare plays – and Will Kemp was a member of the company.

a small court of wanton poets. Haynes, *Sex in Elizabethan England*, p. 51 ff, describes the brilliant Penelope's charms.

Cecil secured Kit as an informer. Marlowe's role as a spy in Strange's milieu is conjecture, though Strange was (albeit possibly reluctantly) a figurehead for Catholics abroad as pretender to the throne, and was under Sir Robert Cecil's surveillance after May 1591 (see Nicholl, *Reckoning*, pp. 227–9). Nicholl believes that, in 1592 at least, Marlowe was working as a 'projector' for Cecil in Strange's milieu (p. 246).

Emilia Bassano. A. L. Rowse famously (if somewhat eccentrically) first proposed Emilia (or Aemilia) Bassano as the Dark Lady. Her biographical details are here taken from his book *Shakespeare the Man* (Macmillan, London, 1988).

Henry Wriothesley – known as 'Rose'. Martin Green, in *Wriothesley's Roses* (Clevedon Books, Baltimore, 1993), pp. 18–24, argues that the family name was pronounced 'Rose-ly', but does not go as far as giving the young earl a floral cognomen.

a huffy scuffle. The contretemps is related by Duncan-Jones, *Ungentle Shakespeare*, p. 105.

'Rose' Wriothesley liked to dress as a woman. The Cobbe portrait was reproduced, with a convincing argument by Anthony Holden for its authenticity and Southampton's cross-dressing, in the *Observer, Review*, 21 April 2002, p. 5.

opens the myth to a strong homoerotic reading. A point made by Duncan-Jones, *Ungentle Shakespeare*, p. 65.

the attentions of minions. Their romps are noted by Duncan-Jones, *Ungentle Shakespeare*, pp. 79–80, and Rowse, *Shakespeare the Man*, pp. 55–6.

'play wantonly with him'. Quoted in Duncan-Jones, *Ungentle Shakespeare*, p. 80.

'fiddling and dancing'. Samuel Stevens describing Margaret Clap's house in 1725, quoted in Alan Bray, *Homosexuality in Renaissance England* (Gay Men's Press, London, 1982), pp. 81 and 82.

'The men [called] one another

"my dear" '. A contemporary account of a drag ball at the molly house in the Old Bailey, quoted in Bray, *Homosexuality*, p. 87.

a 'line of continuity'. Bray, *Homosexuality*, p. 85.

'a clinical, scientific coinage'. Bruce R. Smith, *Homosexual Desire in Shakespeare's England* (University of Chicago Press, Chicago, 1994), p. 11.

'The temptation to debauchery'. Bray, *Homosexuality*, p. 16.

'beds are not only places where people sleep'. See Bray, 'Homosexuality and the Signs of Male Friendship . . .', p. 4; Anne Bacon and Bishop Laud are quoted here also.

'daily conventions of friendship', et al: Bray's terms (Bray, 'Homosexuality and the Signs of Male Friendship . . .', pp. 8–9).

'Unless one were famous and had powerful enemies'. Smith, *Homosexual Desire*, pp. 48–53.

promiscuous and predatory. Duncan-Jones, *Ungentle Shakespeare*, p. 79, quotes Ovid Senior in Jonson's *Poetaster* (who is horrified his son will become 'an ingle for players') as illustration of the wicked reputation of theatre folk. Jonathan Goldberg, *Sodometries* (Stanford University Press, California, 1992), p. 106, cites other objectors, including Stephen Gosson, who complains that theatres 'effeminate the minde, as pricks unto vice'.

'The question confronting a young man'. Smith, *Homosexual Desire*, p. 65.

'a specifically homosexual subjectivity'. See Smith, *Homosexual Desire*, p. 23 and chapters six and seven. He, of course, does not hold that Marlowe wrote the Sonnets.

'Marlowe [was] breaking free'. Holden, *William Shakespeare*, p. 95, who is writing tangentially about Marlowe – his exact claim is: '. . . Shakespeare joined Marlowe in breaking free of the plodding, one-dimensional archetypes of the mediaeval tradition'.

'Marlowe was the first poet to grasp that chance'. Gurr, *Playgoing*, p. 141.

Holinshed's *Chronicles* are a major source for *Edward II* (Bakeless, *Tragicall History*, Vol. 2, p. 8 ff) and subsequent history plays. A new edition did come out in 1587, but that Walsingham gave Marlowe one as a gift is invention.

'a theatrical feat never previously attempted'. Holden, *William Shakespeare*, p. 95, writing on Shakespeare.

CHAPTER NINE *Theatre of Blood*

'as hatefull to the people as the Spaniard himself'. Thomas Wilkes, one of the English members of the *Raad van State*, the governing body of the United Provinces; quoted in Jonathan I. Israel, *Dutch Republic*, pp. 228–9. The portrait of Flushing is accurate, though Elisabeth Brandt is an invention.

a 'projector' to sniff out conspiracy. Nicholl, *Reckoning*, pp. 235–47, makes a convincing case for this. I am indebted to his view of events in Flushing for my account, and have followed his interpretation, though have embellished the antagonism between Marlowe and Baines, and

have invented Baines's methods and motives.

Professor Robert B. Wernham extracted a single letter. Nicholl, *Reckoning*, p. 235.

'to go to the enemy, or to Rome'. The letter, from which the ensuing quotations are taken, is given in its entirety in Nicholl, *Reckoning*, pp. 235–6.

Robert Browne and John Bradstriet. The passport is given in full in Chambers, *Elizabethan Stage*, p. 274, though Marlowe's connection with the players is speculation.

plays by the 'celebrated Herr Christopher Marlowe' at Frankfurt (see Chambers, *Elizabethan Stage*, p. 274; Brennecke, *Shakespeare in Germany 1590–1700*, p. 4).

'fast bound like a thief'. Nicholl, *Reckoning*, p. 247.

two Shoreditch constables. The constables are named, and the document given in full, in Bakeless, *Tragicall History*, Vol. 1, pp. 104–5.

no place on earth like jail. Nashe is quoted in Salgãdo, *Elizabethan Underworld*, p. 180.

'never could my Lord endure [Kit's] name or sight'. Quoted in Nicholl, *Reckoning*, p. 226.

Tom Nashe appears not to know. Both possibilities are mentioned by Duncan-Jones, *Ungentle Shakespeare*, p. 57, though she inclines to the view that Nashe was a collaborator on the play.

'. . . there is an upstart Crow'. Greene, *Groats-worth of Witte*, pp. 45–6.

a long though not unpraiseworthy poem. Emilia Bassano's later career is chronicled by Rowse, *Shakespeare the Man* [2], pp. 97–8.

'breathings of lofty rage'. The translation from the Latin is given by Eccles, *Marlowe in London*, pp. 165–6. The dedication is signed 'C. M.', and though there is some dispute that Marlowe is its author, no other feasible candidate has ever been put forward.

Earl of Pembroke's Men. Schoenbaum, *William Shakespeare*, pp. 165–7, notes that these plays were in the company's repertoire, and speculates that Shakespeare was one of Pembroke's players when Marlowe wrote *Edward II* for them.

considerable periods . . . at Scadbury. It is certain that Kit was at Scadbury in 1593, but these early visits are a supposition – though not unlikely, as 1592 was indeed a bad plague year, and the theatres were closed. The oath that Tom Watson extracts from Walsingham and Poley is an invention.

running a network in the Low Countries. Poley's residence and activities are reported in Bakeless, *Tragicall History*, Vol. 1, p. 104, and Nicholl, *Reckoning*, pp. 250 ff.

William Corkine. My treatment of the Corkine incidents in Canterbury is based on accounts by A. D. Wraight, *The Story that the Sonnets Tell* (Adam Hart, London, 1994), pp. 302–4, and Urry, *Marlowe*, pp. 64–8, who argues for a clerical error and that the two incidents were in fact one.

'plainely and distincktly' read the will. Urry, *Marlowe*, p. 57.

'a scowlde' and 'comon swearer'. Quoted in Urry, *Marlowe*, p. 57.

Robert Poley . . . Paul Ive. Their presence in Canterbury is noted by Urry, *Marlowe*, p. 68.

'Will Hall' is paid a handsome £10. References to this mysterious Will Hall, his work for Anthony Munday and subsequent missions to Denmark, the Low Countries and Prague, are listed in Graham Phillips and Martin Keatman, *The Shakespeare Conspiracy* (Century, London, 1994), p. 158 ff. Some writers have imagined Will Hall to be William Shakespeare.

these men in the same place at the same time. The complex inter-relations between these men, and the Scottish connection, are laid out by Nicholl, *Reckoning*, pp. 145–6, and 257–62. Paul Ive was working on the Canterbury canal (Urry, *Marlowe*, p. 68) and did have espionage connections (Nicholl, *Reckoning*, p. 119), but I have invented the idea that he ran a letter drop. One of William Hall's missions was indeed to deliver a letter from the Cecils to Kelley in Prague (see Phillips and Keatman, *Shakespeare Conspiracy*, p. 158).

'each one in a riddle or sieve'. Elze, 'Supposed Travels . . .', p. 307.

'men of quality to go unto the K of Scots'. Quoted in Nicholl, *Reckoning*, p. 260.

CHAPTER TEN *The Mousetrap*

too weak to go to court. Burghley's increasing infirmity is noted in Read, *Burghley and Queen Elizabeth*, pp. 484–5.

series of articles by Christopher Devlin. Devlin's article, entitled

'The Earl and the Alchemist', appears in three parts in *The Month* (1953, Vol. 9), pp. 25–38, 92–104 and 153–66. Devlin puts forward the view that Cecil engineered a plot to eliminate Stanley as a political factor in the succession – a false conspiracy, rather like the Babington plot – and that his plan misfired. In the chapter that follows, I treat Devlin's theory as fact, and have turned the idea on a notch. I have used the evidence that he assembles – the people involved, the planted letter, the chain of events that leads to things going wrong – but have added another layer to Cecil's motive: that he would use his 'exposure' of the plot to further his political standing. Marlowe's role in the affair is conjecture.

'Supposing you had a mind like Cecil's'. Devlin, 'The Earl and the Alchemist', p. 161.

'a stout man, fifty years of age'. Devlin, 'The Earl and the Alchemist', p. 32, gives the description, but does not ascribe it.

'my friend Richard Hesketh'. Quoted in Devlin, 'The Earl and the Alchemist', p. 30.

a haunch of venison as a gift. Woolley, *Queen's Conjuror*, pp. 315–16, comments on the Cecils' sudden ingratiating of Dr Dee, and suggests a possible link with the Hesketh plot, as they pumped him for information on English papists in Prague. The gift of venison is true; the crawfish, though seasonal, is my invention. That Cecil learned of Kelley as an intelligencer after raiding the secret-service archive is also my suggestion.

'fat and merry', with a limp. The description of Kelley is from Charles Nicholl, 'The Last Years of Edward Kelley, Alchemist to the Emperor', *London Review of Books*, 19 April 2001, p. 3.

rumours of a magic powder. Woolley, *Queen's Conjuror*, pp. 281 and 297.

'defer her charges for this summer for her navy'. Quoted in Nicholl, 'The Last Years . . .', p. 3.

'A guilty man on other grounds'. Devlin, 'The Earl and the Alchemist', pp. 102–3.

Bartholomew Hickman. Woolley, *Queen's Conjuror*, p. 317, outlines Dee's dealings with the whole Hickman clan, and also Bartholomew Hickman's government connections.

'a mixture of the terrible plights of Gloucester . . . and York'. Devlin, 'The Earl and the Alchemist', pp. 102–3.

'Your cousin the baker'. Devlin, 'The Earl and the Alchemist', pp. 34–5.

'the old Earl would have been scared rigid'. Devlin, 'The Earl and the Alchemist', p. 104.

'William Hall' was dispatched to Prague. Payment for this is recorded by the Chamber Treasurer of the time. See Phillips and Keatman, *Shakespeare Conspiracy*, p. 158.

Hesketh picked up the document from Sir Robert Cecil. Devlin, 'The Earl and the Alchemist', p. 93, puts forward a good argument for this, citing correspondence 'To Lord Cobham or Sir Robert Cecil'. My account of Hesketh's journey and subsequent events is a much-simplified version of Devlin, p. 92 ff.

'a dupe in a complicated scheme'. Devlin, 'The Earl and the Alchemist', p. 98.

'a witness in Hesketh's favour'. Devlin, 'The Earl and the Alchemist', p. 154.

'vomits . . . like soot or rusty iron'. Talbot Papers, 'Touching the Death of the Earl of Derby', quoted in Devlin, 'The Earl and the Alchemist', p. 166.

Bartholomew Hickman . . . had ridden north. According to Dee's diary entry for 23 March 1594, quoted in Devlin, 'The Earl and the Alchemist', p. 165.

'A warrant to Henry Maunder'. Marlowe's arrest warrant, Acts of the Privy Council, XXIV, 1593, edited by J. R. Dasent (HMSO, London 1901), p. 244. Cecil's conniving is conjecture.

Richard Cholmeley. Nicholl, *Reckoning*, pp. 265–83, discusses Cholmeley in some detail, and questions the validity of the 'Remembrances' and the accusations of atheism against him. My outline of the Dutch Church Libel, and of Cecil's and Cholmeley's involvement is based on Nicholl's well-argued conclusions (pp. 39–47 and 286–9), but I reshuffle his evidence, giving events a somewhat different slant, assigning other motives to Cecil, and imagining different relationships between the people involved.

For centuries the full text was lost
to us. Nicholl, *Reckoning*, p. 284. A full copy of the text is transcribed on www2.prestel.co.uk/rey/libell/htm.

'in better case and more freedom than her own people'. From one of a number of other 'libels' current at the time; quoted in Nicholl, *Reckoning*, p. 49.

'counterfeiting religion for [their] flight'. See www2.prestel.co.uk/rey/libell/htm lines 30 and 42; spelling modernised.

'Whereas it is pretended that for strangers'. Quoted in Nicholl, *Reckoning*, pp. 290–1.

'With Spanish gold, you all are infected'. See www2.prestel.co.uk/rey/libell/htm, lines 45–51.

'he saith & verily believeth that one Marlowe'. Quoted in Nicholl, *Reckoning*, p. 267; Nicholl discusses the relationship between Drury and Cholmeley on pp. 306–8, but I have turned his evidence in a slightly different direction.

'search in any the chambers, studies, chests'. Quoted in Nicholl, *Reckoning*, p. 42.

'shuffled with some of mine'. In a letter to Sir John Puckering, quoted in Nicholl, *Reckoning*, p. 288.

'This daie Christofer Marley of London, gentleman'. Marlowe's arrest warrant, Acts of the Privy Council, Vol. XXIV, 1593, p. 244.

'In the realities of Elizabethan politics'. Nicholl, *Reckoning*, p. 315, Nicholl puts forward Cecil as the 'only plausible' candidate as Marlowe's protector – but I have Cecil protect Marlowe for entirely different reasons.

'his daily attendaunce on their Lordships'. There is no record of his ever doing this. Haynes, *Elizabethan Secret Services*, p. 119, puts forward the idea that Robert Cecil substituted the daily appearance with a meeting with Poley at Eleanor Bull's establishment. Bakeless, *Tragicall History*, Vol. 1, pp. 141–2, suggests Deptford as the 'natural place to go' for such a meeting, as London was stricken by the plague. **Cecil was waiting to brief him**. Normally a regular attendant at Privy Council meetings, Cecil is inexplicably absent between 24–29 May. Cecil's meeting with Poley, and Poley's subsequent journey to Scadbury, are fictitious.

CHAPTER ELEVEN *The Reckoning*
that mild May morning. The background on Skeres and Ingram Frizer is derived from Nicholl, *Reckoning*, pp. 22–7, and Trow, *Marlowe?* pp. 213–14. I imagine the order in which they arrive, the plan to save Marlowe, and details of diet and climate, but the structure of events is as narrated at the inquest.
'one man's sudden death'. Duncan-Jones, *Ungentle Shakespeare*, p. 28.
'Take iii sponfulls of the galle'. The formula is given in Barbara Howard Traister, *The Notorious Astrological Physician of London* (University of Chicago Press, Chicago, 2001), p. 36.
'payment of a sum of pence, that is, *le recknynge*'. The translation from the Latin of the coroner's report is from Hotson, *Death of Christopher Marlowe*, pp. 31–4.
'one manner of cut'. Phillip Stubbes, *Anatomie of Abuses* (1583,

facsimile reprint, Garland, New York, 1973), no page numbers; *Merchant of Venice* I ii 66–8; Nashe, *Unfortunate Traveller*, p. 77.

INTERLUDE
the Queen's pardon. Eccles, *Marlowe in London*, pp. 24–5, gives the date of the pardon as early as 12 June 1593, but Hotson, *Death of Christopher Marlowe*, pp. 34–7 argues otherwise.
the next twenty years. Bakeless, *Tragicall History*, Vol. 1, pp. 161–71.
'Nicholas Kyrse, alias Skeers'. Nicholl, *Reckoning*, pp. 30 and 336.
'our well-beloved subject R. P.'. Nicholl, *Reckoning*, pp. 336–7, suggests the 'R. P.' is Poley, who is being recommended for the post of yeoman-waiter in the Tower of London, and thus put out to grass as a minor official.
'I do know the law'. Nicholl, *Reckoning*, p. 281.
Baines delivered his 'Note'. Nicholas Davidson, in 'Marlowe and Atheism', in Grantley and Roberts (eds), *Marlowe and English Renaissance Culture*, p. 129, cites a number of cases to show that most of the blasphemies mentioned in the note were neither exceptional nor new. Nicholl, *Reckoning*, p. 310, discusses various opinions on the veracity of the Note, which appear either to refute or validate it entirely, using exactly the same data; on p. 129 Nicholl discusses the closeness of the Note to Baines's 'confession', and on p. 278 notes the three close parallels with further accusations about Cholmeley in a letter to the

authorities by the compiler of the 'Remembrances'.

'A note Containing the opinion'. British Library Harley MS.6848 ff.185–6, transcribed on www2.prestel.co.uk/rey/ baines1.htm.

'Banish me forever'. Historical Manuscripts Commission, *Cecil*, Vol. 4, pp. 366–7 and 357–8, www2.prestel.co.uk/rey/drury.htm.

'soden & fearfull end of his life'. Nicholl, *Reckoning*, pp. 311–12, traces the alterations.

Gabriel Harvey . . . appears not to have known about it. Bakeless, *Tragicall History*, Vol. 1, p. 139.

Kit died of the plague. This is how most biographers interpret a reference in his *New Letter of Notable Contents*, an addition to *Pierce's Supererogation*, published in September 1593, though Nicholl, *Reckoning*, p. 61 ff, argues the poem is not about Marlowe at all.

'Marlin . . . a Poet of scurrilitie'. This and subsequent accounts of Marlowe's death are cited in Bakeless, *Tragicall History*, Vol. 1, pp. 142–53.

his first noticeable appearance in the public arena. Schoenbaum, *William Shakespeare*, pp. 172–6; Wraight, *New Evidence*, pp. 8–9.

Walton himself ended up in jail. The story is related by Nicholl, *Reckoning*, pp. 33 and 335.

PART III

CHAPTER TWELVE *His Exits and His Entrances*

quince marmalade and . . . sea water. The remedies for

seasickness are based on some given by Fynes Moryson, *Itinerary*, Vol. 3, p. 395.

more ships in Vlissingen. Coryate, *Coryats Crudities* p. 652. The inns in Flushing/Vlissingen are invented.

a Dialect of the German toung. Fynes Moryson, in Hughes (ed.), *Shakespeare's Europe*, pp. 377–8.

'a mighty blue feather in a black hat'. Sir Henry describes his disguise and adventures in a letter to Lord Zouche, May 1592, printed in Logan Pearsall Smith, *The Life and Letters of Sir Henry Wotton* (Clarendon, Oxford, 1907), Vol. I, p. 271 ff, also p. 19.

the Dutch-held town of Middelburg. Moryson, *Itinerary*, Vol. 1, p. 430, records the distance as a mile. Charles Nicholl, in 'At Middleborough' in Grantley and Roberts (eds), *Marlowe and English Renaissance Culture*, argues that Middelburg was a centre of clandestine printing and makes a connection with Poley.

Antwerp was in a forlorn condition. The account of Antwerp and the surrounding countryside is based on H. G. Koenigsberger and George L. Mosse, *Europe in the Sixteenth Century* (Longman, London, 1972), pp. 48–52; Israel, *Dutch Republic*, p. 219; Jervis Wegg, *The Decline of Antwerp under Philip of Spain* (Hyperion Press, Connecticut, 1979), p. 311 ff; Ephraim Schmidt, *Geschiedenis van de Joden in Antwerpen* (C. de Vries-Brouwers, Antwerp, 1994), pp. 57–8; John J. Murray, *Antwerp in the Age of Plantin and Brueghel*

(University of Oklahoma Press, Norman, 1970).

'Venice outdone'. Quoted in Murray, *Antwerp in the Age*, p. 43.

her breasts devoured. Hooft cited by Wegg in *Decline of Antwerp*, p. 312.

De Roy Lelie/Het Gulden Cruys. Details of Antwerp's *hoofden* and taverns are from Paul Verhuyck and Corine Kisling, *Het Mandement van Bacchus* (C. de Vries-Brouwers, Antwerp, 1997).

places in the city that Kit had to avoid. The activities of Adrian de Langhe and Jacques Ghibbes, as well as the names of Cecil's agents, are outlined in Haynes, *Elizabethan Secret Services*, p. 158.

Diego Lopez Alleman was a resident of Antwerp at the time, who as a Marrano would have been allowed to own property (see Ephraim Schmidt, *Geschiedenis van de Joden in Antwerpen*, p. 55); and Pieter Bellerus was indeed a local printer and bookseller (see Voet, *Golden Compasses* Vol. 2, *passim*) though their relationship with 'Walter de Hooch' is invented. Christophe Plantin at the 'Gulden Passer' was one of the most renowned publishers of the era.

'a superannuated Virgin'. Quoted in Bates, *Touring in 1600*, p. 122.

'Antwerp . . . surpasses all the towns I have seen'. Quoted in Murray, *Antwerp in the Age*, p. 27.

'Sterrell' . . . bribed one of De Langhe's letter clerks. Mail was kept for a day for weighing in Antwerp, and Sterrell did bribe one of the clerks (see Haynes, *Elizabethan Secret Services*, p. 159),

but the letter cited here is an invention.

the travelling company of Robert Browne certainly was performing at the Frankfurt Book Fair in 1593 (see Brennecke, *Shakespeare in Germany 1590–1700*, p. 5).

assistants as representatives. Voet, *Golden Compasses*, Vol. 2, p. 396, also fn. 4.

Jan van Keerbergen and Martin Nutius are real (see Voet, *Golden Compasses*, Vol. 2, p. 267, and p. 396, fn. 2), but Van Keerbergen's diary is not.

Christendom's foremost book mart. Voet, *Golden Compasses*, Vol. 2, pp. 395–6 describes the importance of the Frankfurt Book Fair in the sixteenth century.

'in a pleasant and fruitfull plaine'. Coryate, *Coryat's Crudities*, p. 588.

'you can hear them discussing philosophy'. Translated from the Latin original of Henri Estienne ('Stephanus'), *Francofordiense Emporium* (1574), by James Westfall Thompson as *The Frankfurt Book Fair* (Caxton Book Club, Chicago, 1911), pp. 169–70.

'had an evil time in carrying books'. Josias Maler's diary is quoted in Thompson (trans.) *Frankfurt Book Fair*, p. 25.

'cheere[d] the tables of the Fair'. Estienne, translated in Thompson, *Frankfurt Book Fair*, p. 147.

125 extra 'strangers'. Figures from Thompson (ed.), *Frankfurt Book Fair*, p. 53.

Love's Labour's Won. Meres, 'Wit's Treasury', p. 281.

Roderigo Lopez, the Queen's physician, did send money to Antwerp, and an anonymous letter

of 18 February 1594, ascribed to
Diego Lopez Alleman, was used at
his trial (see Schmidt, *Geschiedenis
van de Joden*, p. 55; Haynes,
Elizabethan Secret Services,
pp. 135–46).
'Jewish gaberdine'. Umberto Fortis,
The Ghetto on the Lagoon (trans. by
Roberto Matteoda, Storti, Venice,
2001), p. 15, gives the dress
regulations for Jews in Venice; as
does Coryate, *Coryat's Crudities*,
p. 231 – though he records red
hats for Jews of Western origin
and yellow turbans for Levantines.
'a kinde of light yellowish vaile'.
Coryate, *Coryat's Crudities*, p. 232;
McPherson, *Shakespeare, Jonson and
the Myth of Venice*, p. 64, describes
the dress-code anomalies.
**'For when as walking in the Court
of the Ghetto'.** Coryate, *Coryat's
Crudities*, pp. 234–7.
more conservative estimates.
McPherson, *Shakespeare, Jonson and
the Myth of Venice*, p. 64.

CHAPTER THIRTEEN *In the Bleak
Midwinter*
Disgrace and loss of reputation.
Wraight points to this and other
sonnets (such as Sonnets 121 and
112) as belonging to a group with
a theme of disgrace; one which is
closely associated with a group of
sonnets of exile (see Wraight, *The
Story*, p. 11, pp. 57–8). The idea
that the sonnets are Marlowe's
verse letters back to England is
derived from Wraight's writings.
'Odd' Thorpe. The details on
Thomas Thorpe are from Phillips
and Keatman, *Shakespeare
Conspiracy*, p. 161, and Alan and
Veronica Palmer, *Who's Who in*

Shakespeare's England, p. 250,
though he did not, of course,
employ Oliver Laurens.
a lump sum of £1,000. No one
knows for certain how Shakespeare
came by the money to buy a share
in the Lord Chamberlain's
company – the rumour of a
£1,000 gift from the Earl of
Southampton was first recorded in
Nicholas Rowe's biography in
1709, though Schoenbaum is
sceptical (see *William Shakespeare, a
Compact Documentary Life*,
pp. 178–9); Holden, *William
Shakespeare, His Life and Work*,
pp. 129–35, suggests the amount
was a possible pay-off, but for
reasons other than I have
outlined; Duncan-Jones, *Ungentle
Shakespeare*, p. 85, thinks the sum
more likely to have been £100,
used by Shakespeare to buy his
coat of arms, and cites Andrew
Gurr as saying that he probably
paid for his share in the Lord
Chamberlain's Men using play-
scripts carried from other
companies. And so on. It is true,
though, that Southampton broke
off all professional relations with
Shakespeare from this point
forward, and no longer acted as
his patron.
'The gift is small'. Ascription
found in a manuscript compiled
by Sir Francis Fane of Bulbeck
(1611–80), now in the Bodleian
Library, Oxford, quoted in
Holden, *William Shakespeare*,
p. 135.
**one year that Browne did not
travel to Germany.** Schrickx
'English Actors . . .', pp. 156–7,
notes Browne's absence and family

tragedy; Hans Hartleb, *Deutschlands Erster Theaterbau* (Walter de Gruyter, Berlin, 1936), pp. 24–6, points out that while there were English comedians in Kassel (on a likely route to or from Frankfurt) in 1594, it was not Browne's troupe.

a high point of the English comedians' activity. Limon, *Gentlemen of a Company*, pp. 4–5 and 10.

'When I came to the Duke of Brunswick'. Letter to Sir Robert Cecil from Nuernburg, 10 November 1595, quoted in Diana Poulton, *John Dowland* (Faber and Faber, London, 1972), p. 38. The Duke of Brunswick and Maurice of Kassel were indeed renowned for their cultured courts, and played host to such musicians and players.

a small company led by Harry Brodribb. Fantasy, though firmly based on accounts of real troupes travelling at the time.

the annual *Hirschessen*. Hartleb, *Erster Theaterbau*, p. 20, mentions the feast, and cites a letter from the Marburg state archive as evidence that a group of English players, and two lutenists (one of whom was most likely Dowland), attended Maurice.

comedians may have stopped over before. A point made by Schrickx, 'English Actors . . .', p. 155; Hartleb, *Erster Theaterbau*, pp. 24–5.

a paragon among princes. Poulton, *Dowland*, p. 31, points out the differences in temperament between Maurice and Brunswick, and quotes the German historian Johann Janssen on the obscene nature of one of Brunswick's plays.

'a goodly personage, of stature tall'. Nichols, *Progresses and Processions*, Vol. 3, p. 394.

'like the Louvre in Paris, hie and statelie'. Nichols, *Progresses and Processions*, Vol. 3, p. 385.

Dowland . . . was a melancholy man. Poulton, *Dowland*, pp. 76–8, comments on the intensity of Dowland's depression. His relationship with Marlowe is conjecture.

soliloquies of *Hamlet*. This similarity between Dowland's 'ayres' and the soliloquies is noted by Christopher Headington in *The Bodley Head History of Western Music*, (Bodley Head, London, 1974), p. 100–01.

Flow, my tears. John Dowland, from *Second Book of Airs*, transcribed, scored and edited by Edmund Horace Fellowes, in *The English School of Lutenist Song Writers* (Stainer & Bell, London, 1922), p. 8.

detects the same hand. Poulton, *Dowland*, pp. 254–6, though she does admit objections to the idea.

parallels . . . *The Merchant of Venice*. Poulton, *Dowland*, p. 281.

Dowland was in contact with Cecil. Poulton, in *Dowland*, pp. 36–40, reproduces his panic-stricken letter.

the bitterness of the scholar reduced to . . . clowning. A point made by William Bliss, in his largely imagined *The Real Shakespeare* (Sidgwick & Jackson, London, 1947), p. 116.

the ageing Doctor Hugo Blotz was indeed in charge of the Imperial Library, was an advocate of unity and peace, and played host to Sir

Henry Wotton (see Pearsall Smith, *Life and Letters of Sir Henry Wotton*, Vol. I, p. 14). This visit is based on Wotton's – though it is not certain whether Blotius owned a copy of Holinshed.

'*Bugeria* is an Italian word'. Quoted in Goldberg, *Sodometries*, p. 106.

the original Admirable Crichton was indeed the mysterious and multitalented James Crichton of Cluny. His adventures are related in more detail in Douglas Crichton, *The Admirable Crichton* (L. Upcott Gill, London, 1909), and George Pottinger, *The Real Admirable Crichton* (Michael Russell, Norwich, 1995), which includes a reprint of Sir Thomas Urquhart's inventive biographical essay. There were rumours of a second man, 'Crichton, The Survivor' (Pottinger, pp. 96–7).

'he never blotted out a line'. Bate, *Genius of Shakespeare*, pp. 26–7, makes his commentary and quotes the passage from Jonson's literary notebook in full.

a 'Poet-Ape'. Michell, *Who Wrote Shakespeare*, p. 72, points out that most biographers hold Shakespeare to be the main contender for the title, and quotes Jonson's epigram, which hints that the Poet-Ape stole other people's work.

the Chamber Treasurer paid £15 to 'Hall and Wayte'. Noted in Phillips and Keatman, *Shakespeare Conspiracy*, p. 159.

'to guide the Passinger his dangerous way'. Lithgow, *Total Discourse*, p. 335.

'head downewards and heeles

upward'. Moryson, *Itinerary*, Vol. 3, p. 467.

'the fittest time to passe the Alpes'. Moryson, *Itinerary*, Vol. 3, p. 467.

CHAPTER FOURTEEN *Renaissance Man*

an unsolved riddle. The incident is recorded in Schoenbaum, *William Shakespeare*, pp. 198–9.

William Wayte's stepfather. Noted in Schoenbaum, *William Shakespeare*, pp. 198–9, though Hotson's claim is refuted here.

'worldly recognition' . . . 'a gentleman'. Duncan-Jones, *Ungentle Shakespeare*, pp. 83 and 85.

hoarding grain at a time of famine. Shakespeare's hard-nosed business practices are discussed by many, including Duncan-Jones, *Ungentle Shakespeare*, pp. 121–2; Park Honan, *Shakespeare, A Life* (Oxford University Press, Oxford, 1999), pp. 225, 292–3 and 321–2.

The coat of arms. Duncan-Jones, *Ungentle Shakespeare*, pp. 95–7, gives details of the coat of arms, and Shakespeare's dubious means of acquiring it.

Ben Jonson wickedly sent up. Jonson's satire is discussed by Michell, *Who Wrote Shakespeare?*, pp. 72–3.

Malvolio's cross-gartered yellow stockings. Duncan-Jones, *Ungentle Shakespeare*, pp. 157–8, unravels the riddle of the garters, though she sees it as an example of Shakespeare's self-ridicule.

Jan Moretus did not record their names. Voet, *Golden Compasses*, Vol. 2, pp. 174–5 and 187–8, notes that these casual workers often slipped through company records.

knowledge of printers' trade

expressions. W. Jaggard, *Shakespeare, Once a Printer and a Bookman* (Shakespeare Press, Stratford-upon-Avon, 1934), p. 6ff.

at busy times even family members helped out. Voet, *Golden Compasses*, Vol. 2, p. 180, discusses the work arrangements of the proof-readers, and describes how casuals and family were roped in to help; young Christophe's punishment and letter are given in Murray, *Antwerp in the Time*, pp. 99–100.

'they do not laugh'. The rules are given in Voet, *Golden Compasses*, Vol. 2, pp. 184–5.

Lipsius and his dog Mopsus. Master and mutt are mentioned in Mark Morford, 'Justus Lipsius en zijn contubernales', in R. Dusoir et al. (eds), *Justus Lipsius en het Plantijnse Huis* (Museum Plantin-Moretus, Antwerp, 1997), p. 139. The great humanist was a frequent resident at the Gulden Passer, and Rubens was indeed part of the milieu as a friend of the younger Moretus (see Voet, *Golden Compasses*, Vol. 1, pp. 207 and 212). Apart from the public conversation with 'Hooghius', the picture of Lipsius drawn here is based on Morford, Voet and on Francine de Nave, 'Amicitiā et constantiā' and Jeanine de Landtsheer, 'Justus Lipsius en zijn relatie met Johannes I Moretus', in Dusoir et al. (cds), p. 15 ff and p. 82 ff respectively; and Aloïs Gerlo and Hendrik Vervliet, *La Correspondence de Juste Lipse Conservée au Musée Plantin Moretus* (De Nederlandsche Boekhandel, Antwerp, 1967), pp. 52–4. The Rubens letter is an invention,

though he did at times illustrate his correspondence – see Ruth Saunders Magurn (ed.), *The Letters of Peter Paul Rubens* (Harvard University Press, Cambridge, Mass., 1971), p. 42.

'the solemnity and weight of the Senecan iambic'. Eliot, 'Seneca in Elizabethan Translation', in *Selected Essays*, p. 85.

'Blount, I purpose to be blunt'. Thorpe's dedicatory letter to Blount is printed in full in Hoffman, *The Man Who Was Shakespeare?*, p. 191 ff., who proposes that Blount knew Marlowe was alive and that Thorpe had discovered the truth and was 'twitting' him; and by fellow Marlovian, A. D. Wraight, who sees Marlowe floating through St Paul's Churchyard disguised as a Moor (Wraight, *The Story*, pp. 378–80).

intricate set of references. Michell, *Who Wrote Shakespeare?*, pp. 238–9, discusses the allusions in *As You Like It* more fully.

something of a culture-raid. Details of the duke's visit to the Low Countries (with Monteverdi in train), and the visit's musical influence on the composer are from Fabbri, *Monteverdi*, p. 33 ff. It is not certain, but most likely, that this is when Vincenzo recruited both Pourbus and Rubens – see Marie-Anne Lescourret, *Rubens: A Double Life* (Allison & Busby, London, 1993), pp. 24–5.

Lipsius was planning to travel to Rome. Marc Laureys and Jan Papy, ' "The grandeur that was Rome": Lipsius's variaties op een oud thema', in Dusoir et al. (eds), *Justus Lipsius*, pp. 129–30.

'The dizzying display of poetry and philosophy'. Holden, *William Shakespeare*, pp. 190–91.

'a new inwardness, almost independent of dramatic necessity'. Kermode, *Shakespeare's Language*, p. 71 and p. ix. He is, of course, speaking of the conventional Shakespeare.

on horseback to Mantua. This is Rubens's departure date and mode of transport, though it is not known exactly who comprised the party (Lescourret, *Rubens*, pp. 16–17).

CHAPTER FIFTEEN *Under the Mask*

'chosen my Lord the Duke as patron'. The boast reappears in a letter of November 1603, Magurn (ed.), *Letters of Peter Paul Rubens*, p. 38.

while a pageboy to the Countess de Lalaing. Magurn, (ed.), *Letters of Peter Paul Rubens*, p. 14.

'whole *Forests* of *Olive-trees*'. Lassells, *The Voyage of Italy*, p. 2.

'abundance of goodly meadows'. Coryate, *Coryat's Crudities* pp. 119–20.

by sailboat along waterways. Edward Sullivan, 'Shakespeare and the Waterways of North Italy', in *The Nineteenth Century*, August 1908, p. 215 ff, elaborates on this extensive transport system (one which, incidentally, would permit Prospero in *The Tempest* to leave Milan by boat – something which has perplexed some critics).

'wealth of many beautiful and great palaces'. Quoted in Fabbri, *Monteverdi*, pp. 24–5. Vasari's praise came in the second edition

of his *Vite* (1566), correcting an earlier impression.

he handed over an entire estate. Maria Bellonci, *A Prince of Mantua* (Weidenfeld & Nicolson, London, 1956), p. 199.

Vincenzo loved the theatre. Details of the duke's patronage of the arts are from Fabbri, *Monteverdi*, pp. 24–5; Iain Fenlon, *Music and Patronage in Sixteenth-century Mantua* (Cambridge University Press, Cambridge, 1980), pp. 5 and 123; Chambers, *Elizabethan Stage*, p. 261; Denis Stevens (trans.) *The Letters of Claudio Monteverdi* (Clarendon Press, Oxford, 1995), p. 23; Lescourret, *Rubens*, pp. 18–23.

Mantua was gratifyingly cosmopolitan. Fenlon, *Music and Patronage*, p. 10, attests the cosmopolitan nature of Mantua; Lithgow, *Total Discourse*, p. 330, notes the locals' lingering sorrow over the death of the Admirable Crichton.

the Jewish community. Details of the status of Jews in Mantua are from Shlomo Simonsohn, *History of the Jews in the Duchy of Mantua* (Kiryath Sepher, Jerusalem, 1977), pp. 25–41, and Emanuele Colorni, *La Comunità Ebraica Mantovana* (Mantova Ebraica, Mantua, 2000), pp. 26–30.

'he favoured the Jews and spoke kindly to them'. Quoted in Simonsohn, *History of the Jews*, p. 31.

Leone de' Sommi ... Salomone Rossi. Their contribution to Mantuan court life and Italian culture is discussed by Kate Simon in *A Renaissance Tapestry* (Harrap,

London, 1988), pp. 219–22;
Colorni, *Comunità Ebraica
Mantovana*, p. 14; Simonsohn,
History of the Jews, pp. 658 ff and
673 ff.
the double of the great Arlecchino.
Stevens (trans.), *Letters of Claudio
Monteverdi*, pp. 23–4.
**strangely similar to Monteverdi's
Lament of Ariana**. The similarity is
noted in Headington, *History of
Western Music*, pp. 100–01.
Marlowe's involvement is
hypothetical.
a legend of terror. The story is
related in Selwyn Brinton, *The
Gonzaga – Lords of Mantua*
(Methuen, London, 1927), p. 176.
**in Sabbioneta the Teatro
Olimpico**. Sabbioneta – the *città
ideale* – and Vespasiano's theatre
are still very much intact.
**famed as architect, painter and
creator of theatrical effects**.
Romano's versatility is mentioned
in Simon, *Renaissance Tapestry*,
pp. 5, 211 and 216, and Michell
Who Wrote Shakespeare? pp. 224–6.
The tombstone inscriptions were
noted by Vasari and are quoted in
Elze, 'Supposed Travels . . .',
pp. 287–8.
**'work of brush more horrible and
frightening'**. Quoted in Gianna
Suitner and Chiara Tellini Perina,
Palazzo Te in Mantua (Christopher
Evans, Electa, Milan, 1994),
pp. 101–2.
'great gambler, a spendthrift'.
Ludovico Muratori, *Annali*, quoted
in Lescourret, *Rubens*, p. 22.
**at the centre of Mantuan academic
circles**. Fabbri, *Monteverdi*, p. 25,
points out the central role
Vincenzo played among Mantua's

academia. Tasso had been resident
in Mantua, scholarly debates were
common, there were alchemists in
the cellars, and Vincenzo did
commission a gas bomb (see
Bellonci, *Prince of Mantua*, p. 190).
**'you shall see sometimes ten or
twelve Rooms on a floor'**.
Maximilian Misson, *Voyages*, quoted
in John W. Draper, 'Some details
of Italian local colour in *Othello*',
in *Shakespeare Jahrbuch*, LXVIII,
1932, p. 125.
'open their quivers to every arrow'.
Coryate, *Coryat's Crudities*, p. 264.
'a second *Cleopatra*'. Coryate,
Coryat's Crudities, pp. 266–7.
**compose sonnets and discuss
Boccaccio**. Lawner, *I modi*, p. 26,
remarks on these and other talents
of the courtesans.
'the dregs of their olde age'.
Coryate, *Coryat's Crudities*,
pp. 268–9.
**During his 1595 campaign, he had
taken . . . a young Monteverdi**.
Monteverdi's presence on the
campaign is discussed by Fabbri,
Monteverdi, p. 30.
savoured the powers of command.
Bellonci, *Prince of Mantua*,
pp. 180–3, and 228, notes
Leonora's behaviour in power and
her treatment of Francesco.
**'Willm Halle' . . . returned with
intelligence from Denmark**.
Phillips and Keatman, *Shakespeare
Conspiracy*, p. 159.
**Cromwell, written by 'W. S.' was
published by William Jones in
1602**. Listed by Hoffman, *The Man
Who Was Shakespeare*, p. 38.
**one of the most unpleasant . . .
families in the town**. Holden,
William Shakespeare, pp. 202–3,

358

relates Shakespeare's dealings with the nasty Combes.

stooped to collaborate ... *Sir Thomas More*. The original play was by the part-time spy Anthony Munday ('Will Hall's' first employer). Holden, *William Shakespeare*, pp. 197–8, holds that 'by general consent' Shakespeare was one of the five people brought in to undertake rescue work on the play; Schoenbaum, *William Shakespeare, a Compact Documentary Life*, p. 214, is more assertive.

CHAPTER SIXTEEN *Themes and Variations*

an ambassadorial mission to Spain. Lescourret, *Rubens*, pp. 35–9, outlines Rubens's impact on the Mantuan court, and gives details of the Spanish mission. Marlowe's collaboration with someone at court to sabotage the trip is an invention – though Rubens did take an illogical route, and appears to suspect some sort of plotting against him.

an exuberantly decorated silver coach. Details of the gifts are from Magurn (ed. and trans.), *Letters of Peter Paul Rubens*, p. 21 and Bellonci, *Prince of Mantua*, p. 200.

'they almost crossed themselves in astonishment at such a mistake'. Letter I, from Florence, 18 March 1603, in Magurn (ed. and trans.), *Letters of Peter Paul Rubens*, pp. 24–5.

'by the incompetent advice of I know not whom'. As above.

'through a Flemish gentleman in his service'. Letter II, from Pisa, 26 March 1603, in Magurn (ed. and trans.), *Letters of Peter Paul*

Rubens, pp. 26–7. The identity of this 'Flemish gentleman' is a surmise.

'in every detail as to the quantity and quality of the gifts'. This and subsequent quotation from Letter III, from Pisa, 29 March 1603, in Magurn (ed. and trans.), *Letters of Peter Paul Rubens*, p. 27.

King Philip was hunting rabbits. Lescourret, *Rubens*, pp. 36–7.

'guardian and bearer of the works of others'. This and subsequent quotations from Letter VIII, from Valladolid, 24 May 1603, in Magurn (ed. and trans.), *Letters of Peter Paul Rubens*, p. 33.

known among writers for his unstinting largesse. The generosity and intelligence of the Count of Lemos is recorded in William Byron, *Cervantes, A Biography* (Doubleday & Company, New York, 1978), pp. 295, 460 and pp. 475–6. Lope de Vega had indeed been his secretary.

Miguel de Cervantes Saavedra, a protégé of the Count of Lemos. Byron, *Cervantes*, p. 460, mentions the possibility of Lemos's early patronage of Cervantes; Gary MacEóin, *Cervantes* (Bruce Publishing Co., Milwaukee, 1950), p. 158, mentions him as one of the writer's only two protectors.

reading from his manuscript. Byron, *Cervantes*, pp. 413–14, writes that Cervantes read from his manuscript, probably in the small shop Robles had left behind in Madrid when he moved to Valladolid. This reading in the Valladolid shop is conjecture, and Sanchez's eavesdropping an invention.

'a magic book, as close to being a living object'. Byron, *Cervantes*, p. 423.
Christopher Marlor, or Marlowe. Mentioned in F. S. Boas, *Marlowe and His Circle* (Oxford University Press, London, 1931), pp. 18–20. He reappears in the Gatehouse prison in Westminster in 1604, but the name appears to be an alias – he is described as being 'of very low stature, well set, of black round beard'.
'**without cucumbers or other missiles**'. Quoted in Melveena McKendrick, *Cervantes* (Little, Brown and Co., Toronto, 1980), p. 109.
Lope de Vega quick fed voracious audiences. Byron, *Cervantes*, pp. 280 ff. has been useful to me on the relationship between Lope and Cervantes, and the failure of drama for the latter.
called *Cardenio* (and later *Double Falsehood*). Bate, *Genius of Shakespeare*, pp. 76–82, gives the story of the rediscovery of the play, and makes the strongest argument for Fletcher as collaborator and the play's authenticity (Theobald was accused of forgery).
'**impudently grating on a sorry guitar**'. Quoted in Clare Howard, *English Travellers of the Renaissance* (John Lane, London, 1914), p. 134. Other details of travel in Spain based on Howard, pp. 132–5.
Claudio and Claudia Monteverdi. Strange, but true.
'**our Director of Music, who has a wife and other relatives**'. Quoted in Stevens (trans.), *Letters of Claudio Monteverdi*, p. 33, who

writes of the virginity test; Arnold, *Monteverdi*, p. 19, also tells Caterina's tale. Claudia Monteverdi gave birth to a son in May.
Vincenzo quickly commissioned ... *Orfeo*. The background to the first performance of *Orfeo* is given in Fabbri, *Monteverdi*, p. 63 ff.
'**It should be most unusual**'. Quoted in Fabbri, *Monteverdi*, p. 63.
'**They accompanied the music ... with appropriate facial expressions**'. Vincenzo Giustiniani in 'Discorso sopra la musica', probably written around 1630, quoted in Fenlon, *Music and Patronage*, p. 127.
'**When Romeo and Juliet first speak**'. Bate, *Genius of Shakespeare*, p. 279. The reference is to *Romeo and Juliet* I v 92–105.
fine cakes, monstrous sausages ... and for the allures of its female staff. The shop is described in Giancarlo Malacarne and Mauro Bini (eds), *A Tavola Con Gli Dei* (Il Bulino, Modena, 2000), p. 20; the quotation '*in maniera che a poco a poco...*' is from a letter reproduced here from G. Calzona to Duke Gugliemo Gonzaga, 7 July 1565, though the later complaints about a quaint-talking Fleming are invented.
'**The truth is that instead of *Otello* being an Italian opera**'. Quoted in Bate, *Genius of Shakespeare*, p. 285.
one George Wilkins. This unpleasant character, and his collaboration with Shakespeare is chronicled in Duncan-Jones, *Ungentle Shakespeare*, p. 205 ff.
'**that prodigal aristocrats**

squandered, or borrowed'.
Duncan-Jones, *Ungentle Shakespeare*,
pp. 183–4.

Ottavio Benintendi's bad
intentions are revealed by Stevens
(trans.), *Letters of Claudio
Monteverdi*, p. 34.
**Southampton was a major
'adventurer'.** Southampton's
connections with the Virginia
Company are outlined in A. L.
Rowse, *Shakespeare's Southampton,
Patron of Virginia* (Macmillan,
London, 1965), pp. 234–9. His
friend Sir Thomas Gates did
indeed go out to America on the
Sea Venture (or *Sea Adventure*),
which left that June.
he was Will's bastard son. Or so
tradition has it, though in a letter
to the *Times Literary Supplement*, 16
May 2003, Davenant's biographer
Mary Edmond points out that this
is a misinterpretation of a claim of
Davenant's, reported in Aubrey's
Lives, and that Davenant is rather
saying that he is content to be
thought Shakespeare's son as he
writes in the same spirit as his
godfather – an even more
outrageous statement.
the 'Chandos portrait'. The
provenance of the 'Chandos
portrait' is outlined with some
certainty from Davenant onwards
by E. A. Greening Lamborn in
Notes and Queries, Vol. 194, No. 1,
January 1949, pp. 71–2, but the
early provenance is unclear, and it
is not known for sure whether it is
a picture of Shakespeare or not. I
have used Greening Lamborn's
research and mortared in the

gaps. As mentioned in an earlier
note, the computer face-ageing
process is a digital sleight of hand.
**the flagship *Sea Venture* had been
lost in a terrifying storm.** True.
The story of the loss of the *Sea
Venture* and subsequent events
back home is given in Rowse,
Shakespeare's Southampton, p. 239 ff;
and Leo Salingar, in 'The New
World in *The Tempest*', in Jean-
Pierre Maquerlot and Michèle
Willems (eds.), *Travel and Drama
in Shakespeare's Time* (Cambridge
University Press, Cambridge,
1996), p. 209 ff.
command from King James. That
the king commissioned *Henry VIII*
for wedding celebrations of
Princess Elizabeth is one of the
great Shakespearean biographical
traditions. The Chamber Account
does mention an unnamed play
that was cancelled for the 'greater
pleasures' of a masque (see
Schoenbaum, *Shakespeare, a
Compact Documentary Life*, p. 276).
Fletcher's large contribution to
Henry VIII is generally accepted.
**'a pallid, pompous, prettified
version'.** Holden, *William
Shakespeare*, p. 297.
burned the theatre down. A
contemporary account of the blaze
is reproduced in Schoenbaum,
*Shakespeare, a Compact Documentary
Life*, pp. 276–7.
**a confidential report had reached
the Council.** The *True Reportory* was
kept secret, and was not published
until 1625 in Samuel Purchas's
*Hakluytus Posthumus, or, Purchas his
Pilgrimes* (Salingar, 'The New World
in "The Tempest"' in Maquerlot and
Willems (eds), *Travel and Drama in*

Shakespeare's Time, pp. 209–10; Rowse *Shakespeare's Southampton*, pp. 239–40, also Virginia Mason Vaughan's introduction to the 1999 Arden Shakespeare edition of the play, pp. 40–41) – though it must be admitted that other publications in 1610, including the Virginia Company's own *A True Declaration of the estate of the Colonie in Virginia*, were also possible sources. There are parallels between *The Tempest* and *A True Reportory*, and it remains a riddle that the first performance of the play predated the pamphlet's publication. Most commentators explain this by saying that Shakespeare somehow had access to the secret manuscript of *A True Reportory*. I posit another scenario.

pays homage to the *commedia dell'arte*. K. M. Lea, *Italian Popular Comedy* (Russell & Russell, New York, 1962), Vol. II, pp. 445–53, draws these and many other parallels.

Their names both signify 'one who is lucky, prosperous'. This Prospero/Faustus parallel is pointed out by Duncan-Jones, *Ungentle Shakespeare*, p. 237.

AFTERWORD

'nine bones and six hundred barrels of plaster of Paris'. Mark Twain, *Is Shakespeare Dead?* (Harpers & Brothers, New York, 1909), p. 49.

Bibliography

References to Christopher Marlowe's works from *The Complete Plays*, Penguin, London, 1986

References to William Shakespeare's works from *The Complete Works*, Collins, London, 1980

DOCUMENTS

The Baines Note, British Library, Harley MS.6848. ff. 185–6, transcribed on www2.prestel.co.uk/rey/baines1.htm

The Dutch Church Libel, transcribed on www2.prestel.co.uk/rey/libell.htm

The Flushing Letter, Public Record Office, SP 84/44/60, transcribed by R. B. Wernham, *English Historical Review*, 91, 1976, pp. 344–5 and on www2.prestel.co.uk/rey/flushing.htm

Kyd's Accusations, British Library, Harley MS.6848. f. 154, transcribed on www2.prestel.co.uk/rey/kyd1.htm

Kyd's Letter to Sir John Puckering, British Library, Harley MS.6849. f. 218^{r,v}, transcribed on www2.prestel.co.uk/rey/kyd2.htm

Letter from Privy Council, 29 June 1587, Public Record Office, *Privy Council Registers* PC2/14/381, transcribed on www2.prestel.co.uk/rey/pc_cert.htm

Letters from Thomas Drury to Sir Robert Cecil, Historical Manuscripts Commission, *Cecil*, Vol. 4, pp. 366–7, transcribed on www2.prestel.co.uk/rey/drury.htm

Letter from Thomas Drury to Anthony Bacon, Lambeth Palace Library, *Bacon Papers*, MS 649. f. 246, transcribed by S. E. Sprott, *Times Literary Supplement*, 2 August 1974 and on www2.prestel.co.uk/rey/drury.htm

Marlowe's arrest warrant, Acts of the Privy Council, Vol. XXIV, 1592–93, edited by J. R. Dasent, HMSO, London 1901

The 'Remembrances' against Richard Cholmeley, British Library, Harley MS.6848. f. 190^{r,v}, transcribed on www2.prestel.co.uk/rey/chumley1.htm

BOOKS/PERIODICALS

Abicht, Ludo, *De Joden van Antwerpen*, Grammens, Brussels, 1987

Ackroyd, Peter, *London, The Biography*, Chatto & Windus, London, 2000

Ahmed, Anne (ed.), *A Proper Newe Booke of Cokerye*, (reprint of 1557–8 edition), Corpus Christi College, Cambridge, 2002

Anglo, Sydney, *The Martial Arts of Renaissance Europe*, Yale University Press, New Haven, 2000

Arnold, Denis, *Monteverdi*, Oxford University Press, Oxford, 2000

Arnold, Janet, *Patterns of Fashion*, Macmillan, London, 1985

Bakeless, John, *The Tragicall History of Christopher Marlowe*, Volumes 1 and 2, Archon Books, Connecticut, 1964

Barnes, Julian, *Flaubert's Parrot*, Picador, London, 1985

Bate, Jonathan, *The Genius of Shakespeare*, Picador, London, 1997

Bates, E. S., *Touring in 1600*, Constable & Co., London, 1911

Bearman, Robert, *Shakespeare in the Stratford Records*, Alan Sutton, Stroud, 1994

Bellonci, Maria, *A Prince of Mantua*, Weidenfeld & Nicolson, London, 1956

Bindoff, S. T., *Tudor England*, Penguin, London, 1987

Black, J. B., *The Reign of Elizabeth*, Clarendon Press, Oxford, 1992

Black, Maggie, *A Taste of History*, British Museum Press, London, 1997

Bliss, William, *The Real Shakespeare*, Sidgwick & Jackson, London, 1947

Boas, F. S., *Marlowe and His Circle*, Oxford University Press, London, 1931

Bossy, John, *Giordano Bruno and the Embassy Affair*, Yale University Press, New Haven, 1991

—— *Under the Molehill*, Yale University Press, New Haven, 2001

Bray, Alan, *Homosexuality in Renaissance England*, Gay Men's Press, London, 1982

—— 'Homosexuality and the Signs of Male Friendship in Elizabethan England' in *History Workshop Journal*, 29, 1990, pp. 1–19

Breight, Curtis, *Surveillance, Militarism and Drama in the Elizabethan Era*, Macmillan, London, 1996

Brennecke, E., *Shakespeare in Germany 1590–1700*, University of Chicago Press, Chicago, 1964

Brinton, Selwyn, *The Gonzaga – Lords of Mantua*, Methuen, London, 1927

Brunetti, Gino (ed.), *Cucina Mantovana*, Casa Rurale ed Artigiana di Castel Goffredo, Mantua, 1991

Burke, Peter, *Antwerp, A Metropolis in Comparative Perspective*, Martial & Snoeck, Antwerp, 1993

Byron, William, *Cervantes, A Biography*, Doubleday & Company, New York, 1978

Calthrop, Dion Clayton, *English Costume*, Vol. 3, Tudor and Stuart, Adam & Charles Black, London, 1906

Cecil, David, *The Cecils of Hatfield House*, Cardinal, London, 1973

Chambers, E. K., *The Elizabethan Stage*, Oxford University Press, Oxford, 1923

Chappell, William, *Popular Music of the Olden Time*, Cramer, Beale & Chappell, London, 1853

Clubb, Louise George, *Italian Drama in Shakespeare's Time*, Yale University Press, Newhaven, 1989

Cohn, Albert, *Shakespeare in Germany in the Sixteenth and Seventeenth Centuries*, Asher & Co, London, 1865

Collinson, Patrick, 'Walsingham's Plumber' in *London Review of Books*, 5 July 2001, pp. 20–21

Colorni, Emanuele, *La Comunità Ebraica Mantovana*, Mantova Ebraica, Mantua, 2000

Coolidge, W. A. B., *The Alps in Nature and History*, Methuen, London, 1908

Coryate, Thomas, *Coryat's Crudities 1611*, fascimile edition, Scolar Press, London, 1978

Crichton, Douglas, *The Admirable Crichton*, L. Upcott Gill, London, 1909

Cunnington, C. Willett and Phillis, *Handbook of English Costume in the Sixteenth Century*, Faber and Faber, London, 1969

Deacon, Richard, *A History of the British Secret Service*, Grafton, London, 1991

Devlin, Christopher, 'The Earl and the Alchemist' in the *Month*, January 1953, New Series: Vol. 9, Part I, pp. 25–38; Part II, pp. 92–104; Part III, pp. 153–66

De Nave, Francine and Voet, Leon, *Museum Plantin-Moretus*, Ludion, Brussels, 1989

Dodd, A. H., *Elizabethan England*, Book Club Associates, London, 1974

Doran, Susan, *Elizabeth I and Foreign Policy 1558–1603*, Routledge, London, 2000

Dover Wilson, John, *Life in Shakespeare's England*, Cambridge University Press, Cambridge, 1911

Dovey, Zillah, *An Elizabethan Progress*, Sutton Publishing, Stroud, 1999

Dowland, John, *Second Book of Airs*, transcribed, scored and edited by Edmund Horace Fellowes, in *The English School of Lutenist Song Writers*, Stainer & Bell, London, 1922

Draper, John W., 'Shakespeare and the Doge of Venice', in *Journal of English and German Philology*, 46, 1947, pp. 75–81

——— 'Some Details of Italian Local Colour in *Othello*', in *Shakespeare Jahrbuch*, LXVIII, 1932, pp. 125–7

Duncan-Jones, Katherine, *Ungentle Shakespeare*, The Arden Shakespeare, London, 2001.

Dusoir, R. et al. (eds), *Justus Lipsius en het Plantijnse Huis*, Museum Plantin-Moretus, Antwerp, 1997

Earle, John, *Micro-cosmographie* (1628), Scolar Press facsimile, Leeds, 1966

Eccles, Mark, *Christopher Marlowe in London*, Harvard University Press, Cambridge, Mass., 1934

——— *Shakespeare in Warwickshire*, Madison, Wisconsin, 1961

——— Letter, *Times Literary Supplement*, 6 September 1934

Edmond, Mary, *Rare Sir William Davenant*, Manchester University Press, Manchester, 1987

Eliot, T. S., *Selected Essays*, Faber and Faber, New York, 1932

——— *Elizabethan Dramatists*, Faber and Faber, London, 1963

Elze, Karl, 'Der "Rialto" bei Shakespeare', *Shakespeare Jahrbuch*, V, 1870, pp. 367–9

——— 'The Supposed Travels of Shakespeare', in *Essays on Shakespeare*, Macmillan, London, 1874

Estienne, Henri ('Stephanus'), *Francofordiense Emporium*, translated as *The Frankfurt*

Book Fair by James Westfall Thompson, Caxton Book Club, Chicago, 1911

Fabbri, Paolo, *Monteverdi*, translated by Tim Carter, Cambridge University Press, Cambridge, 1994

Falconer, A. F., *Shakespeare and the Sea*, Constable, London, 1964

Fenlon, Iain, *Music and Patronage in Sixteenth Century Mantua*, Cambridge University Press, Cambridge, 1980

Fellowes, Edmund H., *William Byrd*, Oxford University Press, London, 1948

Fortis, Umberto, *The Ghetto on the Lagoon*, translated by Roberto Matteoda, Storti, Venice, 2001

Fox, 'Mr Harrie Cavendish His Journey to and from Constantynople, by Fox his servant', edited by A. C. Wood, reproduced in *Camden Miscellany*, XVII, 1940

Furlotti, Barbara (ed.), *Le Collezioni Gonzaga: II Carteggio tra Bologna, Parma, Piacenza e Mantova (1563–1634)*, Silvana, Milan, 2000

Gerlo, Aloïs and Vervliet, Hendrik, *La Correspondance de Juste Lipse Conservée au Musée Plantin-Moretus*, De Nederlandsche Boekhandel, Antwerp, 1967

Goldberg, Jonathan, *Sodometries*, Stanford University Press, California, 1992

Grantley, Daryll and Roberts, Peter (eds), *Christopher Marlowe and English Renaissance Culture*, Scolar Press, Aldershot, 1996

Gray, Austin K., 'Some Observations on Christopher Marlowe, Government Agent' in *Modern Language Association of America*, 43, 1928, pp. 682–700

Green, Martin, *Wriothesley's Roses*, Clevedon Books, Baltimore, 1993

Greene, Robert, *Groats-worth of Witte, bought with a million of Repentance*, reprint of 1592 edition, Bodley Head Quartos, London, 1923

Greening Lamborn, E. A., 'Great Tew and the Chandos Portrait', in *Notes & Queries*, 194, No. 1, 8 January 1949, pp. 71–2

Grewar, Andrew, 'The Clowning Zanies: Shakespeare and the Actors of the Commedia dell'Arte', *Shakespeare in Southern Africa*, 3, 1989, pp. 9–32

Grillo, Ernesto, *Shakespeare and Italy*, The University Press, Glasgow, 1949

Gurr, Andrew, *Playgoing in Shakespeare's London*, Cambridge University Press, Cambridge, 2000

—— 'Shakespeare's Localities' in Lombardo, Agostino (ed.), *Shakespeare a Verona e nel Veneto*, Accademia di Agricoltura Scienze e Lettere di Verona, Verona, 1987, pp. 55–66

Harley, John, *William Byrd, Gentleman of the Chapel Royal*, Scolar Press, Aldershot, 1997

Harkness, Deborah E., *John Dee's Conversations with Angels*, Cambridge University Press, Cambridge, 1999

Hartleb, Hans, *Deutschlands Erster Theaterbau*, Walter de Gruyter, Berlin, 1936

Harrison, William, *The Description of England*, edited by Georges Edelen, The Folger Shakespeare Library, Washington, 1994

Haynes, Alan, *Sex in Elizabethan England*, Sutton Publishing, Stroud, 1997

—— *The Elizabethan Secret Services*, Sutton Publishing, Stroud, 2000

Headington, Christopher, *The Bodley Head History of Western Music*, Bodley Head, London, 1974

Hentzner, Paul, 'A Journey into England in the Year MDXCVIII', (1598), in *Paul*

Bibliography

Hentzner's Travels in England during the Reign of Queen Elizabeth, translated by Richard Bentley, London, 1797

Herz, E., *Englische Schauspieler und Englisches Schauspiel zur Zeit Shakespeares in Deutschland*, L. Voss, Hamburg, 1903

Hoffman, Calvin, *The Man Who Was Shakespeare*, M. Parrish, London, 1955

Holden, Anthony, *William Shakespeare, His Life and Work*, Abacus, London, 1999

—— 'That's no lady it's . . .', in *Observer, Review*, 21 April 2002, p. 5

Holmes, George (ed.), *Oxford Illustrated History of Italy*, Oxford University Press, Oxford, 1997

Honan, Park, *Shakespeare, A Life*, Oxford University Press, Oxford, 1999

Hotson, Leslie, *The Death of Christopher Marlowe*, Nonesuch Press, London, 1925

—— 'Marlowe Among the Churchwardens', in *Atlantic Monthly*, 138, 1926, pp. 37–44

Howard, Clare, *English Travellers of the Renaissance*, John Lane, London, 1914

Israel, Jonathan I., *The Dutch Republic*, Clarendon Press, Oxford, 1998

Jaffé, Michael, *Rubens and Italy*, Phaidon, Oxford, 1977

Jaggard, W., *Shakespeare, Once a Printer and a Bookman*, Shakespeare Press, Stratford-upon-Avon, 1934

Kemp, Will, *Kemps Nine Daies Wonder*, edited by Susan Yaxley, The Larks Press, Norfolk, 1985

Kermode, Frank, *Shakespeare's Language*, Penguin, London, 2000

Kirkwood, Kenneth, *Did Shakespeare Visit Denmark?*, privately printed, Karachi, 1953

Kirsch, Arthur, 'Virtue, Vice, and Compassion in Montaigne in *The Tempest*', in *Studies in English Literature*, 37, 1997, pp. 337–52

Koenigsberger, H. G., and Mosse, George L., *Europe in the Sixteenth Century*, Longman, London, 1972

Lacey, Robert, *Sir Walter Ralegh*, Phoenix Press, London, 1973

Lassels, Richard, *The Voyage of Italy*, sold by John Starkey in Fleet Street, 1670

Laurence, Anne, *Women in England 1500–1760*, Phoenix Giant, London, 1999

Lawner, Lynne (ed. and trans.), *I modi, the sixteen pleasures*, Peter Owen, London, 1988

Lea, K. M., *Italian Popular Comedy*, 2 vols, Russell & Russell, New York, 1962

Le Carré, John, *The Spy Who Came in from the Cold*, Coronet Books, London, 1963

Leedham-Green, Elisabeth, *A Concise History of the University of Cambridge*, Cambridge University Press, Cambridge, 1996

Lescourret, Marie-Anne, *Rubens: A Double Life*, Allison & Busby, London, 1993

Letts, Malcolm, 'Contributions to the History of European Travel', *Notes & Queries*, 12S, I, 22 January 1916, pp. 61–4

Levith, Murray, *Shakespeare's Italian Settings and Plays*, Macmillan Press, London, 1989

Limon, Jerzy, *Gentlemen of a Company*, Cambridge University Press, Cambridge, 1985

Lintner, Valerio, *Italy*, The Windrush Press, Gloucestershire, 1998

Lithgow, William, *A Total Discourse of Rare Adventures and Painefull Peregrinations of Long Nineteene Yeares of Travayles*, I. Okes, London, 1640

Lytton Sells, A., *The Paradise of Travellers*, George Allen & Unwin, London, 1964

MacEóin, Gary, *Cervantes*, The Bruce Publishing Co., Milwaukee, 1950

McKendrick, Melveena, *Cervantes*, Little, Brown & Co., Toronto, 1980

McLeish, Kenneth and Unwin, Stephen, *A Pocket Guide to Shakespeare's Plays*, Faber and Faber, London, 1998

McPherson, David C., *Shakespeare, Jonson and the Myth of Venice*, Associated University Presses, New Jersey, 1990

McWilliam, G. H., Inaugural Lecture: 'Shakespeare's Italy Revisited', Leicester University Press, Leicester, 1974

Magurn, Ruth Saunders (ed. and trans.), *The Letters of Peter Paul Rubens*, Harvard University Press, Cambridge, Mass., 1971

Malacarne, Giancarlo and Bini, Mauro (eds), *A Tavola Con Gli Dei*, Il Bulino, Modena, 2000

Maquerlot, Jean-Pierre, and Willems, Michèle (eds), *Travel and Drama in Shakespeare's Time*, Cambridge University Press, Cambridge, 1996

Marrapodi, Michele et al. (eds), *Shakespeare's Italy*, Manchester University Press, Manchester, 1997

Meres, Francis *Palladis Tamia, 'Wit's Treasury'*, London, 1598, edited by Don Cameron Allen, Scholar's Facsimiles and Reprints, New York, 1938

Michell, John, *Who Wrote Shakespeare?*, Thames and Hudson, London, 1999

Montaigne, Michel de, *Essays*, translated by J. M. Cohen, Penguin, London, 1993

—— *The Diary of Montaigne's Journey to Italy in 1580 and 1581*, translated by E. J. Trechmann, Hogarth Press, London, 1929

Moore-Smith, G. C., 'Marlowe at Cambridge', *Modern Language Review*, 4, 1909, pp. 167–77

Morrill, John, *Tudor and Stuart Britain*, Oxford University Press, Oxford, 1996

Mortoft, Francis, 'Francis Mortoft: His Book', *Hakluyt Society*, second series, LVII, London, 1925

Moryson, Fynes, *Itinerary*, 4 vols, 1617 edition, reprinted by James MacLehose and Sons, Glasgow, 1906

—— Supplementary material to the *Itinerary* published as *Shakespeare's Europe*, edited by Charles Hughes, Sherratt & Hughes, London, 1903

Murray, John J., *Antwerp in the Time of Plantin and Brueghel*, University of Oklahoma Press, Norman, 1970

Mutinelli, Fabio, *Del Costume Veneziano*, Filippi, Venice, 1984

Nashe, Thomas, *The Unfortunate Traveller*, reprint of 1594 edition, Percy Reprints, Basil Blackwell, Oxford, 1927

—— *Pierce Penilesse, His Supplication to the Divell*, reprint of 1592 edition, Bodley Head Quartos, London, 1924

Nicoll, Allardyce (ed.), *Shakespeare in His Own Age*, Shakespeare Survey, No. 17, Cambridge University Press, Cambridge, 1964

Nicholl, Charles, *The Reckoning*, University of Chicago Press, Chicago, 1992

—— 'The Last Years of Edward Kelley, Alchemist to the Emperor', *London Review of Books*, 19 April 2001, pp. 3–8

Nichols, J., *Progresses and Processions of Queen Elizabeth*, Vol. 3, London, 1823, and reprinted Burt Franklin, New York, 1966

Bibliography

Norwich, John Julius, *A History of Venice*, Penguin, London, 1983

Osley, A. S., *Scribes and Sources*, Faber and Faber, London, 1980

Palmer, Alan and Veronica, *Who's Who in Shakespeare's England*, Methuen, London, 2000

Partridge, A. C., 'Shakespeare and Italy', in *English Studies in Africa*, 4, 1961, pp. 117–27

Pearson, Hesketh, *A Life of Shakespeare*, Hamish Hamilton, London, 1987

Pearsall Smith, Logan, *The Life and Letters of Sir Henry Wotton*, 2 vols, Clarendon, Oxford, 1907

Phillips, Graham and Keatman, Martin, *The Shakespeare Conspiracy*, Century, London, 1994

Piccinelli, Roberta (ed.), *Le Collezioni Gonzaga: Il Carteggio tra Firenze e Mantova (1554–1626)*, Silvana, Milan, 2000

Pottinger, George, *The Real Admirable Crichton*, Michael Russell, Norwich, 1995

Porter, Roy, *London, A Social History*, Penguin, London, 1994

Poulton, Diana, *John Dowland*, Faber and Faber, London, 1972

Praz, Mario, 'Shakespeare's Italy', *Shakespeare Survey*, No. 7, 1954, pp. 95–106

Preston, Jean F. and Yeandle, Laetitia, *English Handwriting 1400–1650*, Pegasus Press, Asheville N.C., 1999

Pritchard, R. E., *Shakespeare's England*, Sutton Publishing, Stroud, 1999

Read, Conyers, *Lord Burghley and Queen Elizabeth*, Jonathan Cape, London, 1960

Rietbergen, P. J. A. N., *A Short History of the Netherlands*, Bekking, Amersfoort, 1998

Ringler, William, 'Stephen Gosson: a Biography and Critical Study', in *Princeton Studies in English*, 25, 1942

Rossetti, Lucia, *The University of Padua*, Erredici, Padua, 1999

Routh, C. R. N., *Who's Who in Tudor England*, Shepheard-Walwyn, London, 1990

Rowse, A. L., *Shakespeare's Southampton, Patron of Virginia*, Macmillan, London, 1965

—— *Shakespeare the Man*, Macmillan, London, 1988

St Clare Byrne, M. (ed.), *The Elizabethan Home*, Cobden-Sanderson, London, 1930

Salgādo, Gāmini, *The Elizabethan Underworld*, Sutton Publishing, Stroud, 1995

Sanderson, John, 'Travels of John Sanderson in the Levant, 1584–1602', reproduced in *The Hakluyt Society*, Second Series, LXVII, 1930

Schoenbaum, S., *William Shakespeare, A Compact Documentary Life*, Oxford University Press, Oxford, 1975

Schmidt, Ephraim, *Geschiedenis van de Joden in Antwerpen*, C. de Vries-Brouwers, Antwerp, 1994

Schrickx, Willem, 'English Actors at the Courts of Wolfenbüttel, Brussels and Graz during the Lifetime of Shakespeare', in *Shakespeare Survey*, No. 33, 1980, pp. 153–68

—— 'Pickleherring and English Actors in Germany', *Shakespeare Survey*, No. 36, 1983, pp. 135–47

Seaton, Ethel, 'Marlowe's Map', in *Essays and Studies*, X, 1924, pp. 13–35

Seng, Peter J., *The Vocal Songs in the Plays of Shakespeare*, Harvard University Press, Cambridge, Mass., 1967

Sim, Alison, *Food and Feast in Tudor England*, Sutton Publishing, Stroud, 1997

—— *Pleasures & Pastimes in Tudor England*, Sutton Publishing, Stroud, 1999

Simon, Kate, *A Renaissance Tapestry*, Harrap, London, 1988

Simonsohn, Shlomo, *History of the Jews in the Duchy of Mantua*, Kiryath Sepher, Jerusalem, 1977

Simpson, Lucie, *The Secondary Heroes of Shakespeare*, The Kingswood Press, London, 1952

Slater, Gilbert, *Seven Shakespeares*, Cecil Palmer, London, 1931

Smith, Bruce R., *Homosexual Desire in Shakespeare's England*, University of Chicago Press, Chicago, 1994

Sobran, Joseph, *Alias Shakespeare*, The Free Press, New York, 1997

Spurling, Hilary, *Elinor Fettiplace's Receipt Book*, Penguin Books, Middlesex, 1987

Starkey, David, *Elizabeth*, Vintage, London, 2001

Stefansson, Jon, 'Shakespeare at Elsinore', in *The Contemporary Review*, LXIX, 1896, pp. 20–40

Stevens, Denis (trans.), *The Letters of Claudio Monteverdi*, Clarendon Press, Oxford, 1995

Stubbes, Phillip, *Anatomie of Abuses*, 1583, facsimile reprint, Garland, New York, 1973

Stow, John, *The Survey of London* (1598), Everyman, London, 1929

Suitner, Gianna and Tellini Perina, Chiara, *Palazzo Te in Mantua*, translated by Christopher Evans, Electa, Milan, 1994

Sullivan, Edward, 'Shakespeare and the Waterways of North Italy', in *The Nineteenth Century*, August 1908, pp. 215–32

Tannenbaum, Samuel, *The Handwriting of the Renaissance*, Routledge, London, 1930

Thompson, J. W. and Padover, S. K., *Secret Diplomacy: A Record of Espionage and Double Dealing 1500–1815*, Jarrolds, London, 1937

Thompson, J. W. (ed.), see Estienne, Henri

Traister, Barbara Howard, *The Notorious Astrological Physician of London*, University of Chicago Press, Chicago, 2001

Trow, M. J., *Who Killed Kit Marlowe?*, Sutton Publishing, Stroud, 2001

Twain, Mark, *Is Shakespeare Dead?*, Harper & Brothers, New York, 1909

Urry, William, *Christopher Marlowe and Canterbury*, Faber and Faber, London, 1988

Verhuyck, Paul and Kisling, Corine, *Het Mandement van Bacchus*, C. de Vries-Brouwers, Antwerp, 1987

Voet, Leon, *The Golden Compasses*, Vols 1 and 2, A. L. Vangendt & Co., Amsterdam, 1969

—— *The Plantin Press (1555–1589)*, Van Hoeve, Amsterdam, 1983

Wegg, Jervis, *The Decline of Antwerp under Philip of Spain*, Hyperion Press, Connecticut, 1979

Whall, W. B., *Shakespeare's Sea Terms Explained*, J. W. Arrowsmith, Bristol, 1910

Williams, Simon, *Shakespeare on the German Stage*, Cambridge University Press, Cambridge, 1990

Woolley, Benjamin, *The Queen's Conjuror*, HarperCollins, London, 2001

Woolfson, Jonathan, *Padua and the Tudors*, James Clarke & Co., Cambridge, 1998

Bibliography

Wraight, A. D., *The Story that the Sonnets Tell*, Adam Hart, London, 1994
—— *New Evidence*, Adam Hart, London, 1996
Zenner, Peter, *The Shakespeare Invention*, Country Books, Bakewell, 1999

Index

373